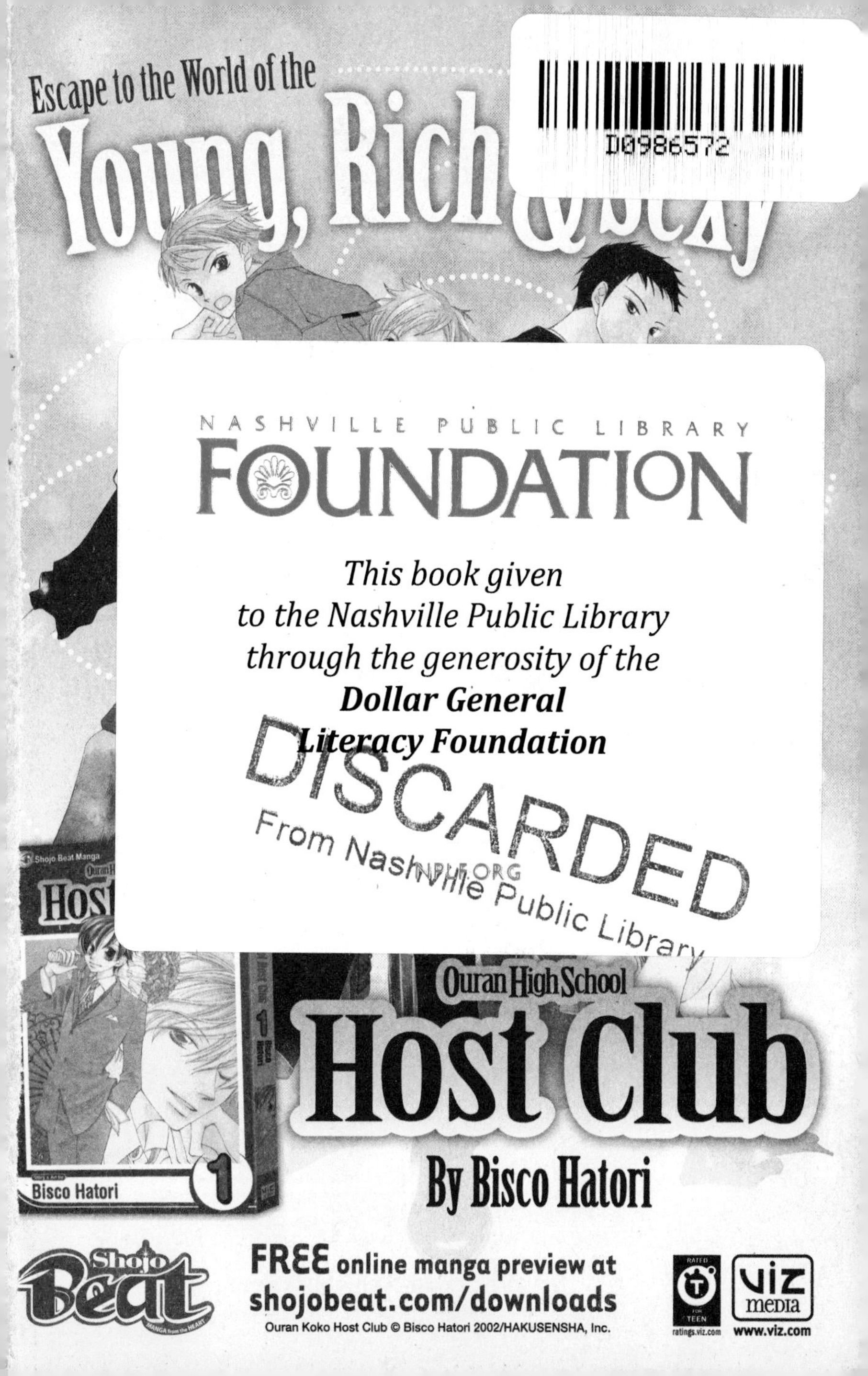
Escape to the World of the
Young, Rich & Sexy
Shojo Beat Manga
Ouran High School
Host Club
1
Bisco Hatori
Ouran High School
Host Club
By Bisco Hatori
Shojo Beat
MANGA from the HEART
FREE online manga preview at
shojobeat.com/downloads
Ouran Koko Host Club © Bisco Hatori 2002/HAKUSENSHA, Inc.
RATED T FOR TEEN
ratings.viz.com
VIZ media
www.viz.com

Don't Hide What's *Inside*

OTOMEN
by AYA KANNO

Despite his tough jock exterior, Asuka Masamune harbors a secret love for sewing, shojo manga, and all things girly. But when he finds himself drawn to his domestically inept classmate Ryo, his carefully crafted persona is put to the test. Can Asuka ever show his true self to anyone, much less to the girl he's falling for?

Find out in the *Otomen* manga—buy yours today!

On sale at www.shojobeat.com
Also available at your local bookstore and comic store.

OTOMEN © Aya Kanno 2006/HAKUSENSHA, Inc.

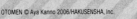

Natsume's BOOK of FRIENDS

STORY and ART by
Yuki Midorikawa

Make Some Unusual New Friends

The power to see hidden spirits has always felt like a curse to troubled high schooler Takashi Natsume. But he's about to discover he inherited a lot more than just the Sight from his mysterious grandmother!

$9.99 USA / $12.99 CAN *
ISBN: 978-1-4215-3243-1

On sale at **store.viz.com**
Also available at your local bookstore or comic store

www.shojobeat.com

Natsume Yujincho © Yuki Midorikawa 2005/HAKUSENSHA, Inc.
* Price subject to change

RATED
T
FOR
TEEN
ratings.viz.com

VIZ
MEDIA
www.viz.com

library wars
Love & War

STORY & ART BY *Kiiro Yumi*   ORIGINAL CONCEPT BY *Hiro Arikawa*

Winning the war on information, one book at a time

When the federal government tries to rid society of "unsuitable" books, an underground group of librarians and bibliophiles vows to fight back.

They are the Library Forces. And this is their story.

$9.99 USA / $12.99 CAN *
ISBN: 978-1-4215-3488-6

Manga on sale at store.viz.com
Also available at your local bookstore or comic store

www.shojobeat.com

Toshokan Sensou LOVE&WAR
© Kiiro Yumi and Hiro Arikawa 2008/HAKUSENSHA, Inc.
* Prices subject to change

www.viz.com

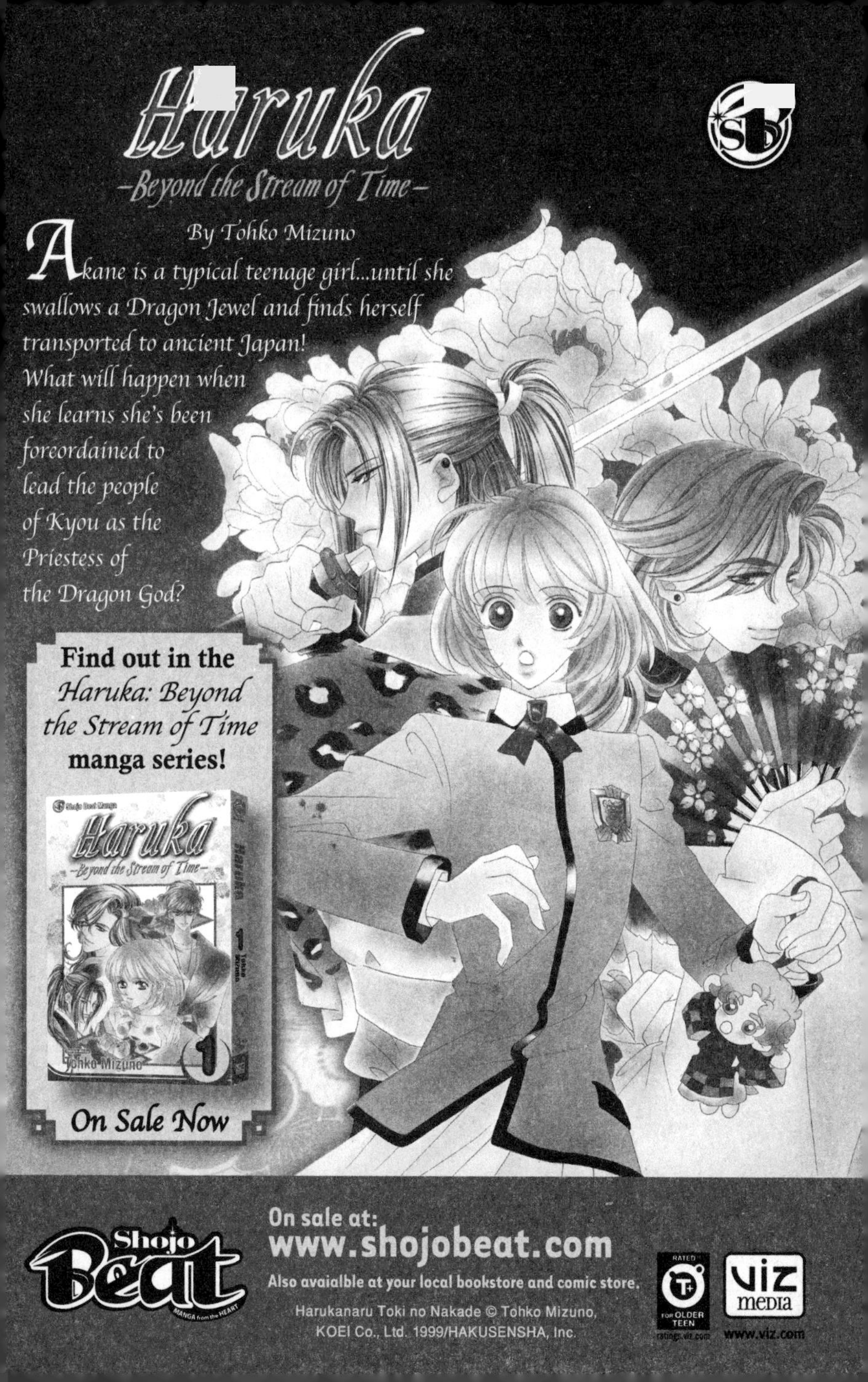
Haruka
-Beyond the Stream of Time-
By Tohko Mizuno
Akane is a typical teenage girl...until she swallows a Dragon Jewel and finds herself transported to ancient Japan! What will happen when she learns she's been foreordained to lead the people of Kyou as the Priestess of the Dragon God?
Find out in the Haruka: Beyond the Stream of Time manga series!
Shojo Beat Manga
Haruka
-Beyond the Stream of Time-
Tohko Mizuno
1
On Sale Now
Shojo Beat
MANGA from the HEART
On sale at:
www.shojobeat.com
Also availalble at your local bookstore and comic store.
Harukanaru Toki no Nakade © Tohko Mizuno, KOEI Co., Ltd. 1999/HAKUSENSHA, Inc.
RATED
T+
FOR OLDER TEEN
ratings.viz.com
viz media
www.viz.com

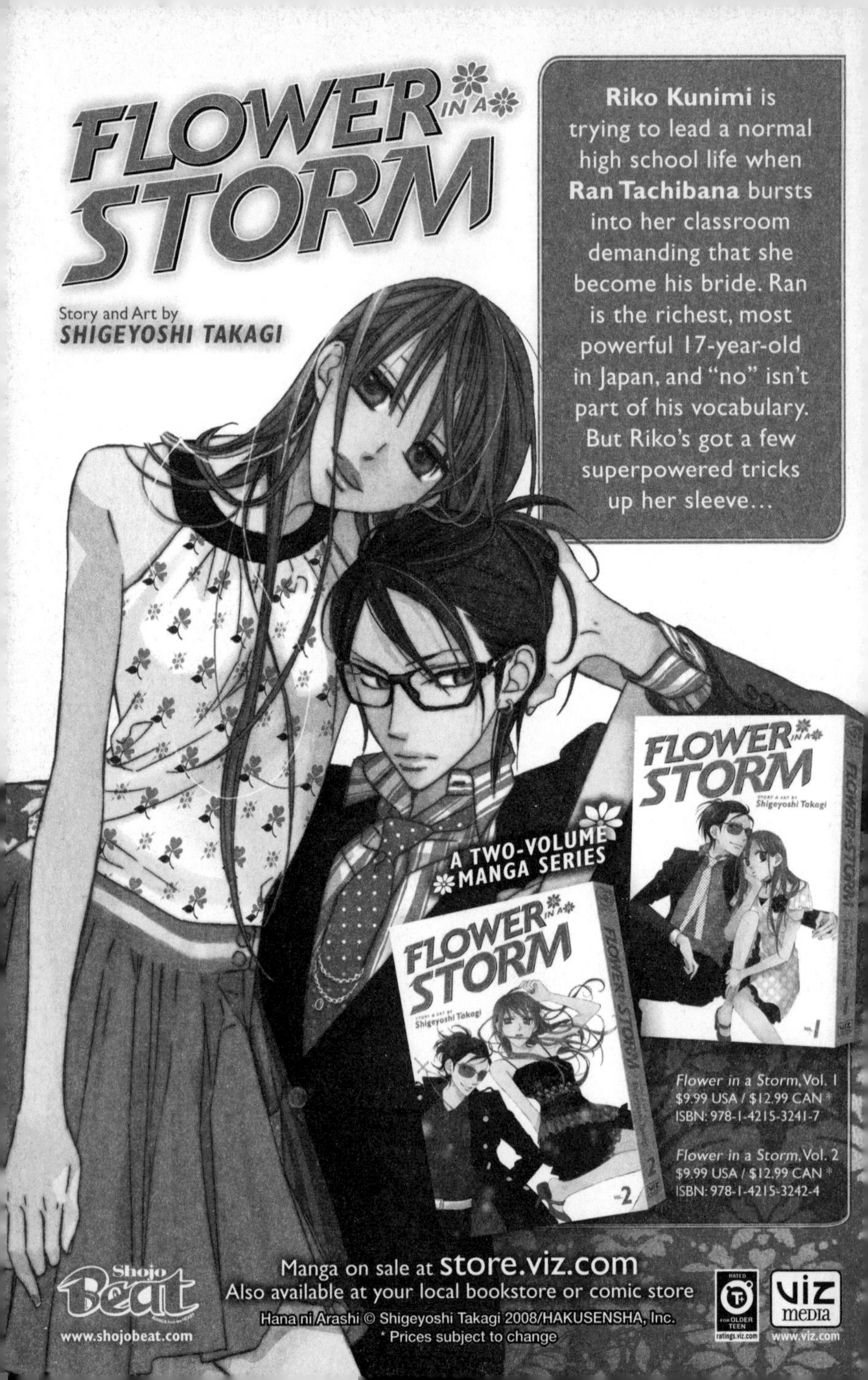
FLOWER IN A STORM
Story and Art by
SHIGEYOSHI TAKAGI
Riko Kunimi is trying to lead a normal high school life when Ran Tachibana bursts into her classroom demanding that she become his bride. Ran is the richest, most powerful 17-year-old in Japan, and "no" isn't part of his vocabulary. But Riko's got a few superpowered tricks up her sleeve...
A TWO-VOLUME MANGA SERIES
FLOWER IN A STORM
Shigeyoshi Takagi
Flower in a Storm, Vol. 1
$9.99 USA / $12.99 CAN *
ISBN: 978-1-4215-3241-7
Flower in a Storm, Vol. 2
$9.99 USA / $12.99 CAN *
ISBN: 978-1-4215-3242-4
Manga on sale at store.viz.com
Also available at your local bookstore or comic store
Hana ni Arashi © Shigeyoshi Takagi 2008/HAKUSENSHA, Inc.
* Prices subject to change
Shojo Beat
www.shojobeat.com
RATED T+ FOR OLDER TEEN
ratings.viz.com
VIZ MEDIA
www.viz.com

Love Kaori Yuki?

Read the rest of VIZ Media's Kaori Yuki collection!

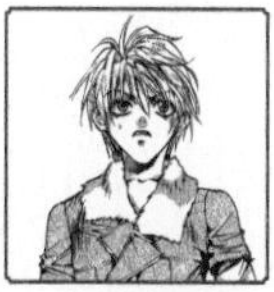

Angel Sanctuary • Rated T+ for Older Teen • 20 Volumes

The angel Alexiel loved God, but she rebelled against Heaven. As punishment, she is sent to Earth to live an endless series of tragic lives. She now inhabits the body of Setsuna Mudo, a troubled teen wrought with forbidden love.

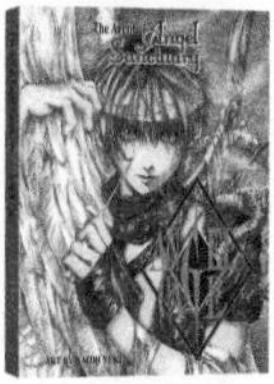

The Art of Angel Sanctuary: Angel Cage

The Art of Angel Sanctuary 2: Lost Angel

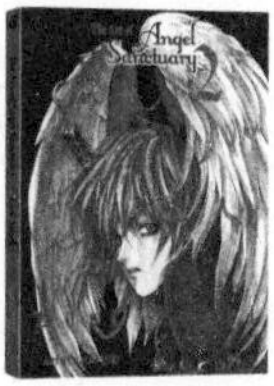

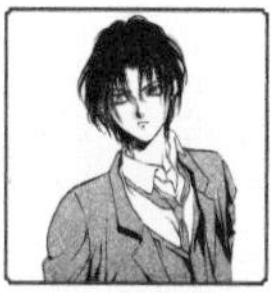

The Cain Saga • Rated M for Mature Readers • 5 Volumes

The prequel to the *Godchild* series, *The Cain Saga* follows the young Cain as he attempts to unravel the secrets of his birth. Delve into the tortured past of Earl Cain C. Hargreaves! Plus bonus short stories in each volume!

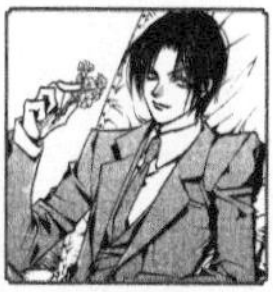

Godchild • Rated T+ for Older Teen • 8 Volumes

In 19th century London, dashing young nobleman Earl Cain Hargreaves weaves his way through the shadowy cobblestone streets that hide the dark secrets of aristocratic society. His mission is to solve the mystery of his shrouded lineage.

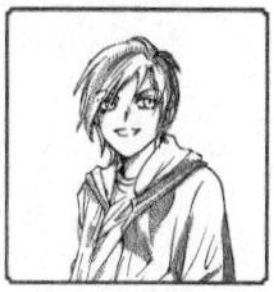

Fairy Cube • Rated T+ for Older Teen • 3 Volumes

Ian and Rin used to just *see* spirits. Now Ian *is* one. Using the Fairy Cube, Ian must figure out how to stop the lizard-spirit Tokage from taking over his life and destroying any chance he has of resurrection.

GRAND GUIGNOL ORCHESTRA
Vol. 5
Shojo Beat Edition

STORY AND ART BY **KAORI YUKI**

Translation **Camellia Nieh**
Touch-up Art & Lettering **Eric Erbes**
Design **Fawn Lau**
Editor **Pancha Diaz**

GUIGNOL KYUTEI GAKUDAN by Kaori Yuki
© Kaori Yuki 2010
All rights reserved.
First published in Japan in 2010 by HAKUSENSHA, Inc., Tokyo.
English language translation rights arranged with HAKUSENSHA, Inc., Tokyo.

The rights of the author(s) of the work(s) in this publication to be so identified
have been asserted in accordance with the Copyright, Designs and Patents Act 1988.
A CIP catalogue record for this book is available from the British Library.

The stories, characters and incidents mentioned in this publication are entirely fictional.

No portion of this book may be reproduced or transmitted in any form or by any means
without written permission from the copyright holders.

Printed in the U.S.A.

Published by VIZ Media, LLC
P.O. Box 77010
San Francisco, CA 94107

10 9 8 7 6 5 4 3 2 1
First printing, December 2011

www.viz.com

PARENTAL ADVISORY
GRAND GUIGNOL ORCHESTRA is rated T+ for Older Teen
and is recommended for ages 16 and up. This volume
contains fantasy violence and some mature themes.
ratings.viz.com

www.shojobeat.com

grand Guignol orchestra

5

STORY AND ART BY

KAORI
YUKI

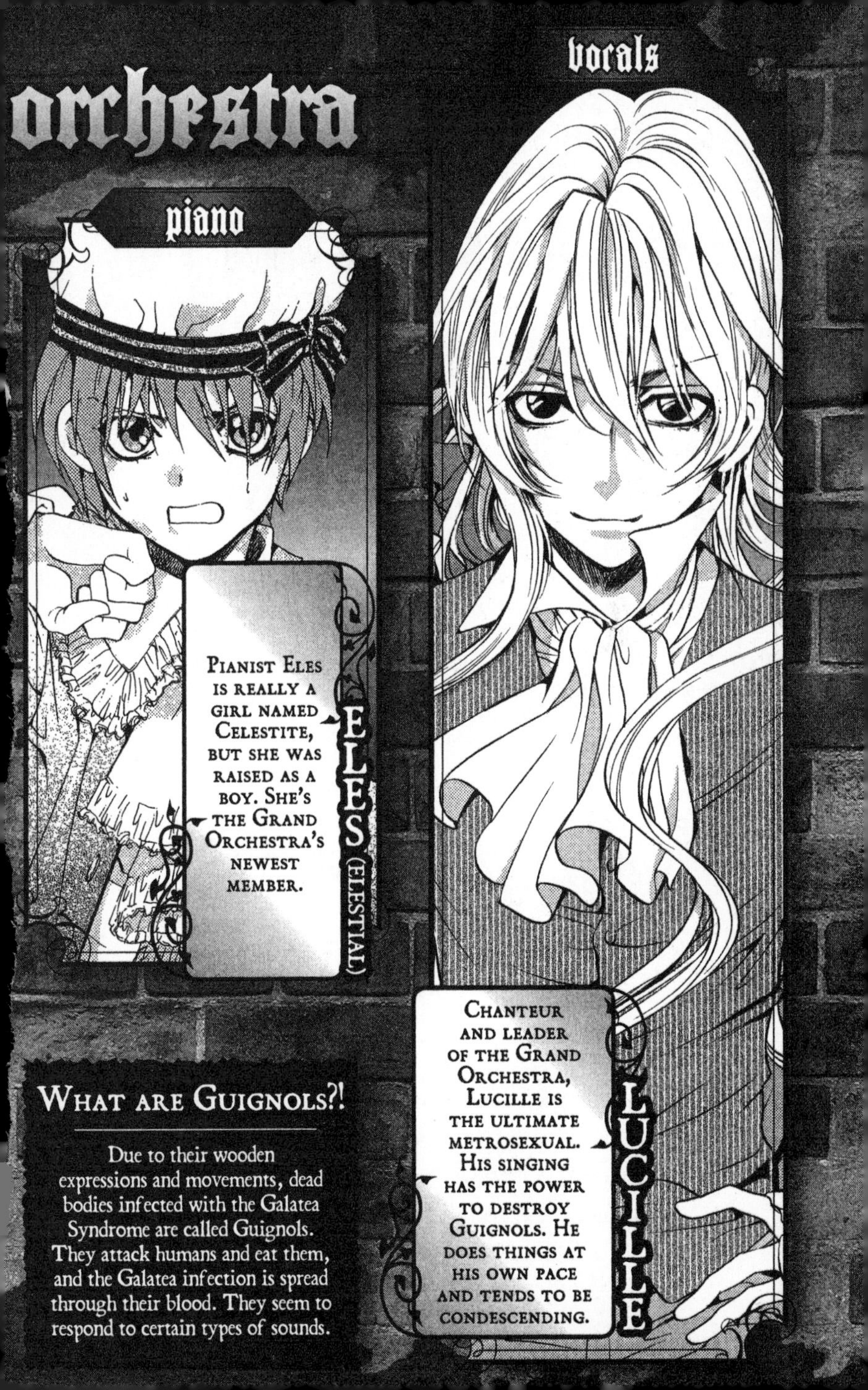
orchestra
vocals
Chanteur and leader of the Grand Orchestra, Lucille is the ultimate metrosexual. His singing has the power to destroy Guignols. He does things at his own pace and tends to be condescending.
LUCILLE
piano
Pianist Eles is really a girl named Celestite, but she was raised as a boy. She's the Grand Orchestra's newest member.
ELES (ELESTIAL)
What are Guignols?!
Due to their wooden expressions and movements, dead bodies infected with the Galatea Syndrome are called Guignols. They attack humans and eat them, and the Galatea infection is spread through their blood. They seem to respond to certain types of sounds.

grand Guignol

Member Introductions

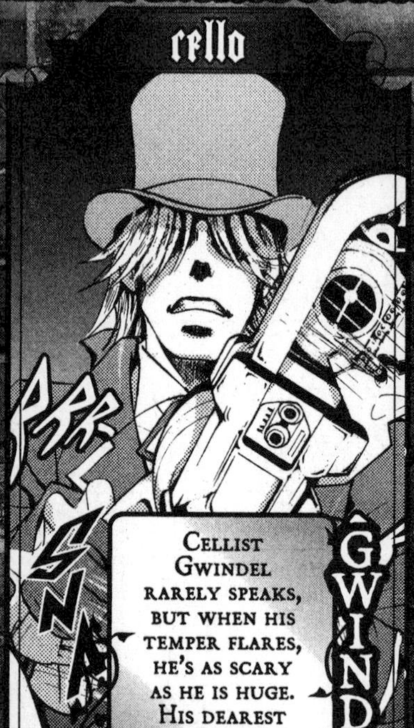
cello
Cellist Gwindel rarely speaks, but when his temper flares, he's as scary as he is huge. His dearest companion is his pet hedgehog.
GWINDEL

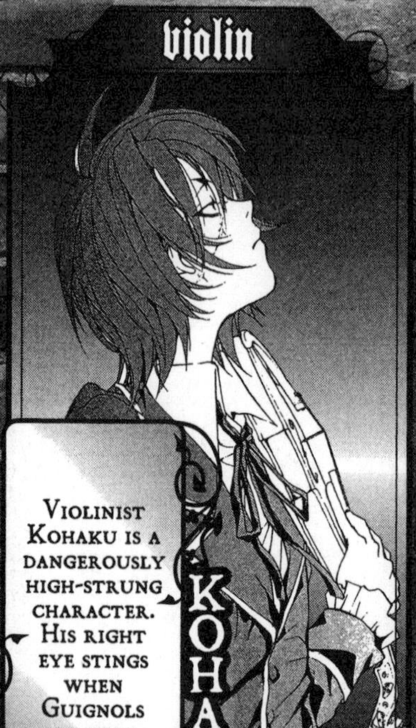
violin
Violinist Kohaku is a dangerously high-strung character. His right eye stings when Guignols are near.
KOHAKU

A bizarre plague that gives rise to man-eating zombies known as Guignols has overtaken the world. Lucille and his gang are the "unofficial" Grand Orchestra, willing to perform any piece of music for the right price. Lucille's Black Hymnal contains songs that can perform all sorts of miracles. What awaits this Guignol-hating group of traveling musicians?

Grand Guignol Orchestra

5

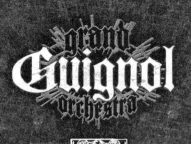

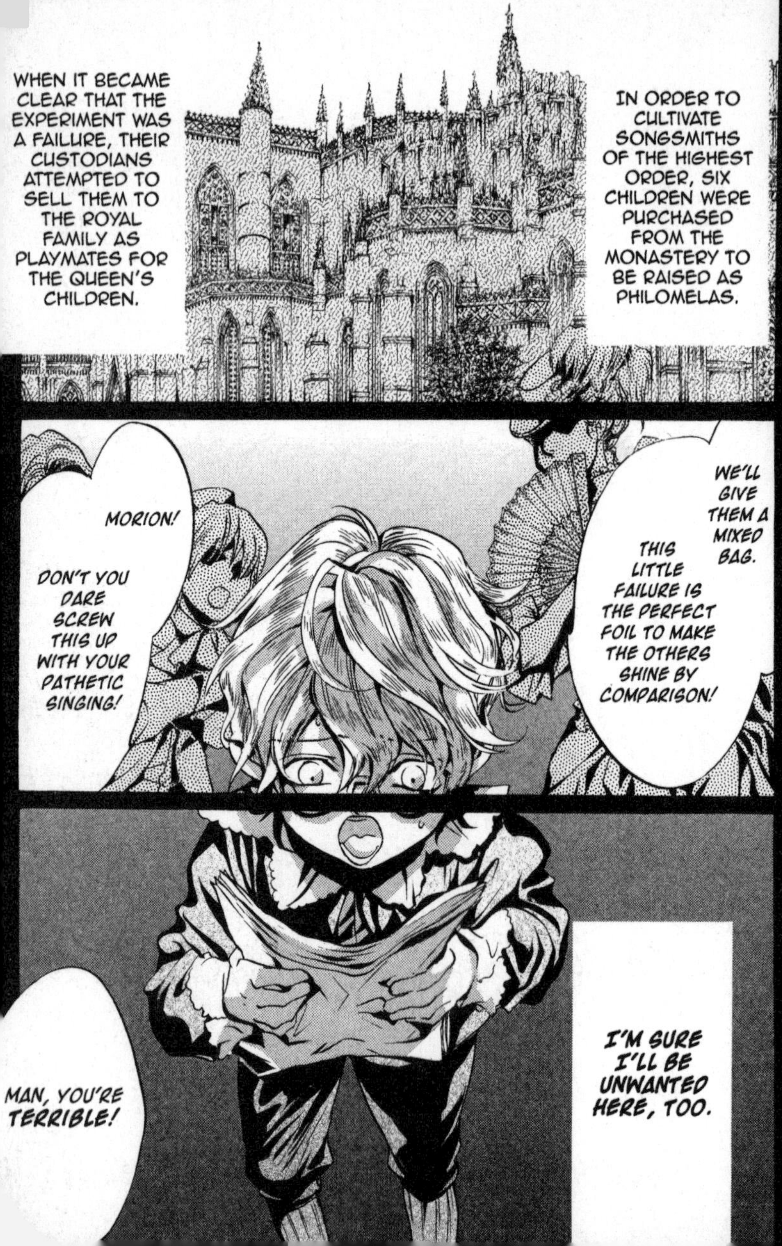
IN ORDER TO CULTIVATE SONGSMITHS OF THE HIGHEST ORDER, SIX CHILDREN WERE PURCHASED FROM THE MONASTERY TO BE RAISED AS PHILOMELAS.
WHEN IT BECAME CLEAR THAT THE EXPERIMENT WAS A FAILURE, THEIR CUSTODIANS ATTEMPTED TO SELL THEM TO THE ROYAL FAMILY AS PLAYMATES FOR THE QUEEN'S CHILDREN.
WE'LL GIVE THEM A MIXED BAG.
THIS LITTLE FAILURE IS THE PERFECT FOIL TO MAKE THE OTHERS SHINE BY COMPARISON!
MORION!
DON'T YOU DARE SCREW THIS UP WITH YOUR PATHETIC SINGING!
I'M SURE I'LL BE UNWANTED HERE, TOO.
MAN, YOU'RE TERRIBLE!

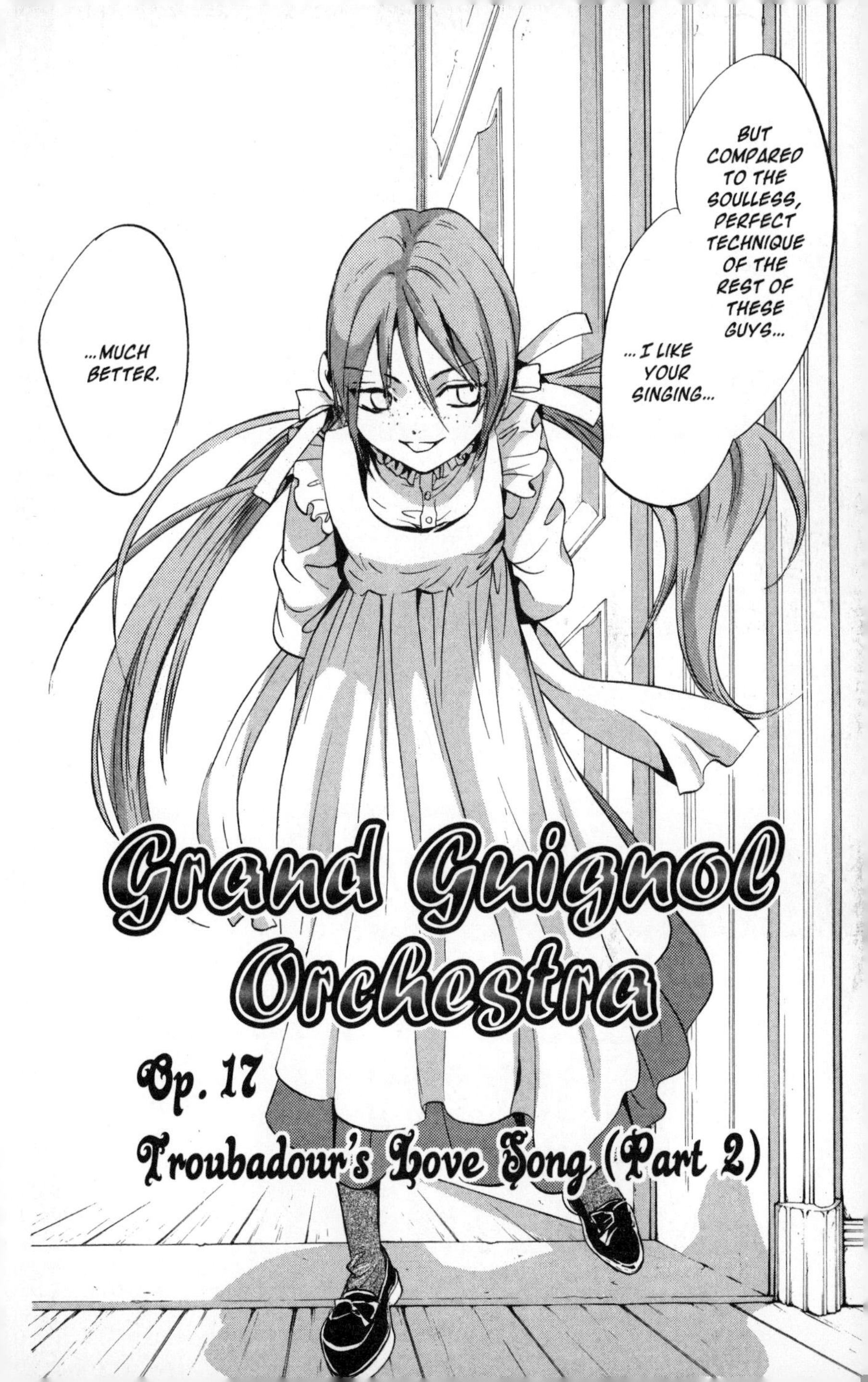
BUT COMPARED TO THE SOULLESS, PERFECT TECHNIQUE OF THE REST OF THESE GUYS...
...I LIKE YOUR SINGING...
...MUCH BETTER.
Grand Guignol Orchestra
Op. 17
Troubadour's Love Song (Part 2)

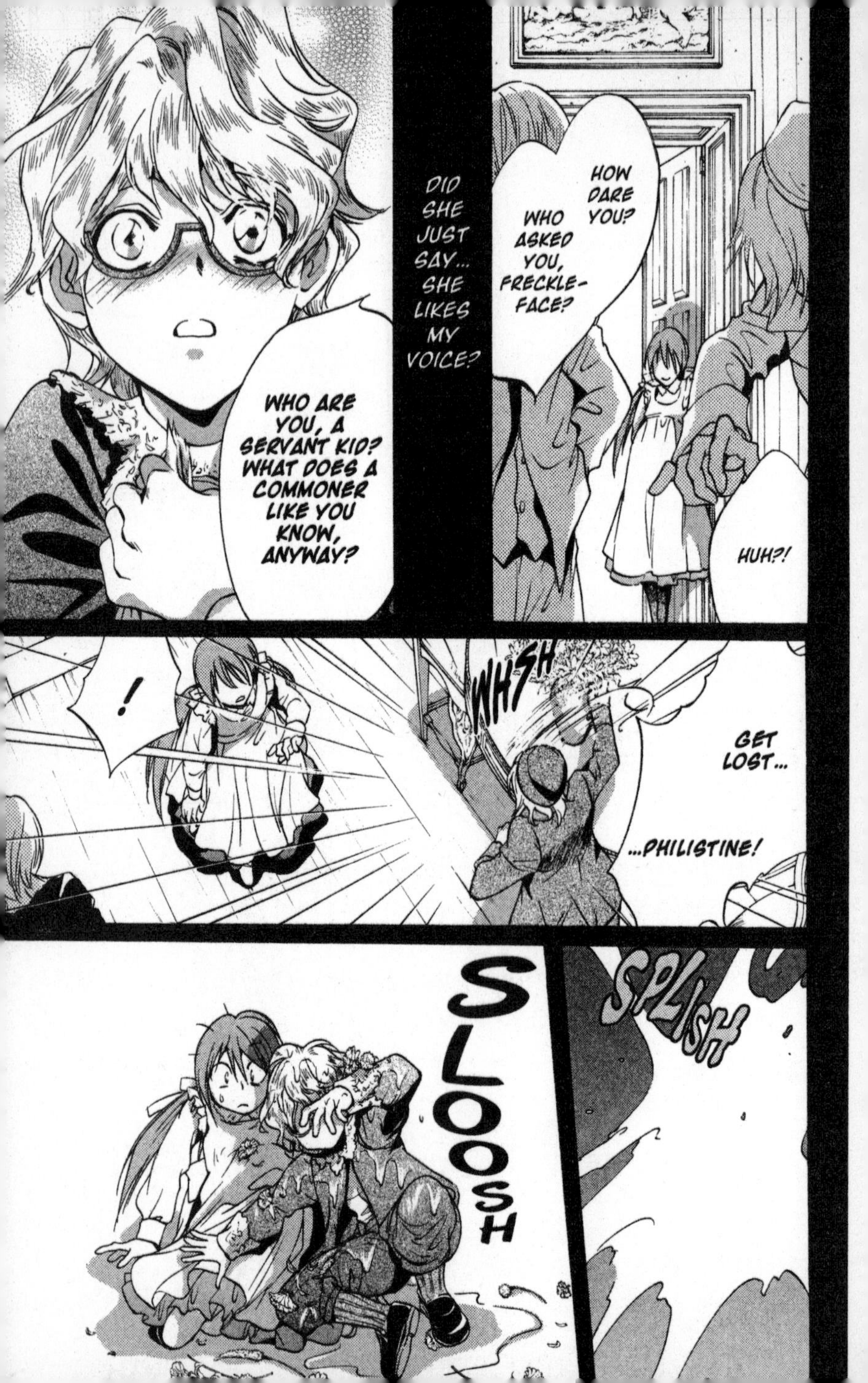
HOW DARE YOU?
WHO ASKED YOU, FRECKLE-FACE?
HUH?!
DID SHE JUST SAY... SHE LIKES MY VOICE?
WHO ARE YOU, A SERVANT KID? WHAT DOES A COMMONER LIKE YOU KNOW, ANYWAY?
GET LOST...
...PHILISTINE!
WHSH
!
SPLISH
SLOOSH

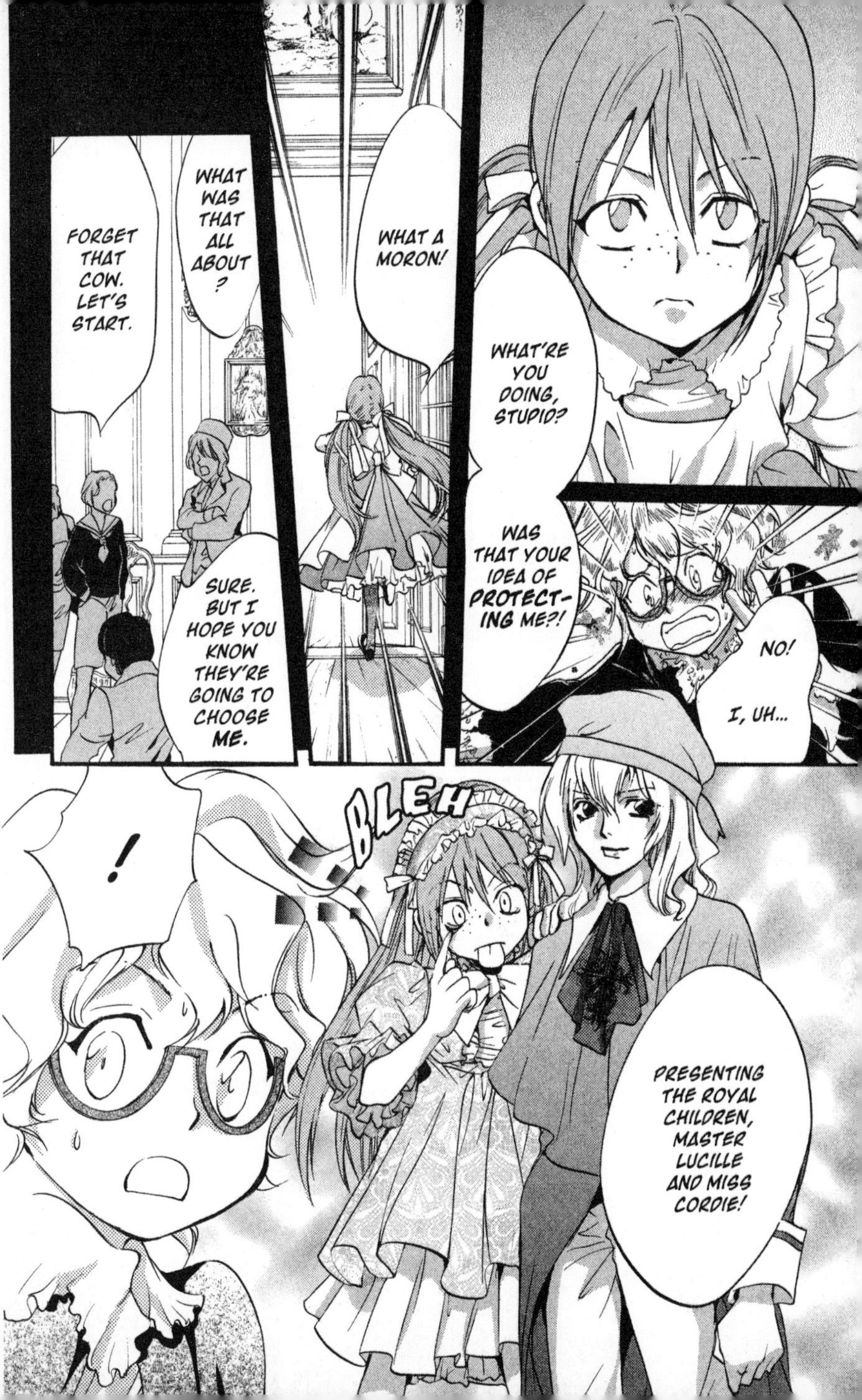
WHAT'RE YOU DOING, STUPID?
WAS THAT YOUR IDEA OF **PROTECTING ME?!**
NO!
I, UH...
WHAT A MORON!
WHAT WAS THAT ALL ABOUT?
FORGET THAT COW. LET'S START.
SURE. BUT I HOPE YOU KNOW THEY'RE GOING TO CHOOSE **ME.**
PRESENTING THE ROYAL CHILDREN, MASTER LUCILLE AND MISS CORDIE!
BLEH
!

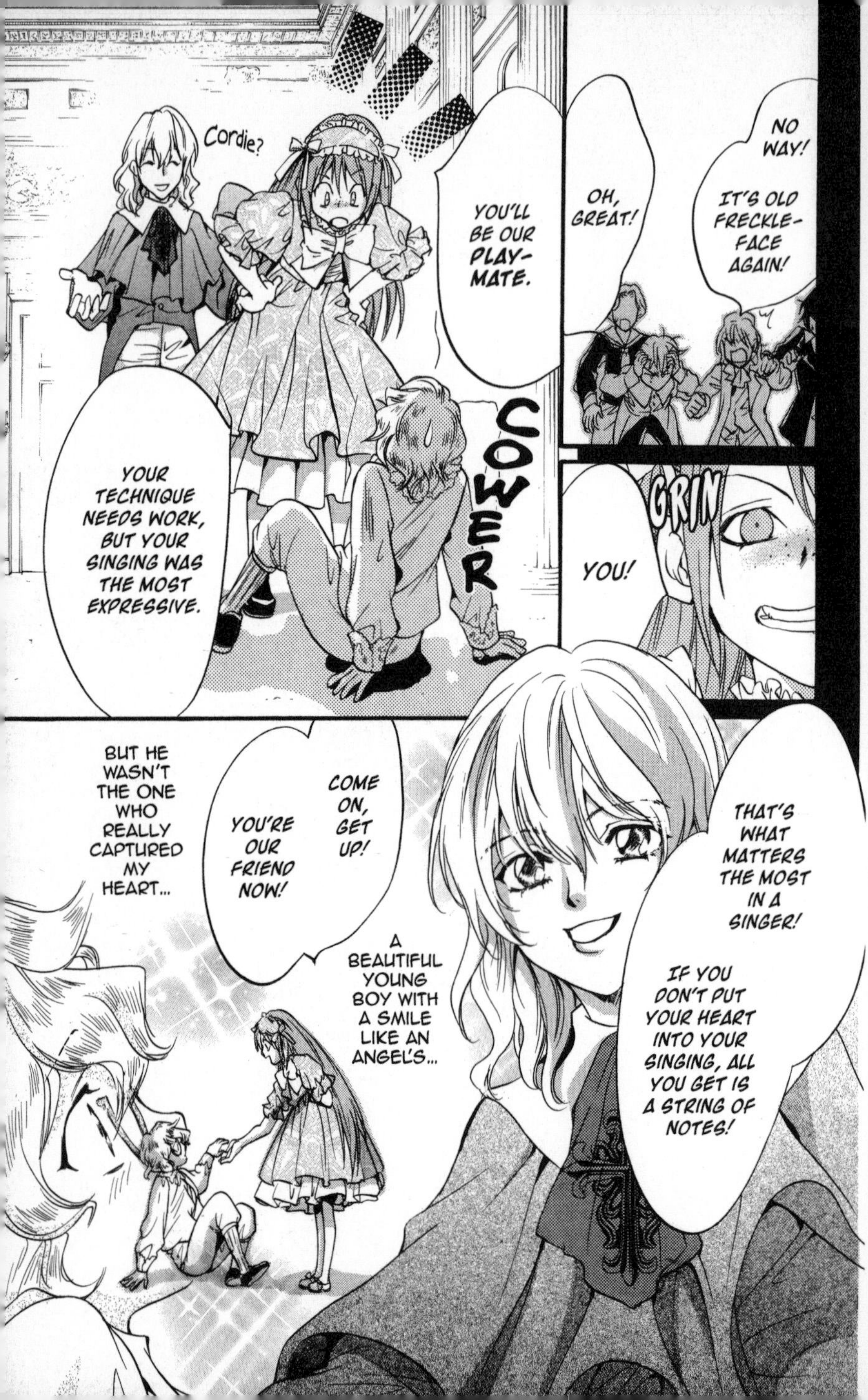
NO WAY! IT'S OLD FRECKLE-FACE AGAIN!
OH, GREAT!
GRIN
YOU!
YOU'LL BE OUR PLAYMATE.
COWER
Cordie?
YOUR TECHNIQUE NEEDS WORK, BUT YOUR SINGING WAS THE MOST EXPRESSIVE.
THAT'S WHAT MATTERS THE MOST IN A SINGER!
IF YOU DON'T PUT YOUR HEART INTO YOUR SINGING, ALL YOU GET IS A STRING OF NOTES!
COME ON, GET UP!
YOU'RE OUR FRIEND NOW!
BUT HE WASN'T THE ONE WHO REALLY CAPTURED MY HEART...
A BEAUTIFUL YOUNG BOY WITH A SMILE LIKE AN ANGEL'S...

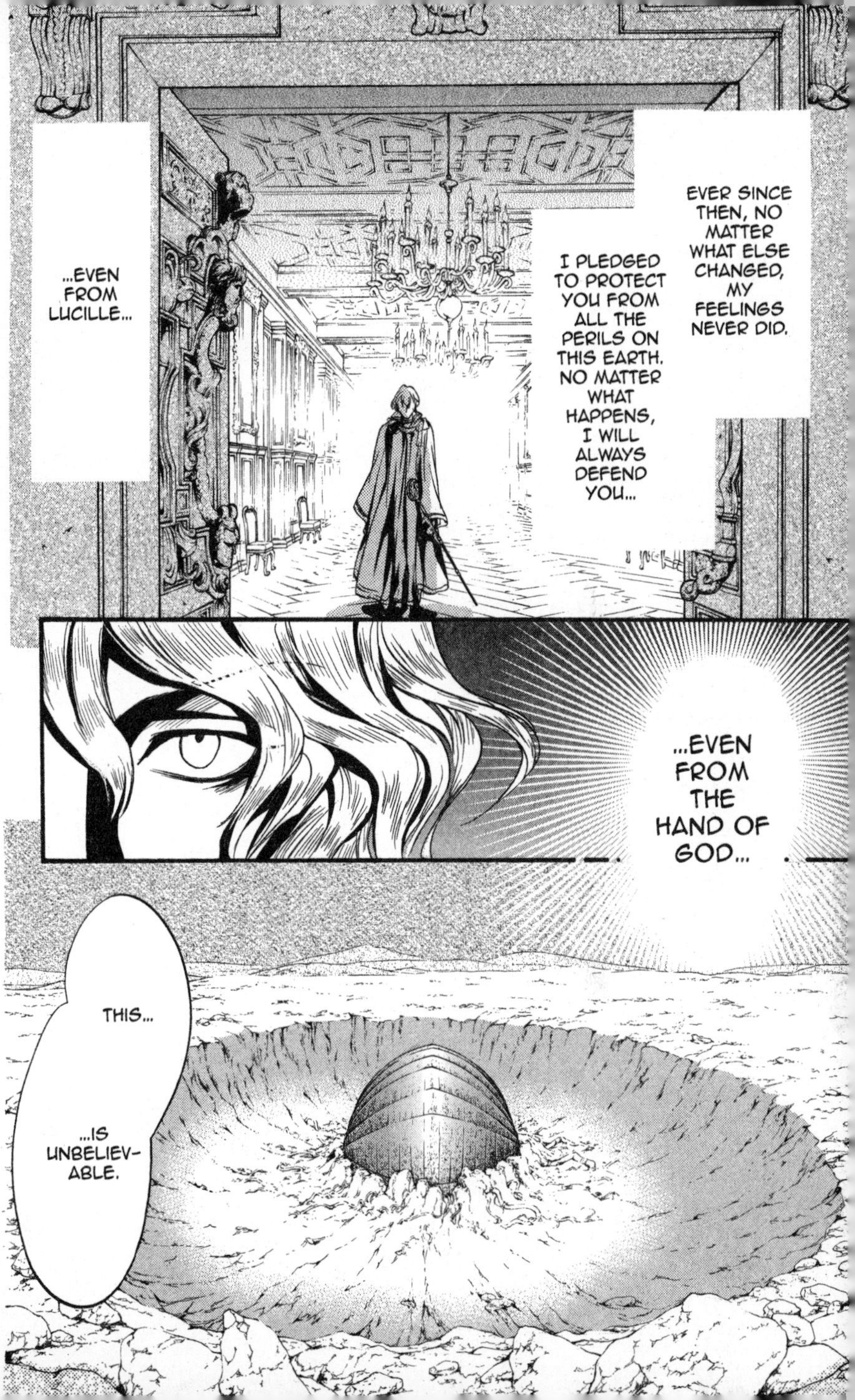
EVER SINCE THEN, NO MATTER WHAT ELSE CHANGED, MY FEELINGS NEVER DID.
I PLEDGED TO PROTECT YOU FROM ALL THE PERILS ON THIS EARTH. NO MATTER WHAT HAPPENS, I WILL ALWAYS DEFEND YOU...
...EVEN FROM LUCILLE...
...EVEN FROM THE HAND OF GOD...
THIS...
...IS UNBELIEV-ABLE.

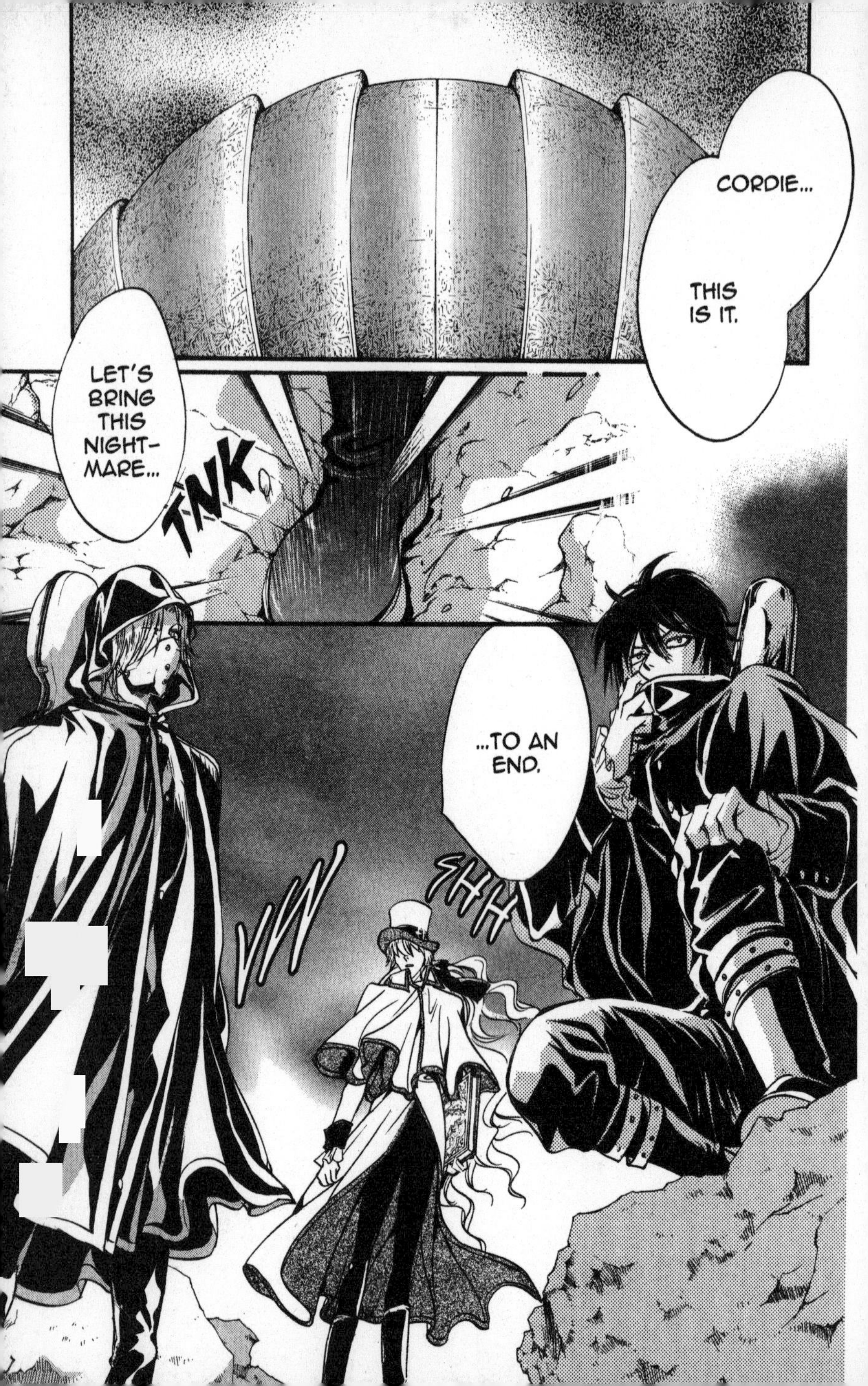
CORDIE... THIS IS IT.
LET'S BRING THIS NIGHT-MARE...
TNK
...TO AN END.
SHH

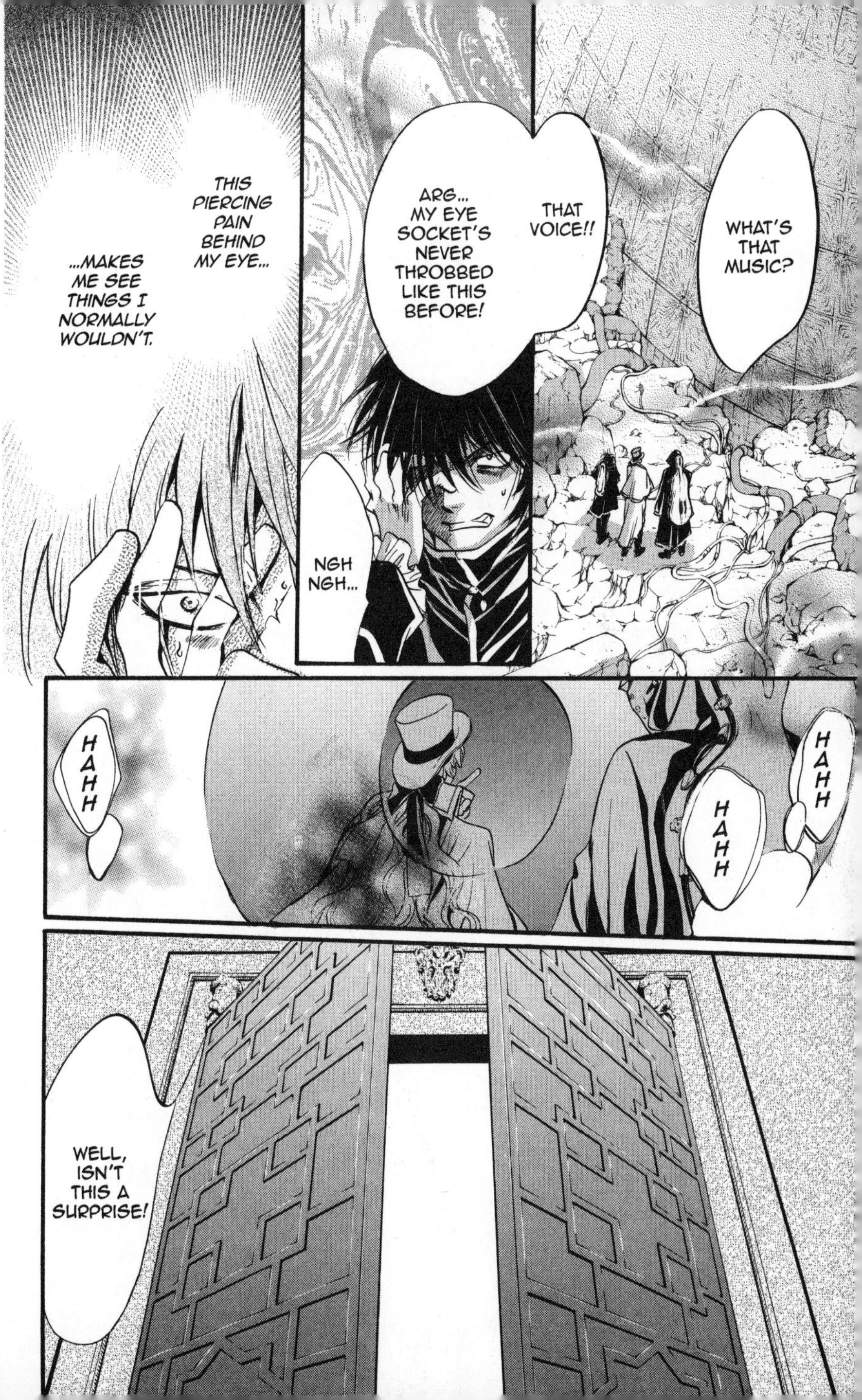
WHAT'S THAT MUSIC?
THAT VOICE!!
ARG... MY EYE SOCKET'S NEVER THROBBED LIKE THIS BEFORE!
NGH NGH...
THIS PIERCING PAIN BEHIND MY EYE...
...MAKES ME SEE THINGS I NORMALLY WOULDN'T.
HAHH
HAHH
HAHH
WELL, ISN'T THIS A SURPRISE!

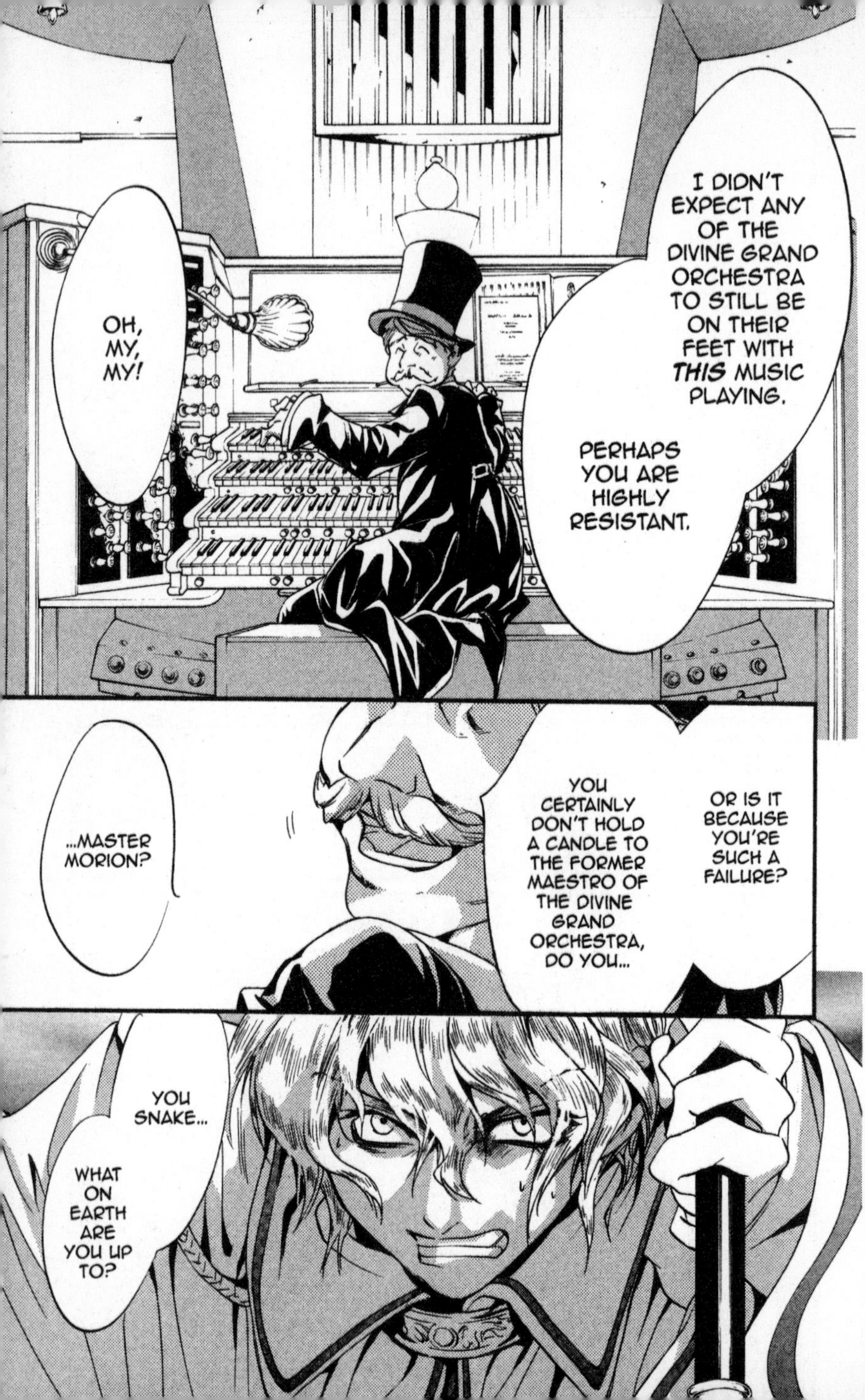

I DIDN'T EXPECT ANY OF THE DIVINE GRAND ORCHESTRA TO STILL BE ON THEIR FEET WITH *THIS* MUSIC PLAYING.
PERHAPS YOU ARE HIGHLY RESISTANT.
OH, MY, MY!
YOU CERTAINLY DON'T HOLD A CANDLE TO THE FORMER MAESTRO OF THE DIVINE GRAND ORCHESTRA, DO YOU...
OR IS IT BECAUSE YOU'RE SUCH A FAILURE?
...MASTER MORION?
YOU SNAKE...
WHAT ON EARTH ARE YOU UP TO?

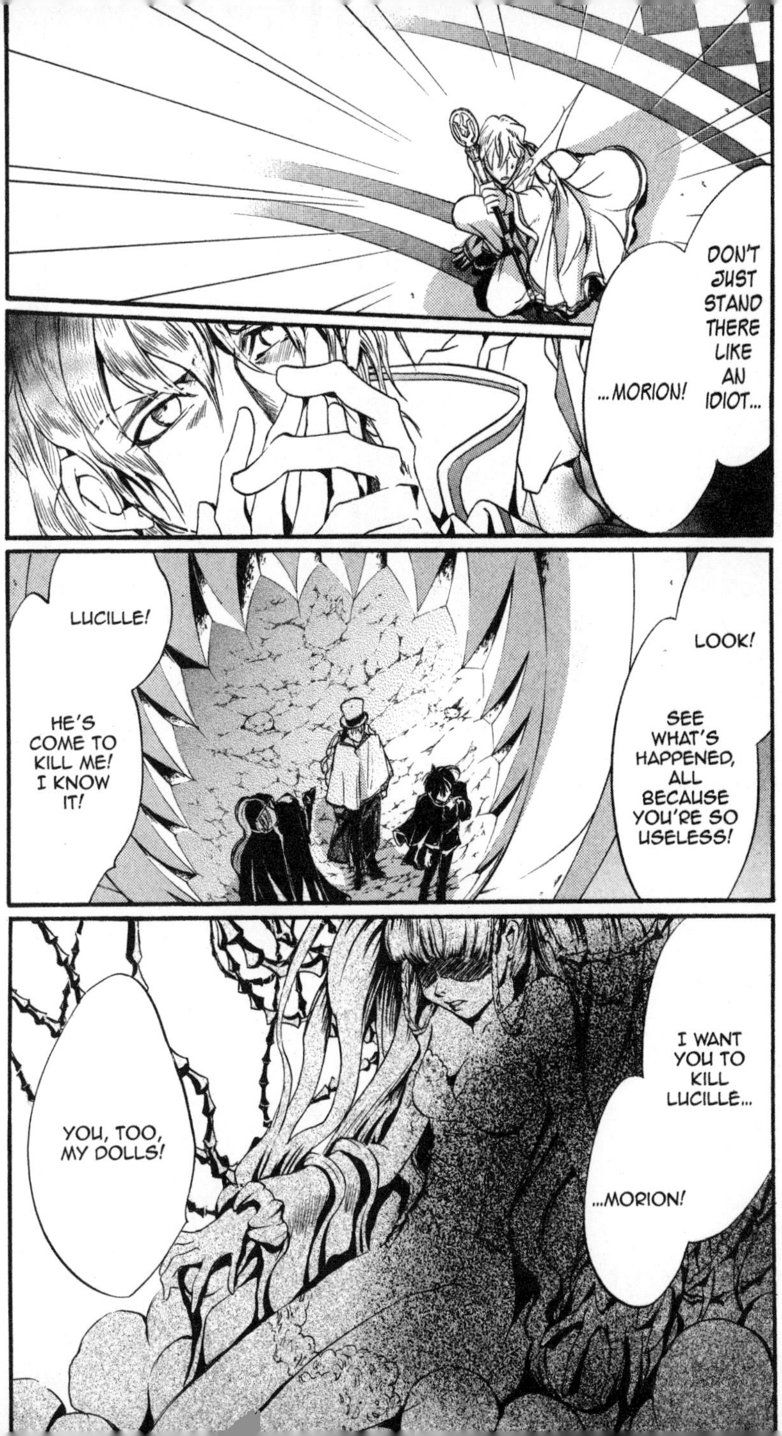
DON'T JUST STAND THERE LIKE AN IDIOT...
...MORION!
LOOK!
SEE WHAT'S HAPPENED, ALL BECAUSE YOU'RE SO USELESS!
LUCILLE!
HE'S COME TO KILL ME! I KNOW IT!
I WANT YOU TO KILL LUCILLE...
...MORION!
YOU, TOO, MY DOLLS!

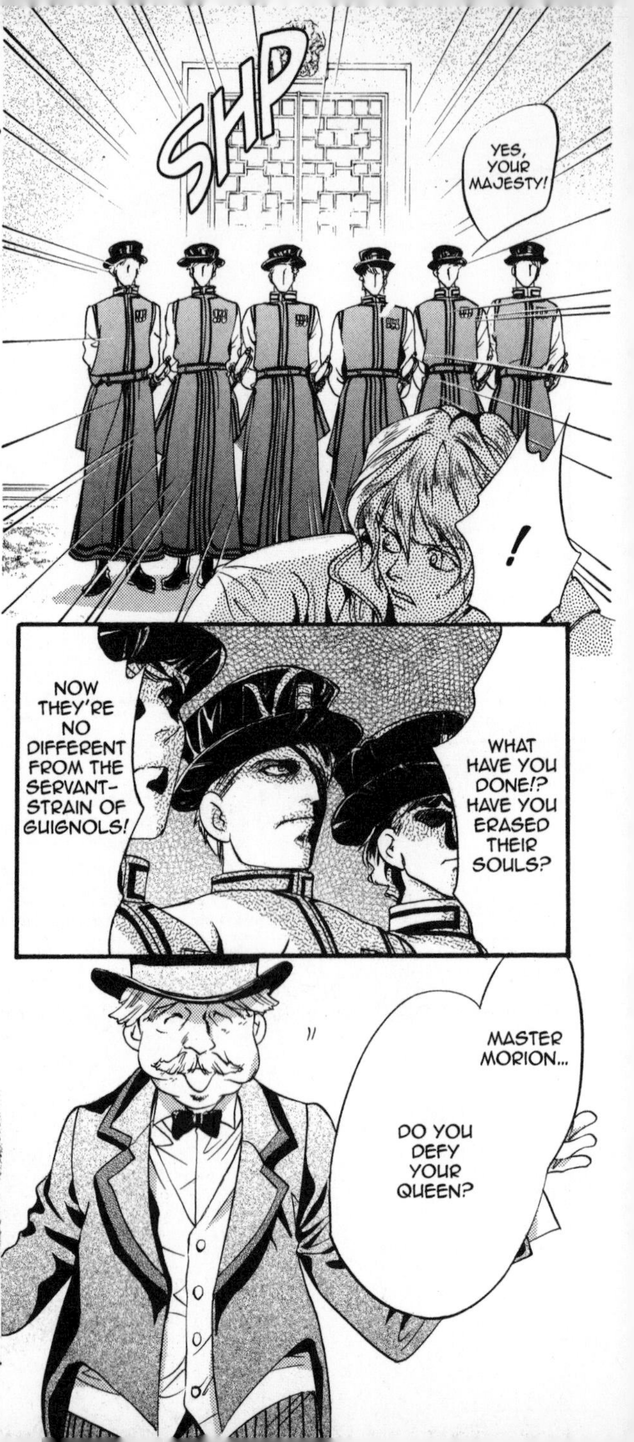
SHP
YES, YOUR MAJESTY!
!
WHAT HAVE YOU DONE!? HAVE YOU ERASED THEIR SOULS?
NOW THEY'RE NO DIFFERENT FROM THE SERVANT-STRAIN OF GUIGNOLS!
MASTER MORION...
DO YOU DEFY YOUR QUEEN?

Hi, there! Here we are in the final volume of *Grand Guignol Orchestra!*

Since this is the final story, it's set in the royal palace. Finally, you'll find out the history between Cordie and Morion, and how Lucille became the way he is. I'm really fond of Morion's character, so I'm glad he's finally getting some action again!

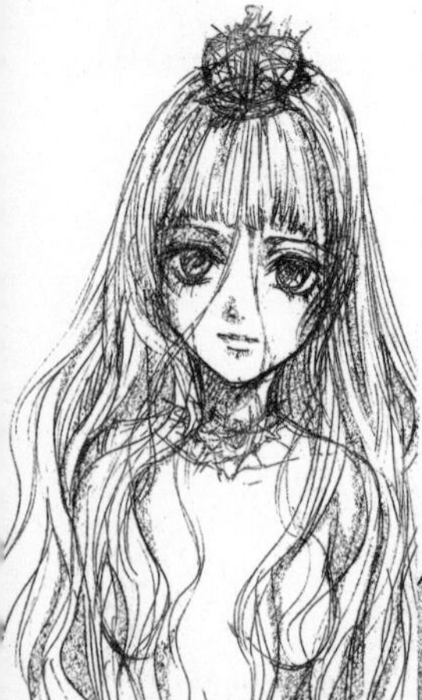

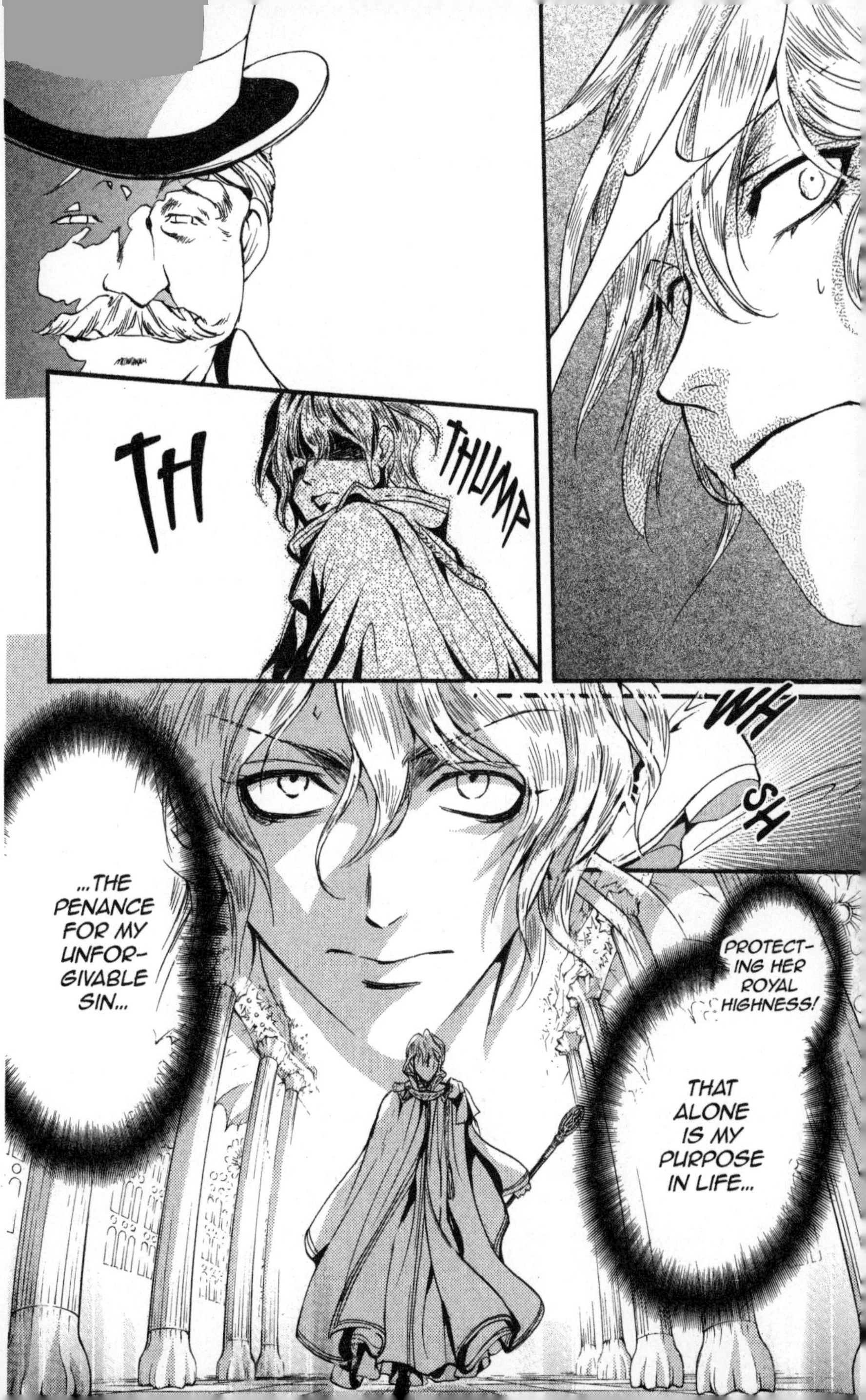
THUMP
TH
WHSH
PROTECT-ING HER ROYAL HIGHNESS!
...THE PENANCE FOR MY UNFORGIVABLE SIN...
THAT ALONE IS MY PURPOSE IN LIFE...

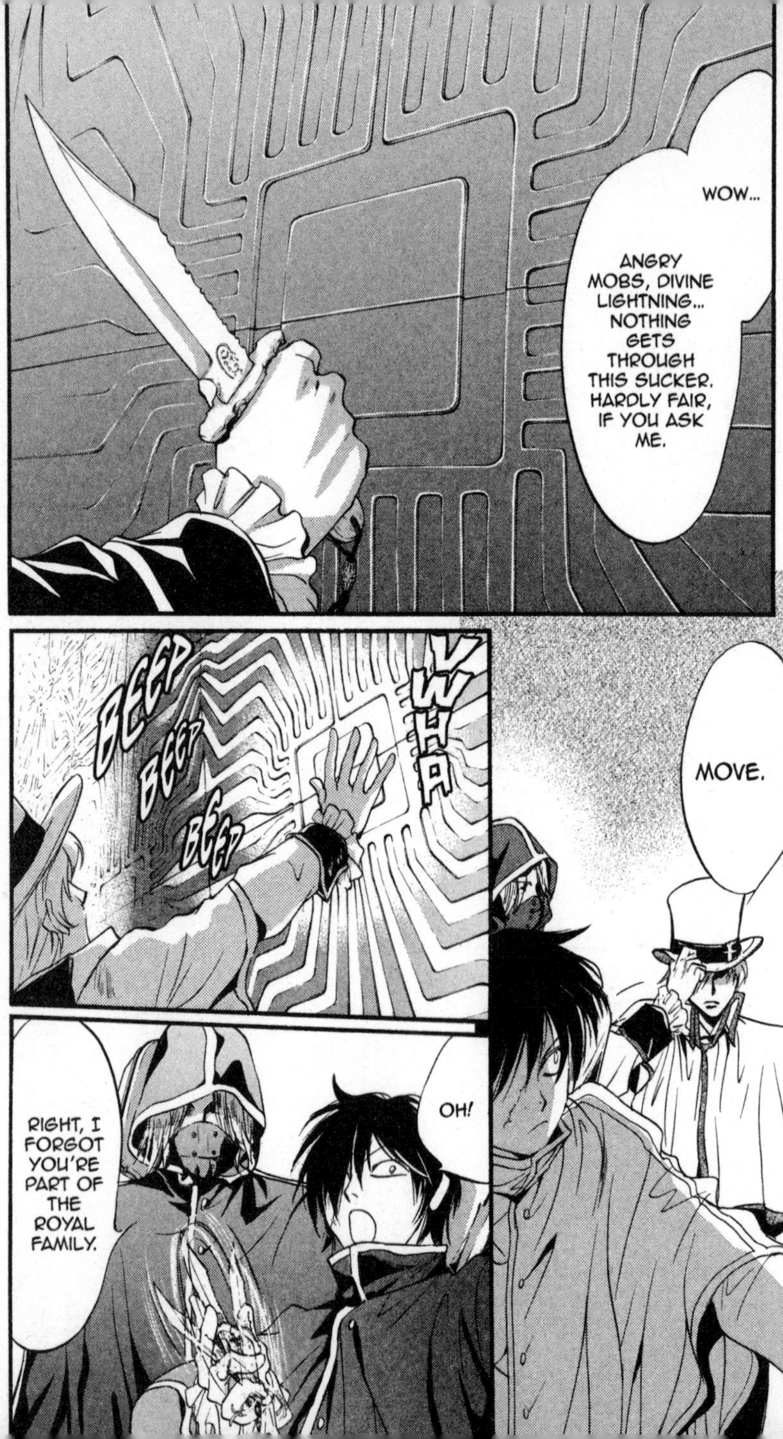
WOW...
ANGRY MOBS, DIVINE LIGHTNING... NOTHING GETS THROUGH THIS SUCKER. HARDLY FAIR, IF YOU ASK ME.
MOVE.
VWHA
BEEP
BEEP
BEEP
OH!
RIGHT, I FORGOT YOU'RE PART OF THE ROYAL FAMILY.

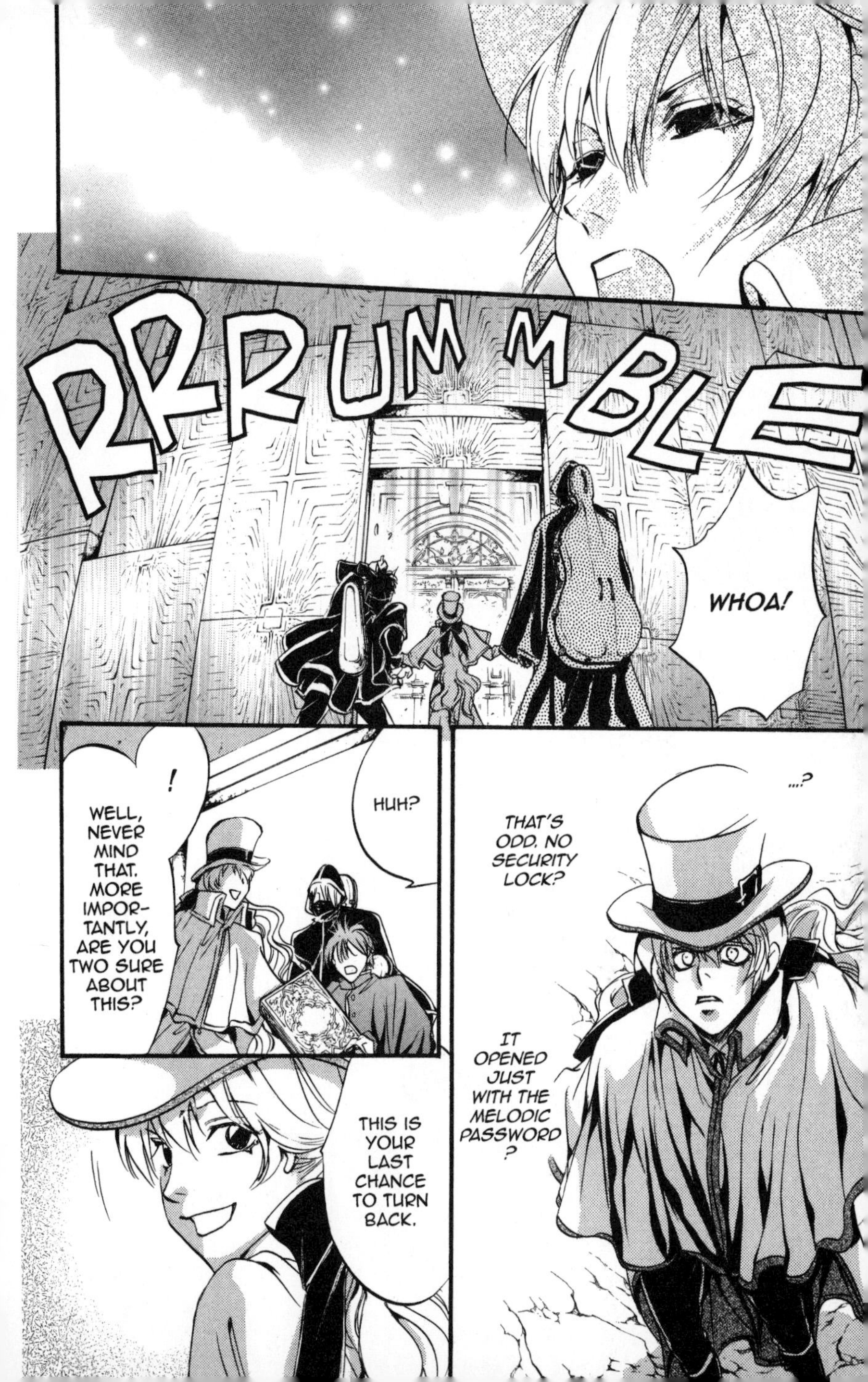
RRRUMMBLE
WHOA!
...?
THAT'S ODD. NO SECURITY LOCK?
IT OPENED JUST WITH THE MELODIC PASSWORD?
HUH?
!
WELL, NEVER MIND THAT. MORE IMPORTANTLY, ARE YOU TWO SURE ABOUT THIS?
THIS IS YOUR LAST CHANCE TO TURN BACK.

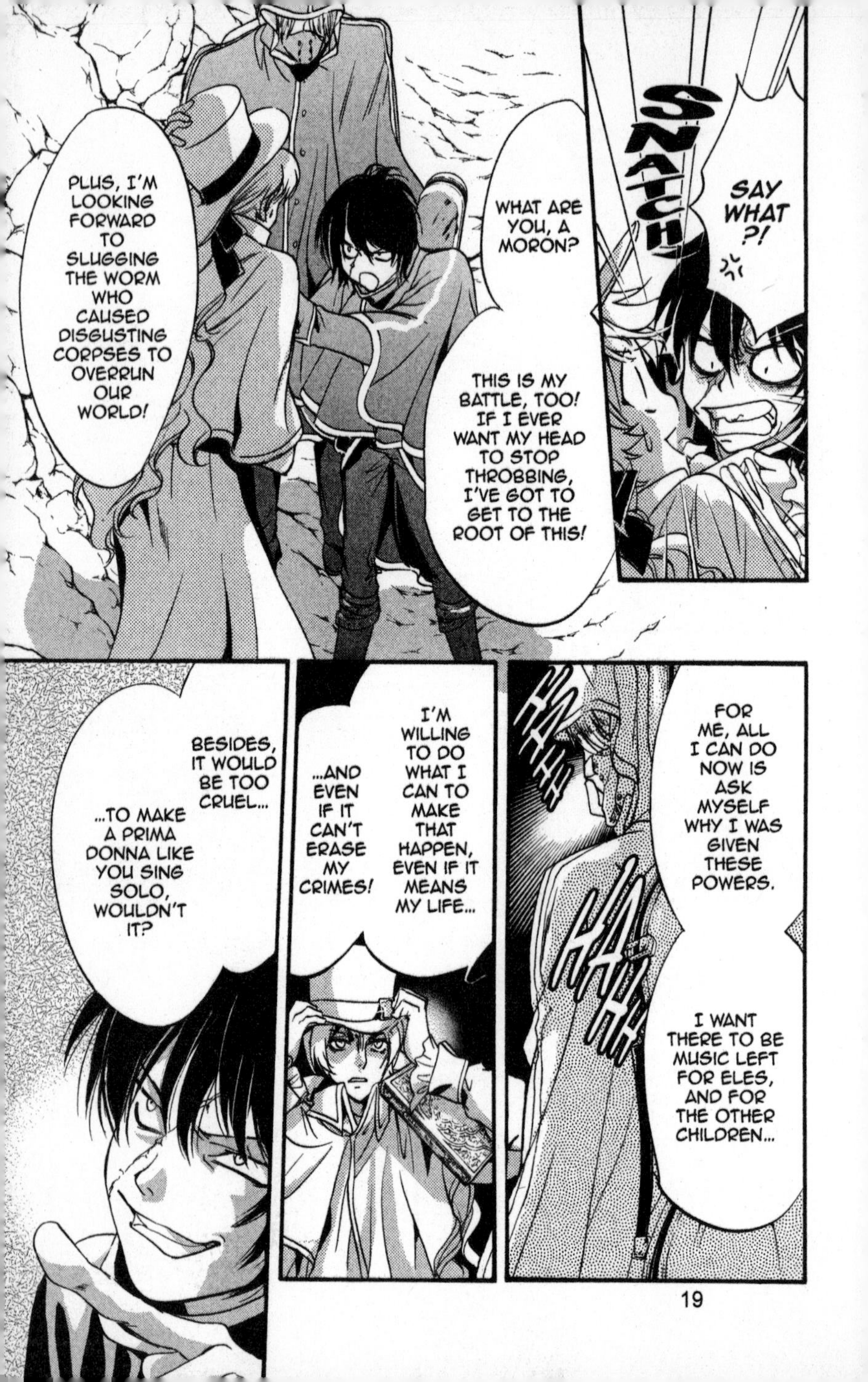
SNATCH
SAY WHAT?!
WHAT ARE YOU, A MORON?
THIS IS MY BATTLE, TOO! IF I EVER WANT MY HEAD TO STOP THROBBING, I'VE GOT TO GET TO THE ROOT OF THIS!
PLUS, I'M LOOKING FORWARD TO SLUGGING THE WORM WHO CAUSED DISGUSTING CORPSES TO OVERRUN OUR WORLD!
FOR ME, ALL I CAN DO NOW IS ASK MYSELF WHY I WAS GIVEN THESE POWERS.
I WANT THERE TO BE MUSIC LEFT FOR ELES, AND FOR THE OTHER CHILDREN...
I'M WILLING TO DO WHAT I CAN TO MAKE THAT HAPPEN, EVEN IF IT MEANS MY LIFE...
...AND EVEN IF IT CAN'T ERASE MY CRIMES!
BESIDES, IT WOULD BE TOO CRUEL...
...TO MAKE A PRIMA DONNA LIKE YOU SING SOLO, WOULDN'T IT?

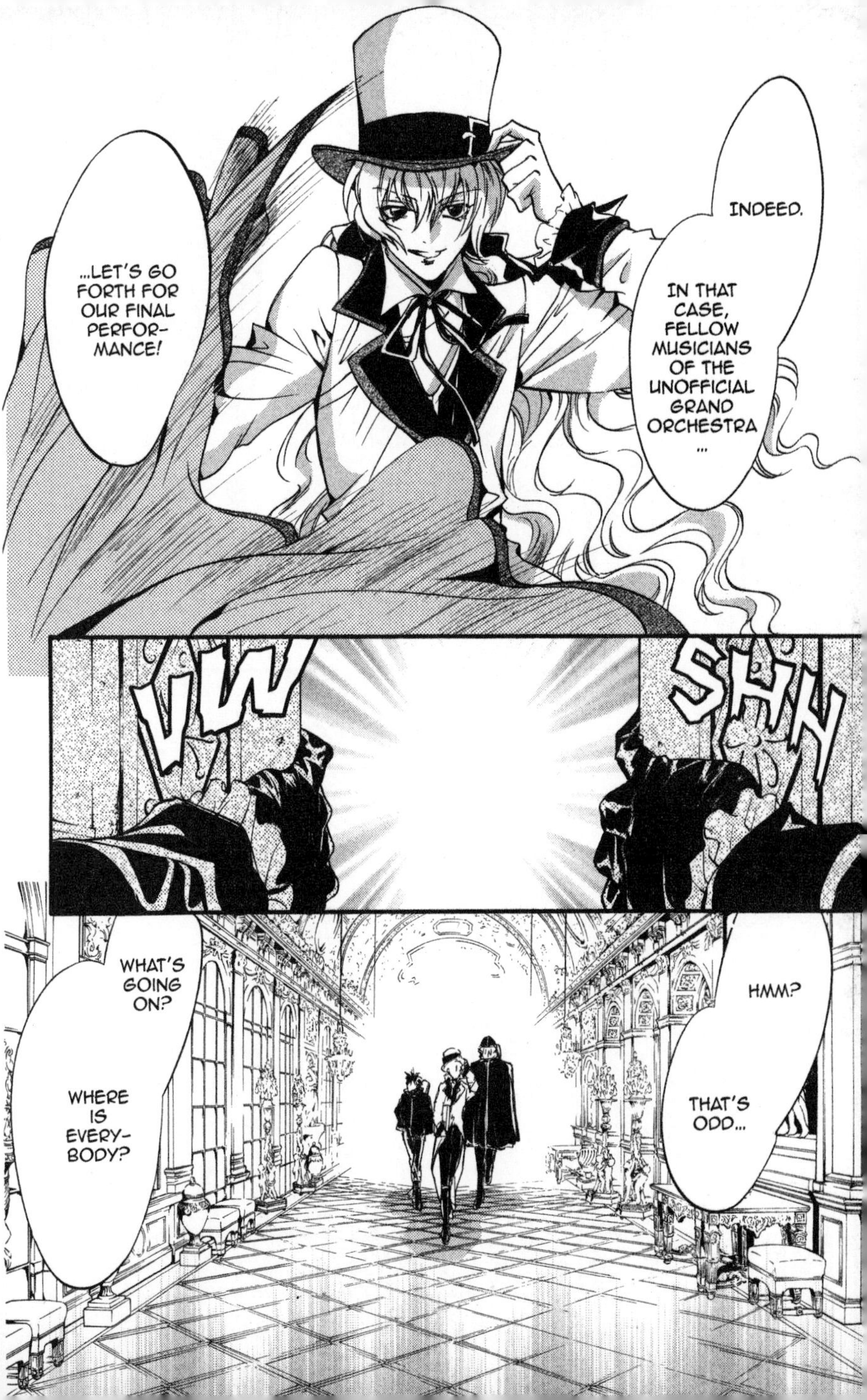
INDEED.
IN THAT CASE, FELLOW MUSICIANS OF THE UNOFFICIAL GRAND ORCHESTRA...
...LET'S GO FORTH FOR OUR FINAL PERFORMANCE!
SHN
VW
HMM?
THAT'S ODD...
WHAT'S GOING ON?
WHERE IS EVERYBODY?

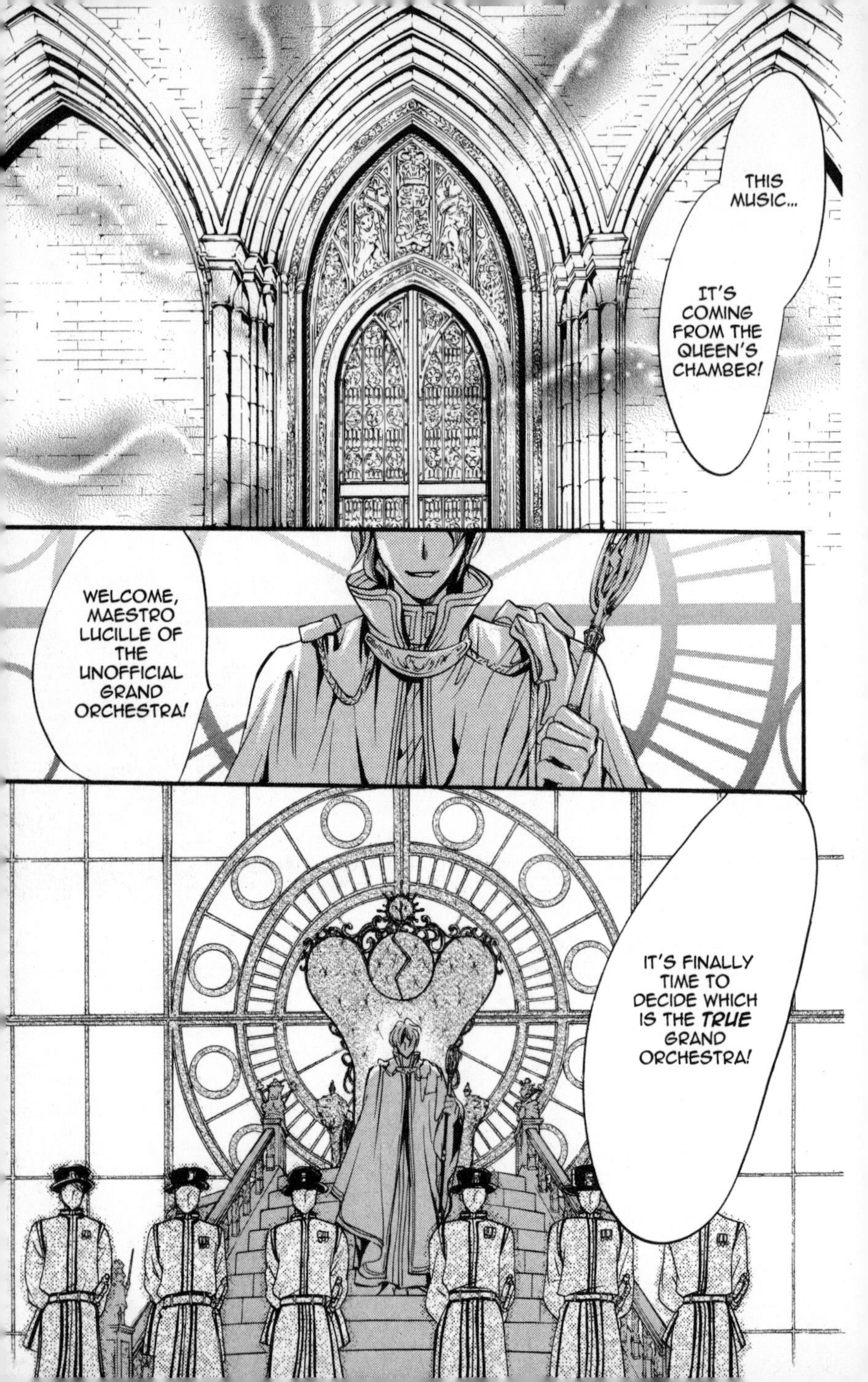
THIS MUSIC...
IT'S COMING FROM THE QUEEN'S CHAMBER!
WELCOME, MAESTRO LUCILLE OF THE UNOFFICIAL GRAND ORCHESTRA!
IT'S FINALLY TIME TO DECIDE WHICH IS THE TRUE GRAND ORCHESTRA!

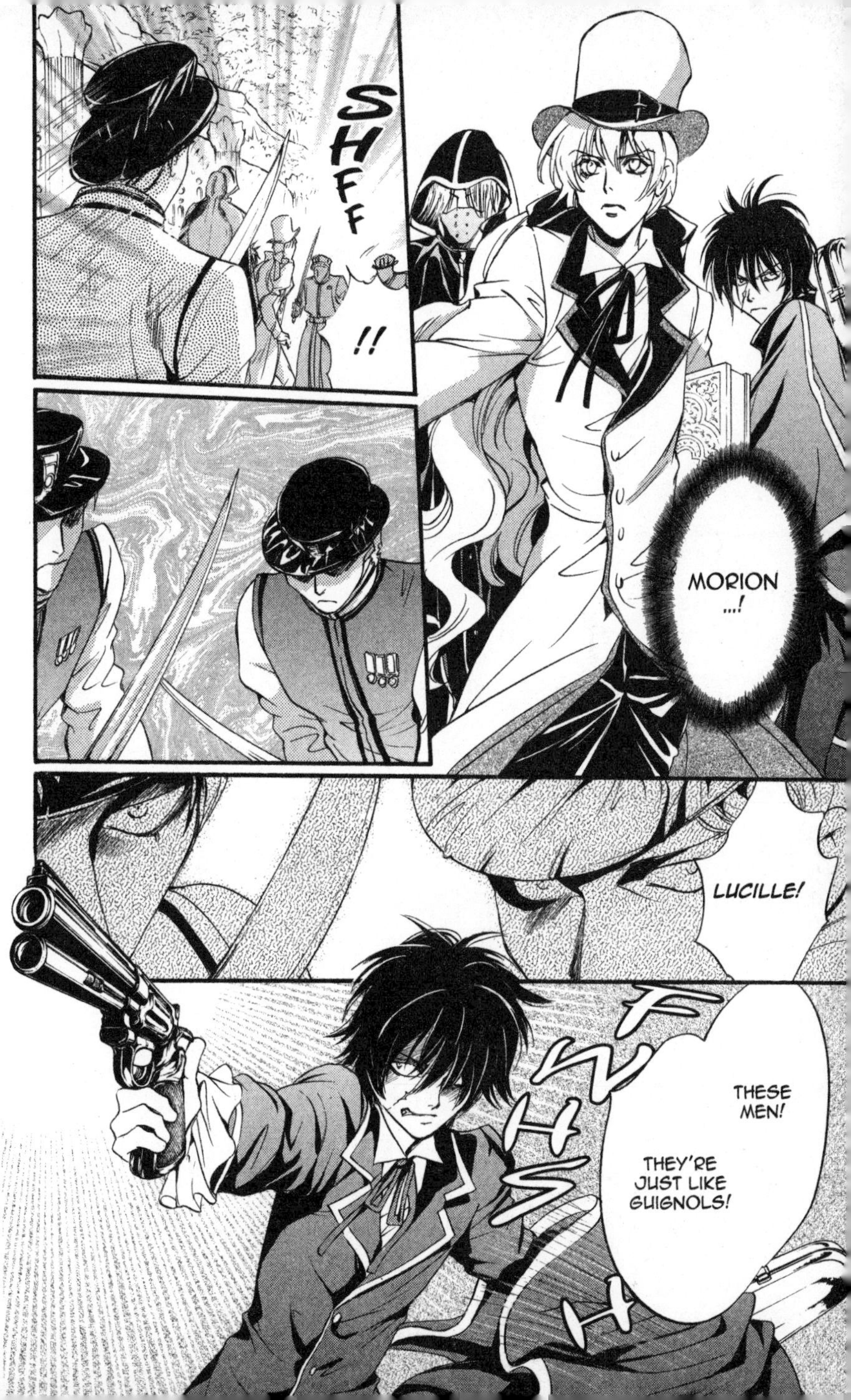
MORION ...!
SHFF
!!
LUCILLE!
THESE MEN!
THEY'RE JUST LIKE GUIGNOLS!

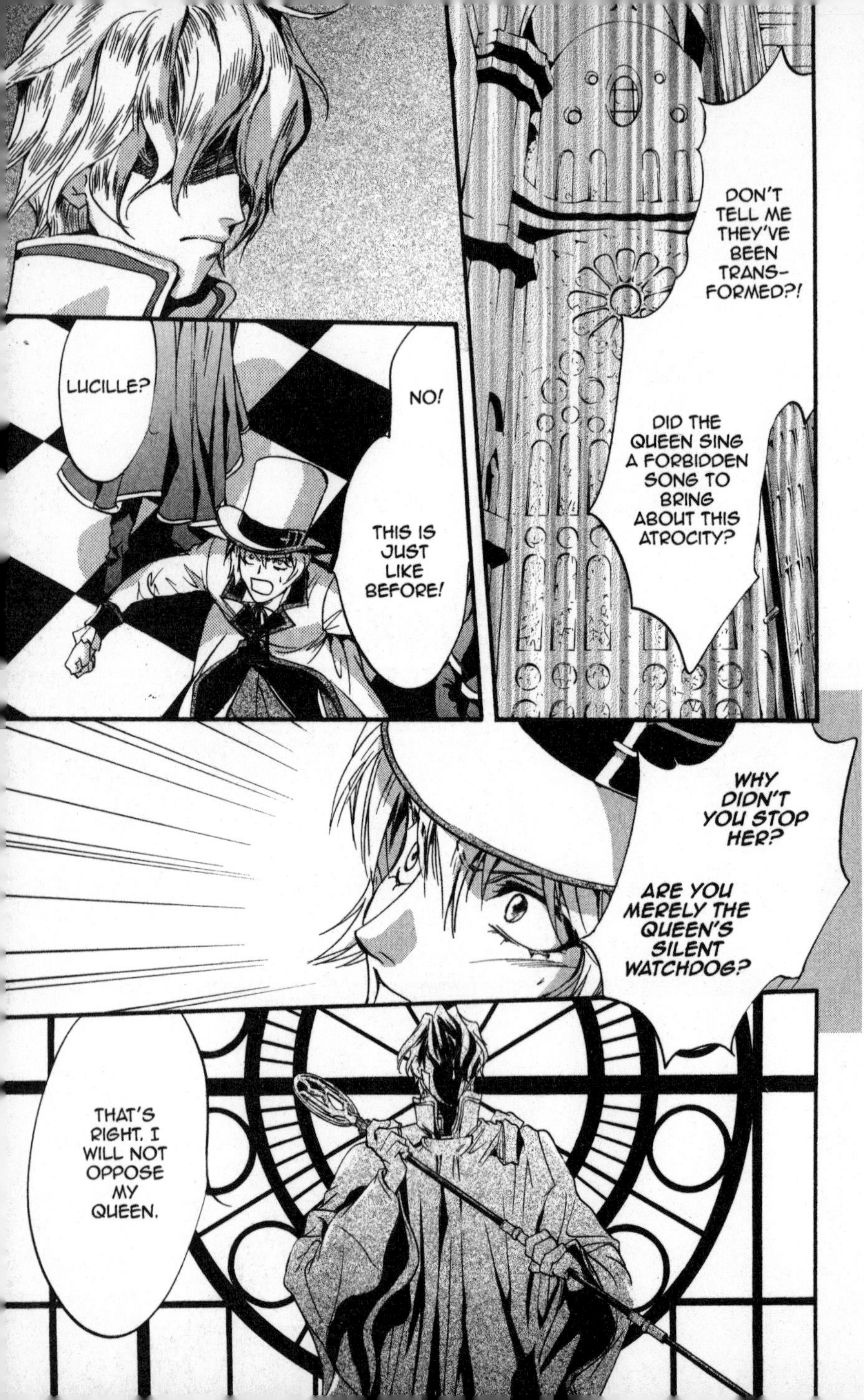
DON'T TELL ME THEY'VE BEEN TRANS-FORMED?!
DID THE QUEEN SING A FORBIDDEN SONG TO BRING ABOUT THIS ATROCITY?
NO!
THIS IS JUST LIKE BEFORE!
LUCILLE?
WHY DIDN'T YOU STOP HER?
ARE YOU MERELY THE QUEEN'S SILENT WATCHDOG?
THAT'S RIGHT. I WILL NOT OPPOSE MY QUEEN.

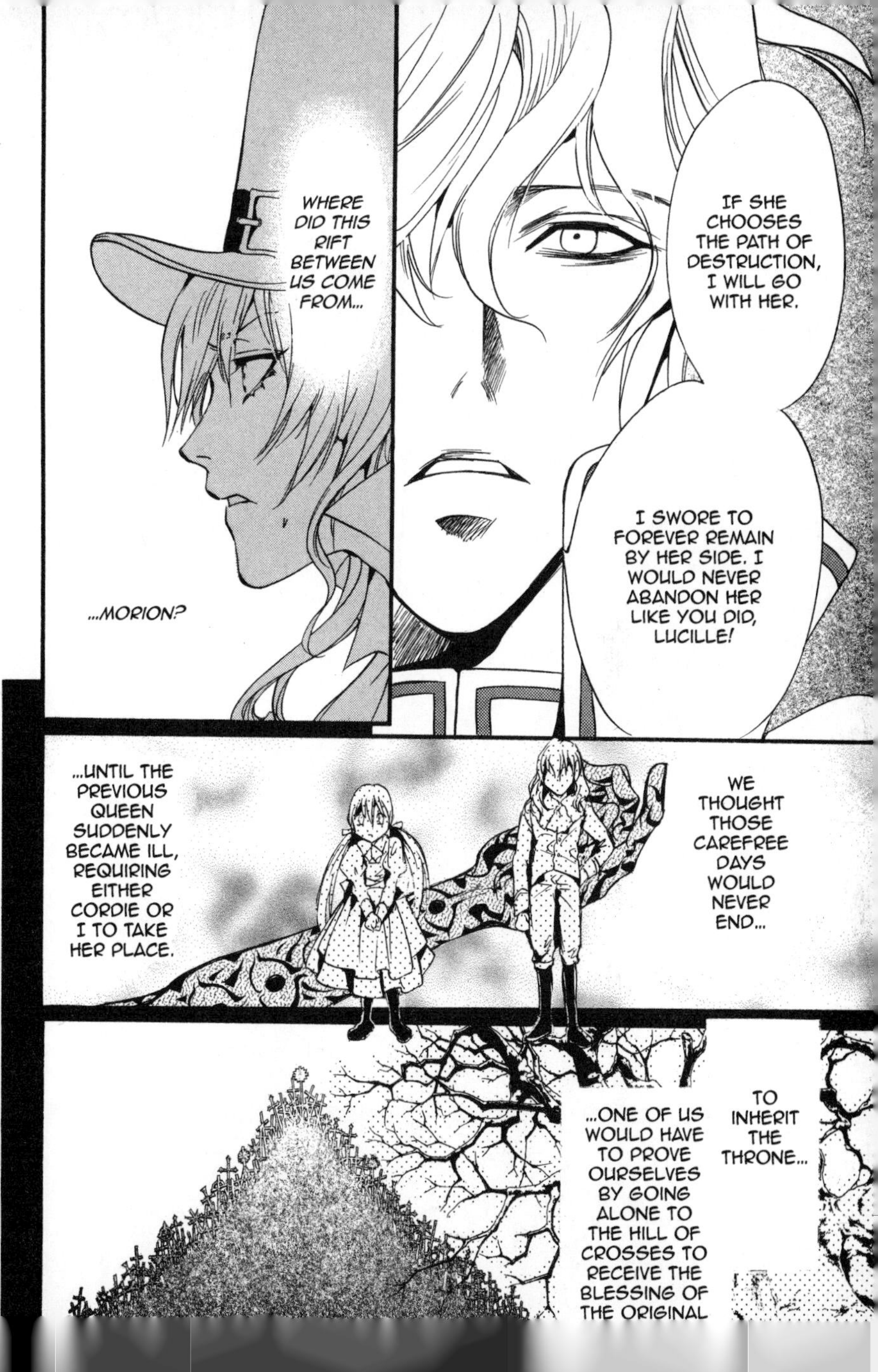
IF SHE CHOOSES THE PATH OF DESTRUCTION, I WILL GO WITH HER.
I SWORE TO FOREVER REMAIN BY HER SIDE. I WOULD NEVER ABANDON HER LIKE YOU DID, LUCILLE!
WHERE DID THIS RIFT BETWEEN US COME FROM...
...MORION?
WE THOUGHT THOSE CAREFREE DAYS WOULD NEVER END...
...UNTIL THE PREVIOUS QUEEN SUDDENLY BECAME ILL, REQUIRING EITHER CORDIE OR I TO TAKE HER PLACE.
TO INHERIT THE THRONE...
...ONE OF US WOULD HAVE TO PROVE OURSELVES BY GOING ALONE TO THE HILL OF CROSSES TO RECEIVE THE BLESSING OF THE ORIGINAL

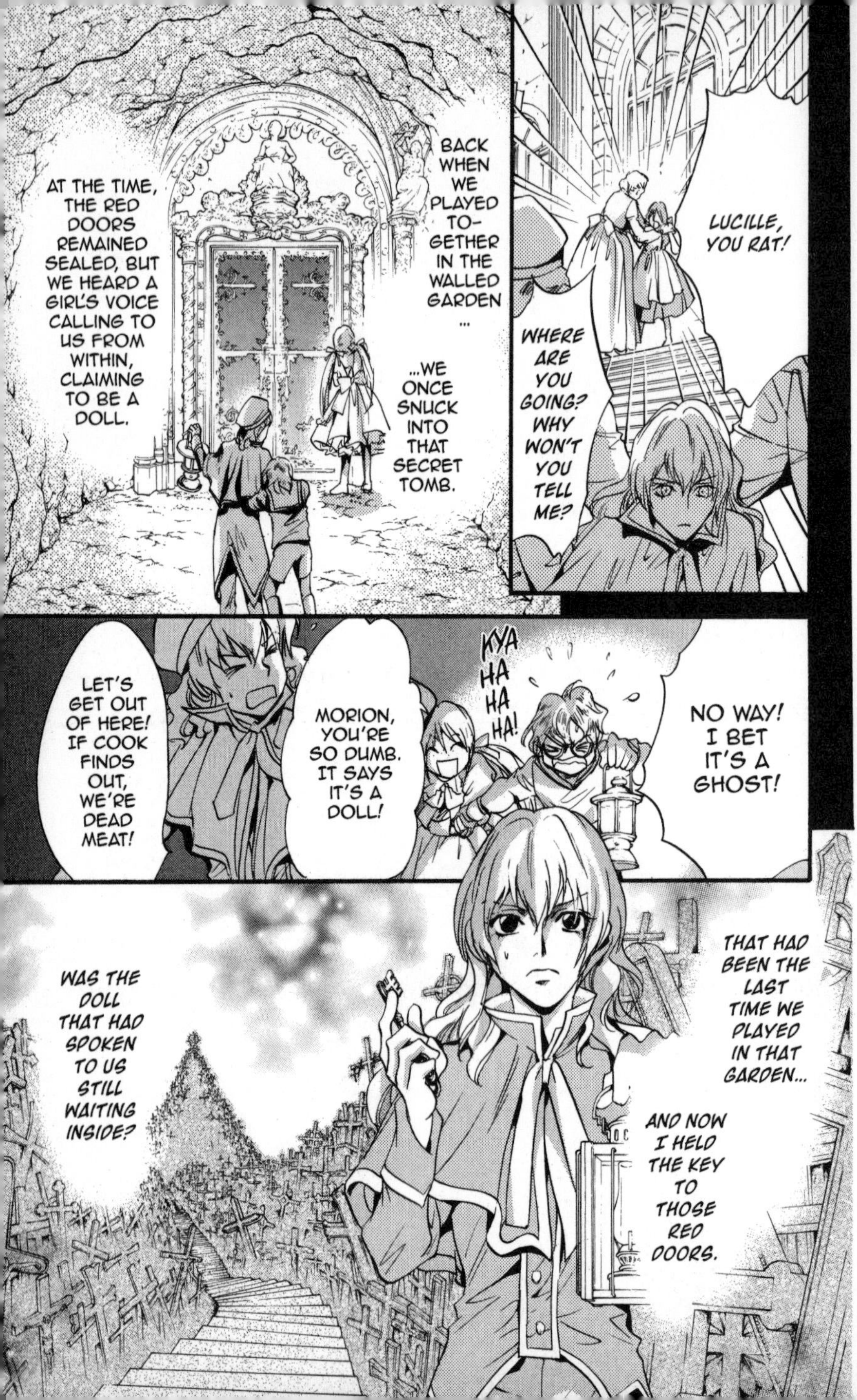
LUCILLE, YOU RAT!
WHERE ARE YOU GOING? WHY WON'T YOU TELL ME?
BACK WHEN WE PLAYED TO-GETHER IN THE WALLED GARDEN ...
...WE ONCE SNUCK INTO THAT SECRET TOMB.
AT THE TIME, THE RED DOORS REMAINED SEALED, BUT WE HEARD A GIRL'S VOICE CALLING TO US FROM WITHIN, CLAIMING TO BE A DOLL.
NO WAY! I BET IT'S A GHOST!
KYA HA HA HA!
MORION, YOU'RE SO DUMB. IT SAYS IT'S A DOLL!
LET'S GET OUT OF HERE! IF COOK FINDS OUT, WE'RE DEAD MEAT!
THAT HAD BEEN THE LAST TIME WE PLAYED IN THAT GARDEN...
AND NOW I HELD THE KEY TO THOSE RED DOORS.
WAS THE DOLL THAT HAD SPOKEN TO US STILL WAITING INSIDE?

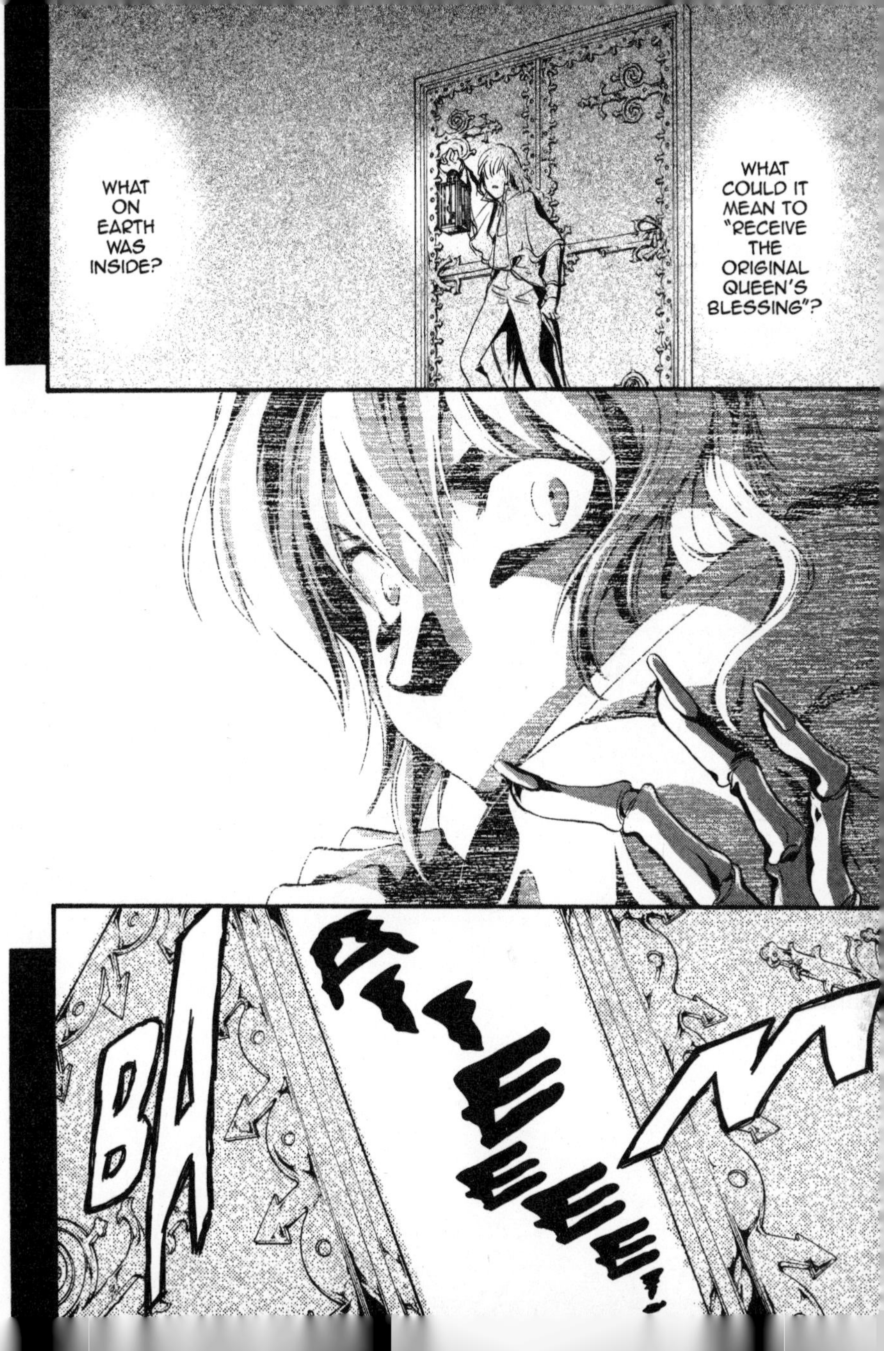
WHAT COULD IT MEAN TO "RECEIVE THE ORIGINAL QUEEN'S BLESSING"?
WHAT ON EARTH WAS INSIDE?

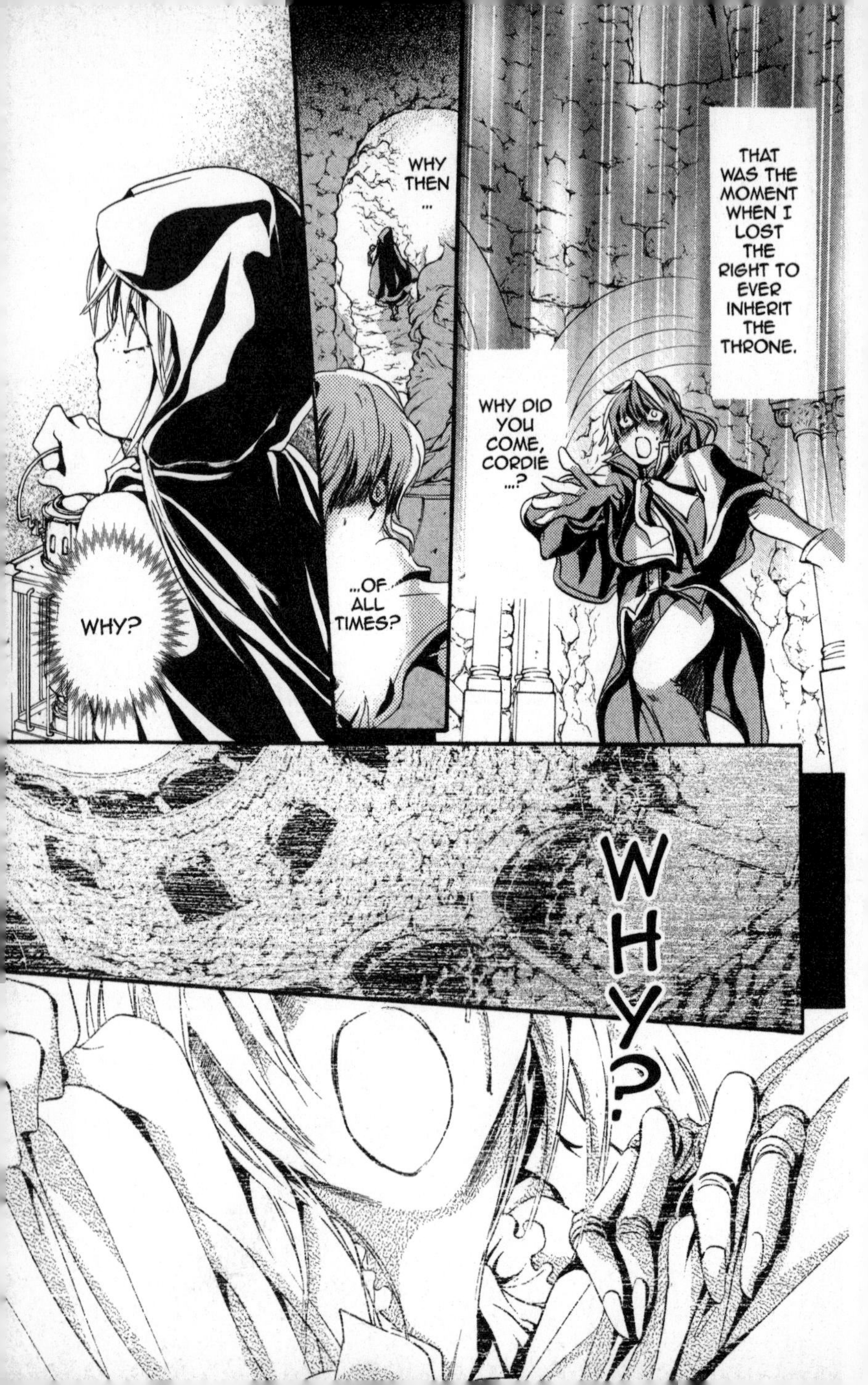
THAT WAS THE MOMENT WHEN I LOST THE RIGHT TO EVER INHERIT THE THRONE.
WHY DID YOU COME, CORDIE ...?
WHY THEN ...
...OF ALL TIMES?
WHY?
WHY?

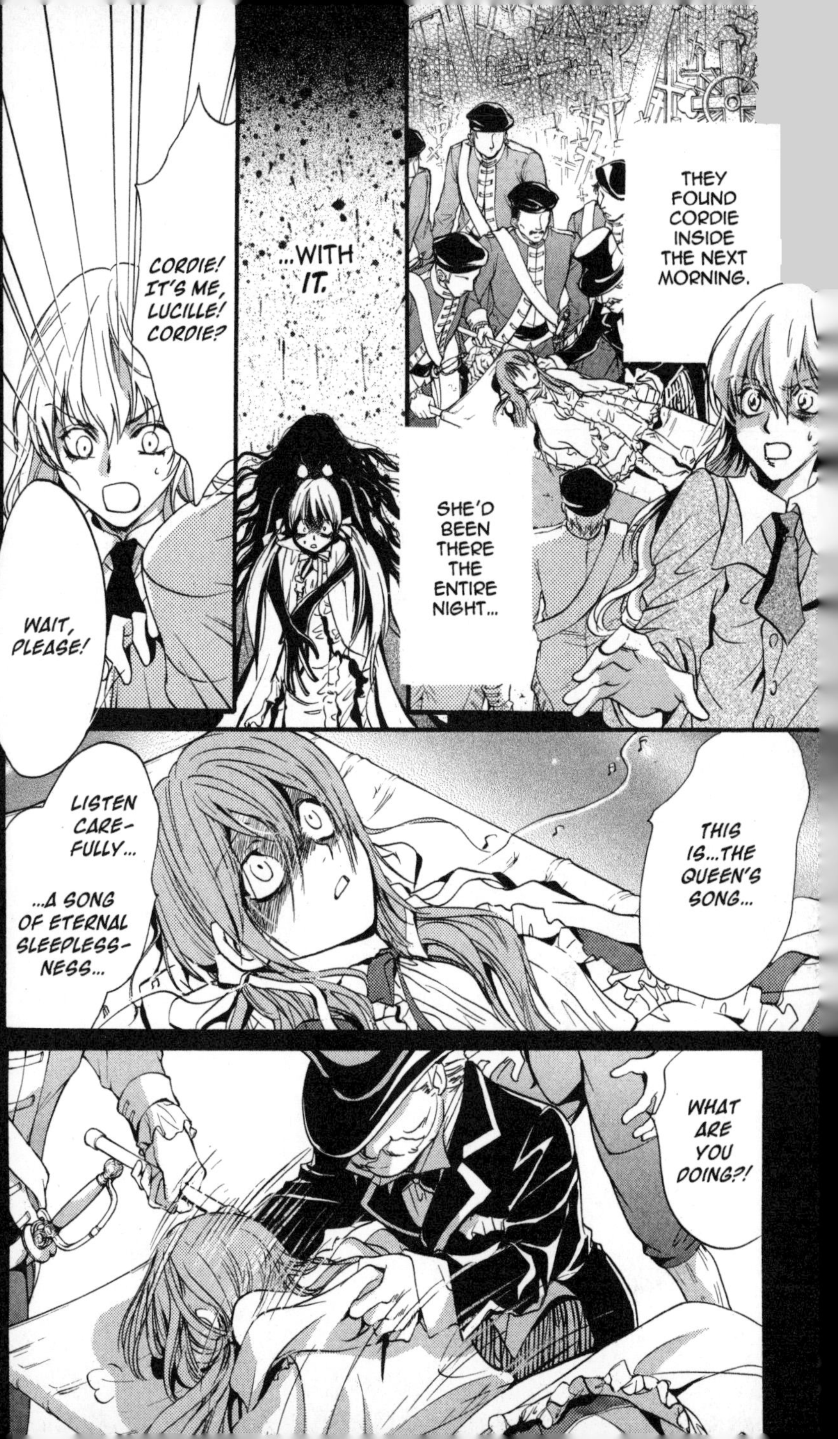
THEY FOUND CORDIE INSIDE THE NEXT MORNING.
SHE'D BEEN THERE THE ENTIRE NIGHT...
...WITH IT.
CORDIE! IT'S ME, LUCILLE! CORDIE?
WAIT, PLEASE!
THIS IS...THE QUEEN'S SONG...
LISTEN CAREFULLY...
...A SONG OF ETERNAL SLEEPLESS-NESS...
WHAT ARE YOU DOING?!

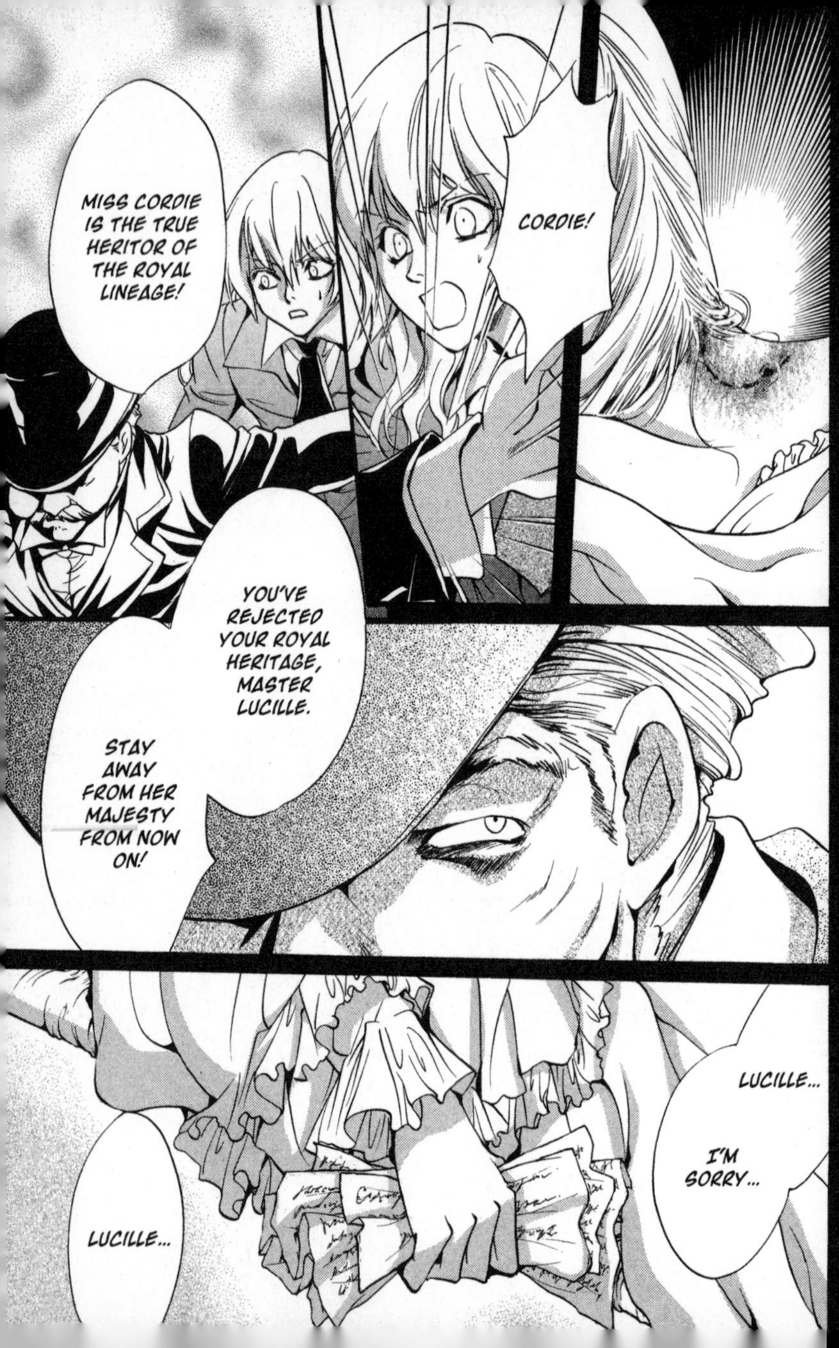
CORDIE!
MISS CORDIE IS THE TRUE HERITOR OF THE ROYAL LINEAGE!
YOU'VE REJECTED YOUR ROYAL HERITAGE, MASTER LUCILLE.
STAY AWAY FROM HER MAJESTY FROM NOW ON!
LUCILLE...
I'M SORRY...
LUCILLE...

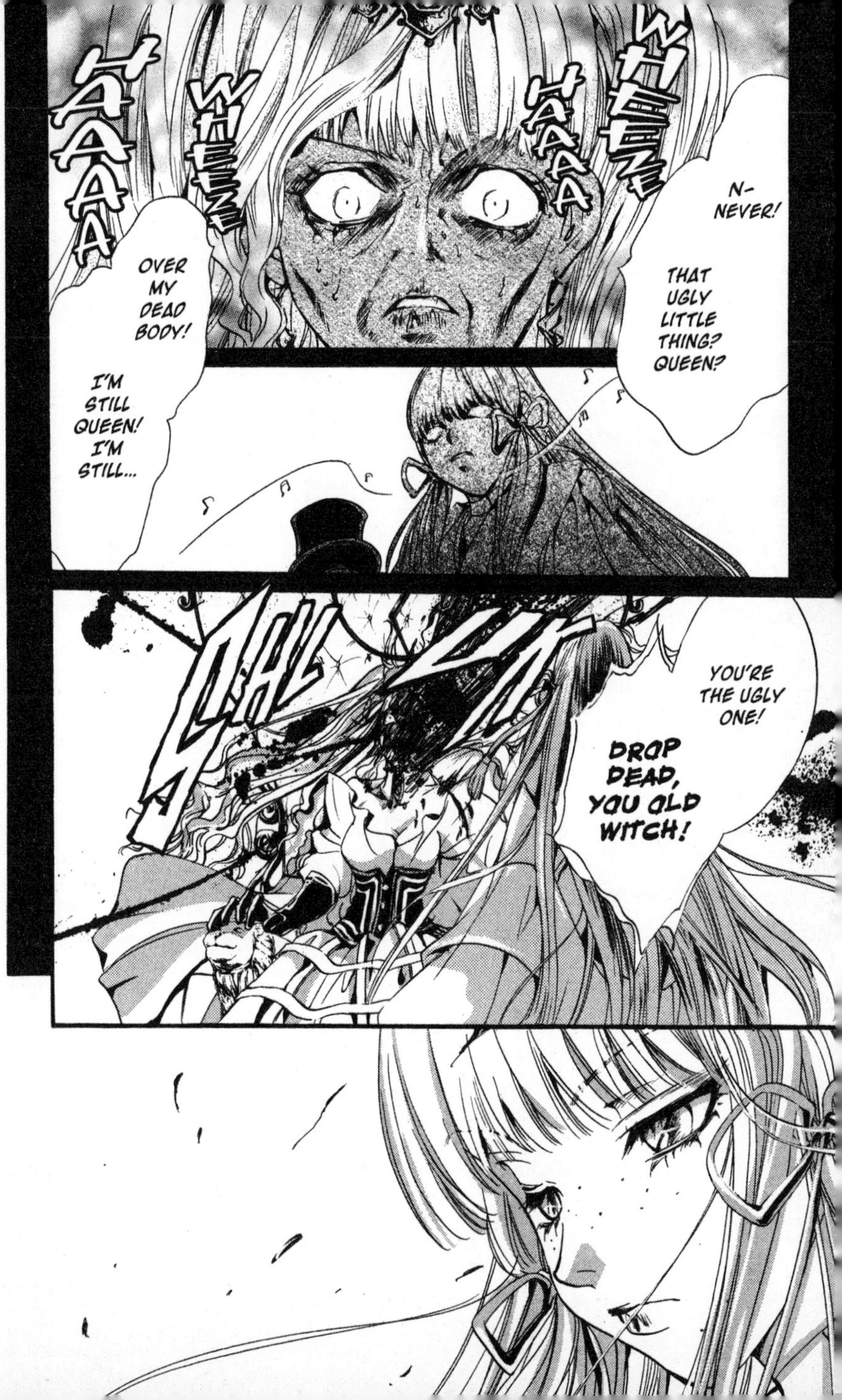
WHEEZE
N-NEVER!
HAAAA
THAT UGLY LITTLE THING? QUEEN?
WHEEZE
HAAAAA
OVER MY DEAD BODY!
I'M STILL QUEEN! I'M STILL...
YOU'RE THE UGLY ONE!
DROP DEAD, YOU OLD WITCH!

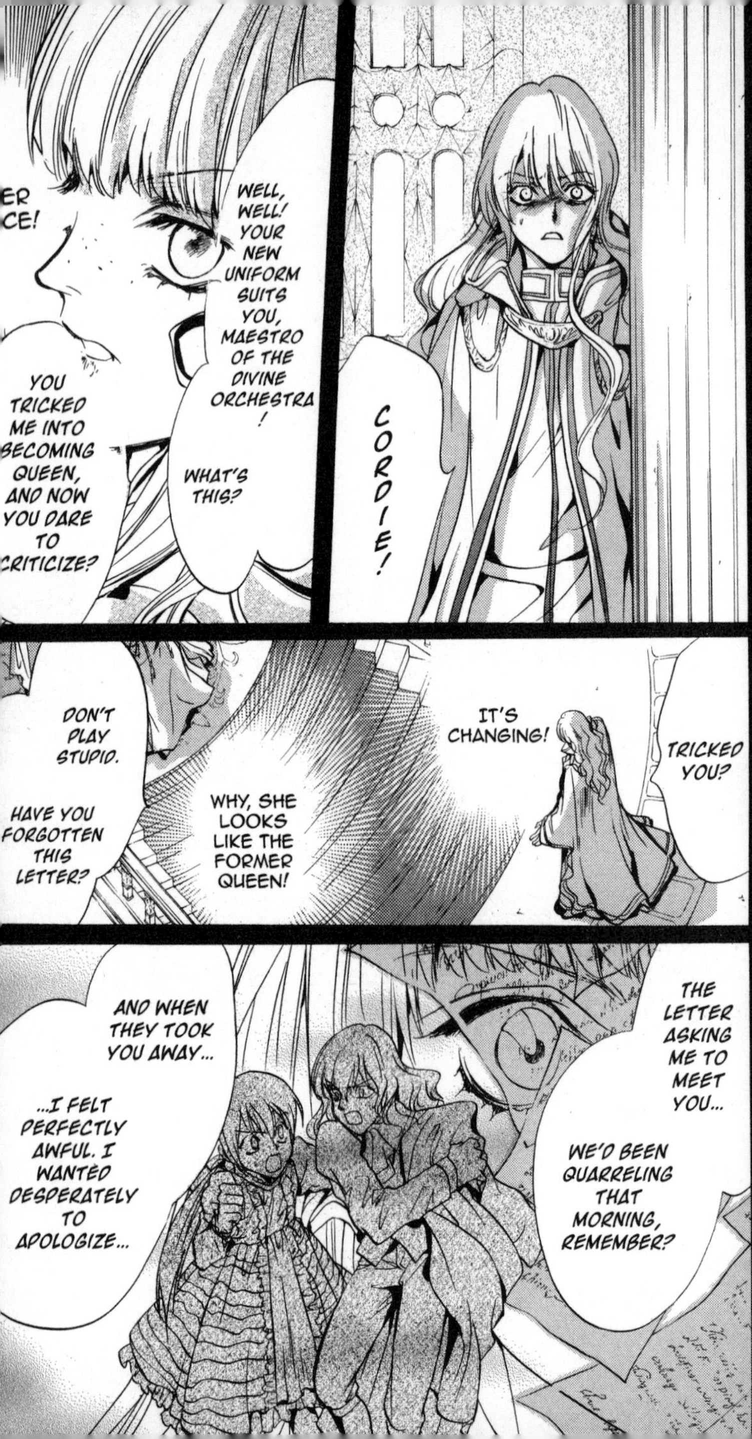
CORDIE!
WELL, WELL! YOUR NEW UNIFORM SUITS YOU, MAESTRO OF THE DIVINE ORCHESTRA!
WHAT'S THIS?
YOU TRICKED ME INTO BECOMING QUEEN, AND NOW YOU DARE TO CRITICIZE?
TRICKED YOU?
IT'S CHANGING!
WHY, SHE LOOKS LIKE THE FORMER QUEEN!
DON'T PLAY STUPID.
HAVE YOU FORGOTTEN THIS LETTER?
THE LETTER ASKING ME TO MEET YOU...
WE'D BEEN QUARRELING THAT MORNING, REMEMBER?
AND WHEN THEY TOOK YOU AWAY...
...I FELT PERFECTLY AWFUL. I WANTED DESPERATELY TO APOLOGIZE...

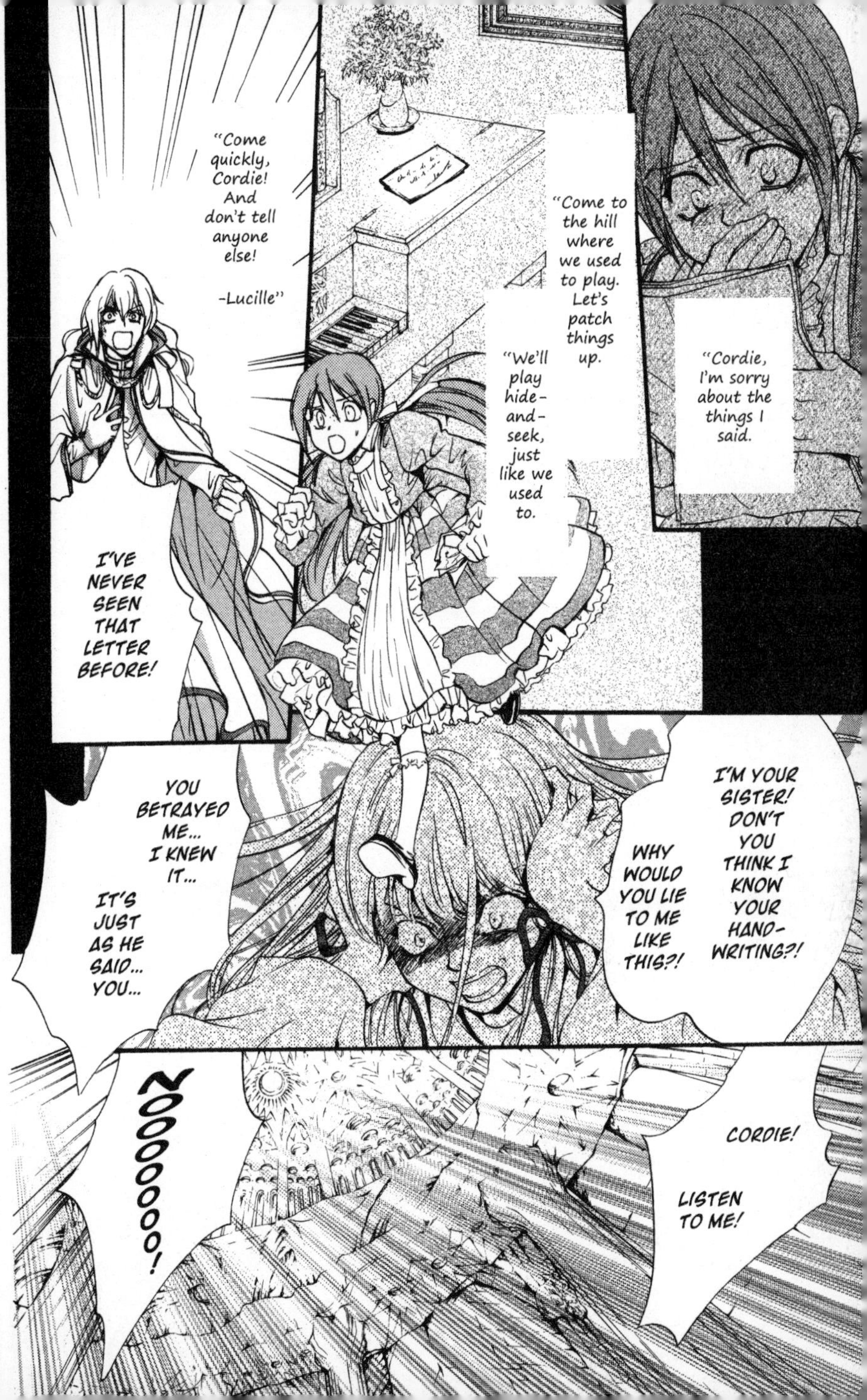
"Cordie, I'm sorry about the things I said.
"Come to the hill where we used to play. Let's patch things up.
"We'll play hide-and-seek, just like we used to.
"Come quickly, Cordie! And don't tell anyone else!
-Lucille"
I'VE NEVER SEEN THAT LETTER BEFORE!
I'M YOUR SISTER! DON'T YOU THINK I KNOW YOUR HAND-WRITING?!
WHY WOULD YOU LIE TO ME LIKE THIS?!
YOU BETRAYED ME... I KNEW IT...
IT'S JUST AS HE SAID... YOU...
CORDIE!
LISTEN TO ME!
NOOOOOOOO!

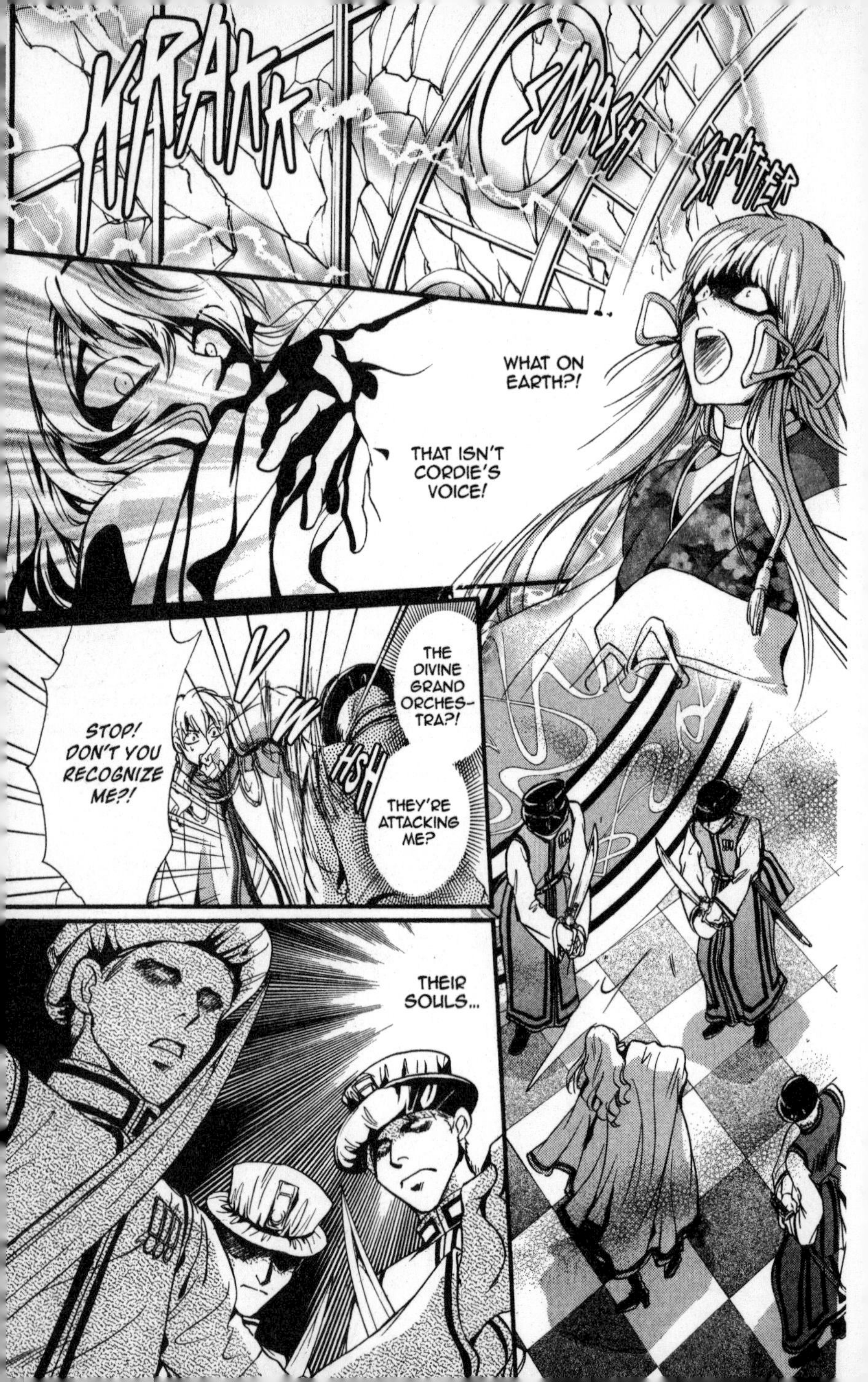
SHATTER
SMASH
KRAKK
WHAT ON EARTH?!
THAT ISN'T CORDIE'S VOICE!
THE DIVINE GRAND ORCHESTRA?!
THEY'RE ATTACKING ME?
HSH
STOP! DON'T YOU RECOGNIZE ME?!
THEIR SOULS...

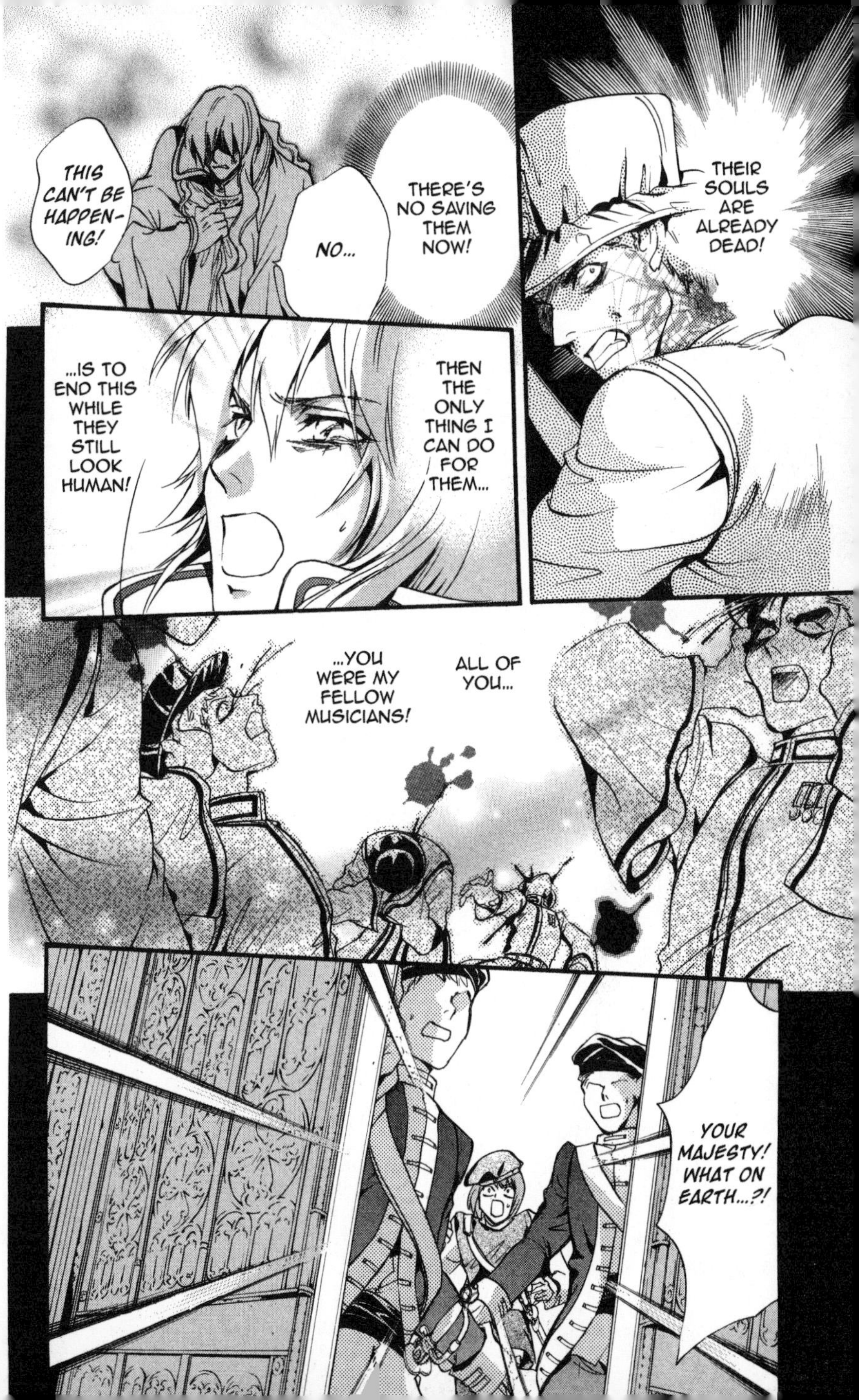
THEIR SOULS ARE ALREADY DEAD!
THERE'S NO SAVING THEM NOW!
NO...
THIS CAN'T BE HAPPEN-ING!
THEN THE ONLY THING I CAN DO FOR THEM...
...IS TO END THIS WHILE THEY STILL LOOK HUMAN!
ALL OF YOU...
...YOU WERE MY FELLOW MUSICIANS!
YOUR MAJESTY! WHAT ON EARTH...?!

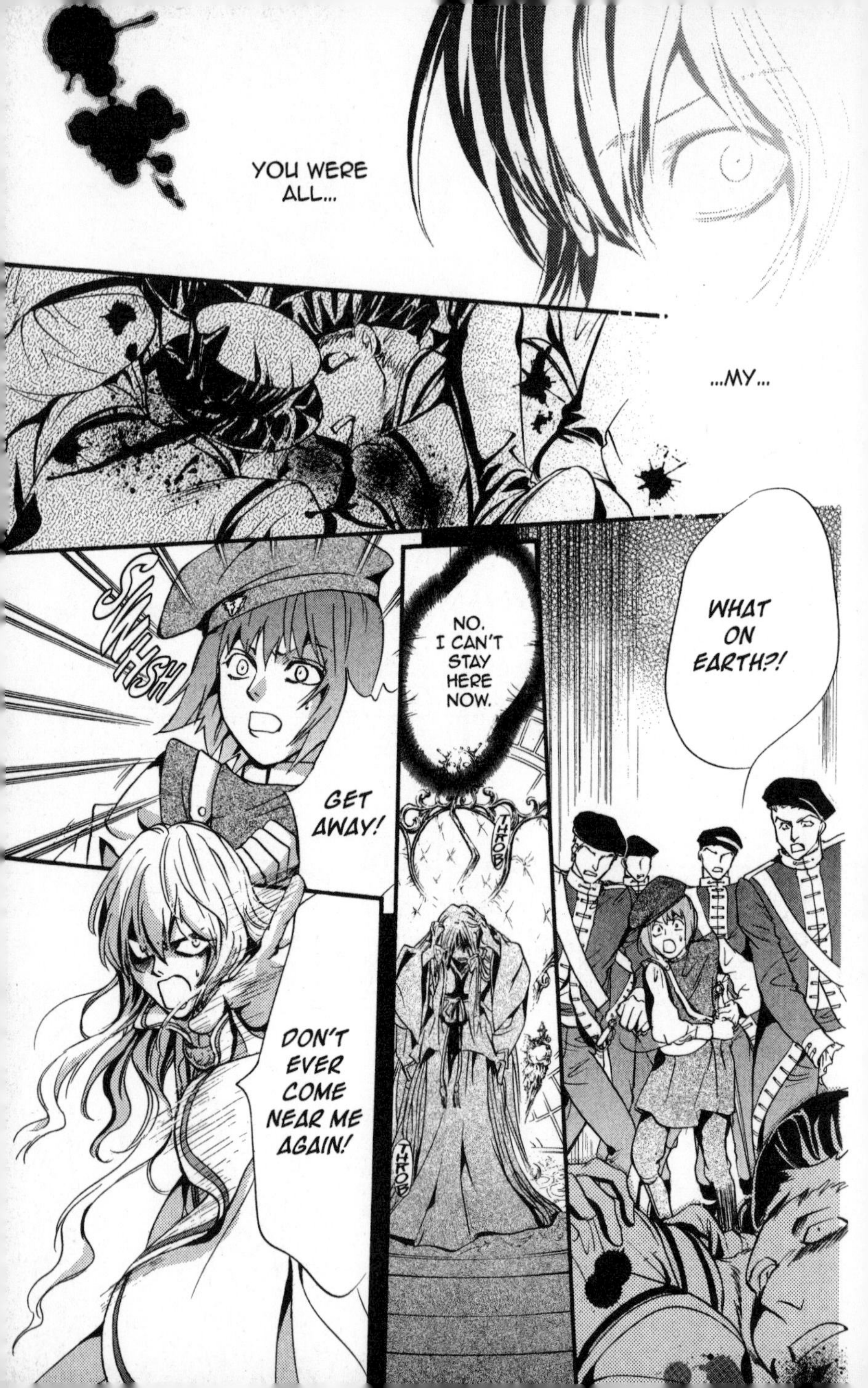
YOU WERE ALL...
...MY...
WHAT ON EARTH?!
NO. I CAN'T STAY HERE NOW.
THROB
THROB
GET AWAY!
DON'T EVER COME NEAR ME AGAIN!

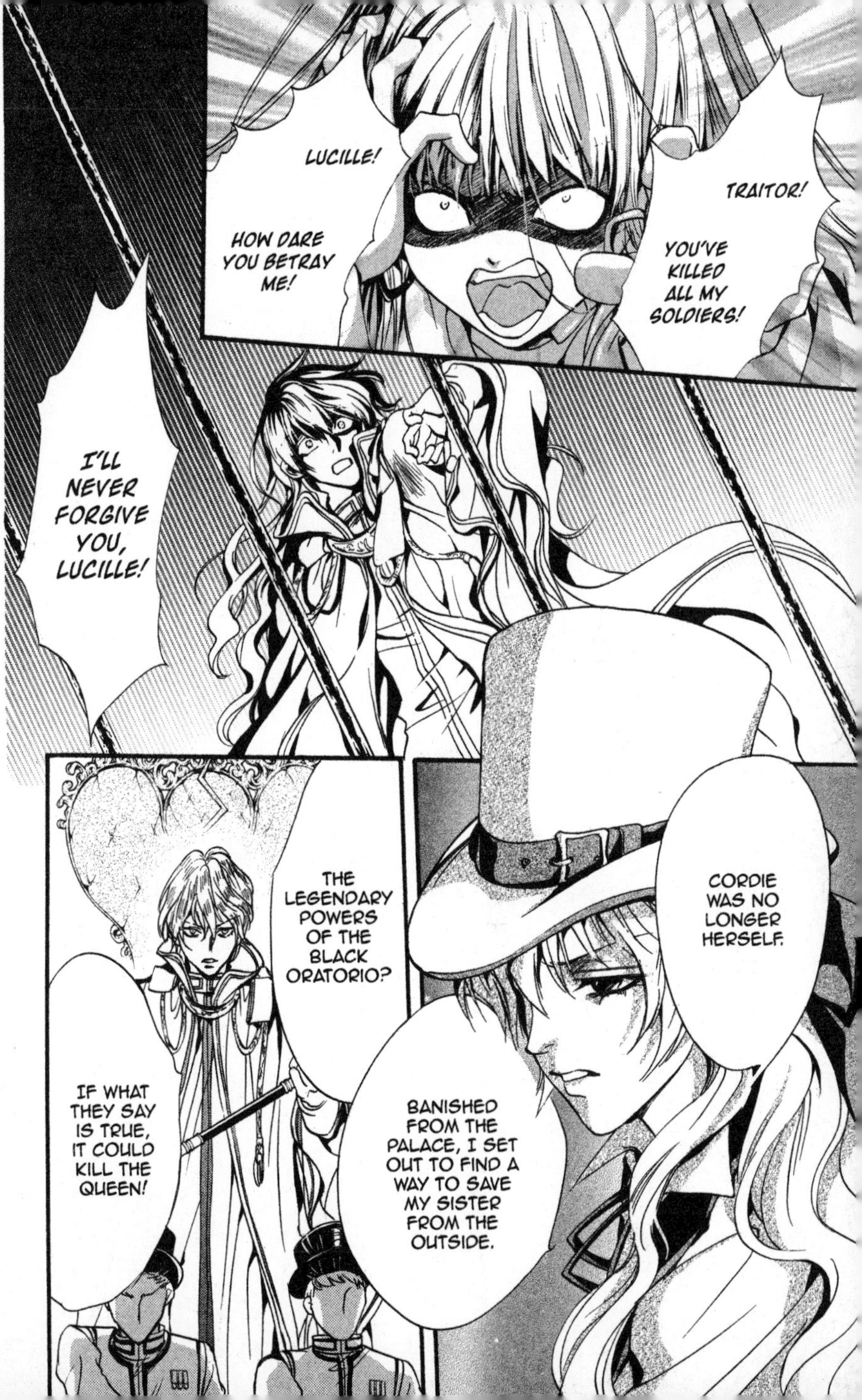
TRAITOR!
YOU'VE KILLED ALL MY SOLDIERS!
LUCILLE!
HOW DARE YOU BETRAY ME!
I'LL NEVER FORGIVE YOU, LUCILLE!
CORDIE WAS NO LONGER HERSELF.
BANISHED FROM THE PALACE, I SET OUT TO FIND A WAY TO SAVE MY SISTER FROM THE OUTSIDE.
THE LEGENDARY POWERS OF THE BLACK ORATORIO?
IF WHAT THEY SAY IS TRUE, IT COULD KILL THE QUEEN!

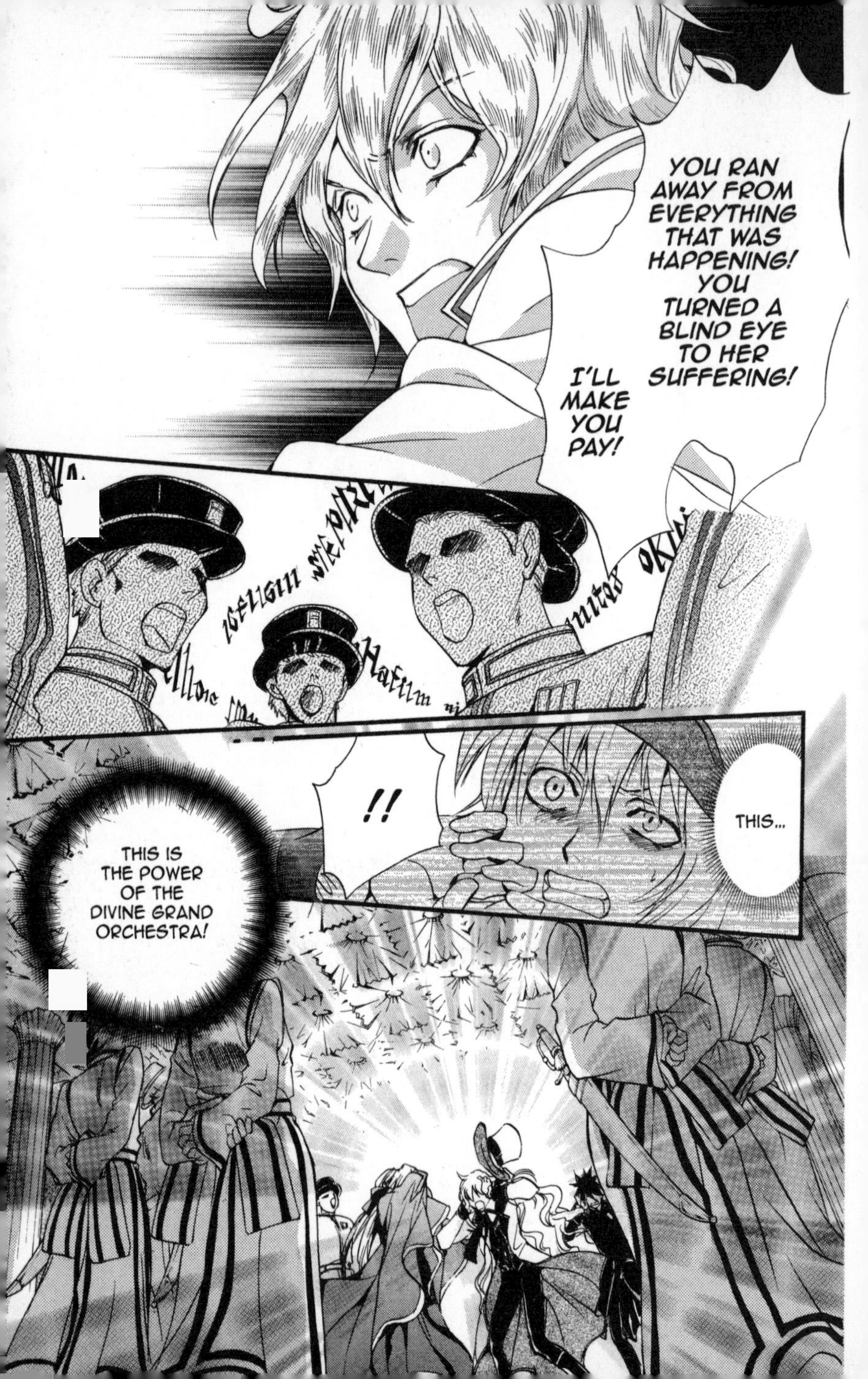
YOU RAN AWAY FROM EVERYTHING THAT WAS HAPPENING! YOU TURNED A BLIND EYE TO HER SUFFERING!
I'LL MAKE YOU PAY!
THIS...
!!
THIS IS THE POWER OF THE DIVINE GRAND ORCHESTRA!

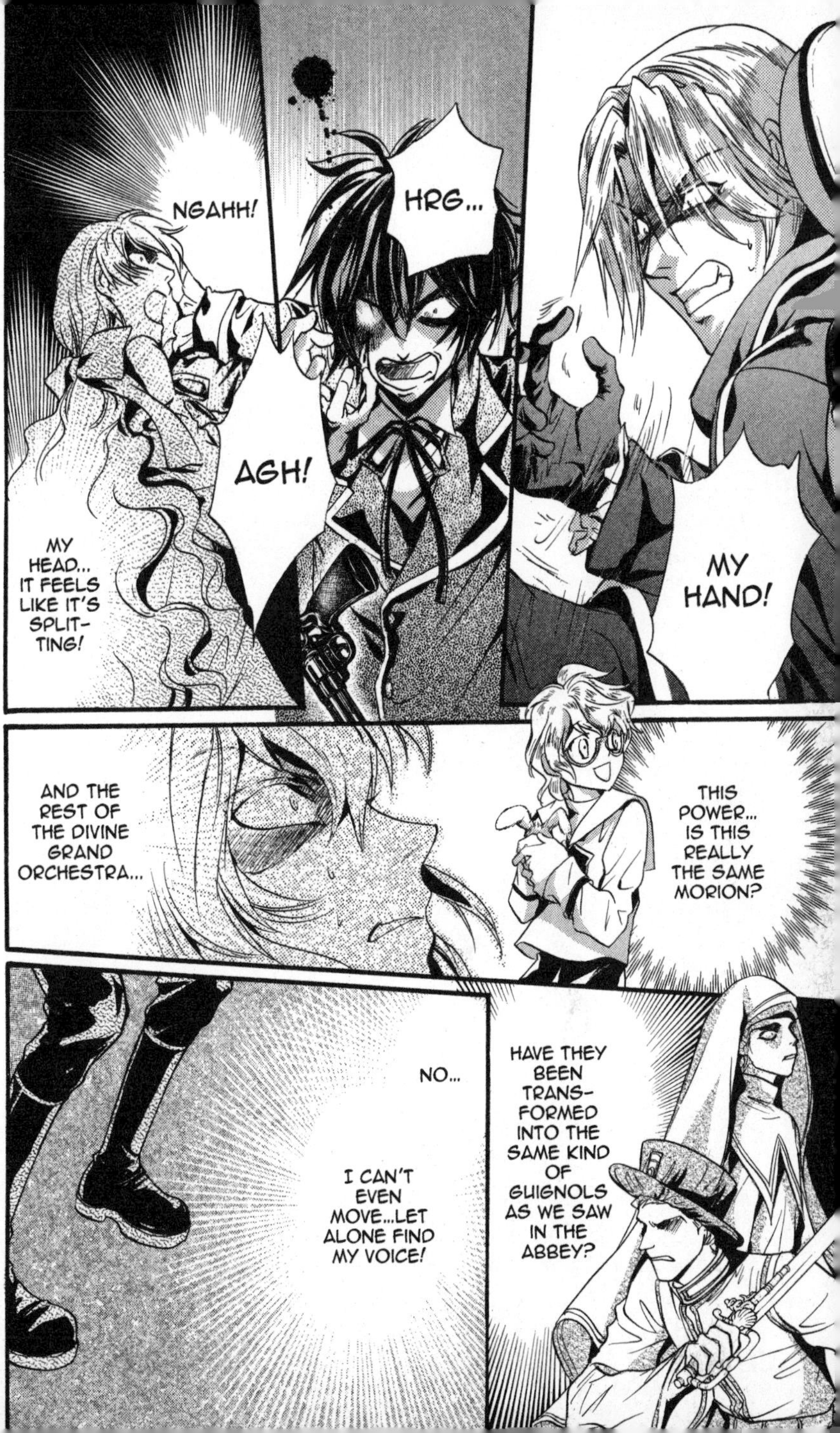
MY HAND!
HRG...
AGH!
NGAHH!
MY HEAD... IT FEELS LIKE IT'S SPLIT-TING!
THIS POWER... IS THIS REALLY THE SAME MORION?
AND THE REST OF THE DIVINE GRAND ORCHESTRA...
HAVE THEY BEEN TRANS-FORMED INTO THE SAME KIND OF GUIGNOLS AS WE SAW IN THE ABBEY?
NO...
I CAN'T EVEN MOVE...LET ALONE FIND MY VOICE!

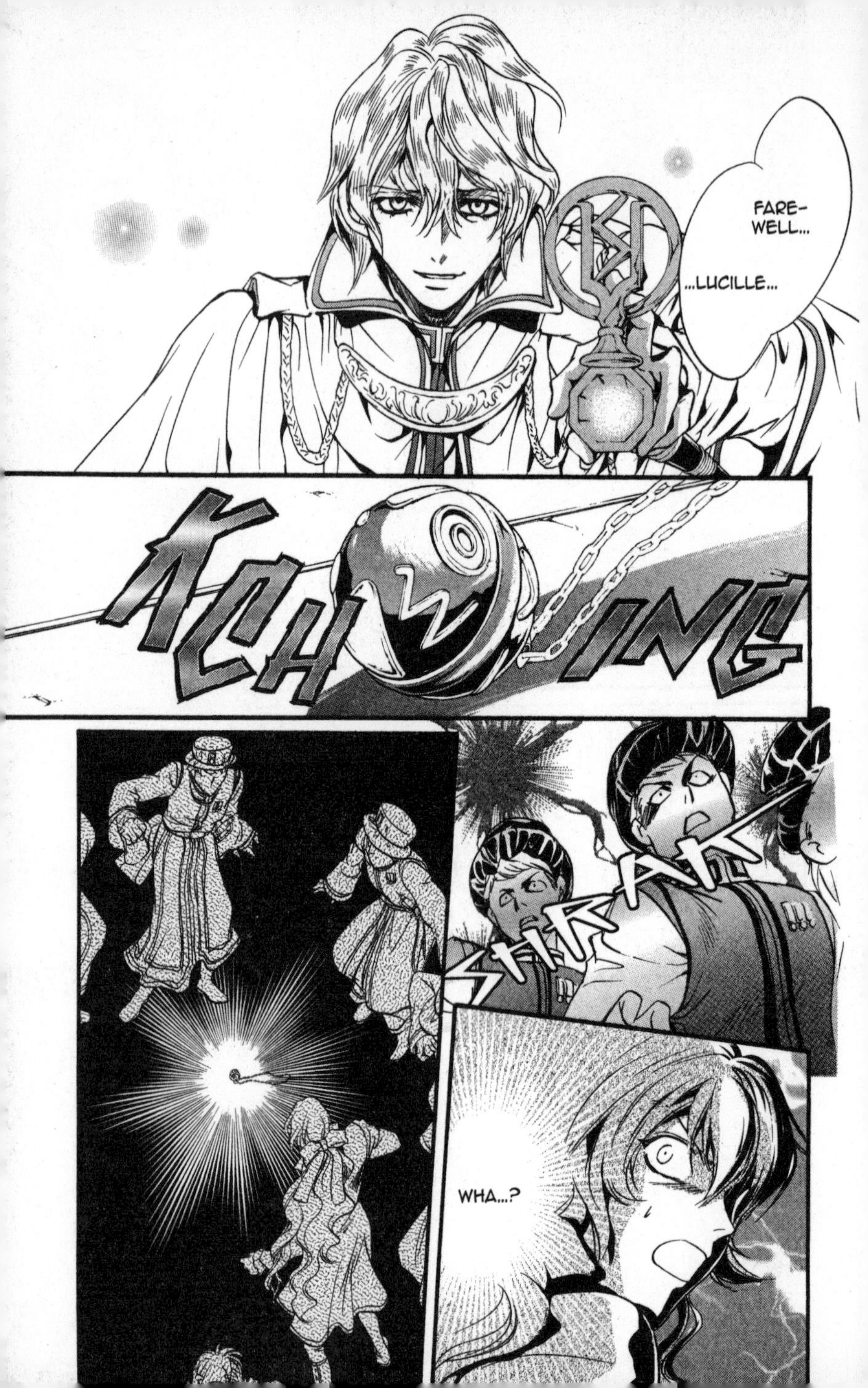

FARE-WELL...
...LUCILLE...
KCHING
SHRAK
WHA...?

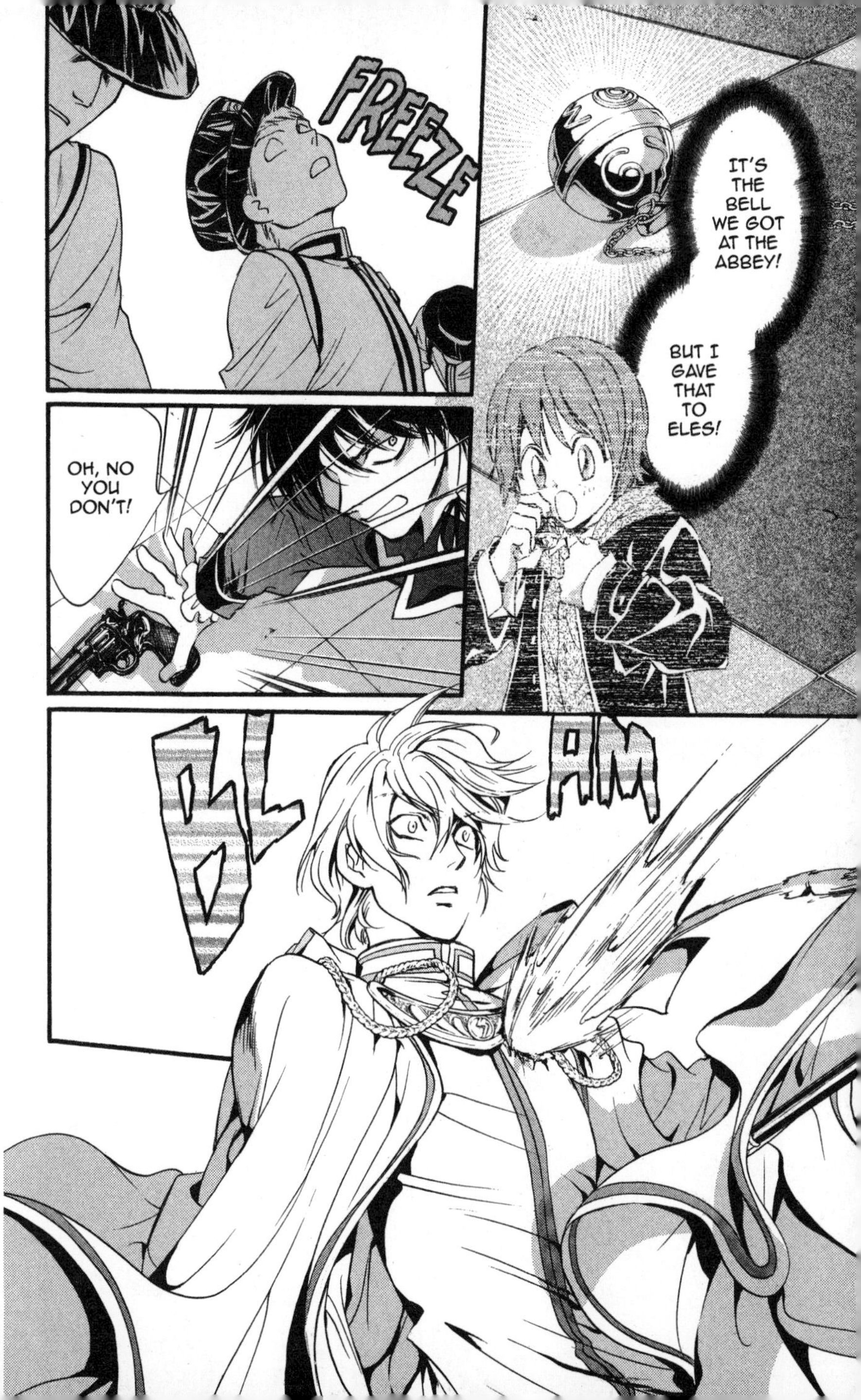
IT'S THE BELL WE GOT AT THE ABBEY!
BUT I GAVE THAT TO ELES!
FREEZE
OH, NO YOU DON'T!
BLAM

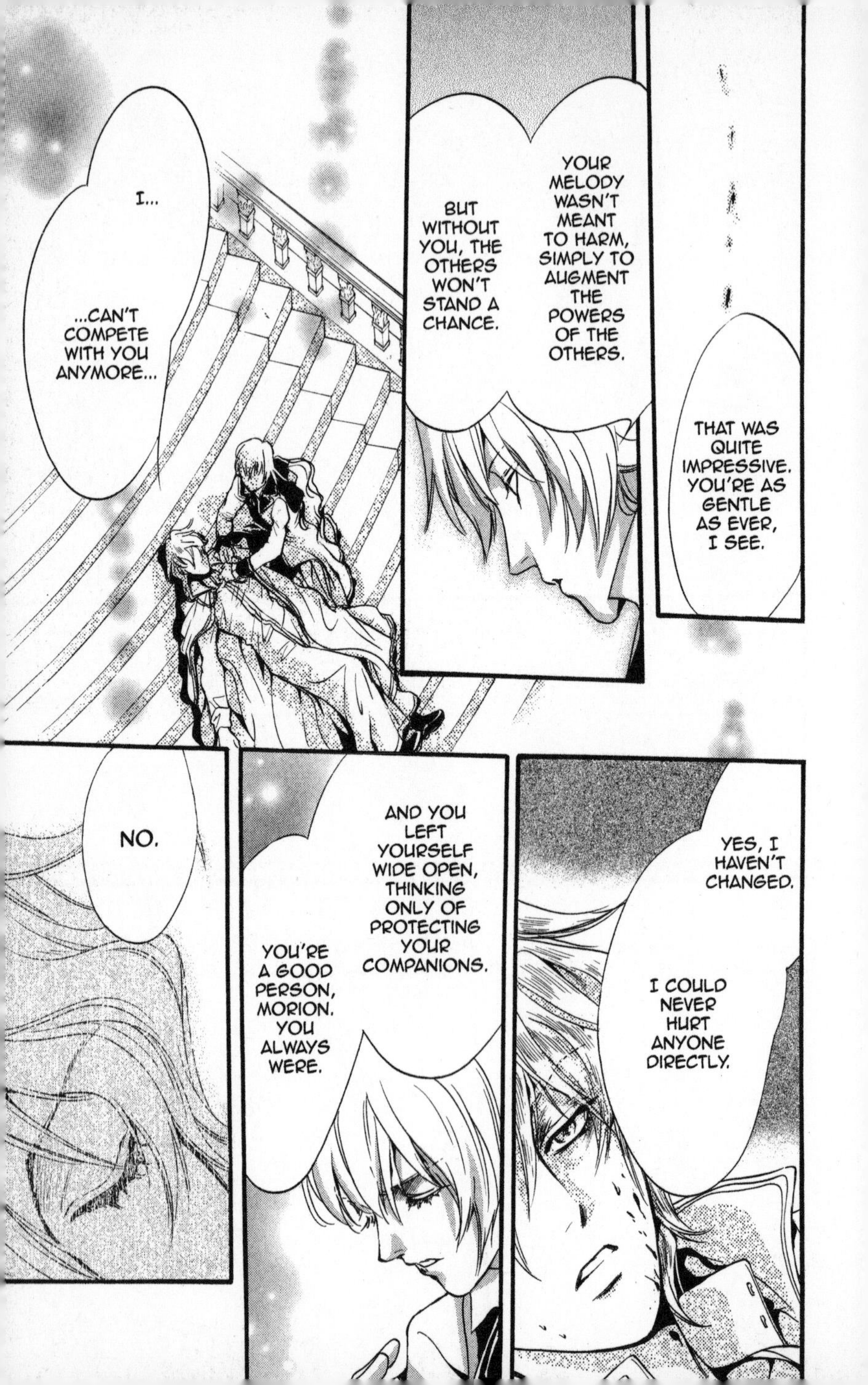
THAT WAS QUITE IMPRESSIVE. YOU'RE AS GENTLE AS EVER, I SEE.
YOUR MELODY WASN'T MEANT TO HARM, SIMPLY TO AUGMENT THE POWERS OF THE OTHERS.
BUT WITHOUT YOU, THE OTHERS WON'T STAND A CHANCE.
I...
...CAN'T COMPETE WITH YOU ANYMORE...
YES, I HAVEN'T CHANGED.
I COULD NEVER HURT ANYONE DIRECTLY.
AND YOU LEFT YOURSELF WIDE OPEN, THINKING ONLY OF PROTECTING YOUR COMPANIONS.
YOU'RE A GOOD PERSON, MORION. YOU ALWAYS WERE.
NO.

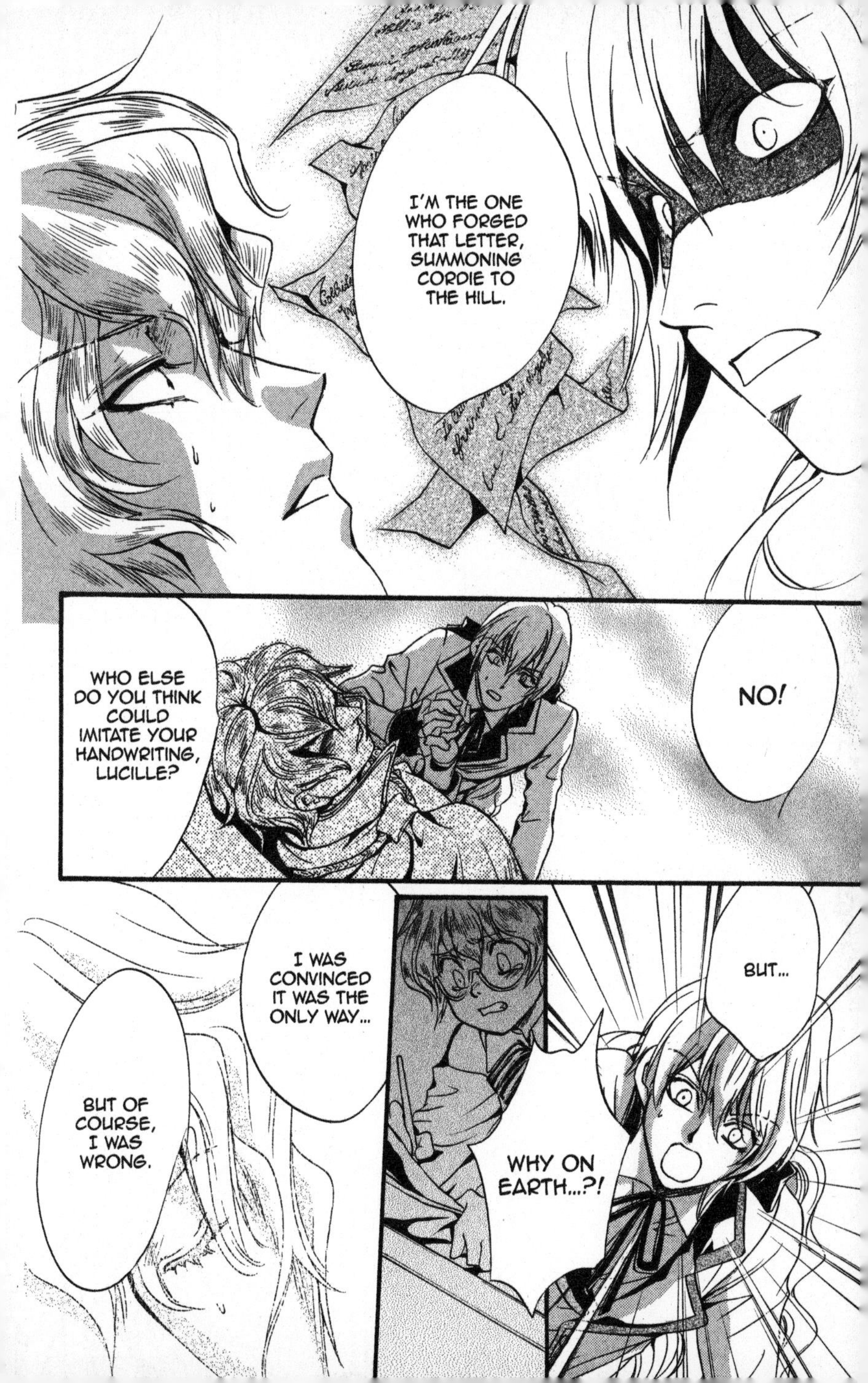
I'M THE ONE WHO FORGED THAT LETTER, SUMMONING CORDIE TO THE HILL.
NO!
WHO ELSE DO YOU THINK COULD IMITATE YOUR HANDWRITING, LUCILLE?
BUT...
WHY ON EARTH...?!
I WAS CONVINCED IT WAS THE ONLY WAY...
BUT OF COURSE, I WAS WRONG.

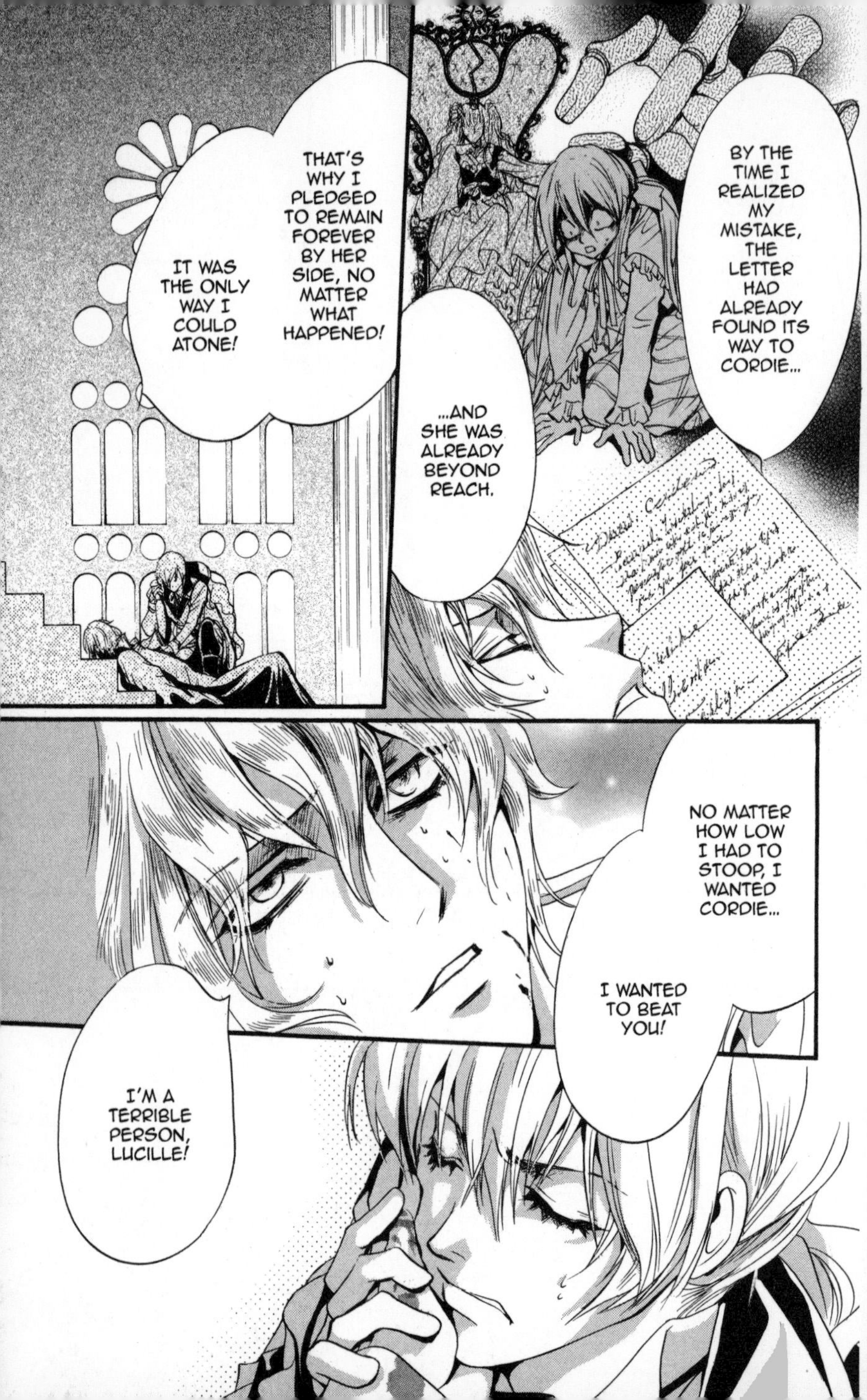
BY THE TIME I REALIZED MY MISTAKE, THE LETTER HAD ALREADY FOUND ITS WAY TO CORDIE...
...AND SHE WAS ALREADY BEYOND REACH.
THAT'S WHY I PLEDGED TO REMAIN FOREVER BY HER SIDE, NO MATTER WHAT HAPPENED!
IT WAS THE ONLY WAY I COULD ATONE!
NO MATTER HOW LOW I HAD TO STOOP, I WANTED CORDIE...
I WANTED TO BEAT YOU!
I'M A TERRIBLE PERSON, LUCILLE!

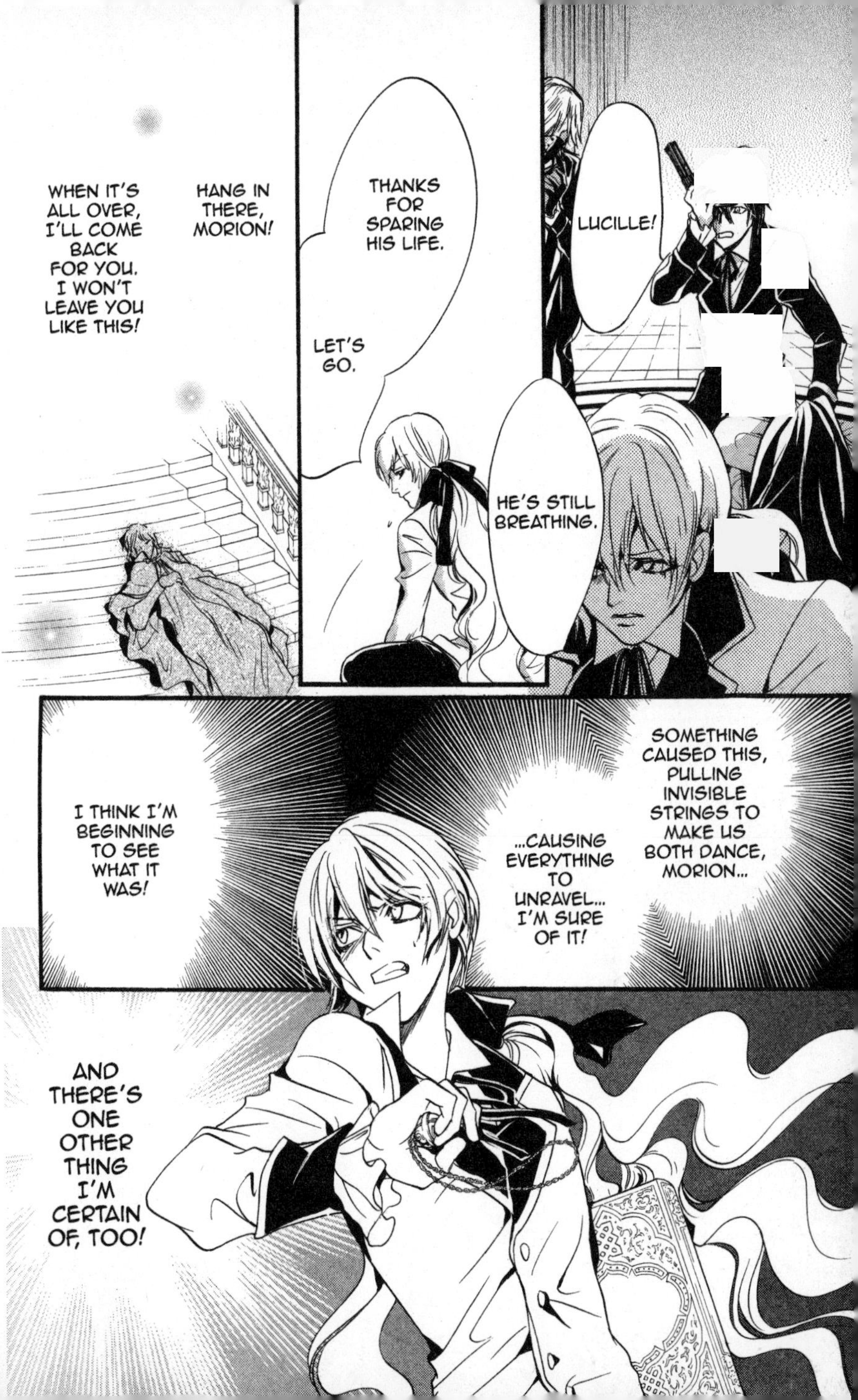
LUCILLE!
HE'S STILL BREATHING.
THANKS FOR SPARING HIS LIFE.
LET'S GO.
HANG IN THERE, MORION!
WHEN IT'S ALL OVER, I'LL COME BACK FOR YOU. I WON'T LEAVE YOU LIKE THIS!
SOMETHING CAUSED THIS, PULLING INVISIBLE STRINGS TO MAKE US BOTH DANCE, MORION...
...CAUSING EVERYTHING TO UNRAVEL... I'M SURE OF IT!
I THINK I'M BEGINNING TO SEE WHAT IT WAS!
AND THERE'S ONE OTHER THING I'M CERTAIN OF, TOO!

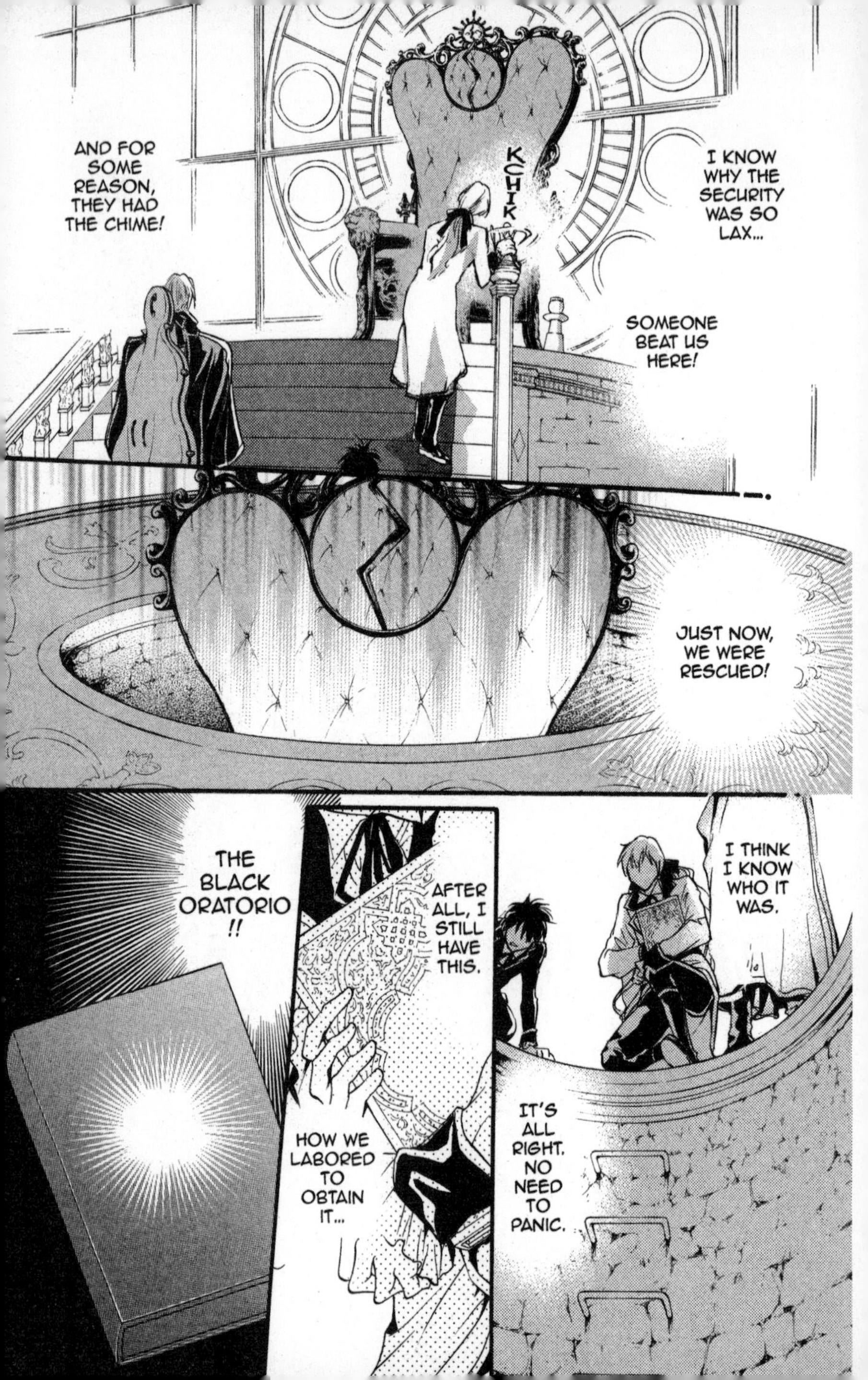
I KNOW WHY THE SECURITY WAS SO LAX...
SOMEONE BEAT US HERE!
KCHIK
AND FOR SOME REASON, THEY HAD THE CHIME!
JUST NOW, WE WERE RESCUED!
I THINK I KNOW WHO IT WAS.
IT'S ALL RIGHT. NO NEED TO PANIC.
AFTER ALL, I STILL HAVE THIS.
HOW WE LABORED TO OBTAIN IT...
THE BLACK ORATORIO !!

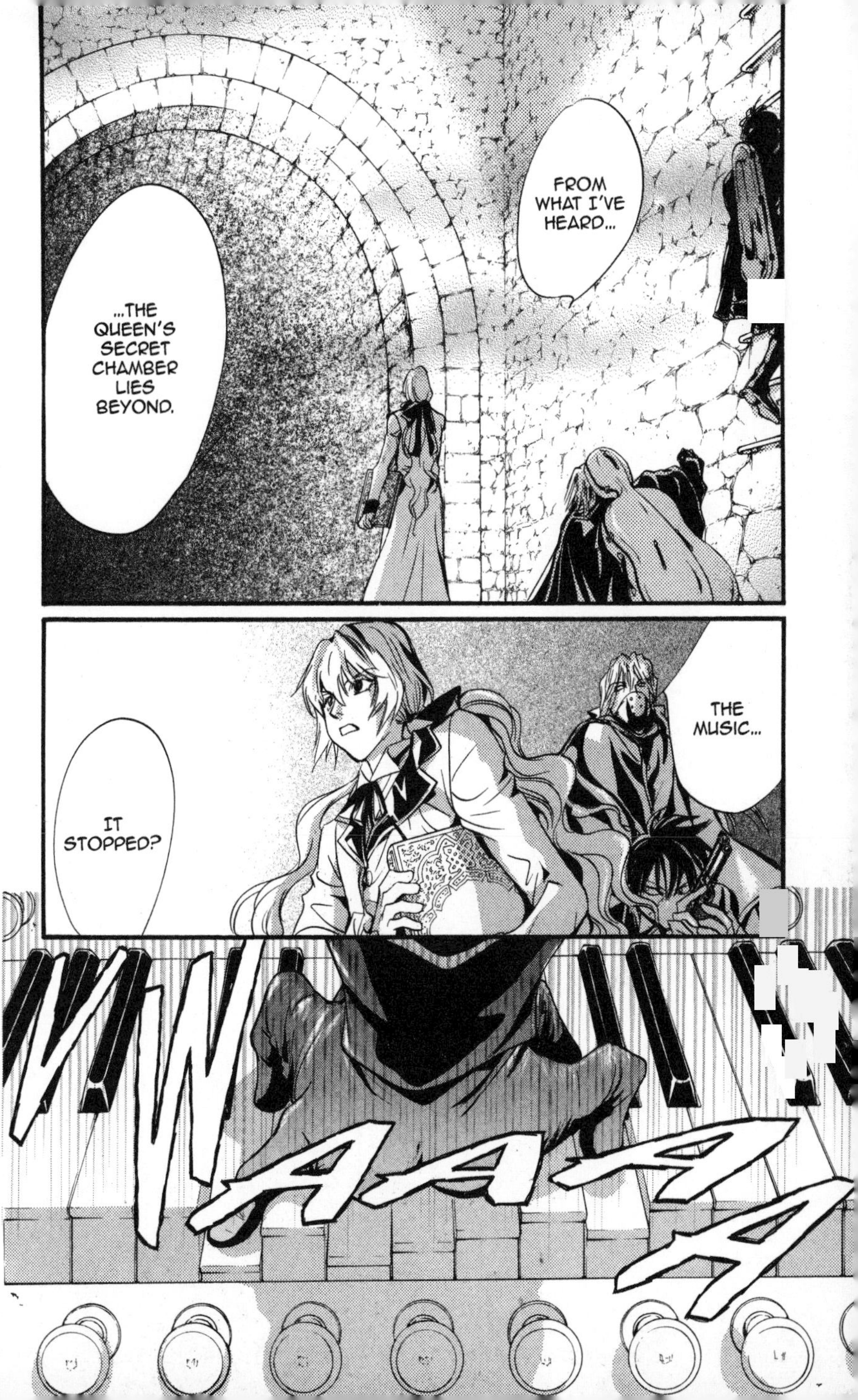
FROM WHAT I'VE HEARD...
...THE QUEEN'S SECRET CHAMBER LIES BEYOND.
THE MUSIC...
IT STOPPED?
VWWAAAA

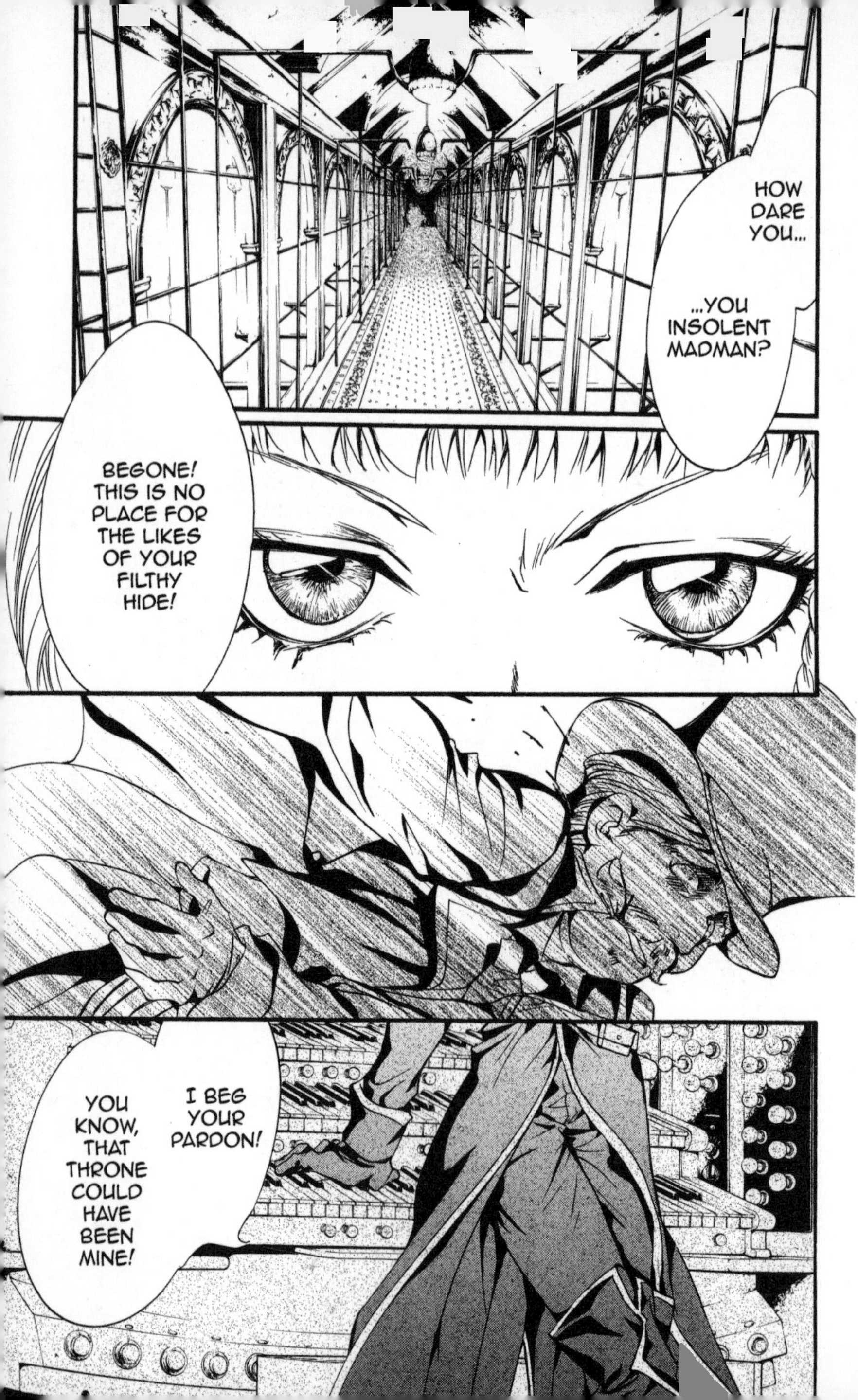
HOW DARE YOU...
...YOU INSOLENT MADMAN?
BEGONE! THIS IS NO PLACE FOR THE LIKES OF YOUR FILTHY HIDE!
I BEG YOUR PARDON!
YOU KNOW, THAT THRONE COULD HAVE BEEN MINE!

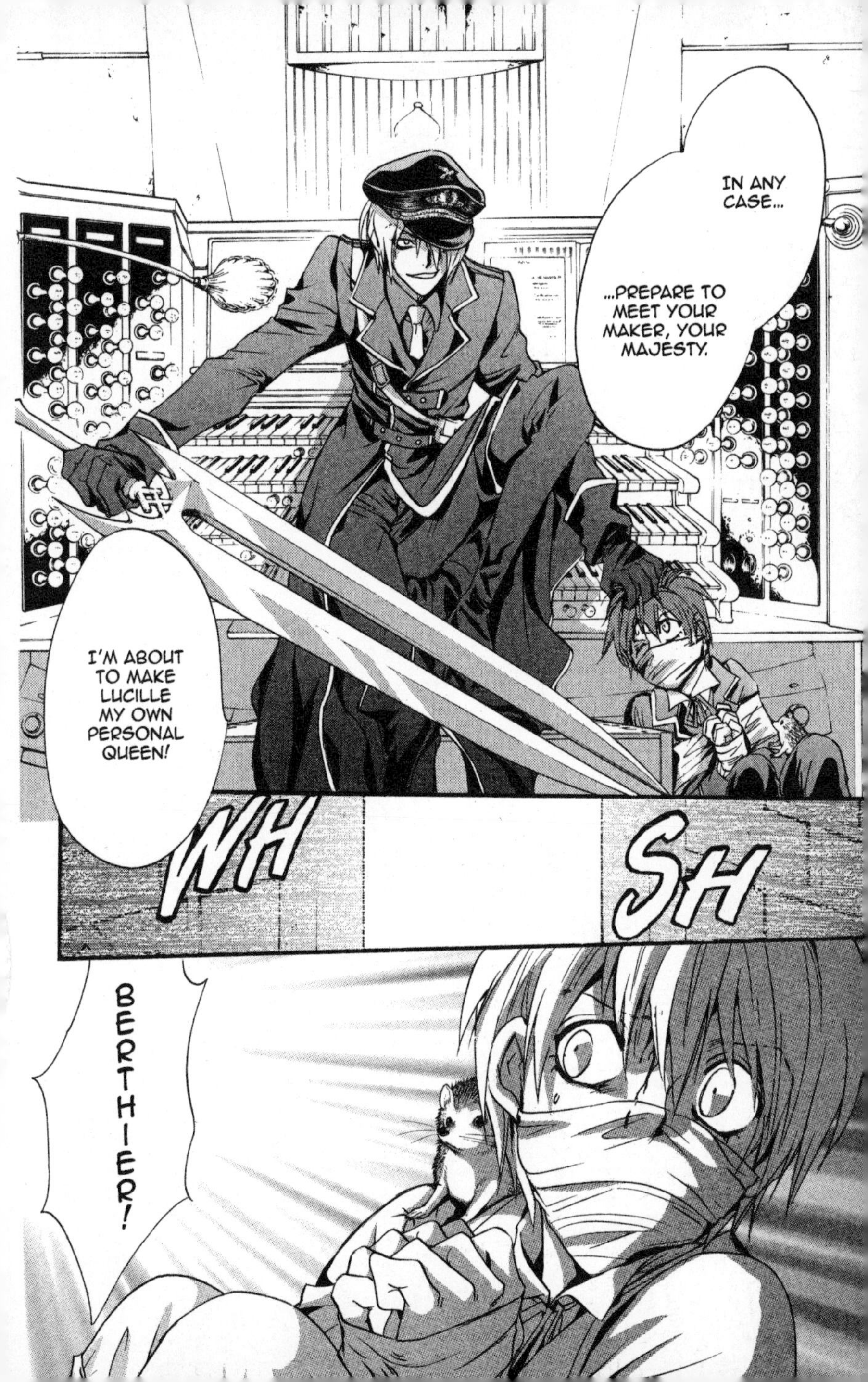
IN ANY CASE...
...PREPARE TO MEET YOUR MAKER, YOUR MAJESTY.
I'M ABOUT TO MAKE LUCILLE MY OWN PERSONAL QUEEN!
WH SH
BERTHIER!

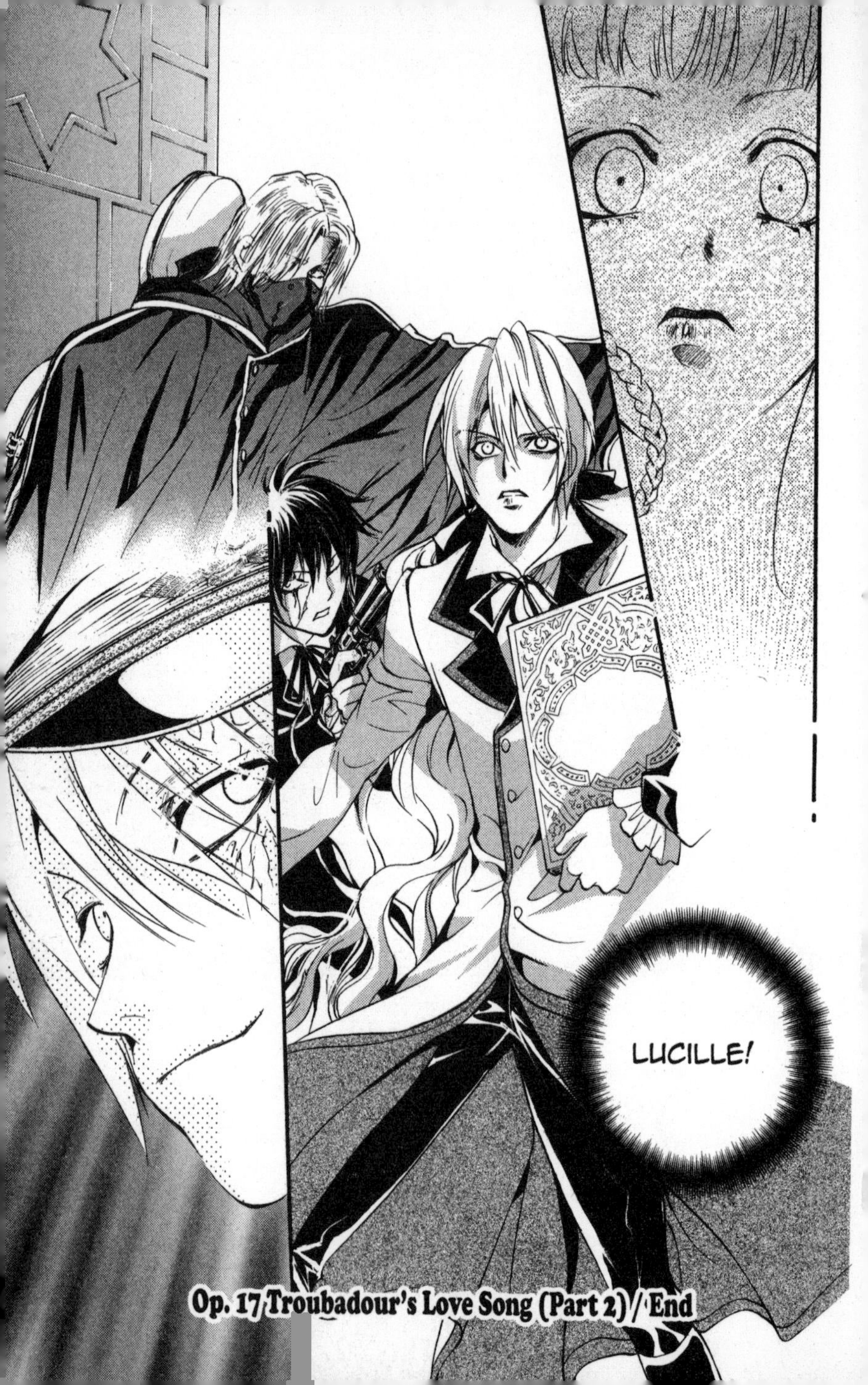
!
LUCILLE!
Op. 17 Troubadour's Love Song (Part 2) / End

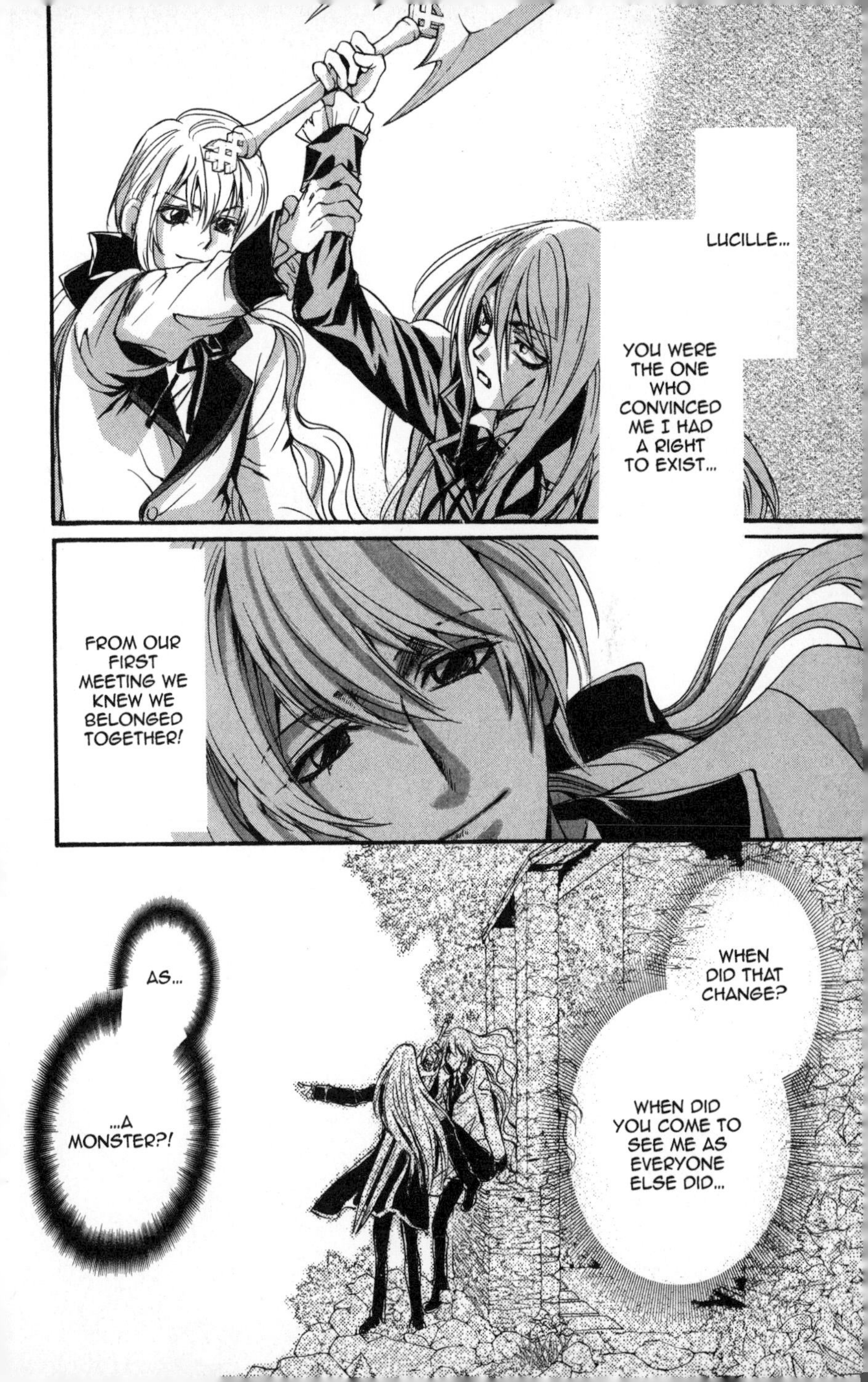
LUCILLE...
YOU WERE THE ONE WHO CONVINCED ME I HAD A RIGHT TO EXIST...
FROM OUR FIRST MEETING WE KNEW WE BELONGED TOGETHER!
WHEN DID THAT CHANGE?
WHEN DID YOU COME TO SEE ME AS EVERYONE ELSE DID...
AS...
...A MONSTER?!

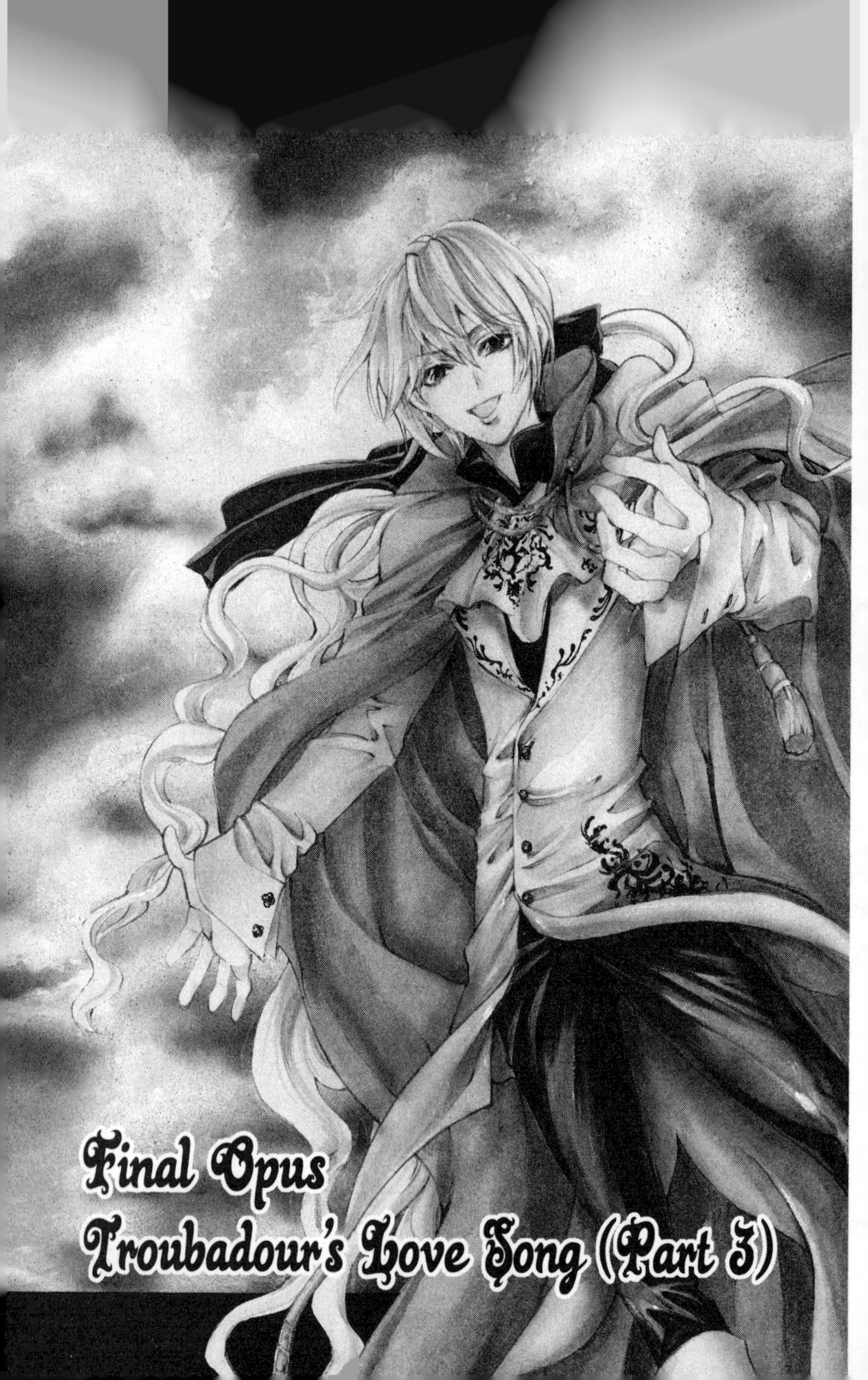
Final Opus
Troubadour's Love Song (Part 3)

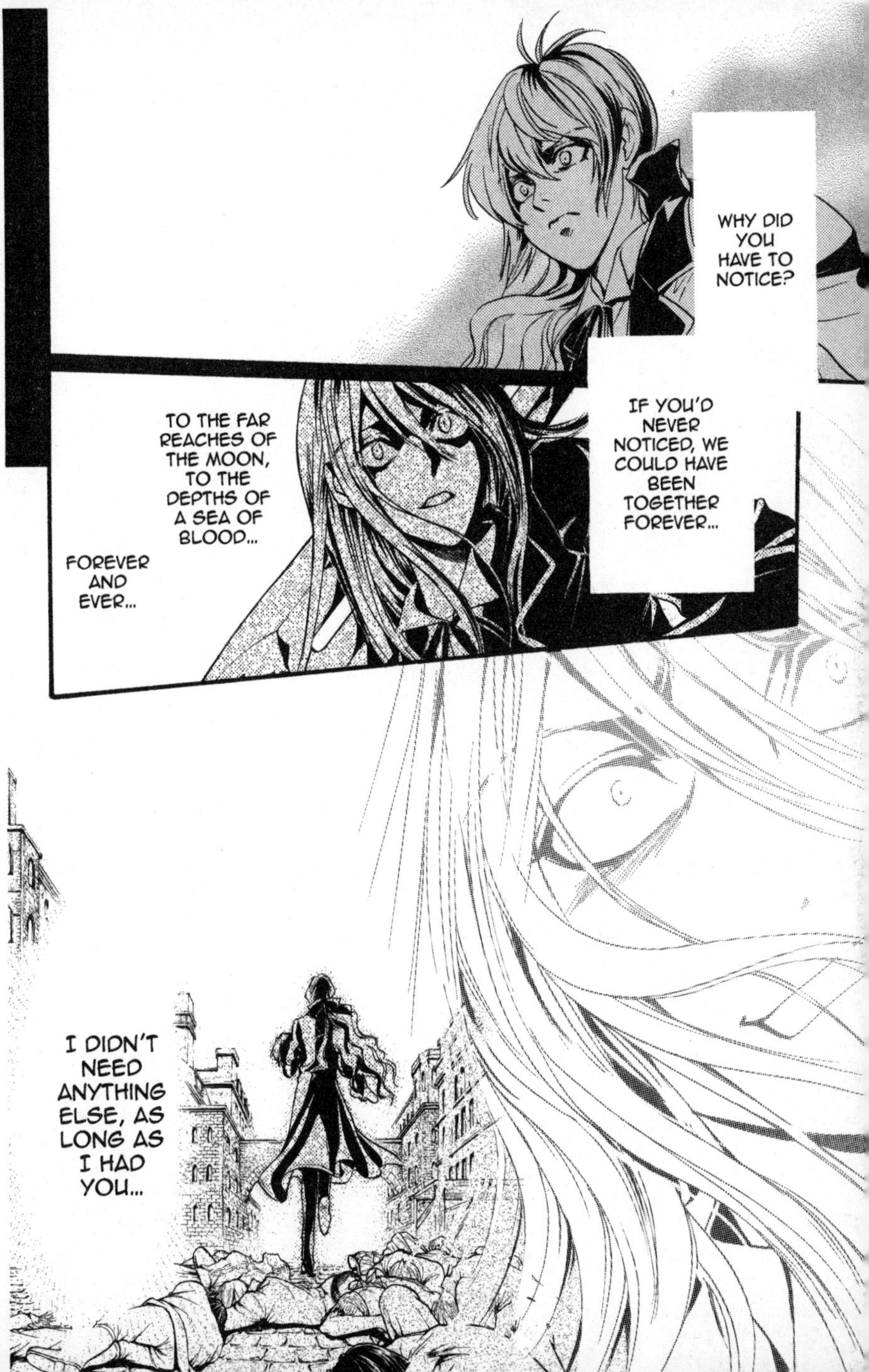
WHY DID YOU HAVE TO NOTICE?
IF YOU'D NEVER NOTICED, WE COULD HAVE BEEN TOGETHER FOREVER...
TO THE FAR REACHES OF THE MOON, TO THE DEPTHS OF A SEA OF BLOOD...
FOREVER AND EVER...
I DIDN'T NEED ANYTHING ELSE, AS LONG AS I HAD YOU...

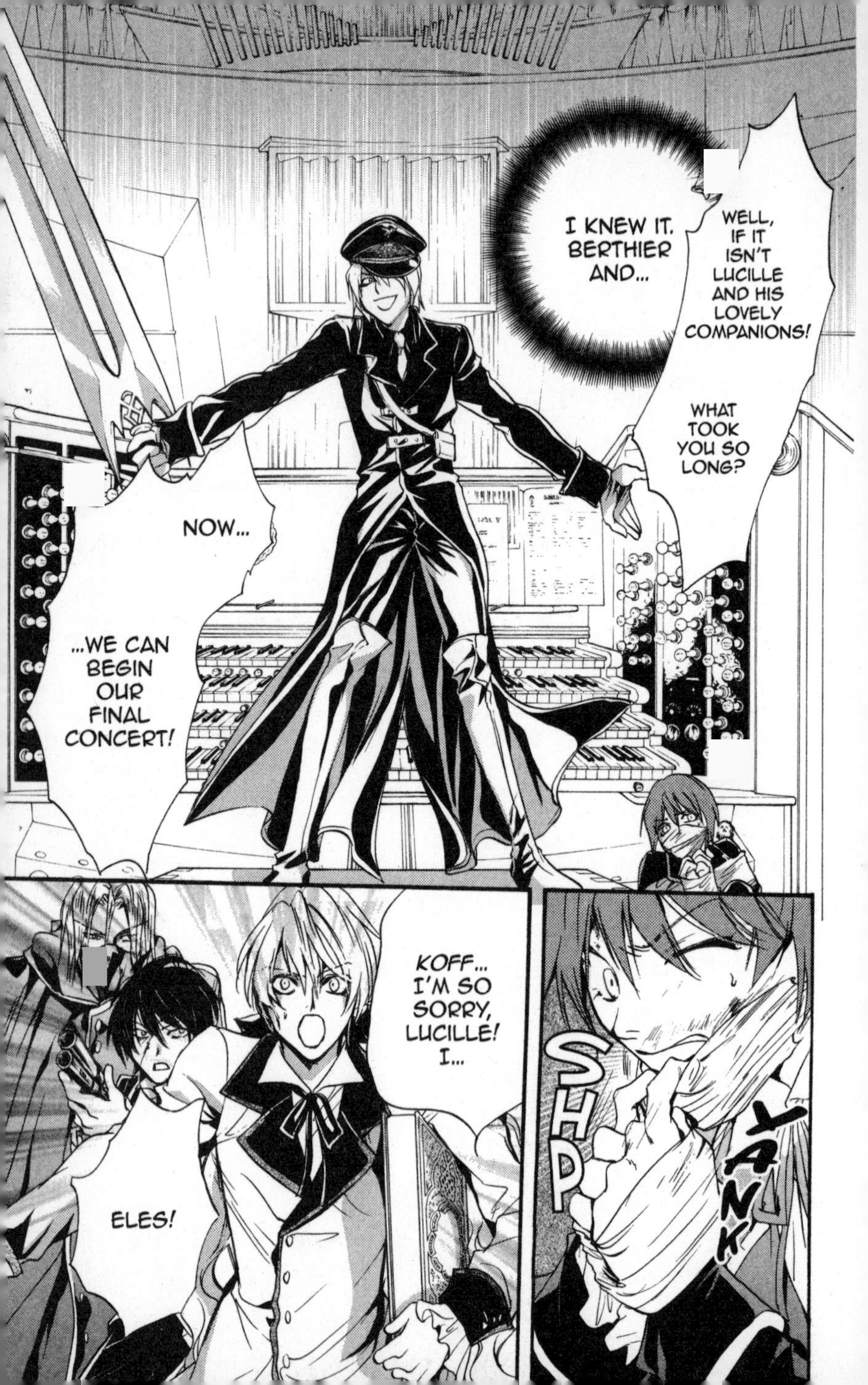
WELL, IF IT ISN'T LUCILLE AND HIS LOVELY COMPANIONS!
WHAT TOOK YOU SO LONG?
I KNEW IT. BERTHIER AND...
NOW...
...WE CAN BEGIN OUR FINAL CONCERT!
YANK
SHP
KOFF... I'M SO SORRY, LUCILLE! I...
ELES!

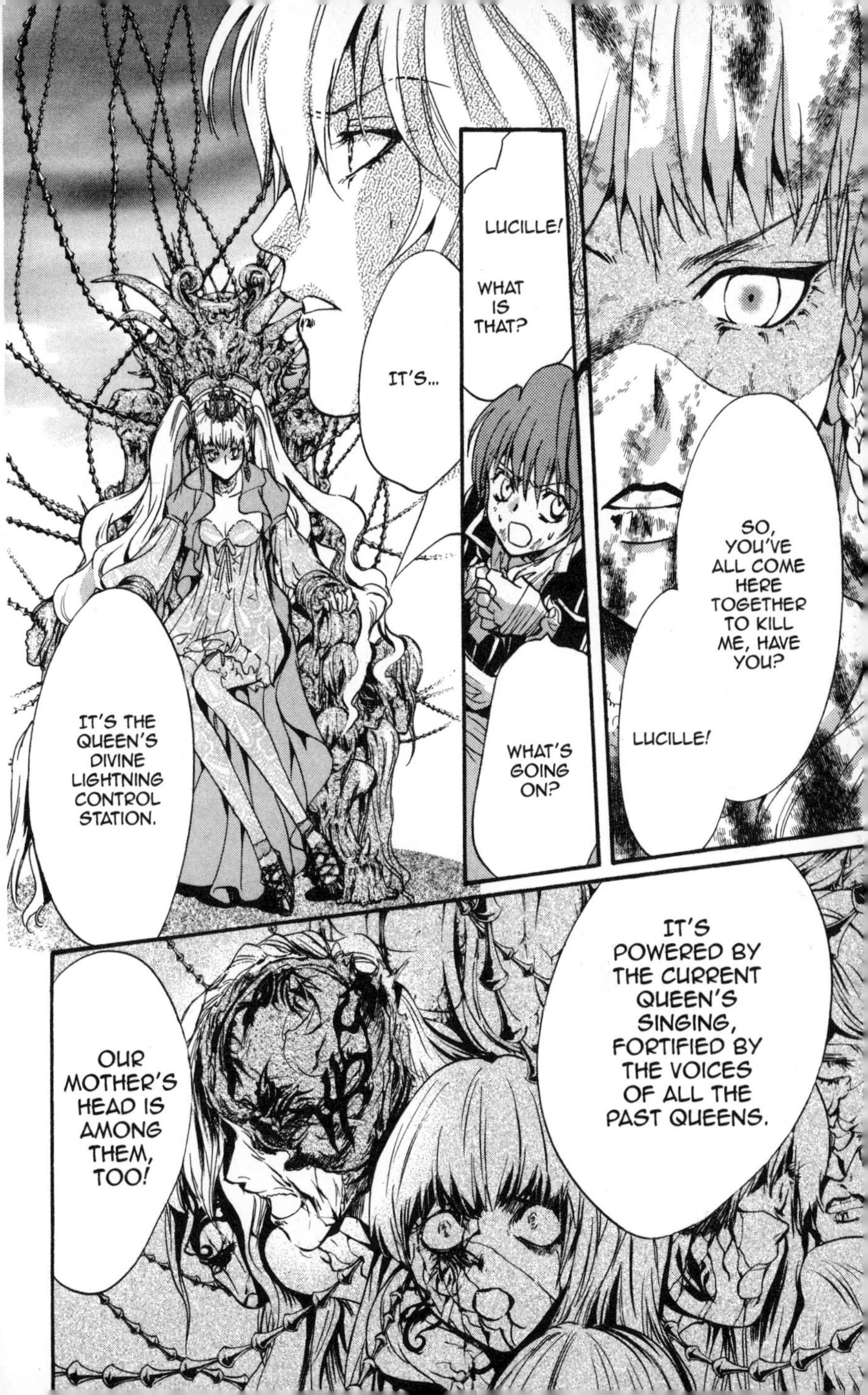
SO, YOU'VE ALL COME HERE TOGETHER TO KILL ME, HAVE YOU?
LUCILLE!
LUCILLE!
WHAT IS THAT?
WHAT'S GOING ON?
IT'S...
IT'S THE QUEEN'S DIVINE LIGHTNING CONTROL STATION.
IT'S POWERED BY THE CURRENT QUEEN'S SINGING, FORTIFIED BY THE VOICES OF ALL THE PAST QUEENS.
OUR MOTHER'S HEAD IS AMONG THEM, TOO!

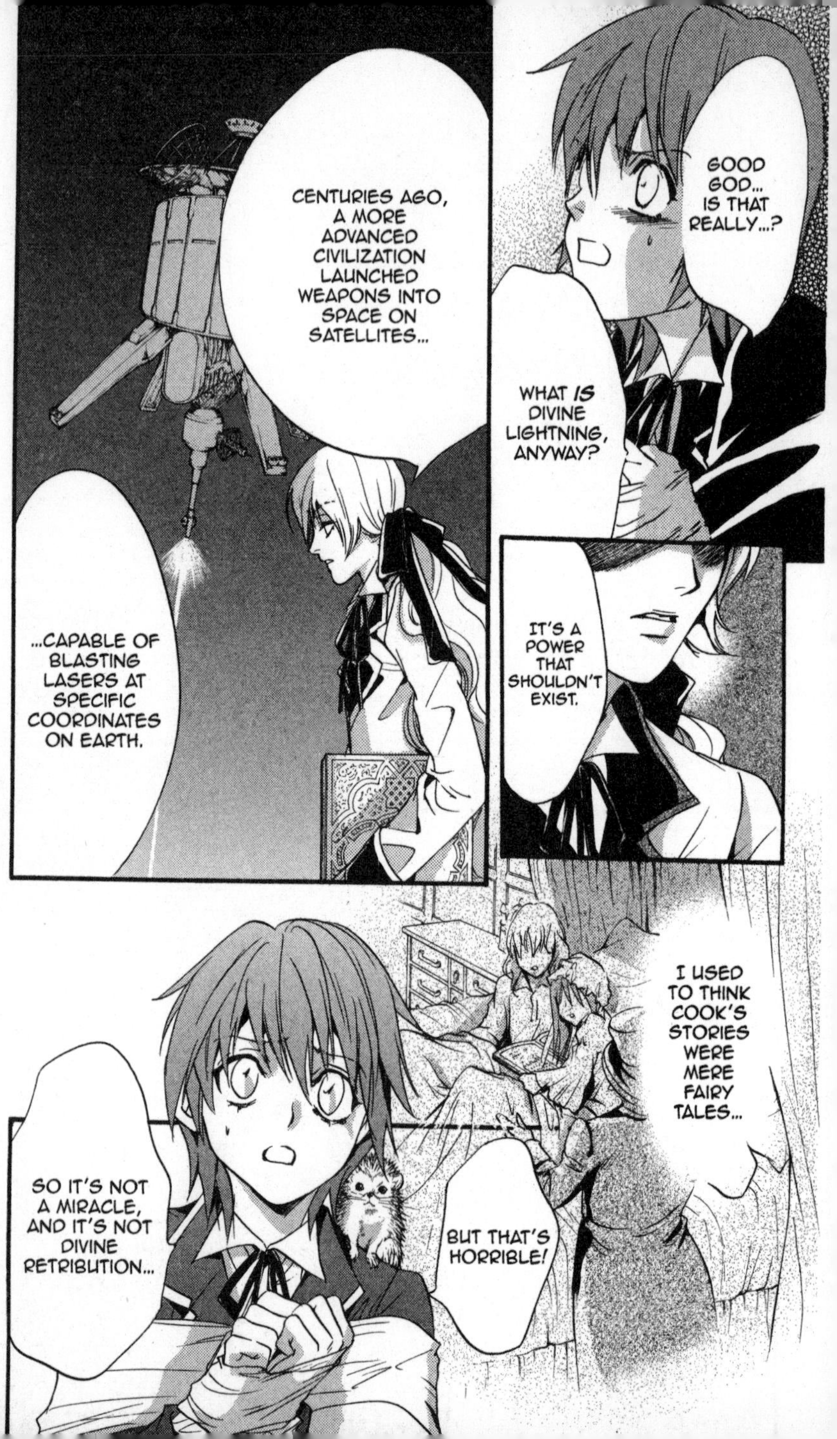
GOOD GOD... IS THAT REALLY...?
WHAT *IS* DIVINE LIGHTNING, ANYWAY?
IT'S A POWER THAT SHOULDN'T EXIST.
CENTURIES AGO, A MORE ADVANCED CIVILIZATION LAUNCHED WEAPONS INTO SPACE ON SATELLITES...
...CAPABLE OF BLASTING LASERS AT SPECIFIC COORDINATES ON EARTH.
I USED TO THINK COOK'S STORIES WERE MERE FAIRY TALES...
SO IT'S NOT A MIRACLE, AND IT'S NOT DIVINE RETRIBUTION...
BUT THAT'S HORRIBLE!

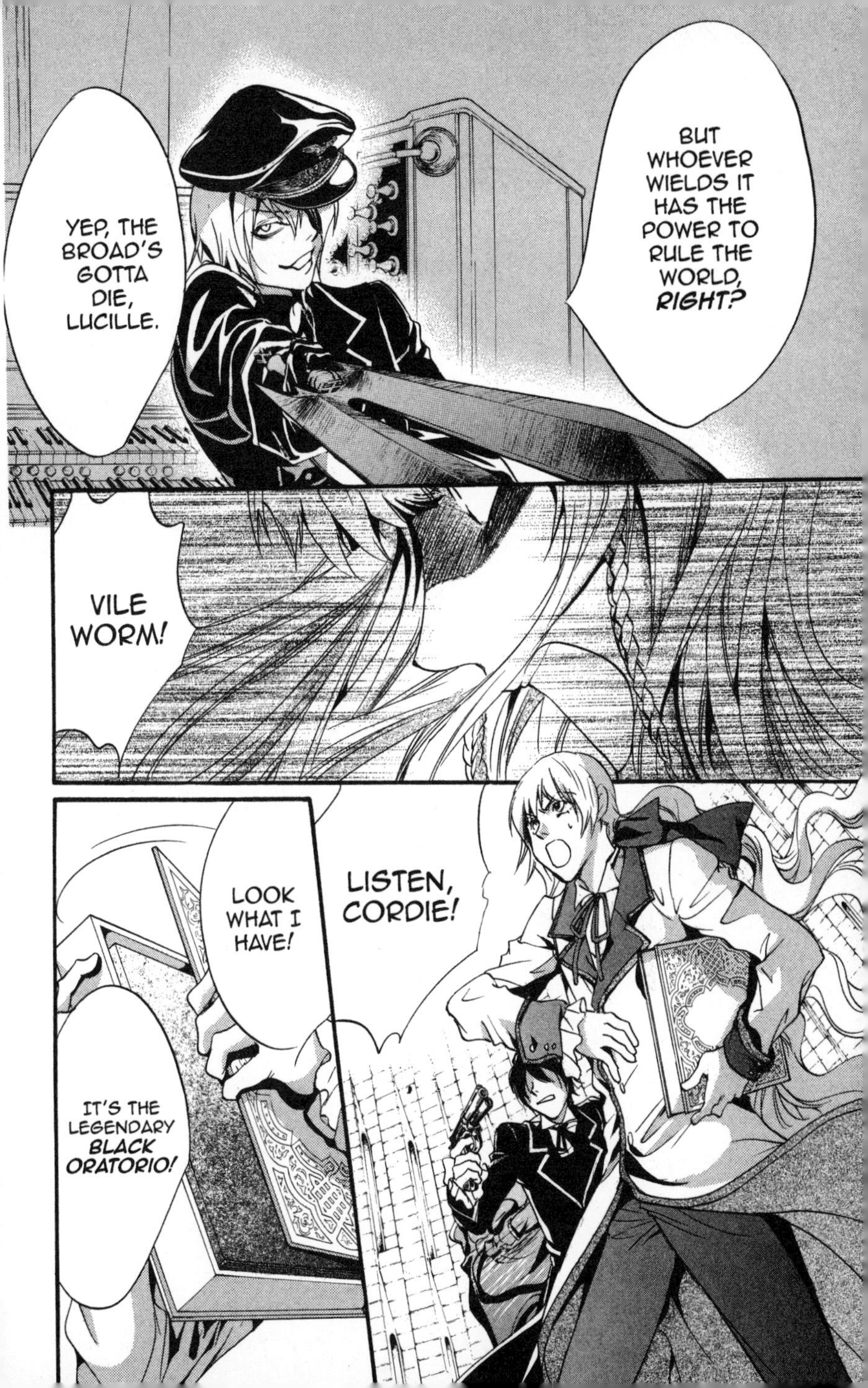
BUT WHOEVER WIELDS IT HAS THE POWER TO RULE THE WORLD, *RIGHT?*
YEP, THE BROAD'S GOTTA DIE, LUCILLE.
VILE WORM!
LISTEN, CORDIE!
LOOK WHAT I HAVE!
IT'S THE LEGENDARY *BLACK ORATORIO!*

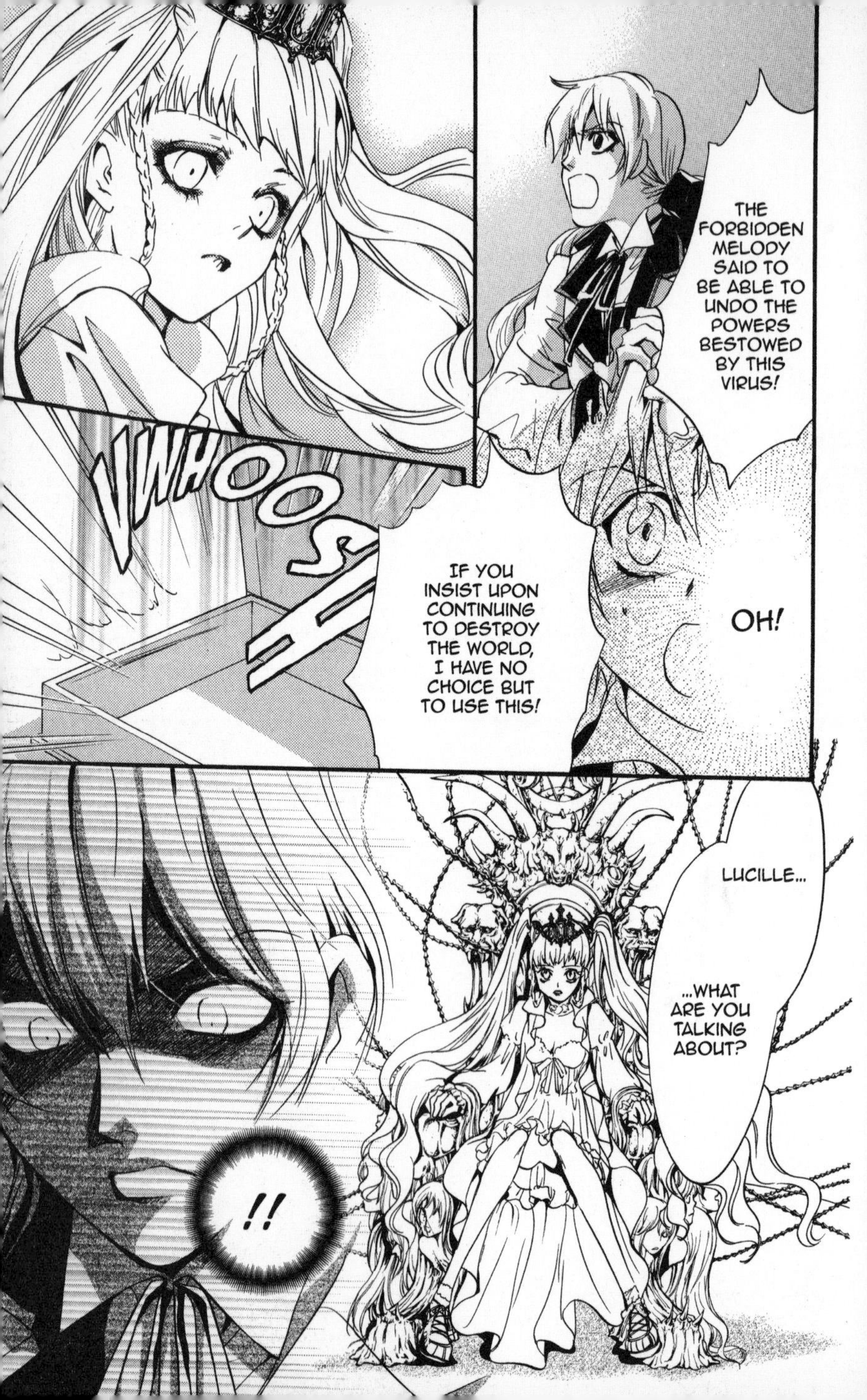
THE FORBIDDEN MELODY SAID TO BE ABLE TO UNDO THE POWERS BESTOWED BY THIS VIRUS!
OH!
IF YOU INSIST UPON CONTINUING TO DESTROY THE WORLD, I HAVE NO CHOICE BUT TO USE THIS!
VWHOOSH
LUCILLE...
...WHAT ARE YOU TALKING ABOUT?
!!

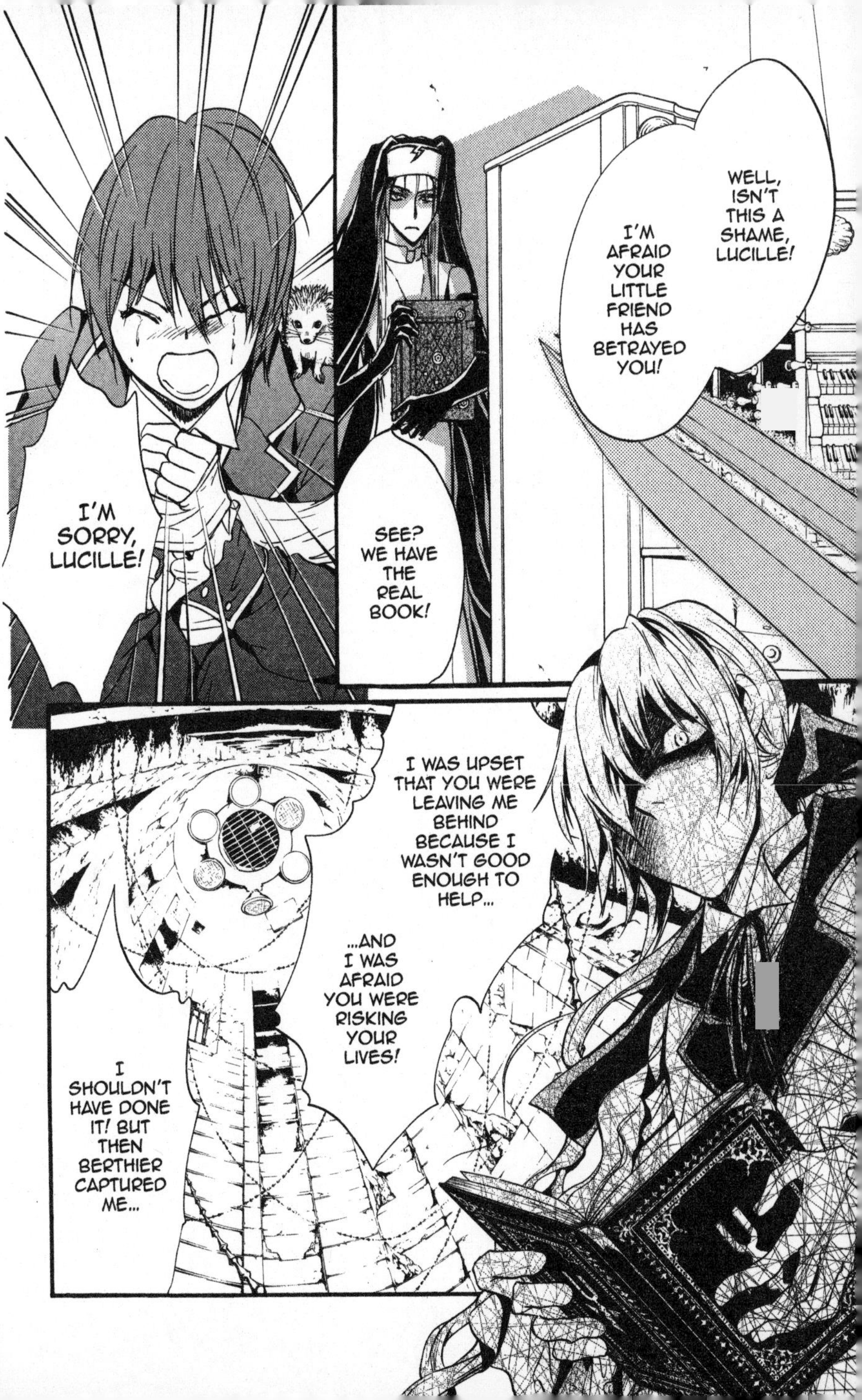
WELL, ISN'T THIS A SHAME, LUCILLE!
I'M AFRAID YOUR LITTLE FRIEND HAS BETRAYED YOU!
SEE? WE HAVE THE REAL BOOK!
I'M SORRY, LUCILLE!
I WAS UPSET THAT YOU WERE LEAVING ME BEHIND BECAUSE I WASN'T GOOD ENOUGH TO HELP...
...AND I WAS AFRAID YOU WERE RISKING YOUR LIVES!
I SHOULDN'T HAVE DONE IT! BUT THEN BERTHIER CAPTURED ME...

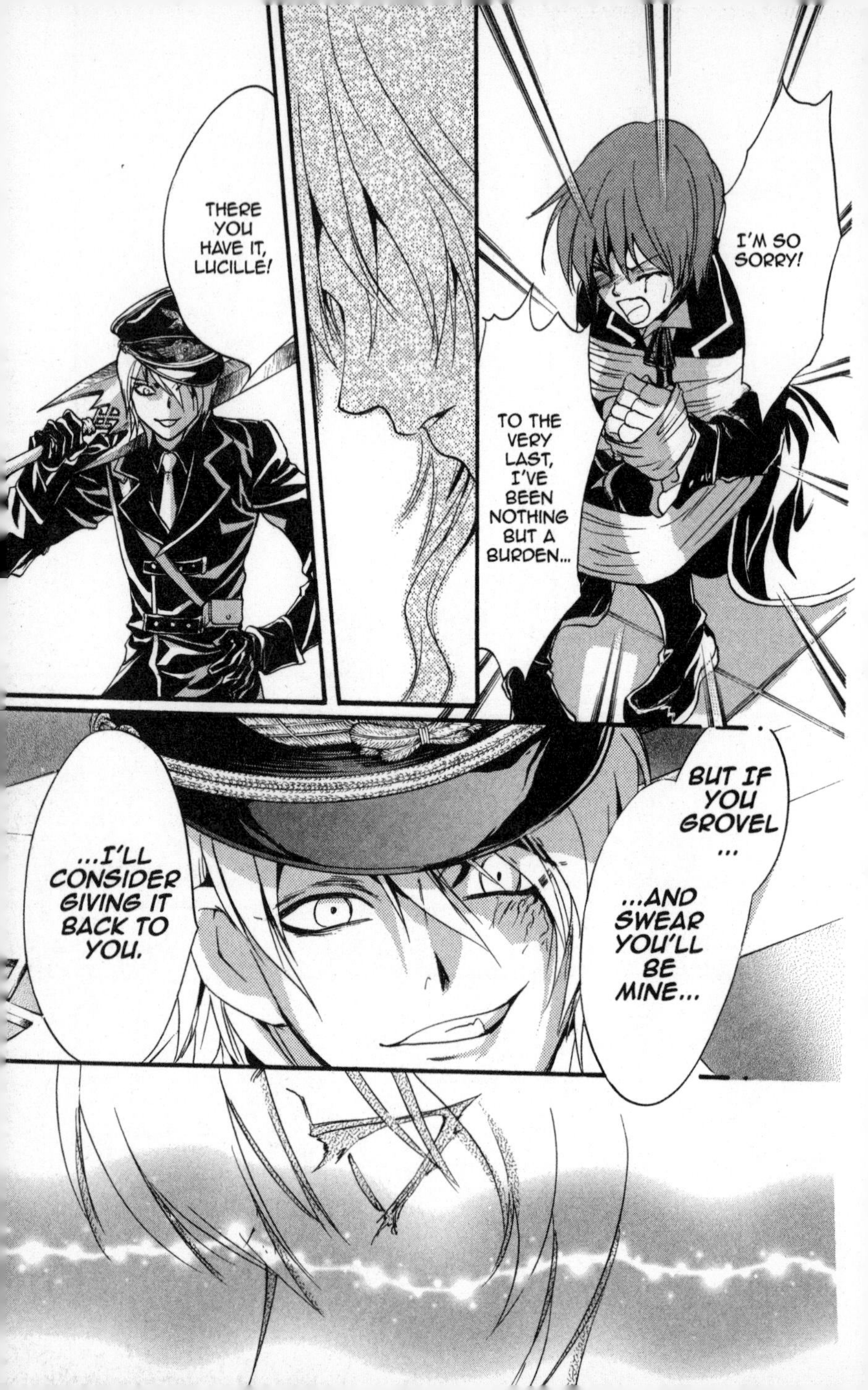
I'M SO SORRY!
TO THE VERY LAST, I'VE BEEN NOTHING BUT A BURDEN...
THERE YOU HAVE IT, LUCILLE!
BUT IF YOU GROVEL ...
...AND SWEAR YOU'LL BE MINE...
...I'LL CONSIDER GIVING IT BACK TO YOU.

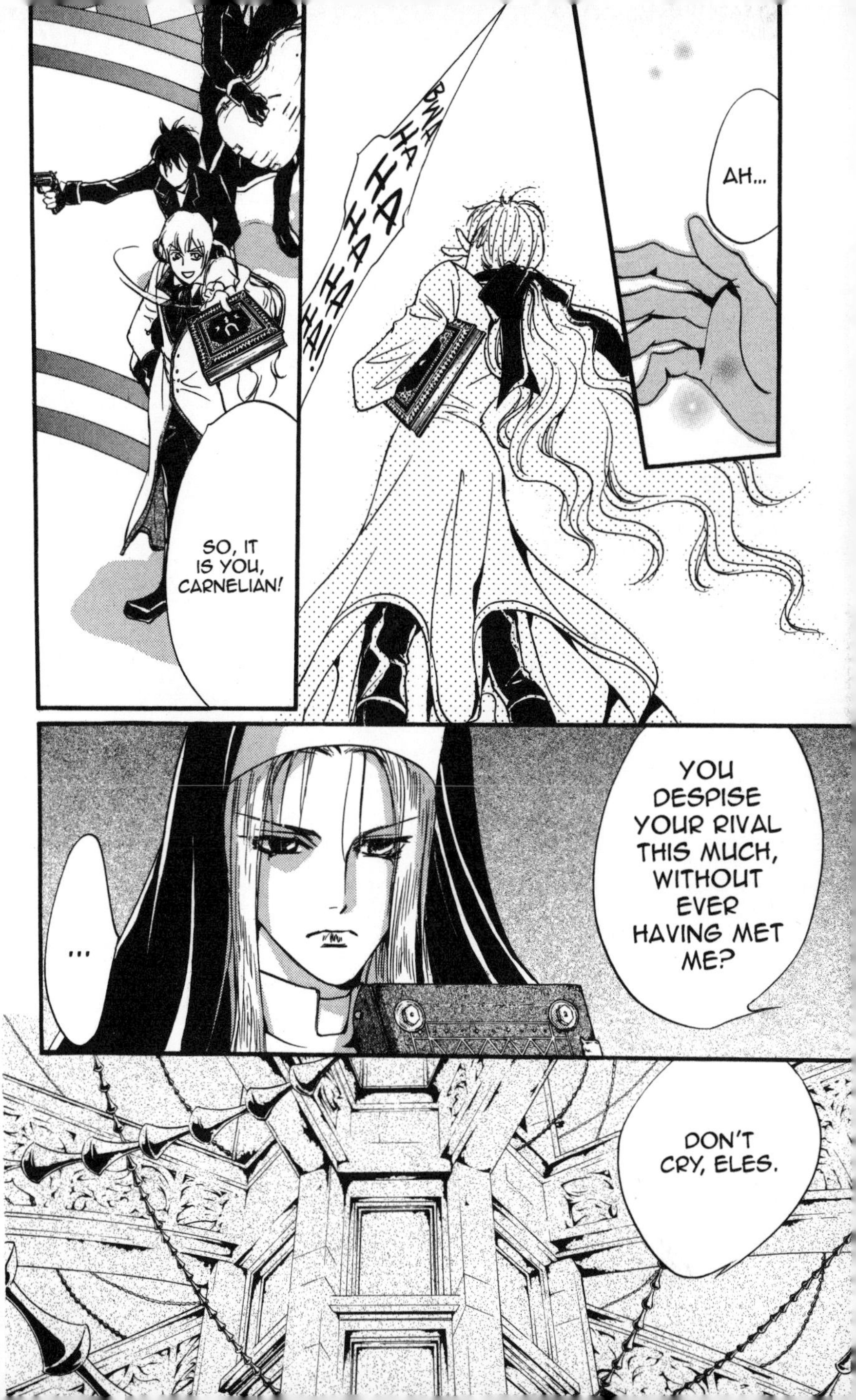
AH...
BWA HA HA HA HA HA!!
SO, IT IS YOU, CARNELIAN!
YOU DESPISE YOUR RIVAL THIS MUCH, WITHOUT EVER HAVING MET ME?
...
DON'T CRY, ELES.

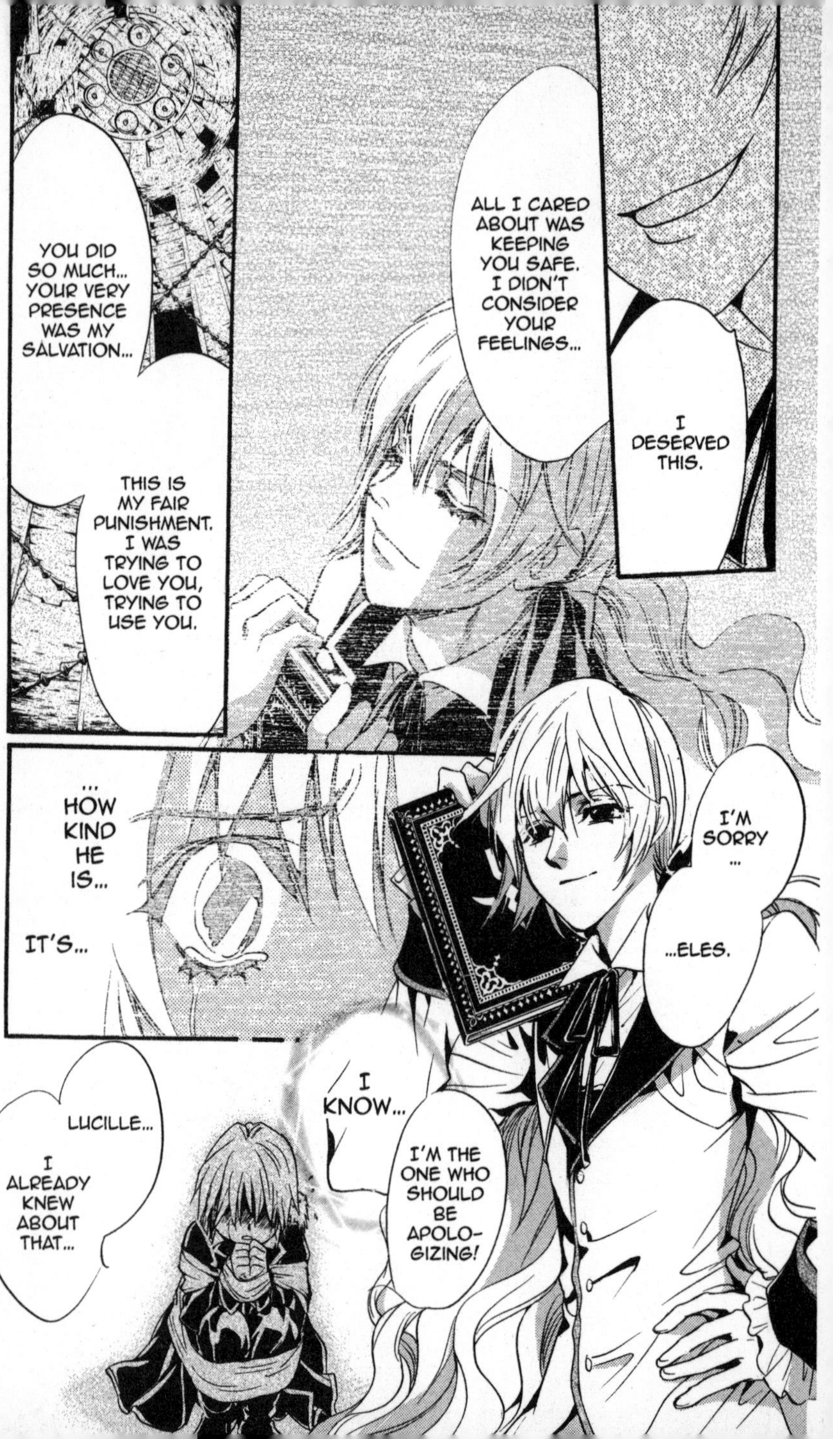
ALL I CARED ABOUT WAS KEEPING YOU SAFE. I DIDN'T CONSIDER YOUR FEELINGS...
I DESERVED THIS.
YOU DID SO MUCH... YOUR VERY PRESENCE WAS MY SALVATION...
THIS IS MY FAIR PUNISHMENT. I WAS TRYING TO LOVE YOU, TRYING TO USE YOU.
I'M SORRY...
...ELES.
...HOW KIND HE IS...
IT'S...
I KNOW...
I'M THE ONE WHO SHOULD BE APOLO-GIZING!
LUCILLE...
I ALREADY KNEW ABOUT THAT...

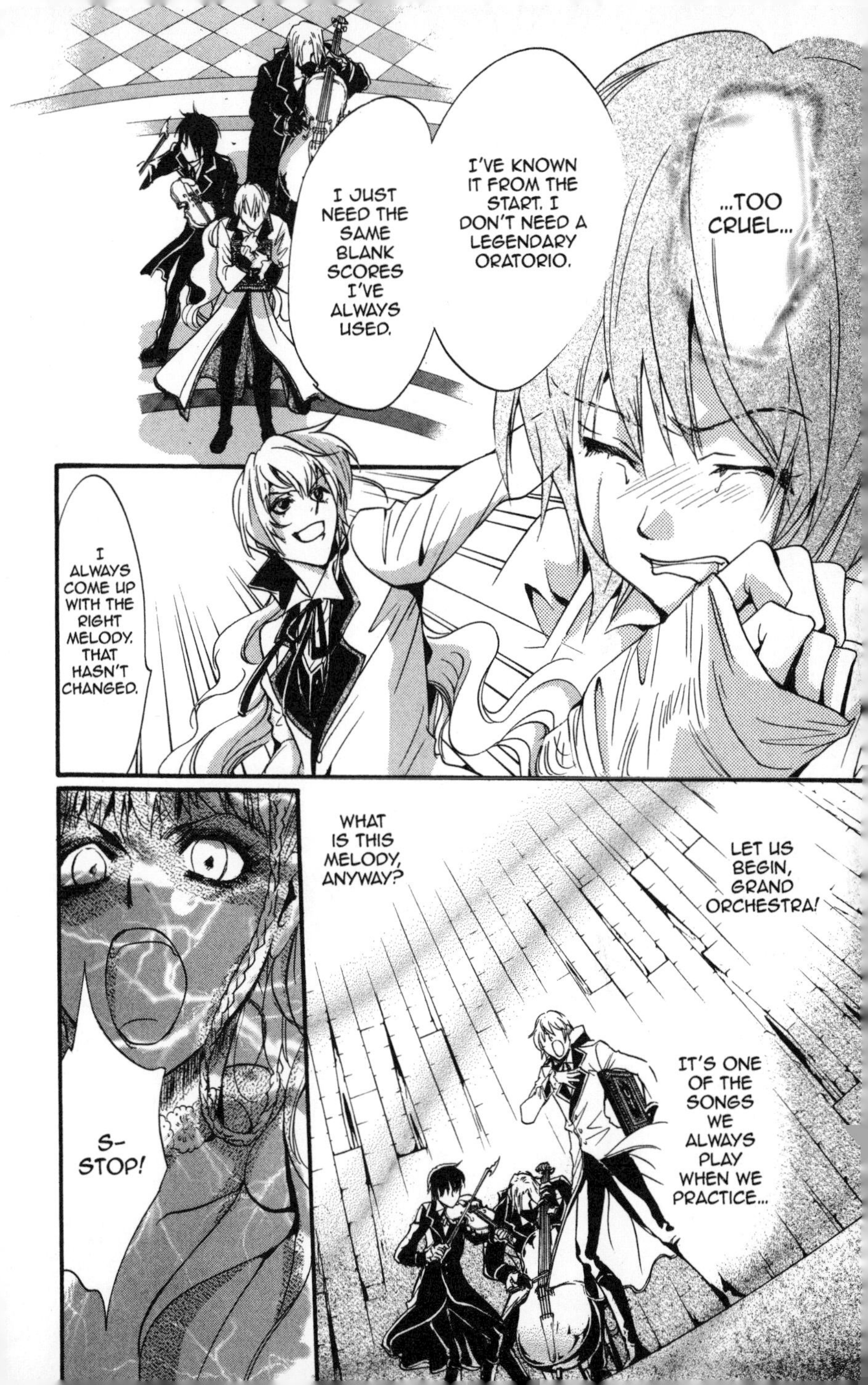
...TOO CRUEL...
I'VE KNOWN IT FROM THE START. I DON'T NEED A LEGENDARY ORATORIO.
I JUST NEED THE SAME BLANK SCORES I'VE ALWAYS USED.
I ALWAYS COME UP WITH THE RIGHT MELODY. THAT HASN'T CHANGED.
LET US BEGIN, GRAND ORCHESTRA!
WHAT IS THIS MELODY, ANYWAY?
IT'S ONE OF THE SONGS WE ALWAYS PLAY WHEN WE PRACTICE...
S-STOP!

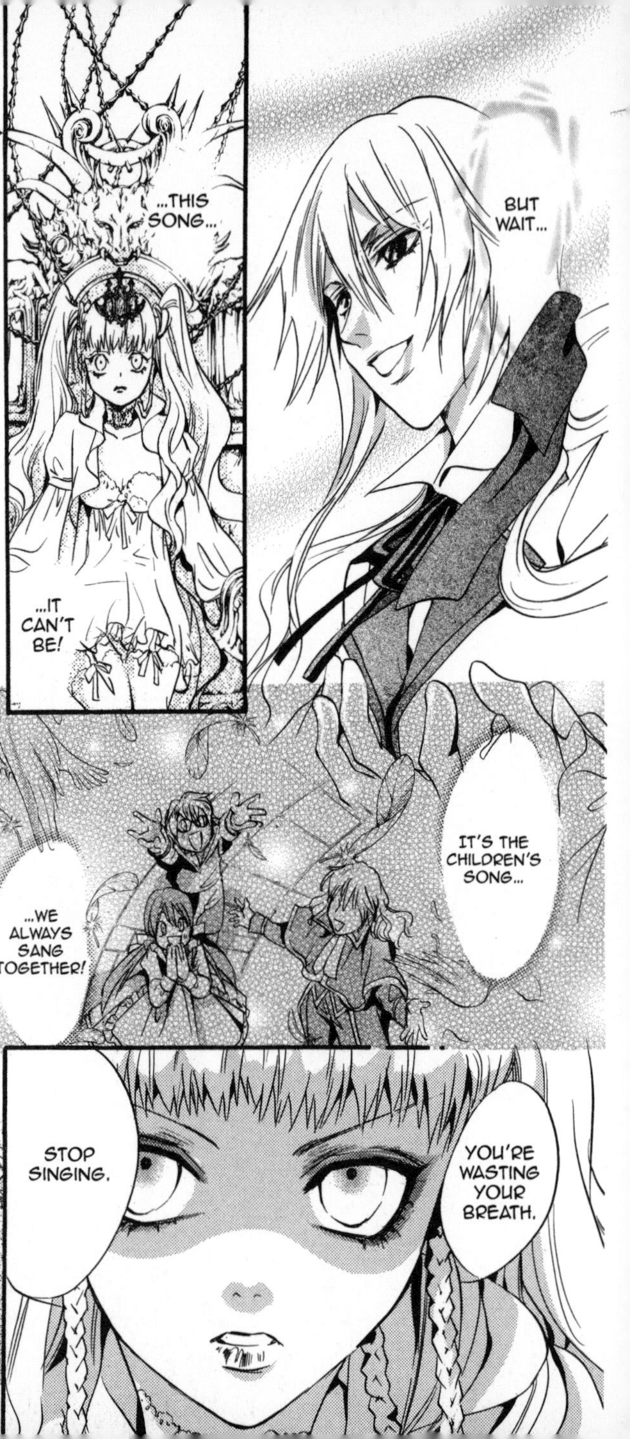
BUT WAIT...
...THIS SONG...
...IT CAN'T BE!
IT'S THE CHILDREN'S SONG...
...WE ALWAYS SANG TOGETHER!
YOU'RE WASTING YOUR BREATH.
STOP SINGING.

As you may already suspect, I had originally intended for Carnelian to have a somewhat—okay, a very different role in the story. It didn't work out due to page constraints, and there were so many things I had to make sure to get in...poor excuses, I know! But I think I managed to wrap the story up the way I had originally intended.

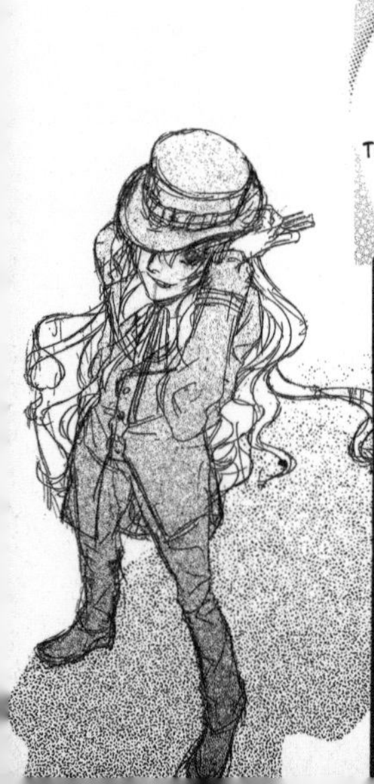

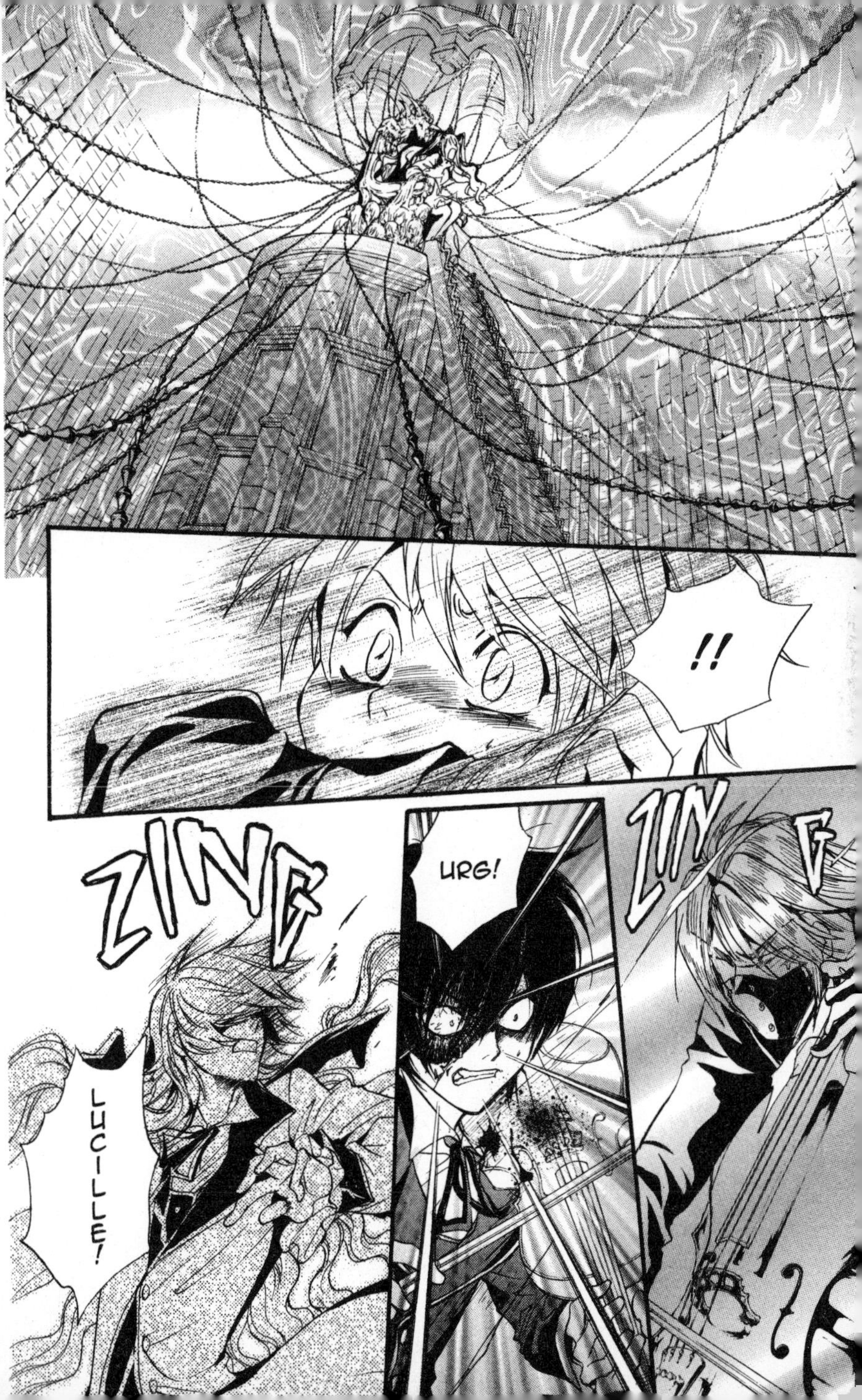
!!
ZING
URG!
ZING
LUCILLE!

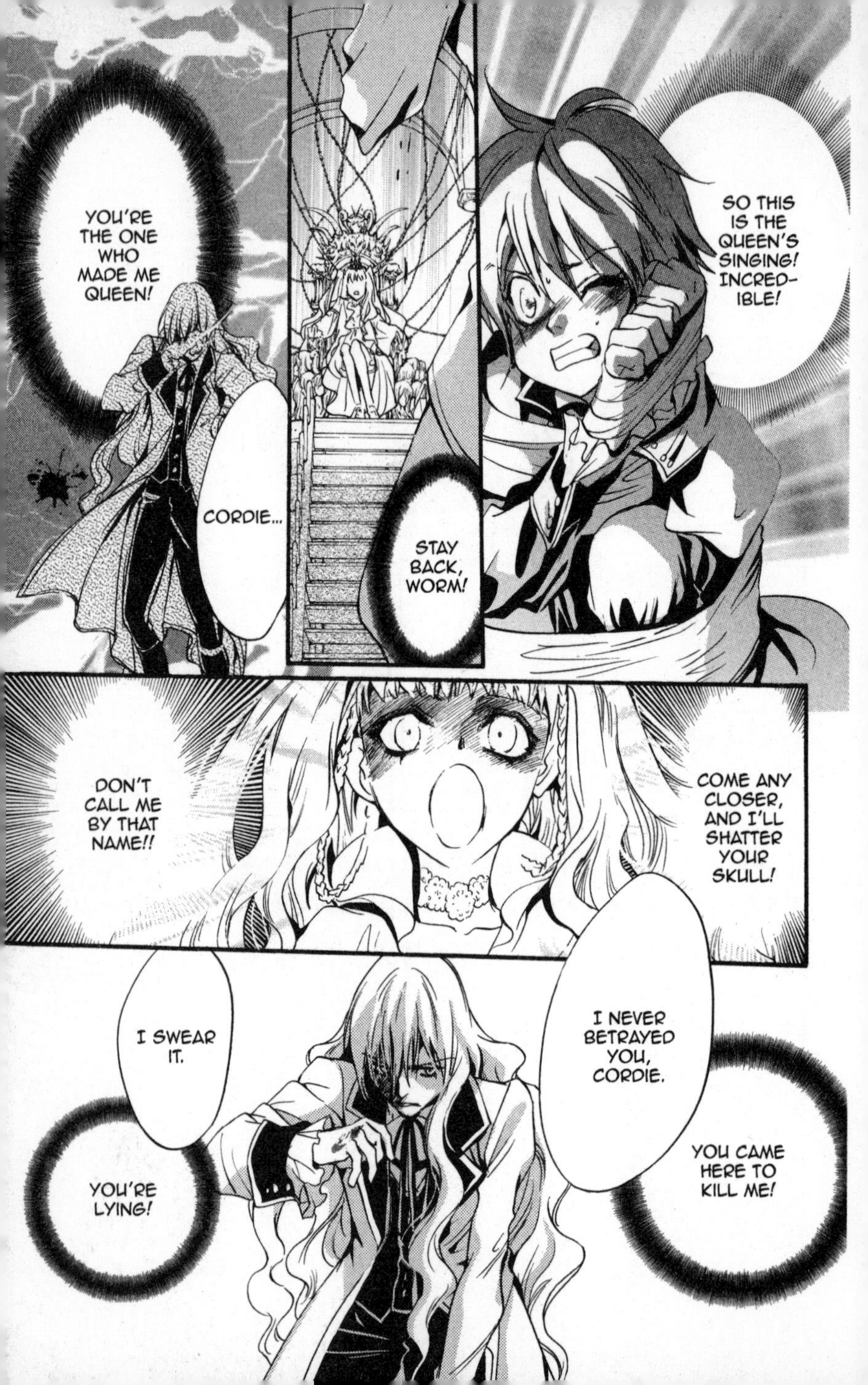
SO THIS IS THE QUEEN'S SINGING! INCRED-IBLE!
STAY BACK, WORM!
YOU'RE THE ONE WHO MADE ME QUEEN!
CORDIE...
COME ANY CLOSER, AND I'LL SHATTER YOUR SKULL!
DON'T CALL ME BY THAT NAME!!
I NEVER BETRAYED YOU, CORDIE.
YOU CAME HERE TO KILL ME!
I SWEAR IT.
YOU'RE LYING!

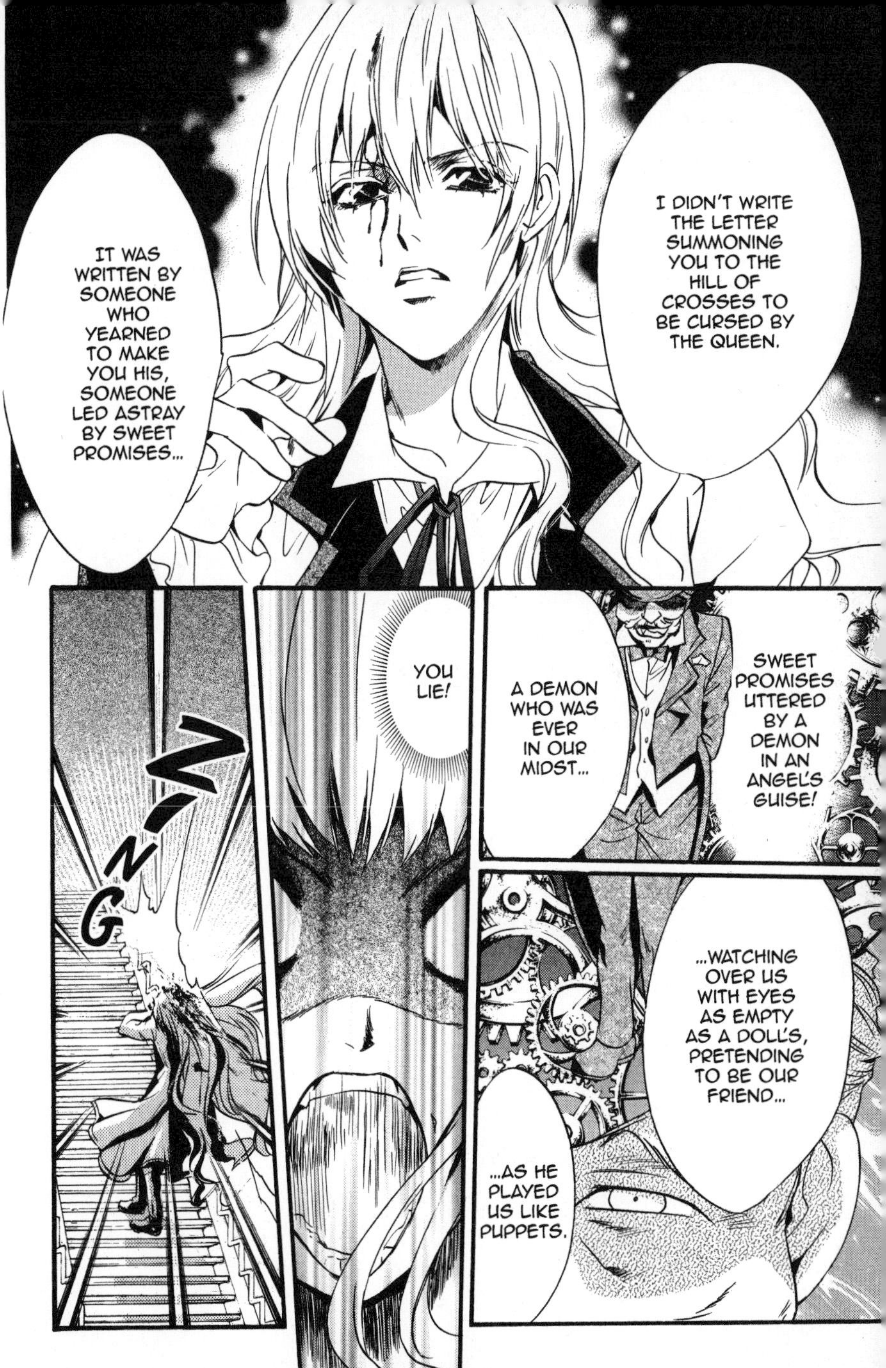
I DIDN'T WRITE THE LETTER SUMMONING YOU TO THE HILL OF CROSSES TO BE CURSED BY THE QUEEN.
IT WAS WRITTEN BY SOMEONE WHO YEARNED TO MAKE YOU HIS, SOMEONE LED ASTRAY BY SWEET PROMISES...
SWEET PROMISES UTTERED BY A DEMON IN AN ANGEL'S GUISE!
A DEMON WHO WAS EVER IN OUR MIDST...
...WATCHING OVER US WITH EYES AS EMPTY AS A DOLL'S, PRETENDING TO BE OUR FRIEND...
...AS HE PLAYED US LIKE PUPPETS.
YOU LIE!
GN-N

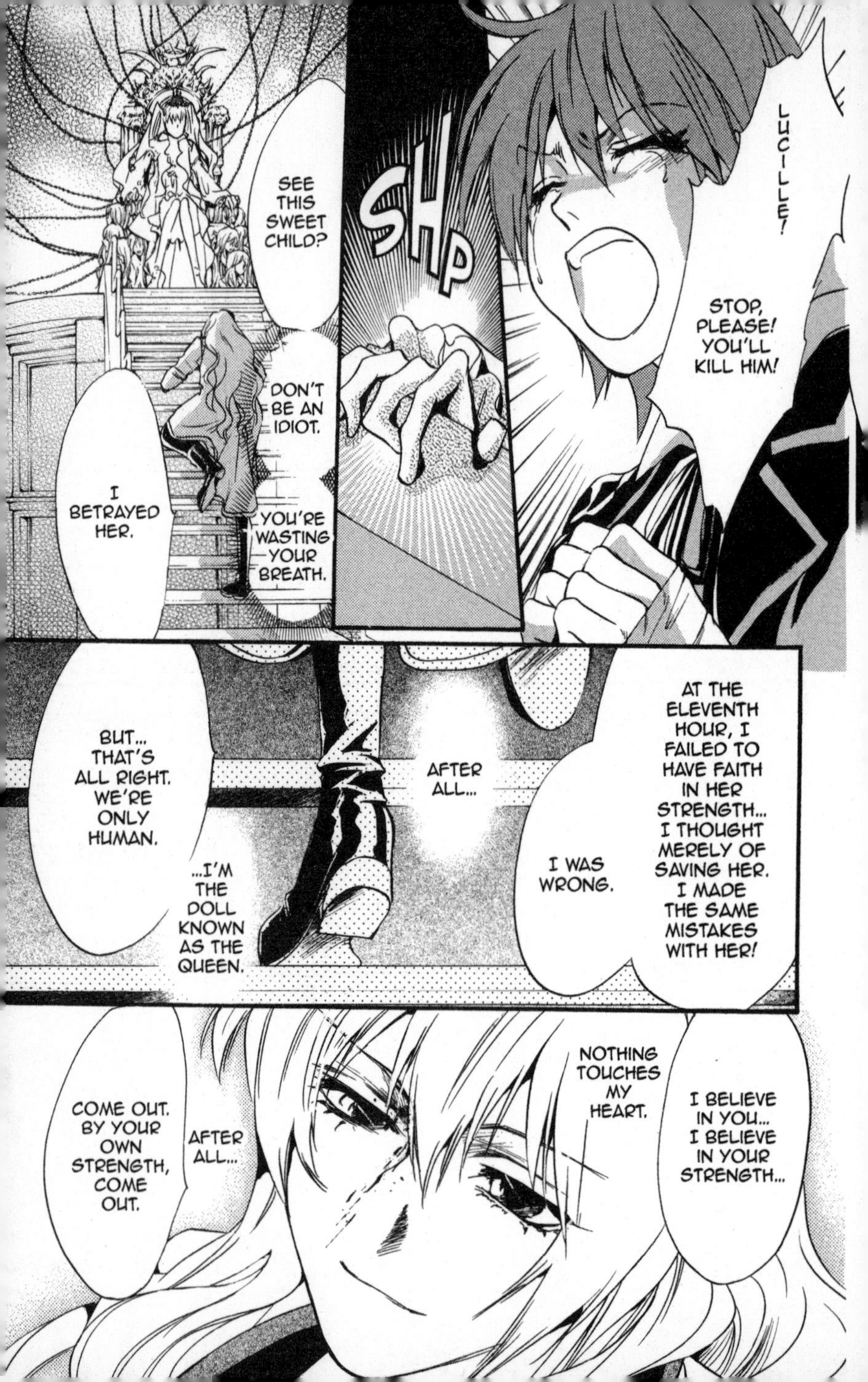
LUCILLE!
STOP, PLEASE! YOU'LL KILL HIM!
SHP
SEE THIS SWEET CHILD?
DON'T BE AN IDIOT.
YOU'RE WASTING YOUR BREATH.
I BETRAYED HER.
AT THE ELEVENTH HOUR, I FAILED TO HAVE FAITH IN HER STRENGTH... I THOUGHT MERELY OF SAVING HER. I MADE THE SAME MISTAKES WITH HER!
I WAS WRONG.
AFTER ALL...
...I'M THE DOLL KNOWN AS THE QUEEN.
BUT... THAT'S ALL RIGHT. WE'RE ONLY HUMAN.
I BELIEVE IN YOU... I BELIEVE IN YOUR STRENGTH...
NOTHING TOUCHES MY HEART.
AFTER ALL...
COME OUT. BY YOUR OWN STRENGTH, COME OUT.

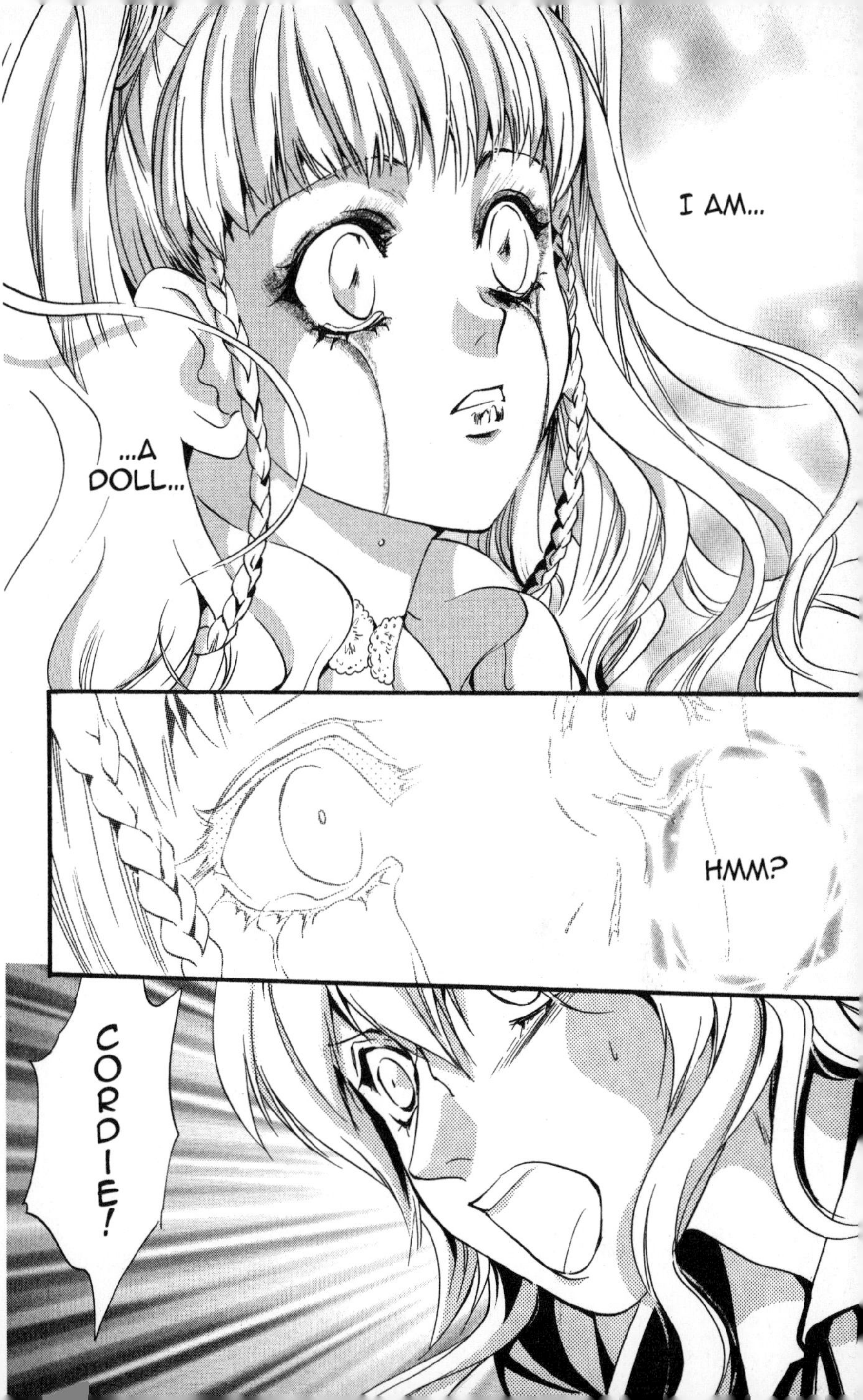
I AM...
...A DOLL...
HMM?
CORDIE!

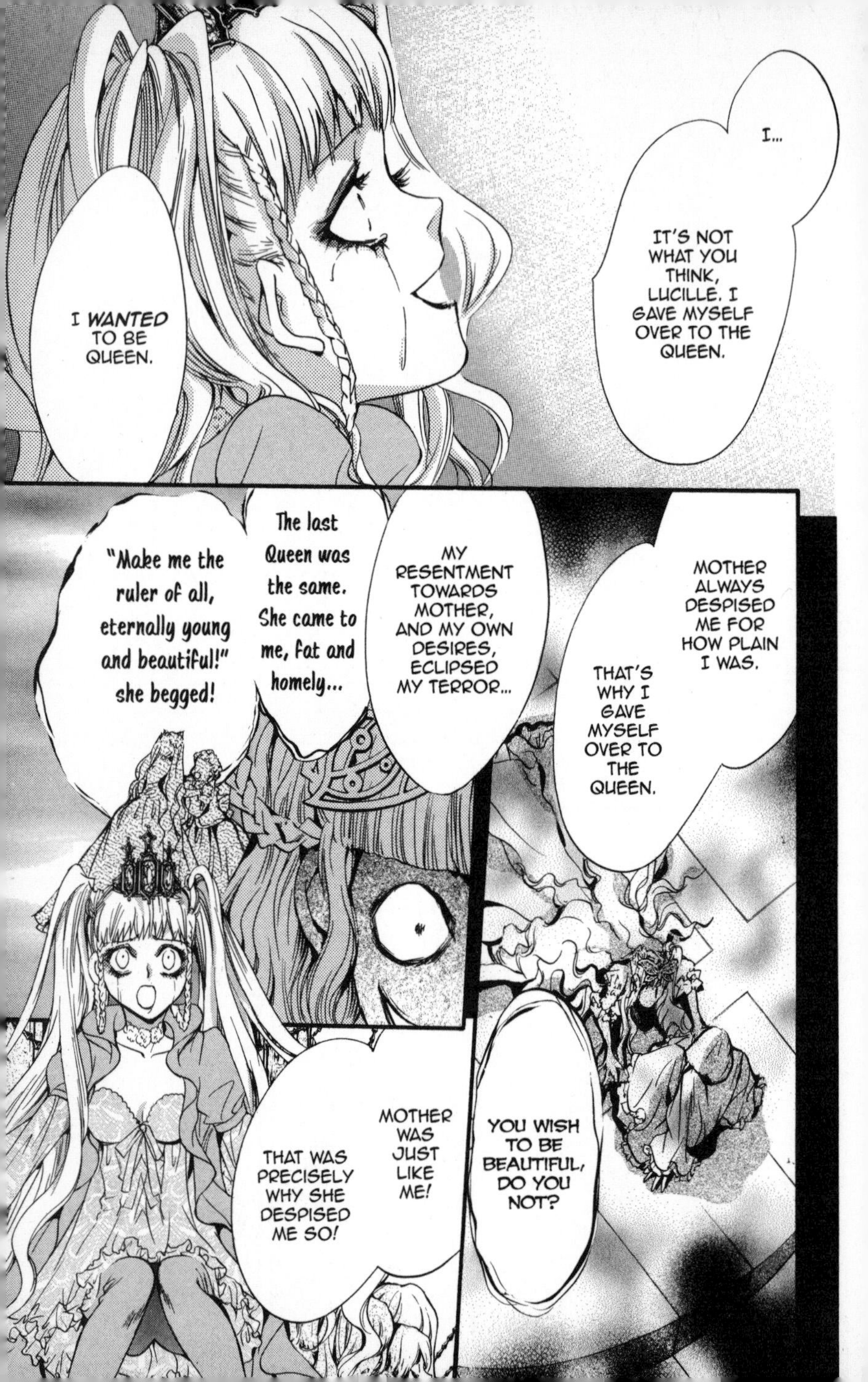
I...
IT'S NOT WHAT YOU THINK, LUCILLE. I GAVE MYSELF OVER TO THE QUEEN.
I *WANTED* TO BE QUEEN.
MOTHER ALWAYS DESPISED ME FOR HOW PLAIN I WAS.
THAT'S WHY I GAVE MYSELF OVER TO THE QUEEN.
YOU WISH TO BE BEAUTIFUL, DO YOU NOT?
MY RESENTMENT TOWARDS MOTHER, AND MY OWN DESIRES, ECLIPSED MY TERROR...
The last Queen was the same. She came to me, fat and homely...
"Make me the ruler of all, eternally young and beautiful!" she begged!
MOTHER WAS JUST LIKE ME!
THAT WAS PRECISELY WHY SHE DESPISED ME SO!

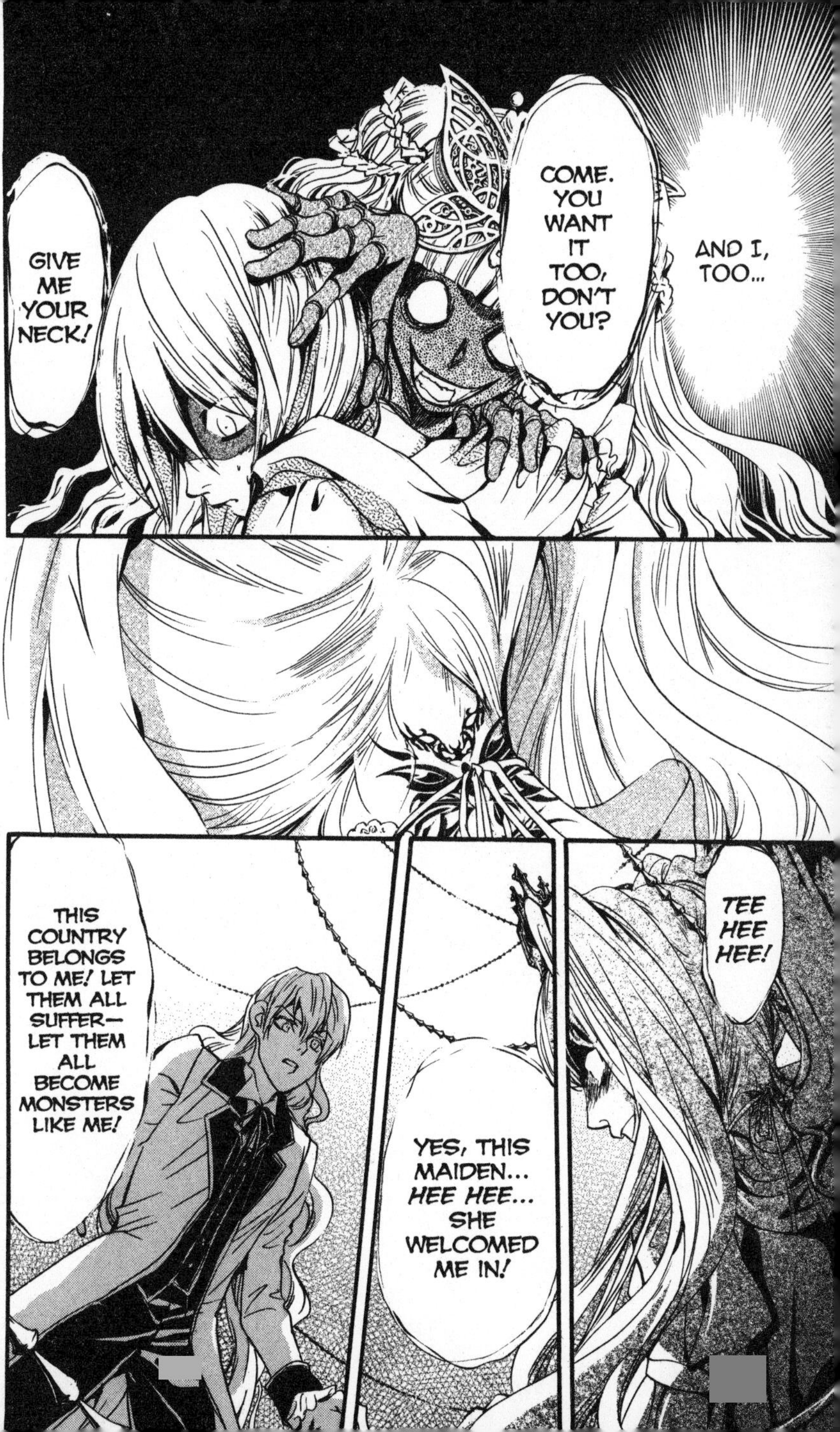
AND I, TOO...
COME. YOU WANT IT TOO, DON'T YOU?
GIVE ME YOUR NECK!
TEE HEE HEE!
YES, THIS MAIDEN... *HEE HEE...* SHE WELCOMED ME IN!
THIS COUNTRY BELONGS TO ME! LET THEM ALL SUFFER— LET THEM ALL BECOME MONSTERS LIKE ME!

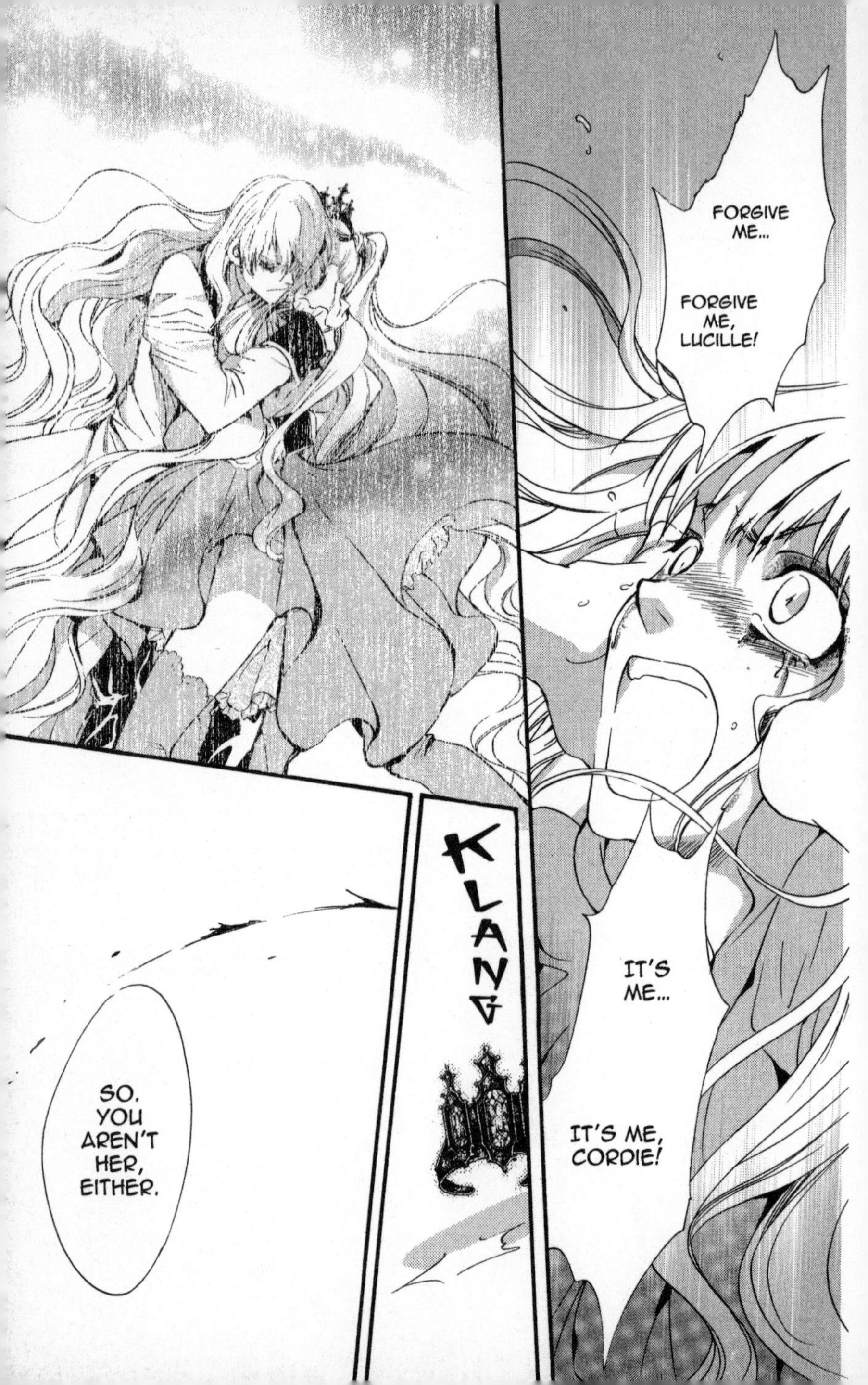
FORGIVE ME...
FORGIVE ME, LUCILLE!
IT'S ME...
IT'S ME, CORDIE!
KLANG
SO. YOU AREN'T HER, EITHER.

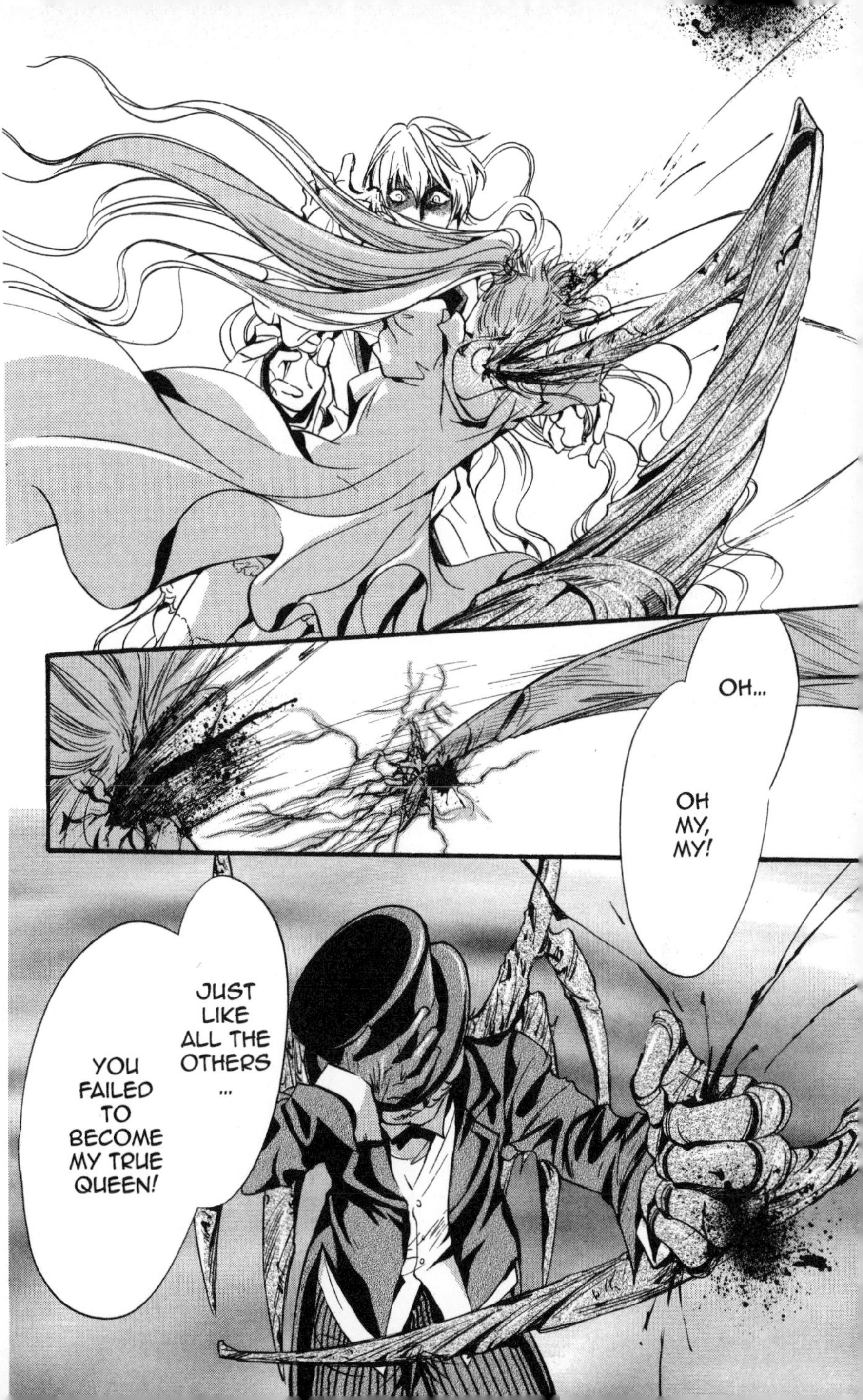
OH...
OH MY, MY!
JUST LIKE ALL THE OTHERS ...
YOU FAILED TO BECOME MY TRUE QUEEN!

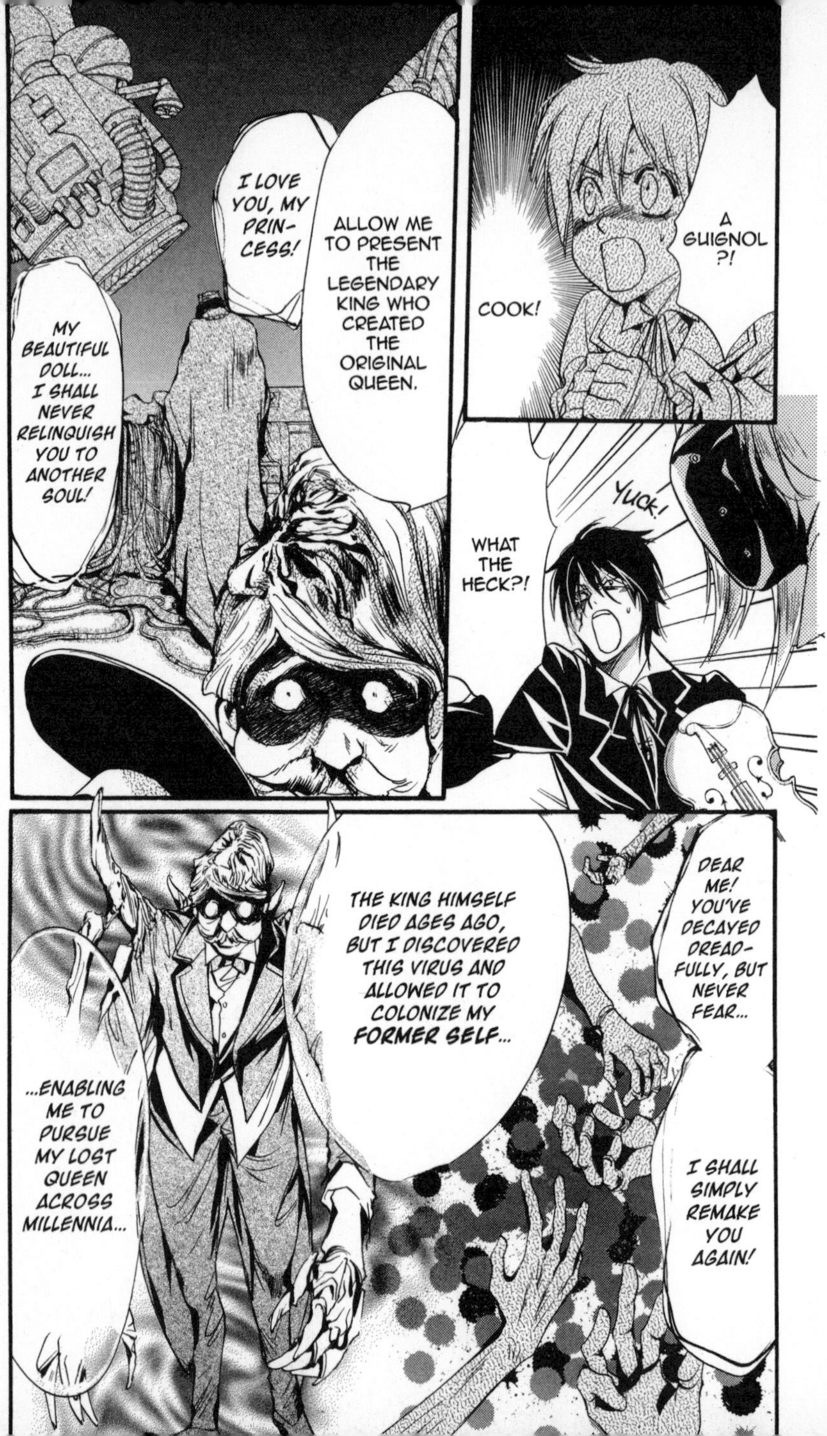
A GUIGNOL ?!
COOK!
YUCK!
WHAT THE HECK?!
ALLOW ME TO PRESENT THE LEGENDARY KING WHO CREATED THE ORIGINAL QUEEN.
I LOVE YOU, MY PRIN-CESS!
MY BEAUTIFUL DOLL... I SHALL NEVER RELINQUISH YOU TO ANOTHER SOUL!
DEAR ME! YOU'VE DECAYED DREAD-FULLY, BUT NEVER FEAR...
I SHALL SIMPLY REMAKE YOU AGAIN!
THE KING HIMSELF DIED AGES AGO, BUT I DISCOVERED THIS VIRUS AND ALLOWED IT TO COLONIZE MY **FORMER SELF**...
...ENABLING ME TO PURSUE MY LOST QUEEN ACROSS MILLENNIA...

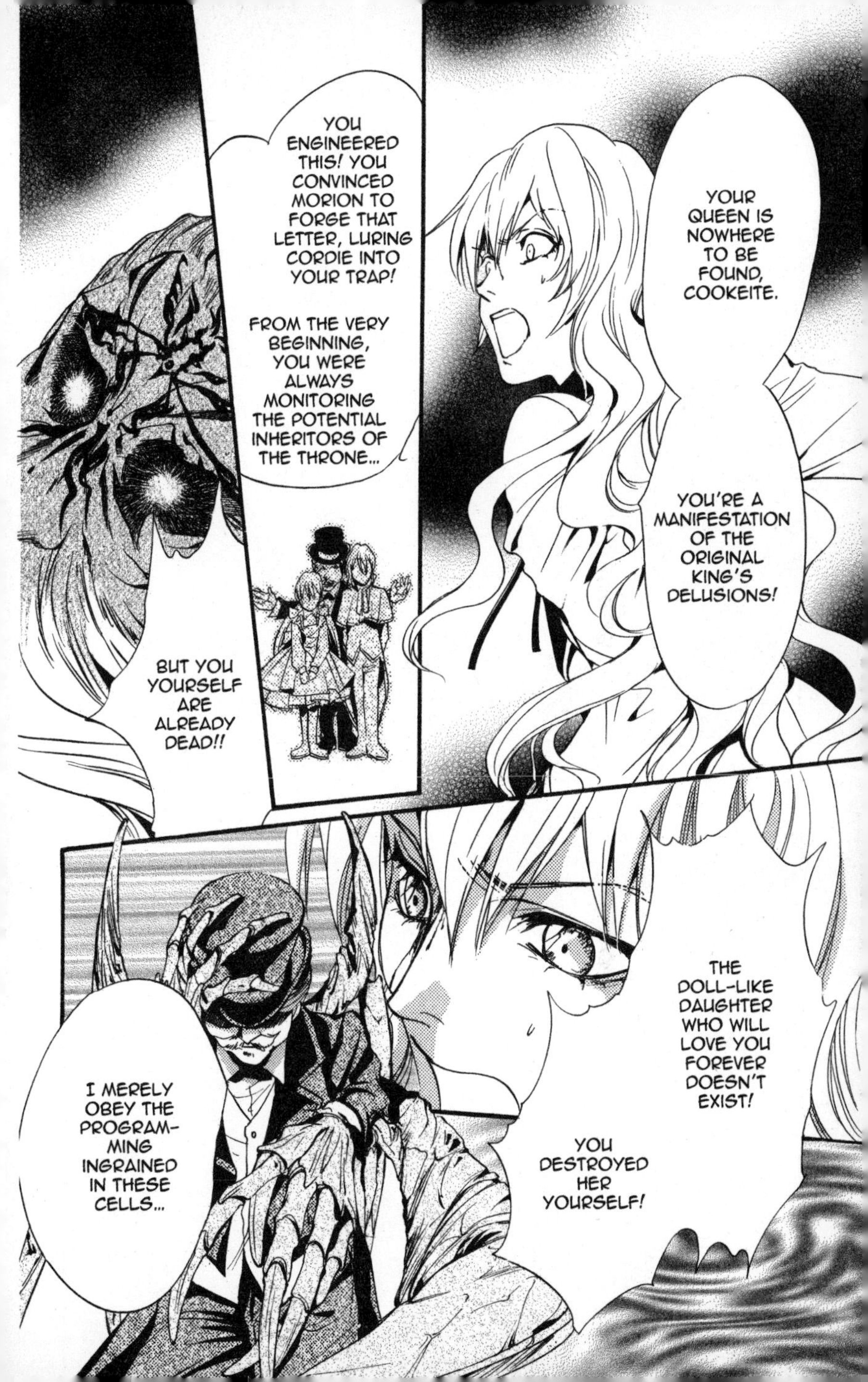
YOUR QUEEN IS NOWHERE TO BE FOUND, COOKEITE.
YOU'RE A MANIFESTATION OF THE ORIGINAL KING'S DELUSIONS!
YOU ENGINEERED THIS! YOU CONVINCED MORION TO FORGE THAT LETTER, LURING CORDIE INTO YOUR TRAP!
FROM THE VERY BEGINNING, YOU WERE ALWAYS MONITORING THE POTENTIAL INHERITORS OF THE THRONE...
BUT YOU YOURSELF ARE ALREADY DEAD!!
THE DOLL-LIKE DAUGHTER WHO WILL LOVE YOU FOREVER DOESN'T EXIST!
YOU DESTROYED HER YOURSELF!
I MERELY OBEY THE PROGRAM-MING INGRAINED IN THESE CELLS...

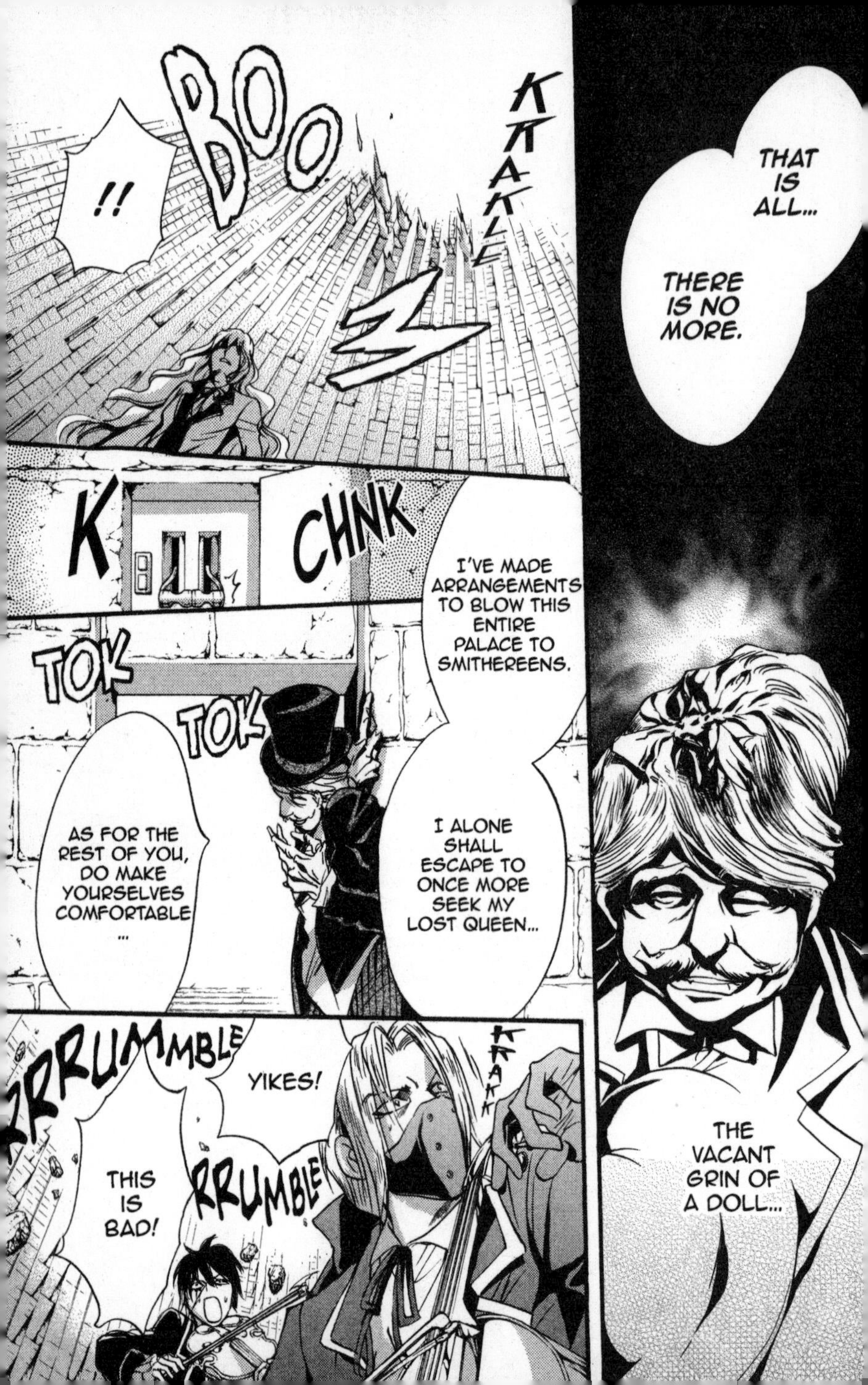
THAT IS ALL...
THERE IS NO MORE.
THE VACANT GRIN OF A DOLL...
KRAKKLE
BOOOM
!!
I'VE MADE ARRANGEMENTS TO BLOW THIS ENTIRE PALACE TO SMITHEREENS.
CHNK
K
TOK
TOK
I ALONE SHALL ESCAPE TO ONCE MORE SEEK MY LOST QUEEN...
AS FOR THE REST OF YOU, DO MAKE YOURSELVES COMFORTABLE...
KRAKK
YIKES!
RRUMBLE
THIS IS BAD!
RRRUMMBLE

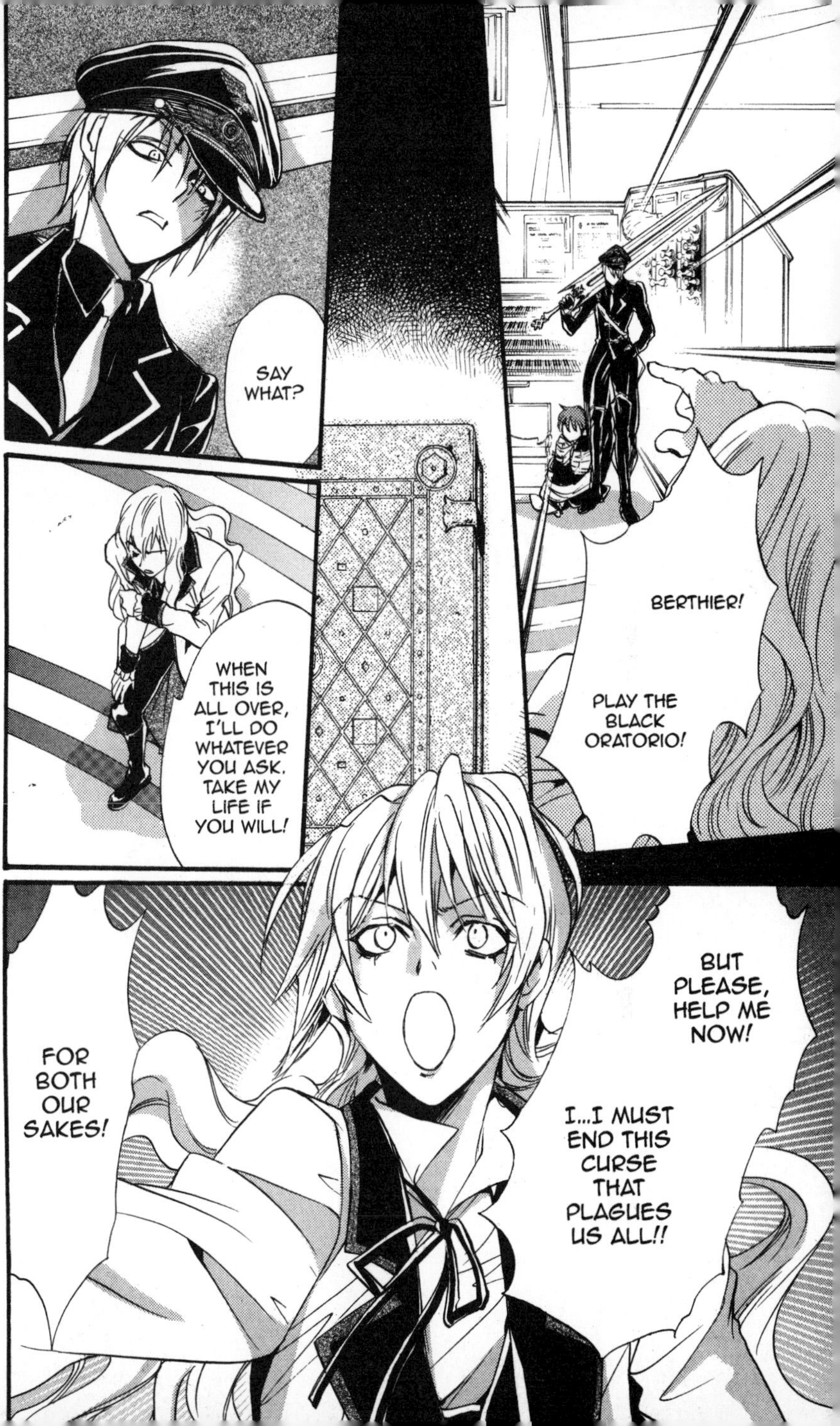
BERTHIER!
PLAY THE BLACK ORATORIO!
SAY WHAT?
WHEN THIS IS ALL OVER, I'LL DO WHATEVER YOU ASK. TAKE MY LIFE IF YOU WILL!
BUT PLEASE, HELP ME NOW!
I...I MUST END THIS CURSE THAT PLAGUES US ALL!!
FOR BOTH OUR SAKES!

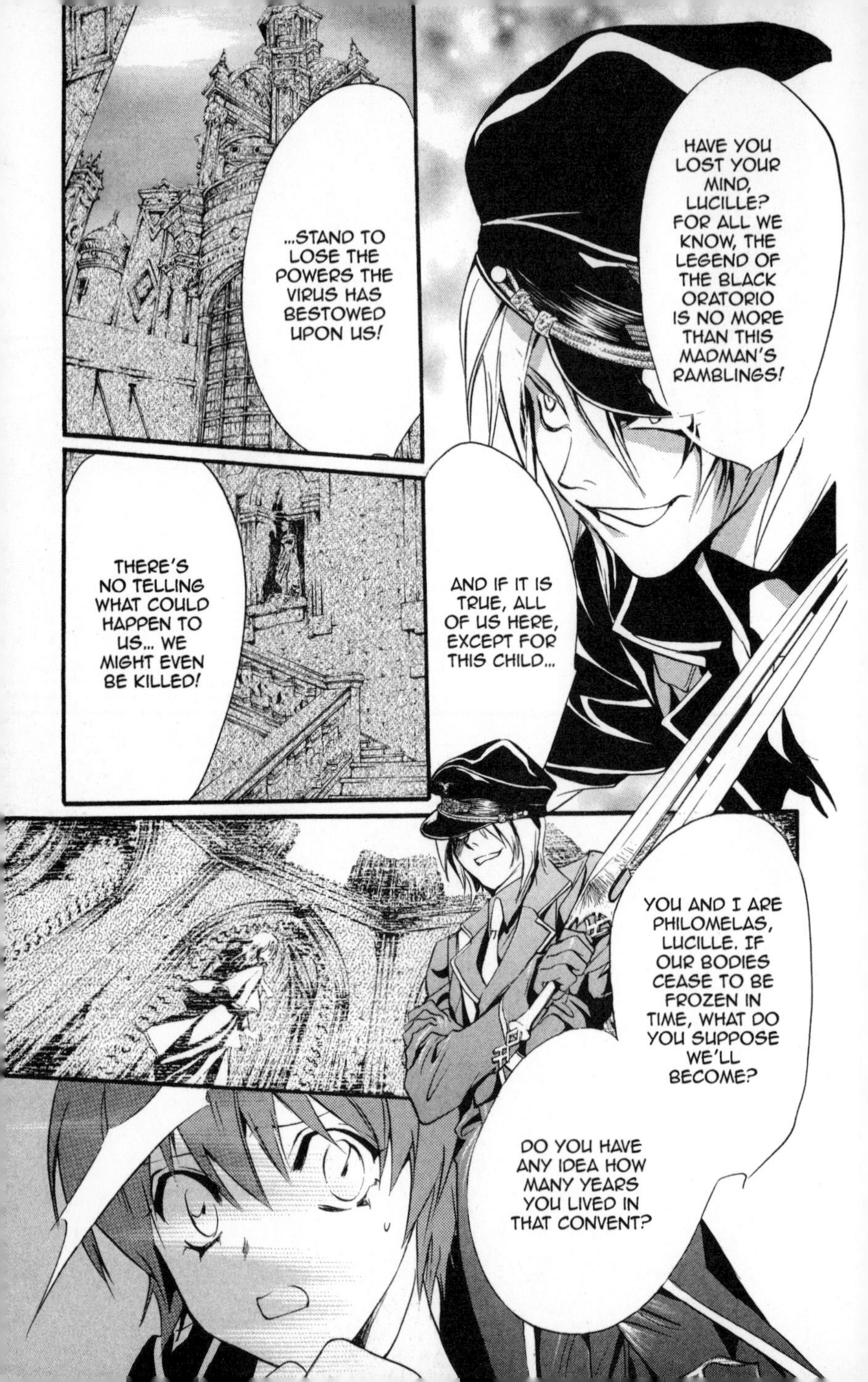
HAVE YOU LOST YOUR MIND, LUCILLE? FOR ALL WE KNOW, THE LEGEND OF THE BLACK ORATORIO IS NO MORE THAN THIS MADMAN'S RAMBLINGS!
AND IF IT IS TRUE, ALL OF US HERE, EXCEPT FOR THIS CHILD...
...STAND TO LOSE THE POWERS THE VIRUS HAS BESTOWED UPON US!
THERE'S NO TELLING WHAT COULD HAPPEN TO US... WE MIGHT EVEN BE KILLED!
YOU AND I ARE PHILOMELAS, LUCILLE. IF OUR BODIES CEASE TO BE FROZEN IN TIME, WHAT DO YOU SUPPOSE WE'LL BECOME?
DO YOU HAVE ANY IDEA HOW MANY YEARS YOU LIVED IN THAT CONVENT?

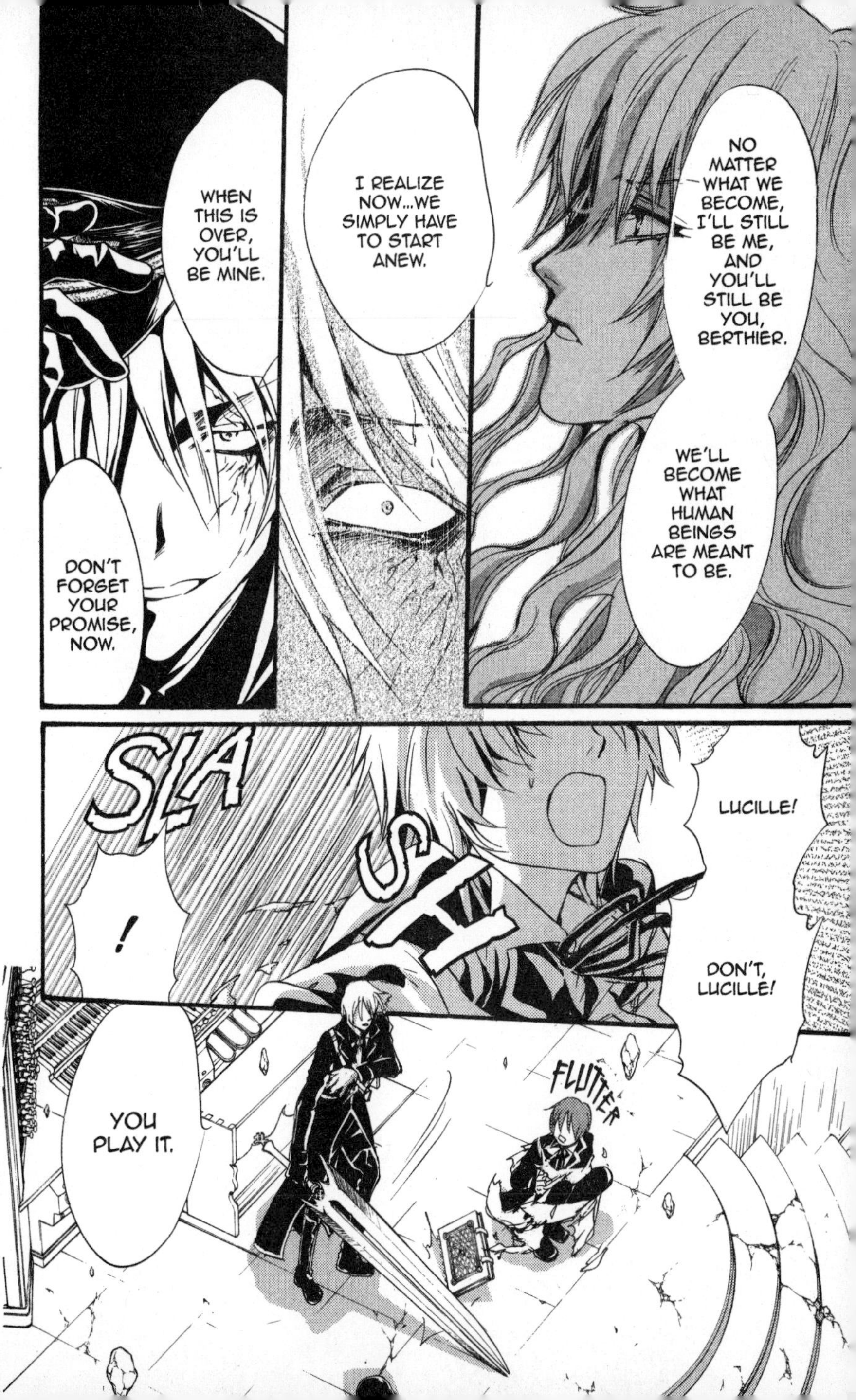
NO MATTER WHAT WE BECOME, I'LL STILL BE ME, AND YOU'LL STILL BE YOU, BERTHIER.
WE'LL BECOME WHAT HUMAN BEINGS ARE MEANT TO BE.
I REALIZE NOW...WE SIMPLY HAVE TO START ANEW.
WHEN THIS IS OVER, YOU'LL BE MINE.
DON'T FORGET YOUR PROMISE, NOW.
LUCILLE!
DON'T, LUCILLE!
SLASH
!
FLUTTER
YOU PLAY IT.

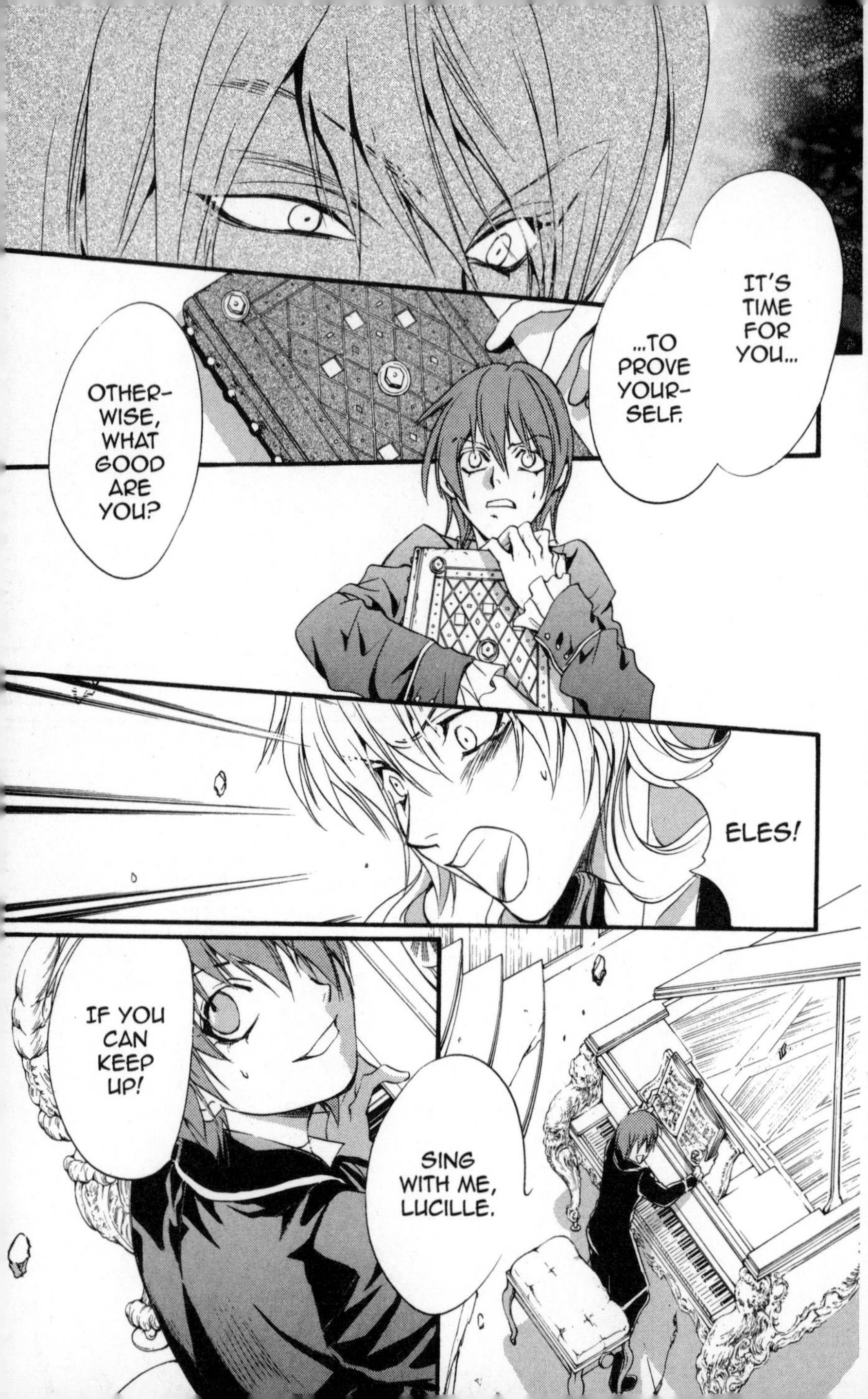
IT'S TIME FOR YOU...
...TO PROVE YOURSELF.
OTHERWISE, WHAT GOOD ARE YOU?
ELES!
SING WITH ME, LUCILLE.
IF YOU CAN KEEP UP!

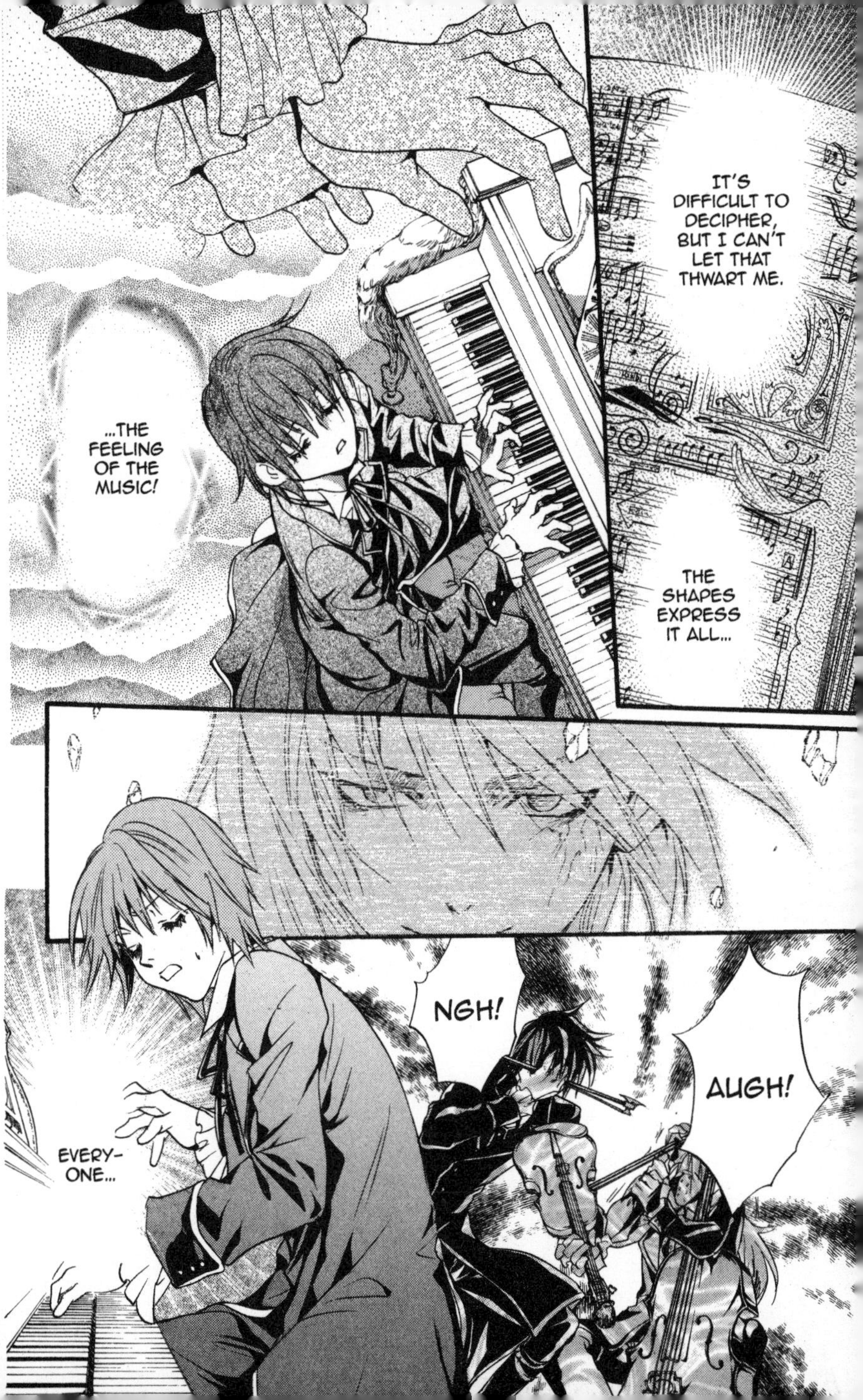
IT'S DIFFICULT TO DECIPHER, BUT I CAN'T LET THAT THWART ME.
THE SHAPES EXPRESS IT ALL...
...THE FEELING OF THE MUSIC!
AUGH!
NGH!
EVERY-ONE...

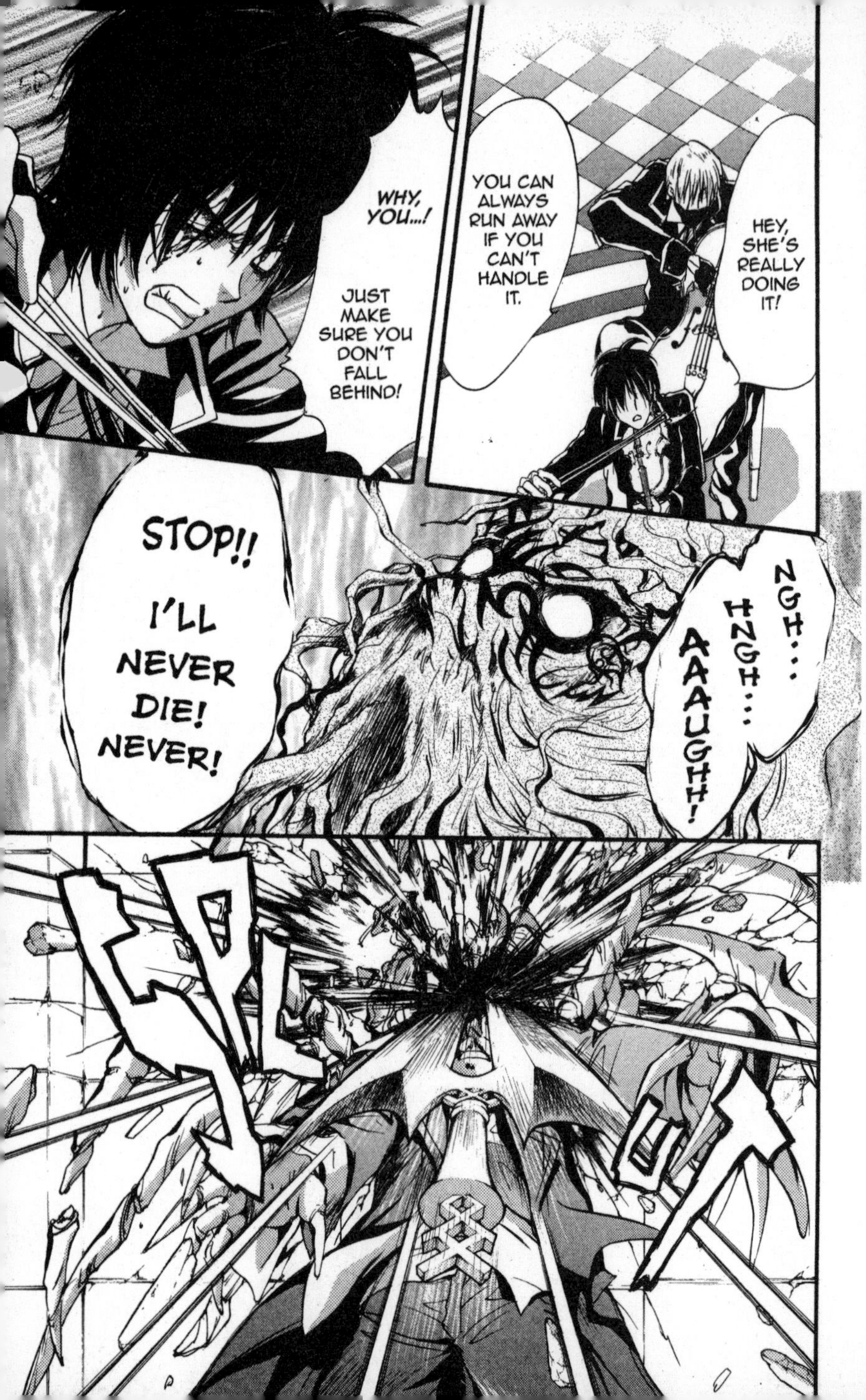
HEY, SHE'S REALLY DOING IT!
YOU CAN ALWAYS RUN AWAY IF YOU CAN'T HANDLE IT.
WHY, YOU...!
JUST MAKE SURE YOU DON'T FALL BEHIND!
NGH... HNGH... AAAUGH!
STOP!!
I'LL NEVER DIE! NEVER!

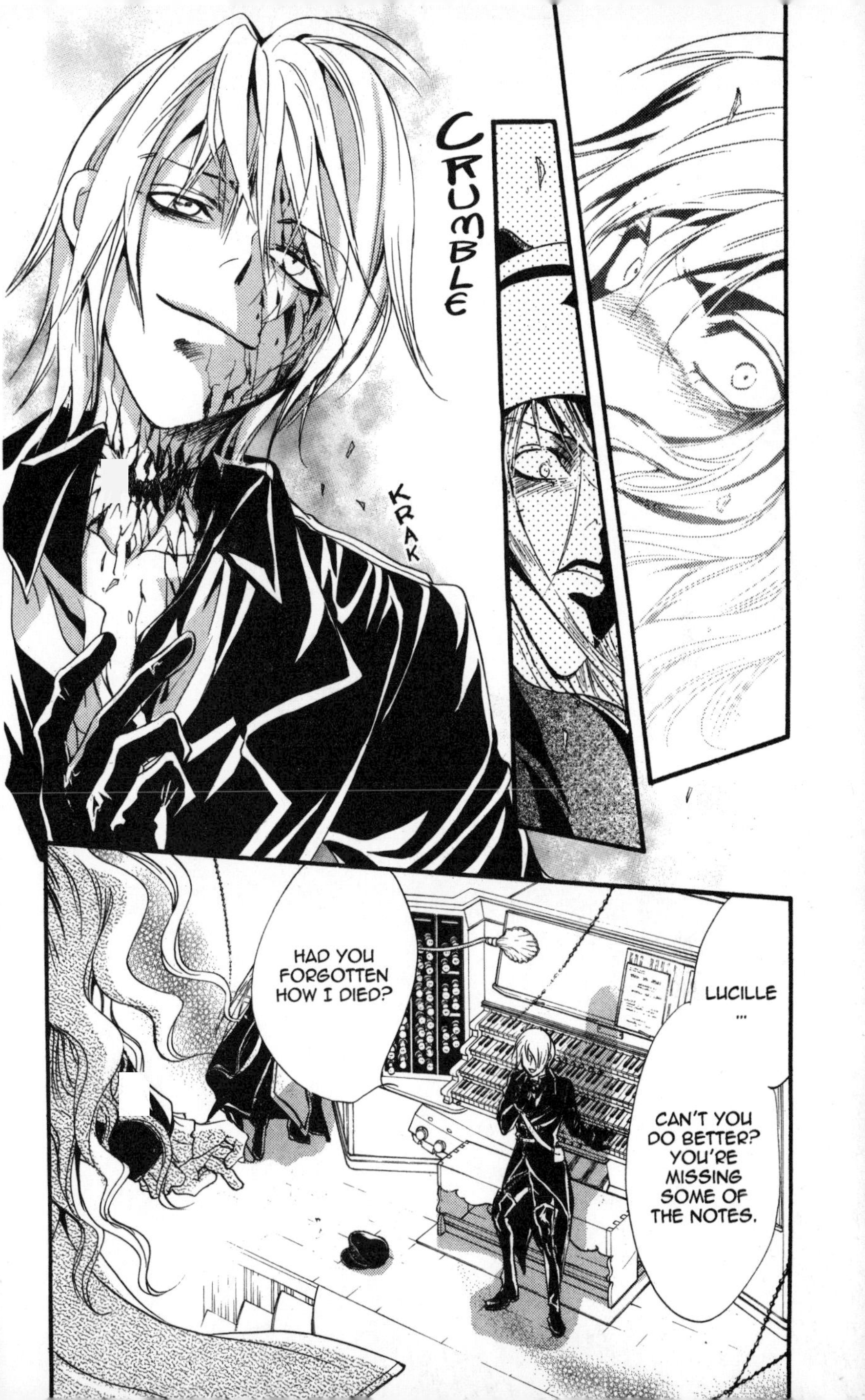
CRUMBLE
KRAK
LUCILLE ...
CAN'T YOU DO BETTER? YOU'RE MISSING SOME OF THE NOTES.
HAD YOU FORGOTTEN HOW I DIED?

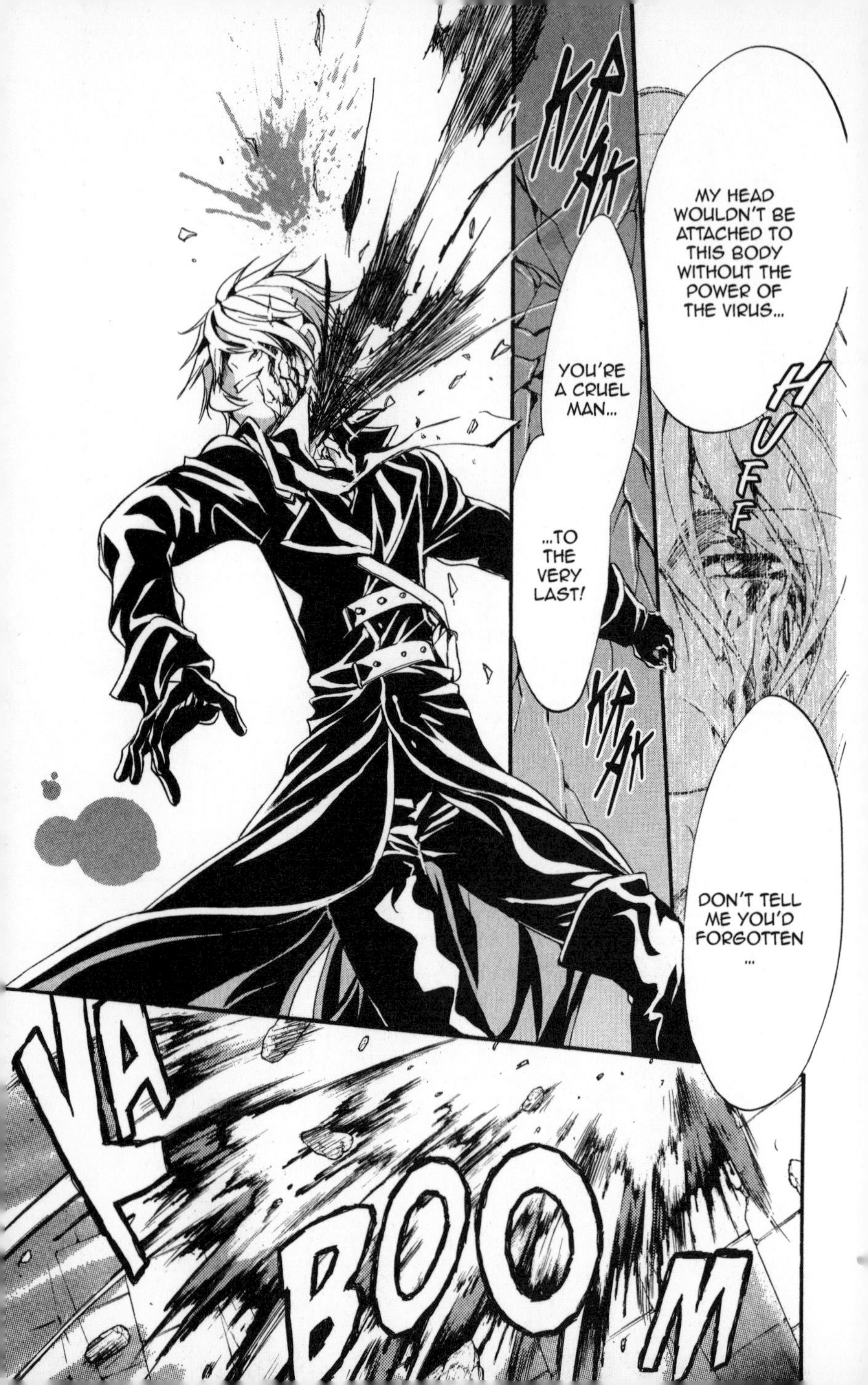
MY HEAD WOULDN'T BE ATTACHED TO THIS BODY WITHOUT THE POWER OF THE VIRUS...
KRAK
HUFF
YOU'RE A CRUEL MAN...
...TO THE VERY LAST!
KRAK
DON'T TELL ME YOU'D FORGOTTEN...
KA BOOM

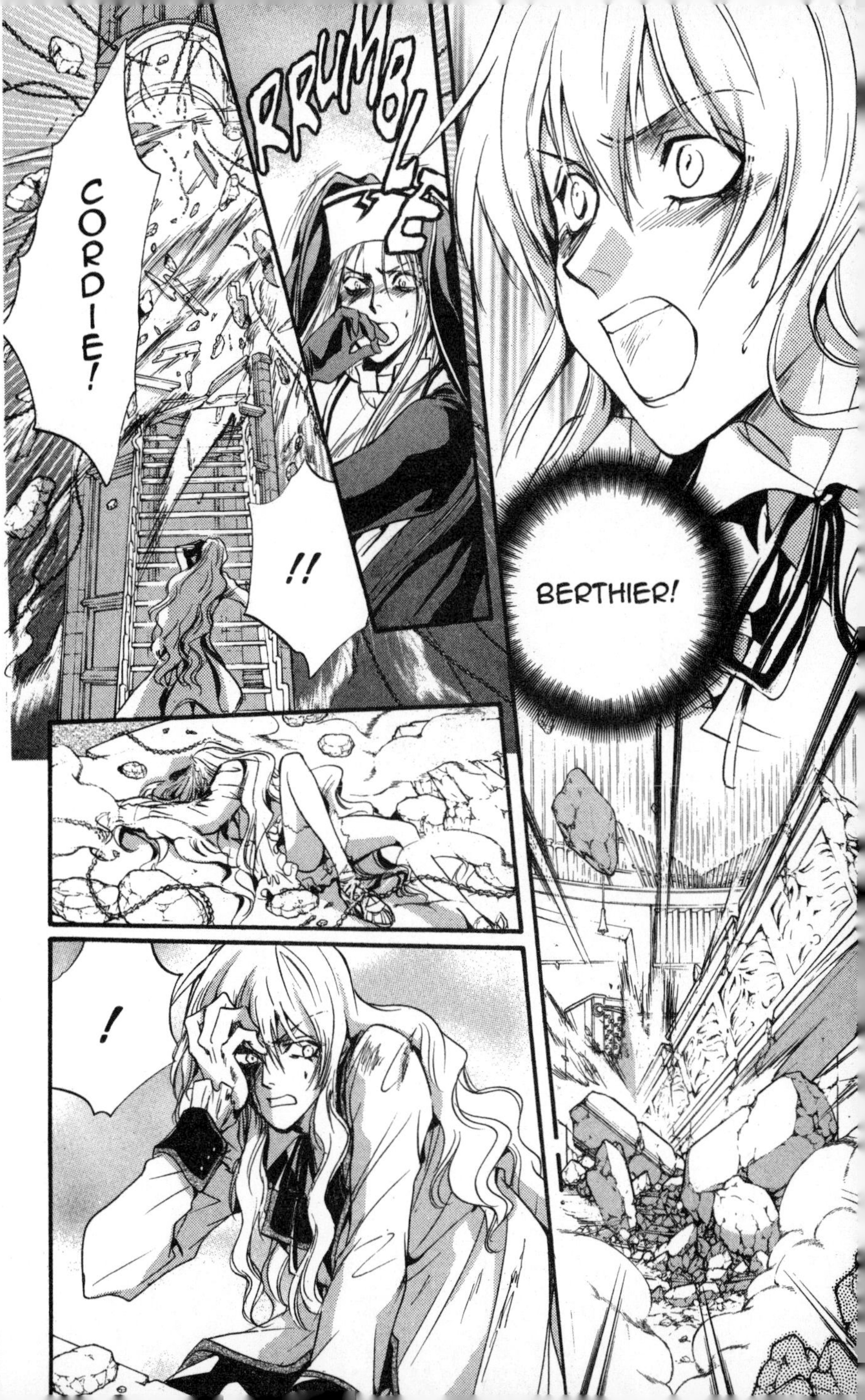
BERTHIER!
RRUMBLE
!!
CORDIE!
!

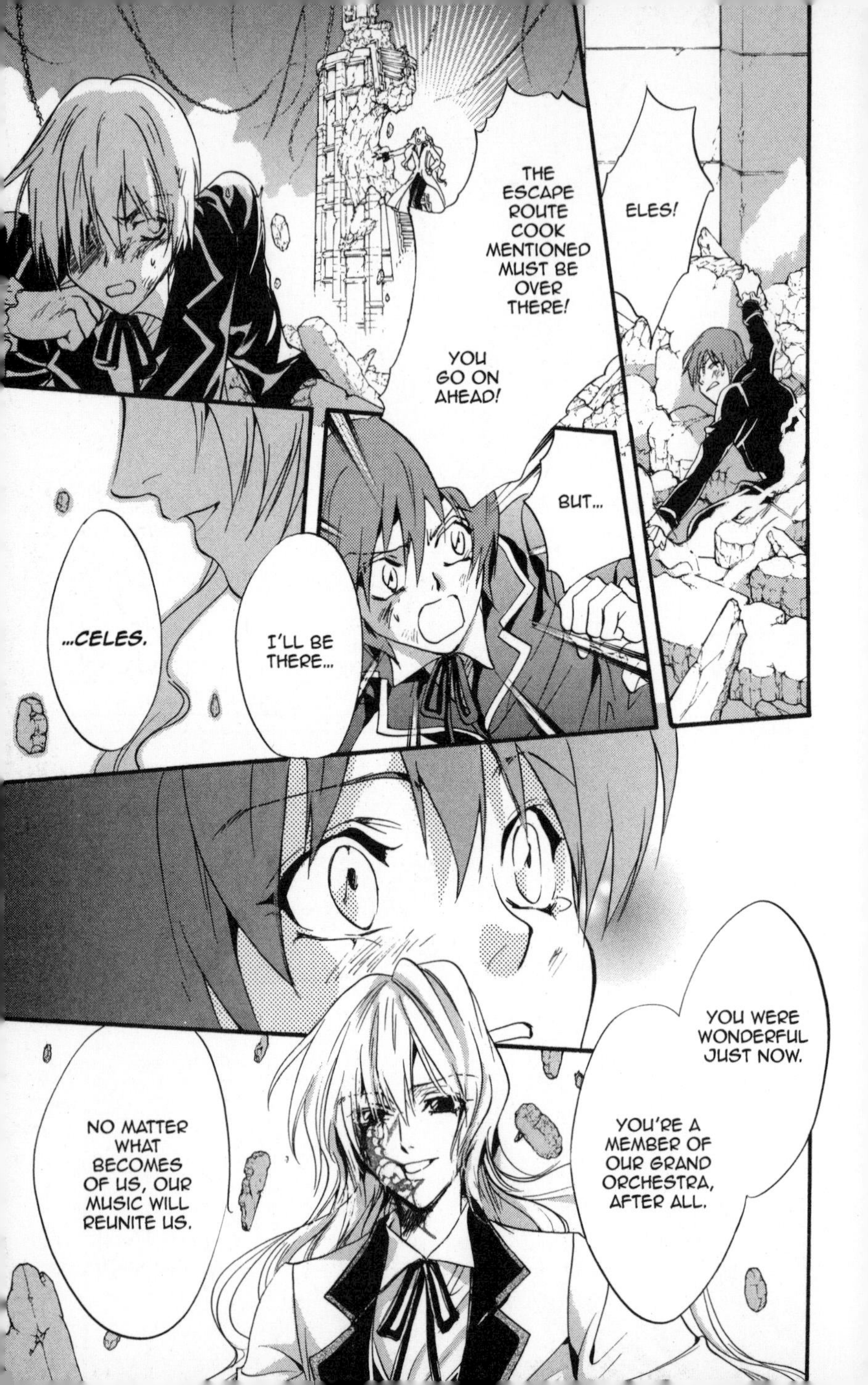
ELES!
THE ESCAPE ROUTE COOK MENTIONED MUST BE OVER THERE!
YOU GO ON AHEAD!
BUT...
I'LL BE THERE...
...CELES.
YOU WERE WONDERFUL JUST NOW.
YOU'RE A MEMBER OF OUR GRAND ORCHESTRA, AFTER ALL.
NO MATTER WHAT BECOMES OF US, OUR MUSIC WILL REUNITE US.

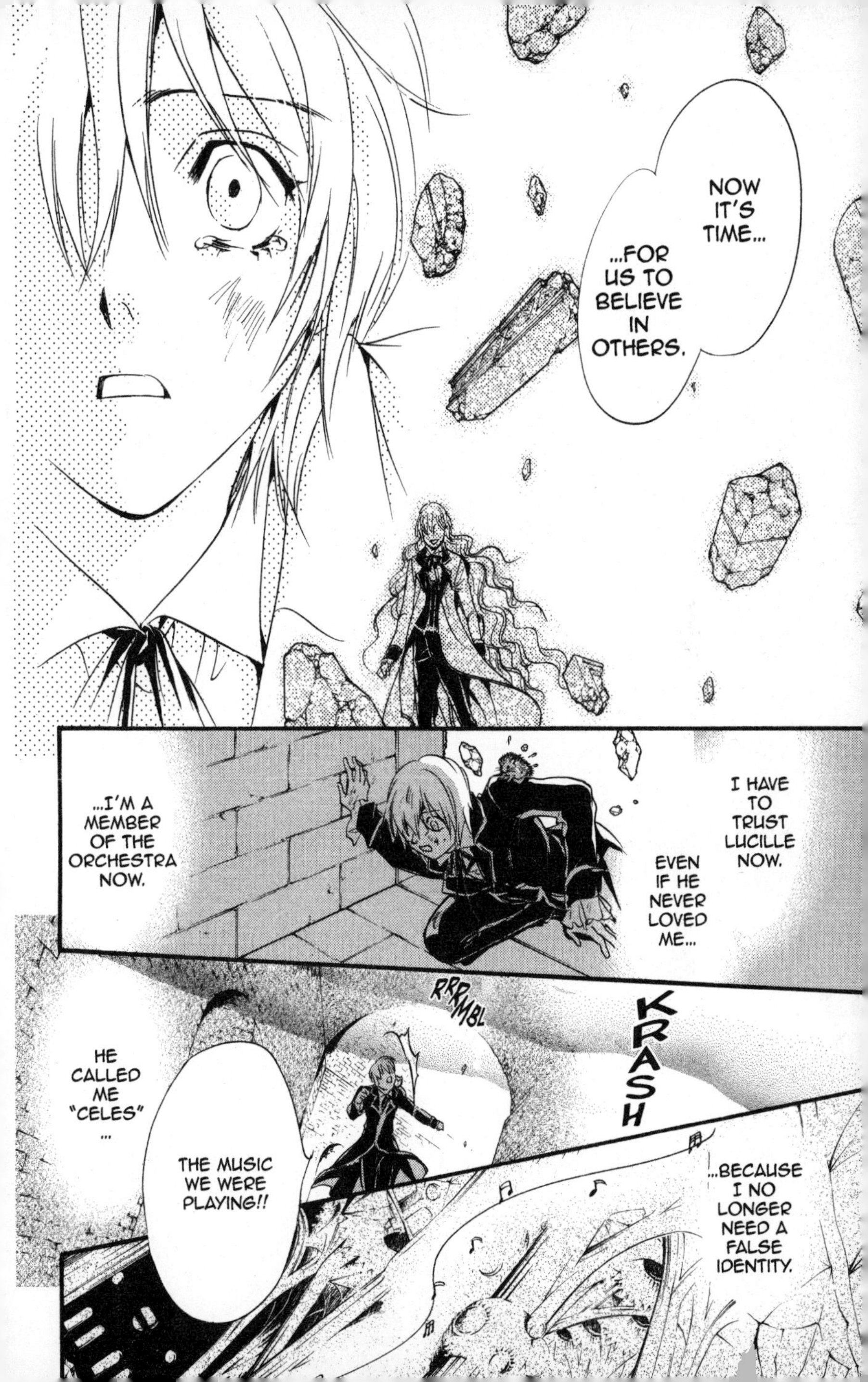
NOW IT'S TIME...
...FOR US TO BELIEVE IN OTHERS.
I HAVE TO TRUST LUCILLE NOW.
EVEN IF HE NEVER LOVED ME...
...I'M A MEMBER OF THE ORCHESTRA NOW.
RRRMBL
KRASH
...BECAUSE I NO LONGER NEED A FALSE IDENTITY.
THE MUSIC WE WERE PLAYING!!
HE CALLED ME "CELES" ...

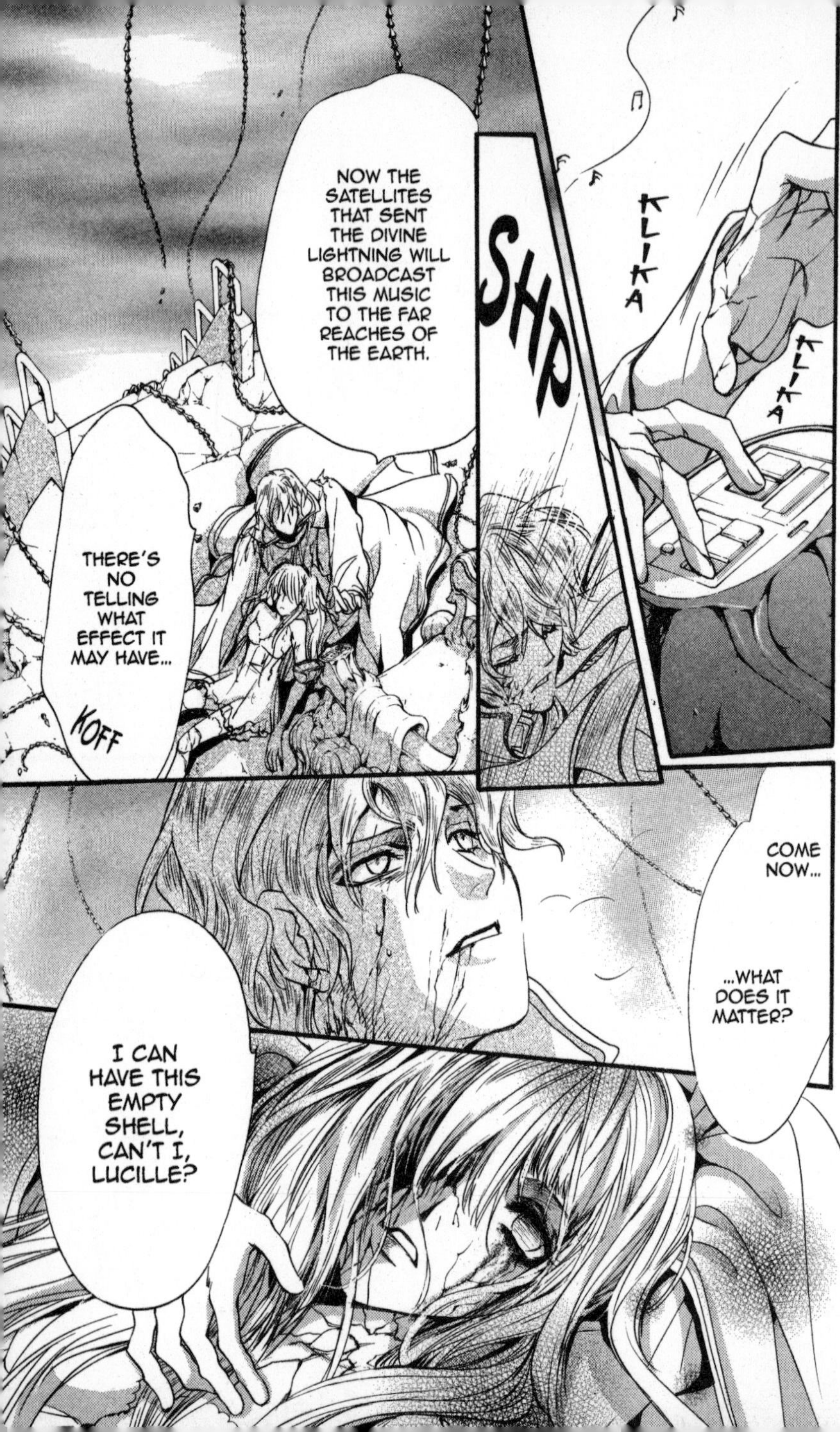
KLIKA
KLIKA
SHP
NOW THE SATELLITES THAT SENT THE DIVINE LIGHTNING WILL BROADCAST THIS MUSIC TO THE FAR REACHES OF THE EARTH.
THERE'S NO TELLING WHAT EFFECT IT MAY HAVE...
KOFF
COME NOW...
...WHAT DOES IT MATTER?
I CAN HAVE THIS EMPTY SHELL, CAN'T I, LUCILLE?

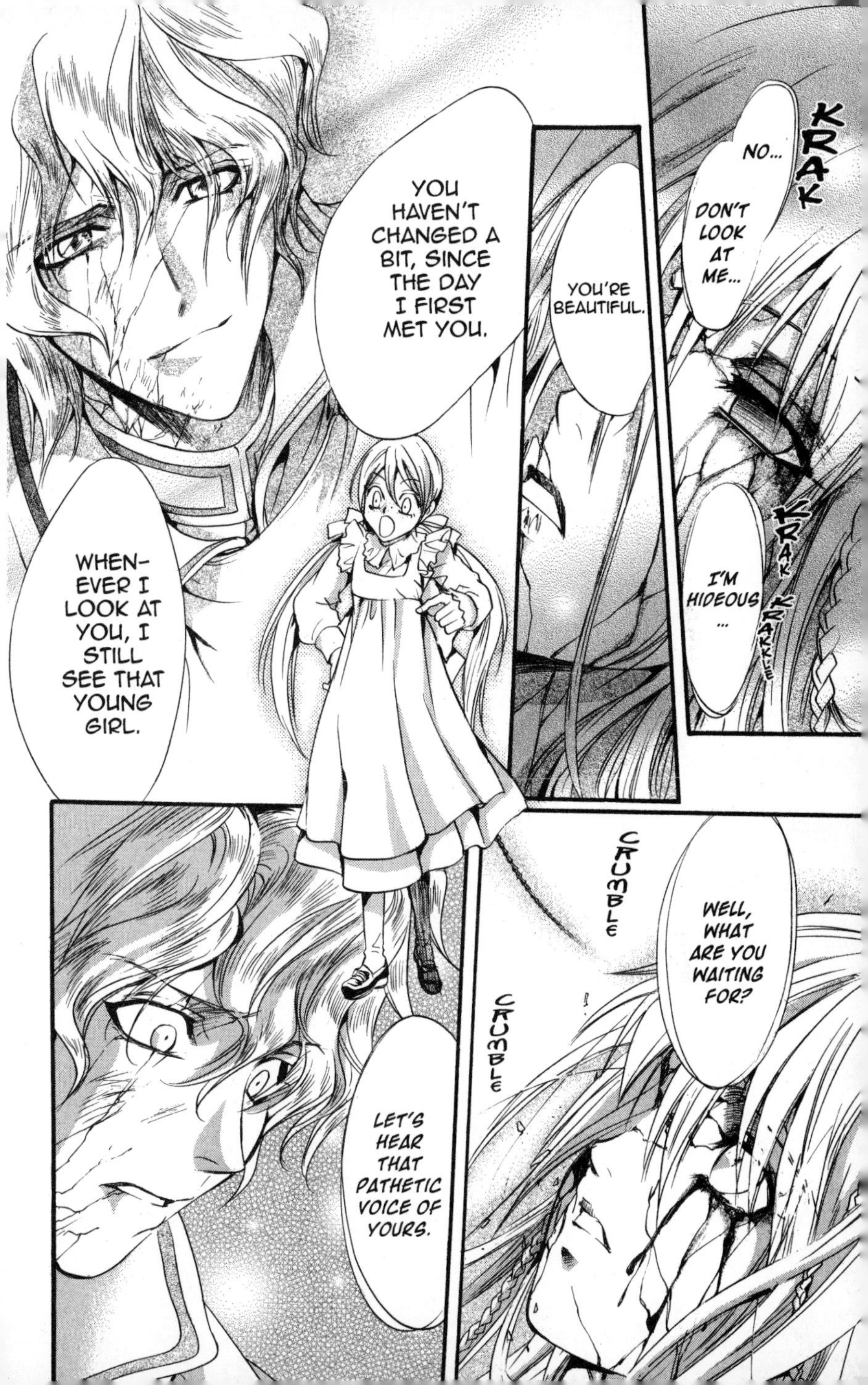
KRAK
NO...
DON'T LOOK AT ME...
KRAK
I'M HIDEOUS...
KRAKKLE
YOU'RE BEAUTIFUL.
YOU HAVEN'T CHANGED A BIT, SINCE THE DAY I FIRST MET YOU.
WHEN-EVER I LOOK AT YOU, I STILL SEE THAT YOUNG GIRL.
CRUMBLE
CRUMBLE
WELL, WHAT ARE YOU WAITING FOR?
LET'S HEAR THAT PATHETIC VOICE OF YOURS.

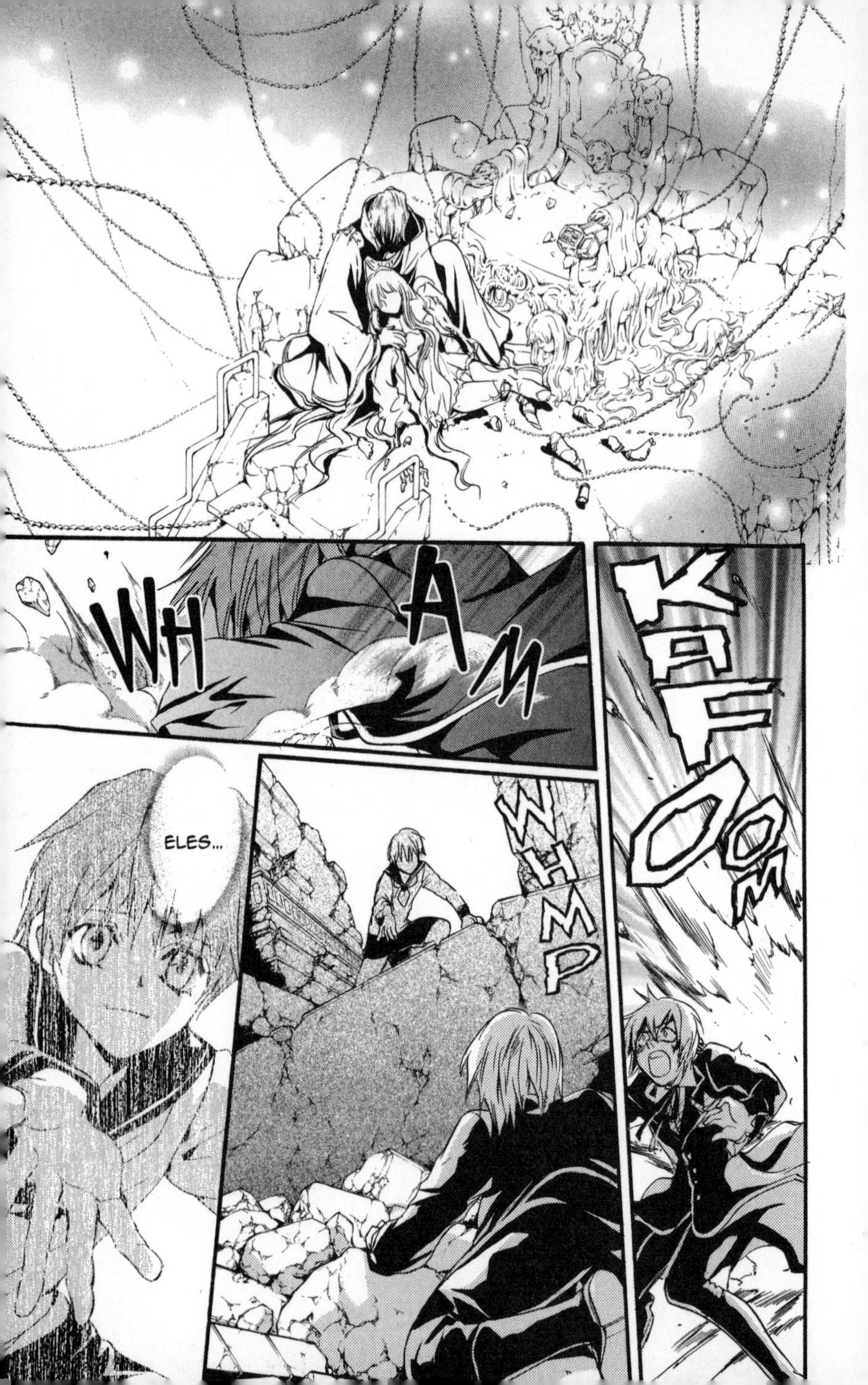
KAFOOM
WHAM
WHMP
ELES...

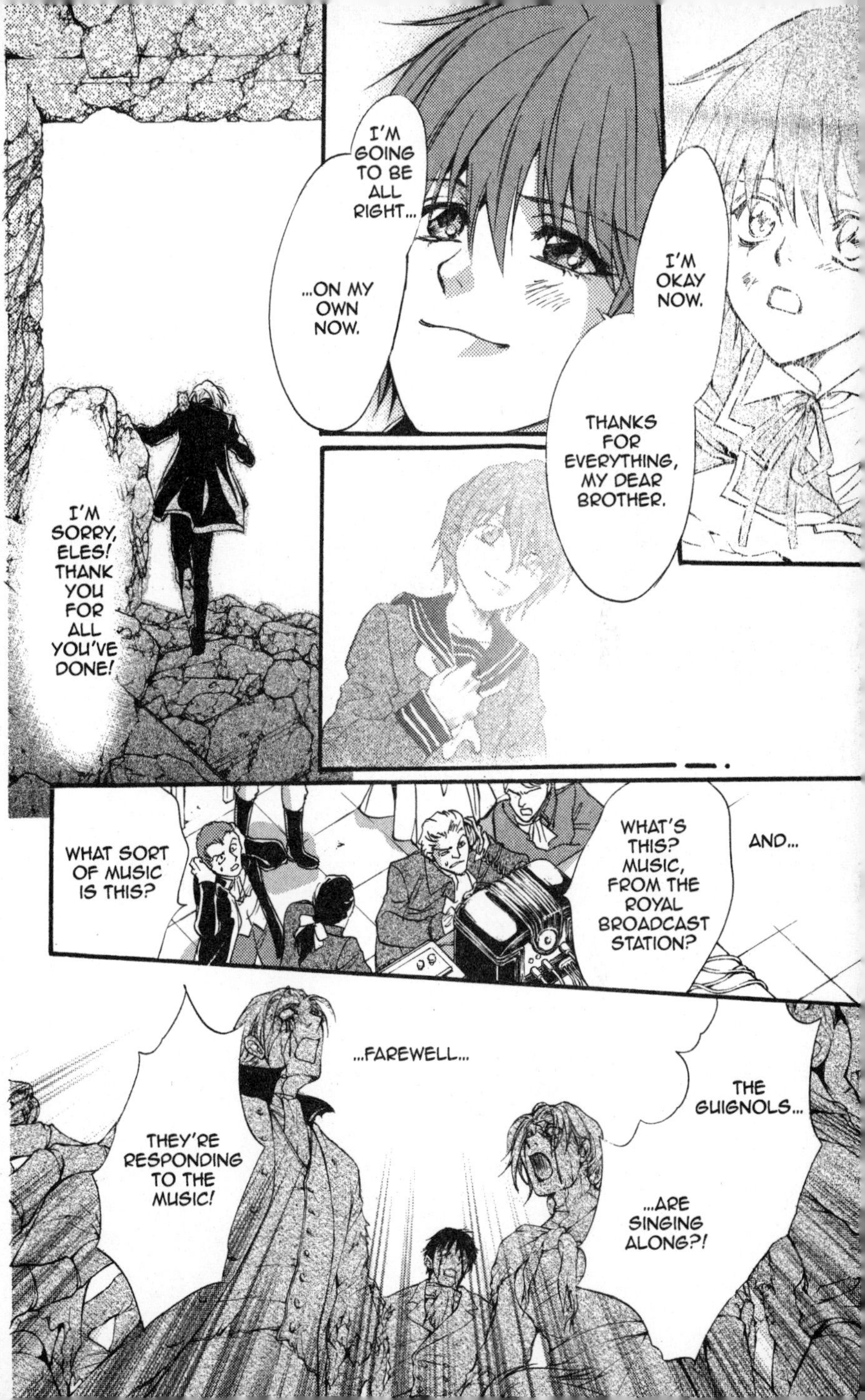
I'M OKAY NOW.
I'M GOING TO BE ALL RIGHT...
...ON MY OWN NOW.
THANKS FOR EVERYTHING, MY DEAR BROTHER.
I'M SORRY, ELES! THANK YOU FOR ALL YOU'VE DONE!
AND...
WHAT'S THIS? MUSIC, FROM THE ROYAL BROADCAST STATION?
WHAT SORT OF MUSIC IS THIS?
THE GUIGNOLS...
...ARE SINGING ALONG?!
...FAREWELL...
THEY'RE RESPONDING TO THE MUSIC!

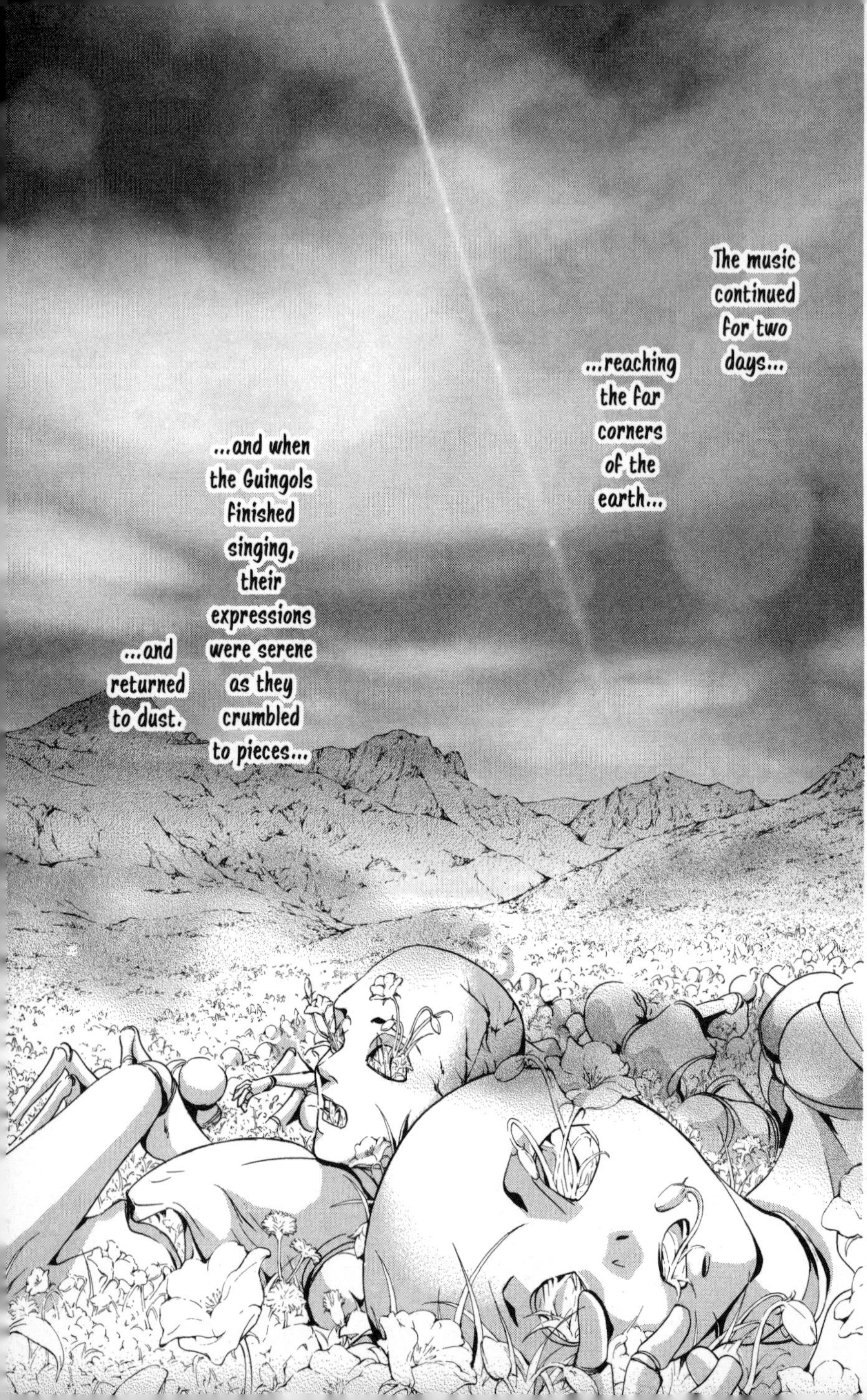
The music continued for two days...
...reaching the far corners of the earth...
...and when the Guingols finished singing, their expressions were serene as they crumbled to pieces...
...and returned to dust.

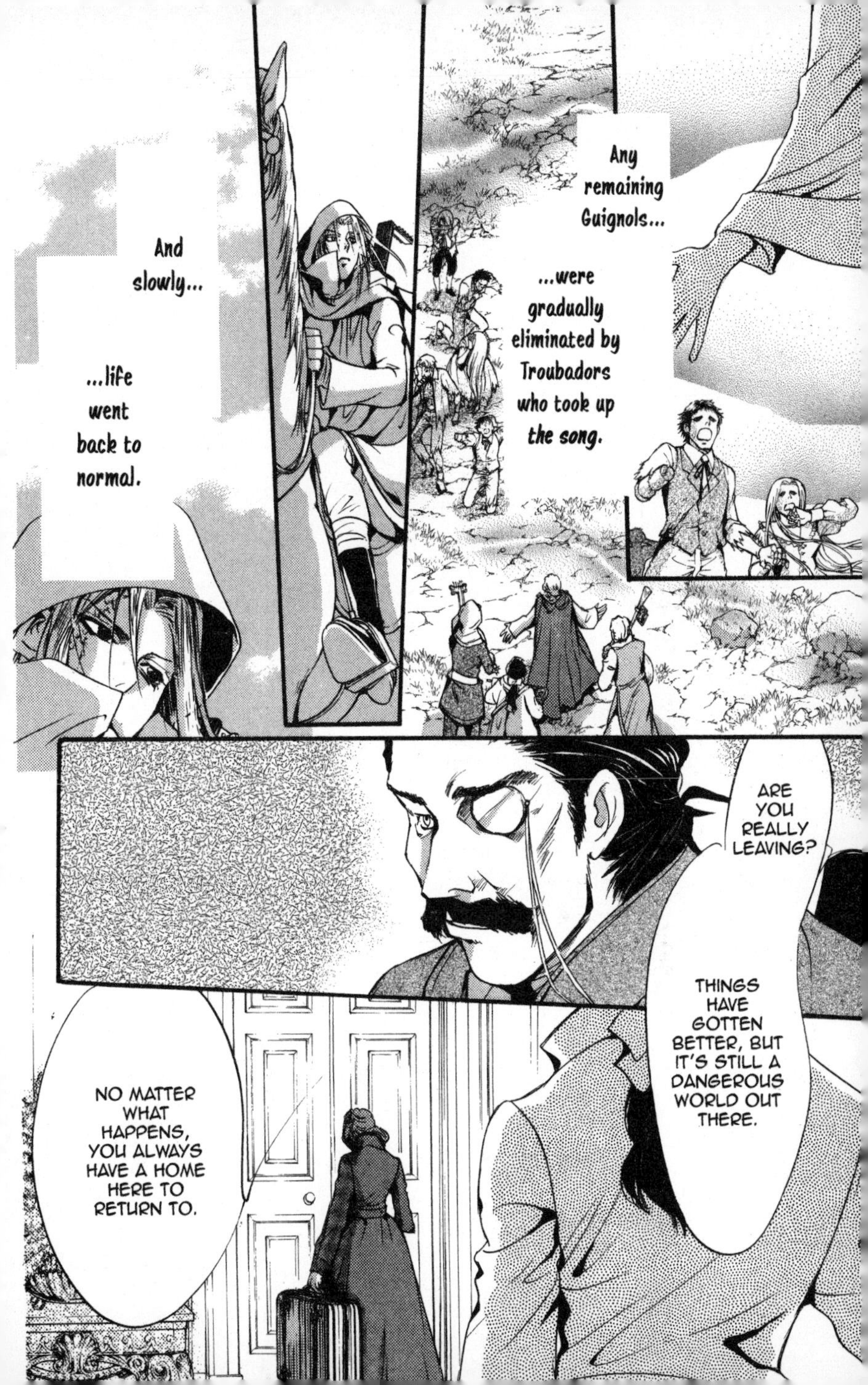
Any remaining Guignols...
...were gradually eliminated by Troubadors who took up the song.
And slowly...
...life went back to normal.
ARE YOU REALLY LEAVING?
THINGS HAVE GOTTEN BETTER, BUT IT'S STILL A DANGEROUS WORLD OUT THERE.
NO MATTER WHAT HAPPENS, YOU ALWAYS HAVE A HOME HERE TO RETURN TO.

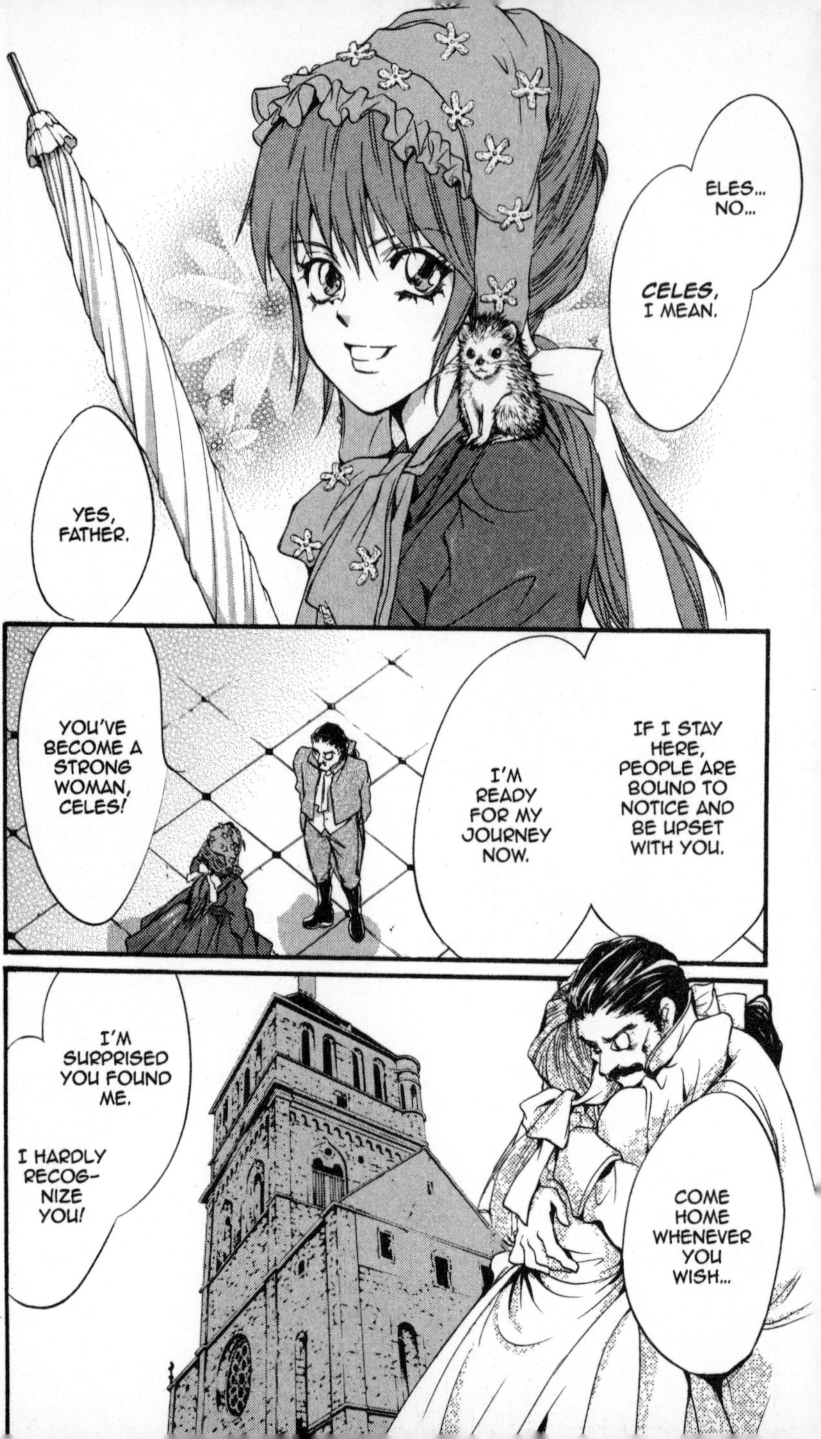
ELES... NO...
CELES, I MEAN.
YES, FATHER.
IF I STAY HERE, PEOPLE ARE BOUND TO NOTICE AND BE UPSET WITH YOU.
I'M READY FOR MY JOURNEY NOW.
YOU'VE BECOME A STRONG WOMAN, CELES!
COME HOME WHENEVER YOU WISH...
I'M SURPRISED YOU FOUND ME.
I HARDLY RECOG-NIZE YOU!

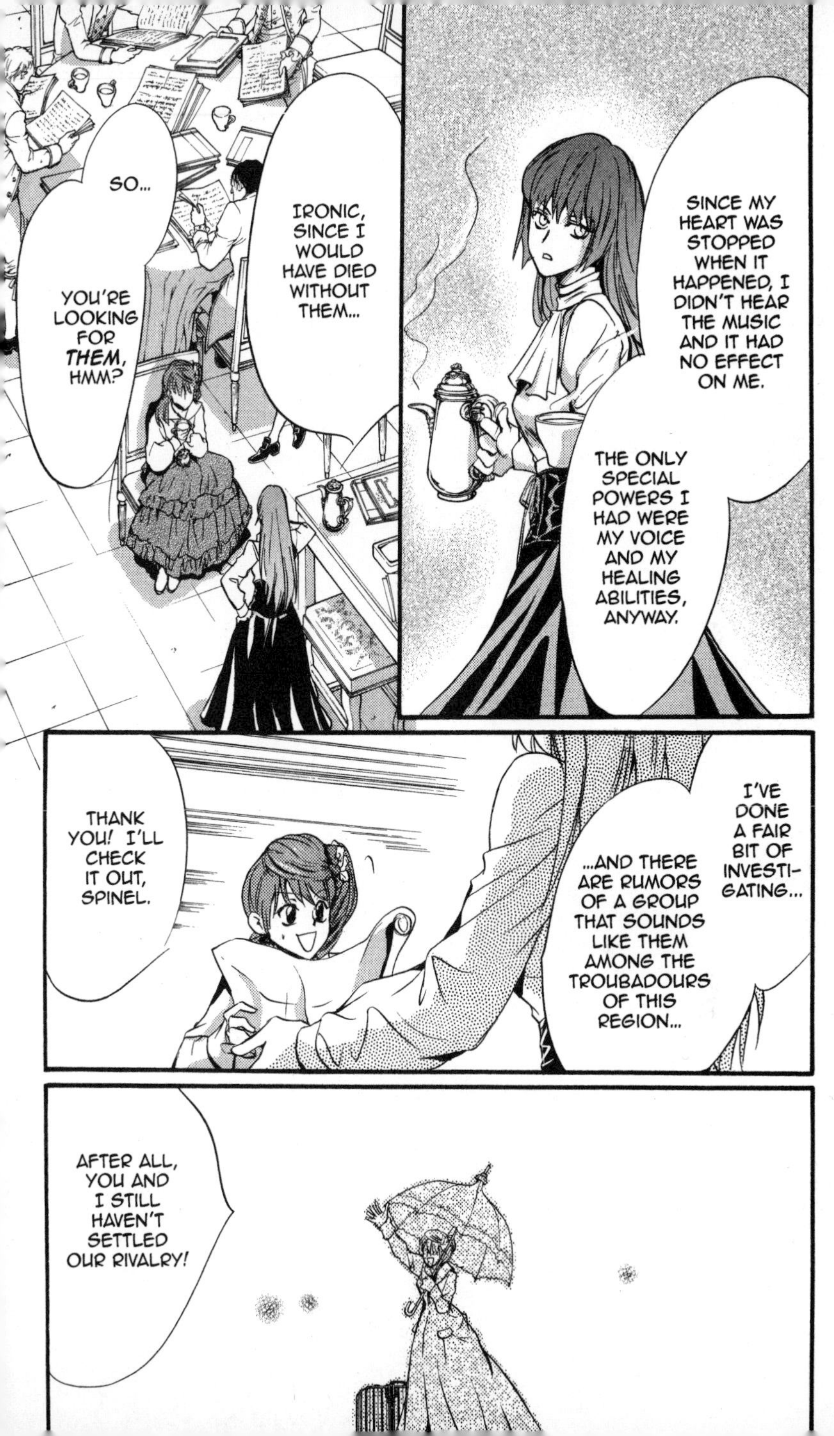
SINCE MY HEART WAS STOPPED WHEN IT HAPPENED, I DIDN'T HEAR THE MUSIC AND IT HAD NO EFFECT ON ME.
THE ONLY SPECIAL POWERS I HAD WERE MY VOICE AND MY HEALING ABILITIES, ANYWAY.
IRONIC, SINCE I WOULD HAVE DIED WITHOUT THEM...
SO... YOU'RE LOOKING FOR *THEM*, HMM?
I'VE DONE A FAIR BIT OF INVESTI-GATING...
...AND THERE ARE RUMORS OF A GROUP THAT SOUNDS LIKE THEM AMONG THE TROUBADOURS OF THIS REGION...
THANK YOU! I'LL CHECK IT OUT, SPINEL.
AFTER ALL, YOU AND I STILL HAVEN'T SETTLED OUR RIVALRY!

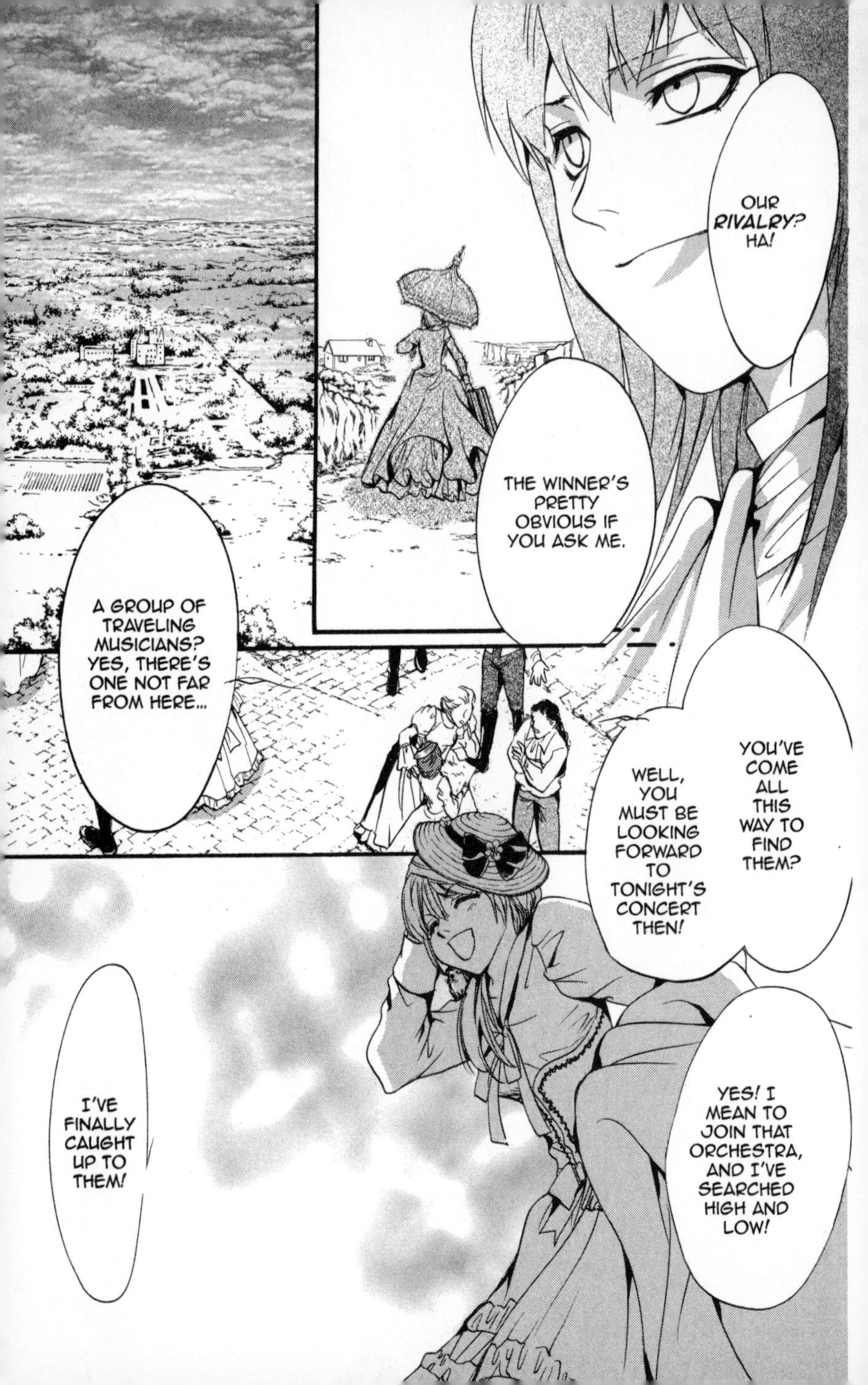
OUR RIVALRY? HA!
THE WINNER'S PRETTY OBVIOUS IF YOU ASK ME.
A GROUP OF TRAVELING MUSICIANS? YES, THERE'S ONE NOT FAR FROM HERE...
YOU'VE COME ALL THIS WAY TO FIND THEM?
WELL, YOU MUST BE LOOKING FORWARD TO TONIGHT'S CONCERT THEN!
YES! I MEAN TO JOIN THAT ORCHESTRA, AND I'VE SEARCHED HIGH AND LOW!
I'VE FINALLY CAUGHT UP TO THEM!

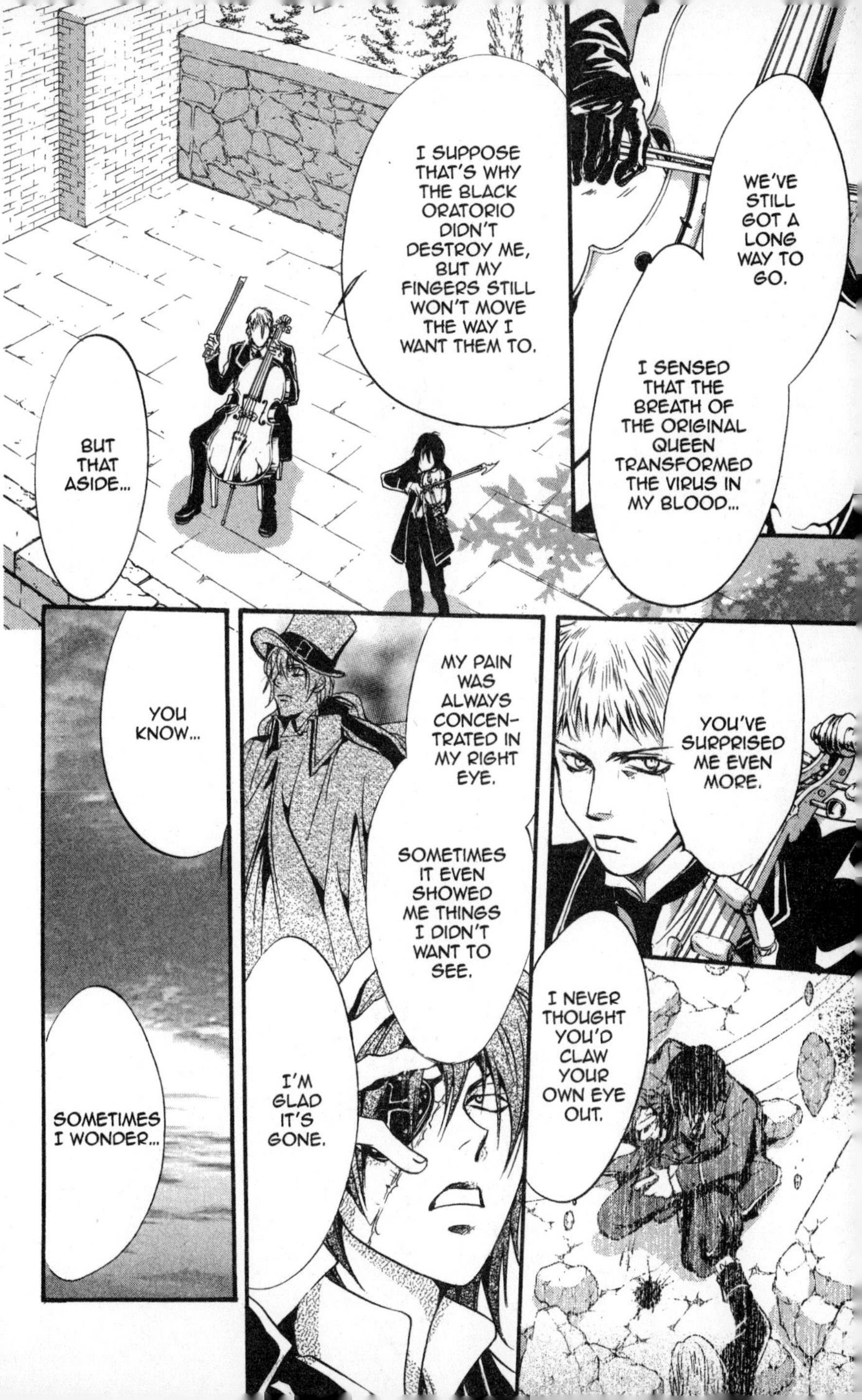

WE'VE STILL GOT A LONG WAY TO GO.
I SENSED THAT THE BREATH OF THE ORIGINAL QUEEN TRANSFORMED THE VIRUS IN MY BLOOD...
I SUPPOSE THAT'S WHY THE BLACK ORATORIO DIDN'T DESTROY ME, BUT MY FINGERS STILL WON'T MOVE THE WAY I WANT THEM TO.
BUT THAT ASIDE...
YOU'VE SURPRISED ME EVEN MORE.
I NEVER THOUGHT YOU'D CLAW YOUR OWN EYE OUT.
MY PAIN WAS ALWAYS CONCEN-TRATED IN MY RIGHT EYE.
SOMETIMES IT EVEN SHOWED ME THINGS I DIDN'T WANT TO SEE.
I'M GLAD IT'S GONE.
YOU KNOW...
SOMETIMES I WONDER...

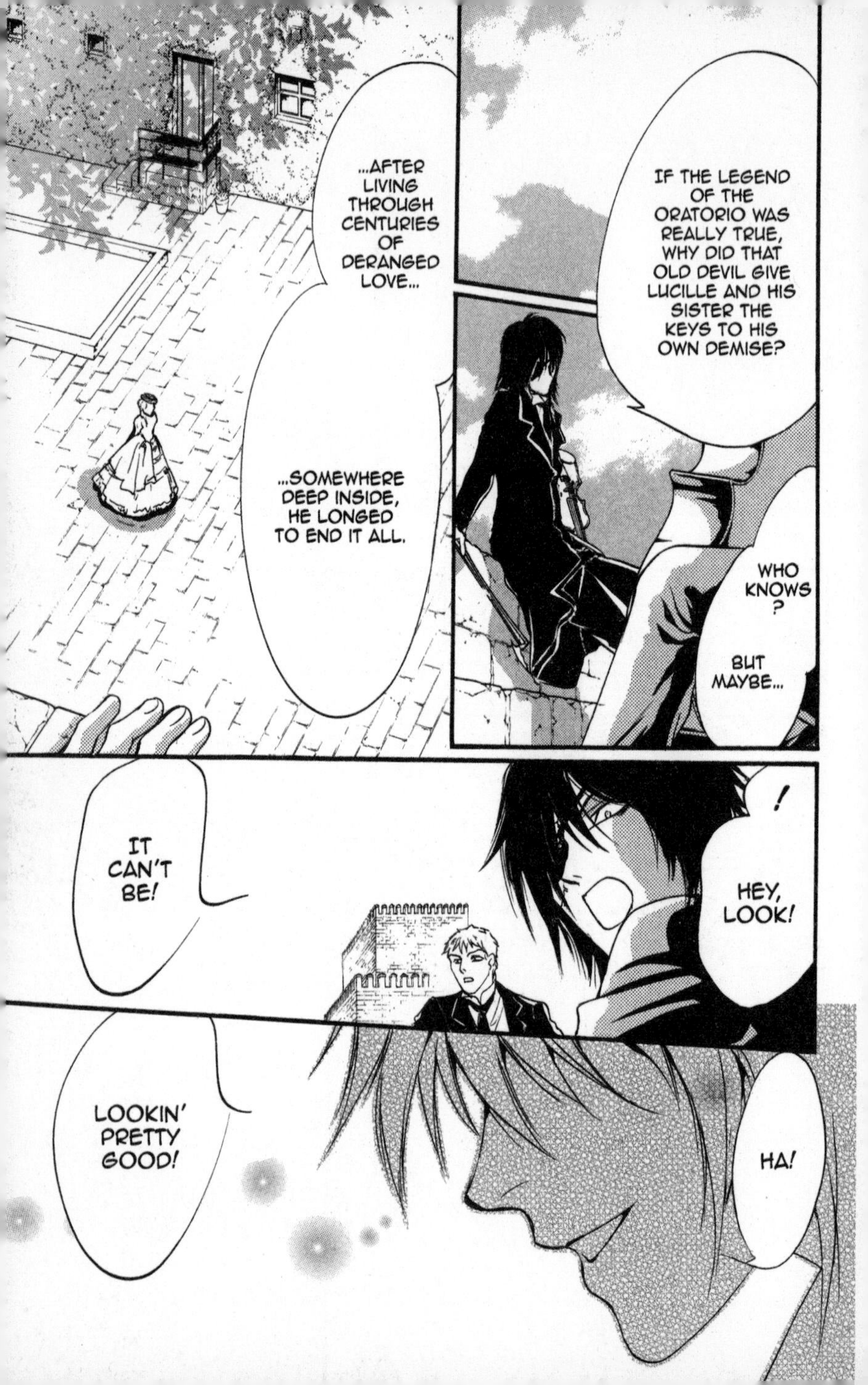
IF THE LEGEND OF THE ORATORIO WAS REALLY TRUE, WHY DID THAT OLD DEVIL GIVE LUCILLE AND HIS SISTER THE KEYS TO HIS OWN DEMISE?
WHO KNOWS?
BUT MAYBE...
...AFTER LIVING THROUGH CENTURIES OF DERANGED LOVE...
...SOMEWHERE DEEP INSIDE, HE LONGED TO END IT ALL.
!
HEY, LOOK!
IT CAN'T BE!
HA!
LOOKIN' PRETTY GOOD!

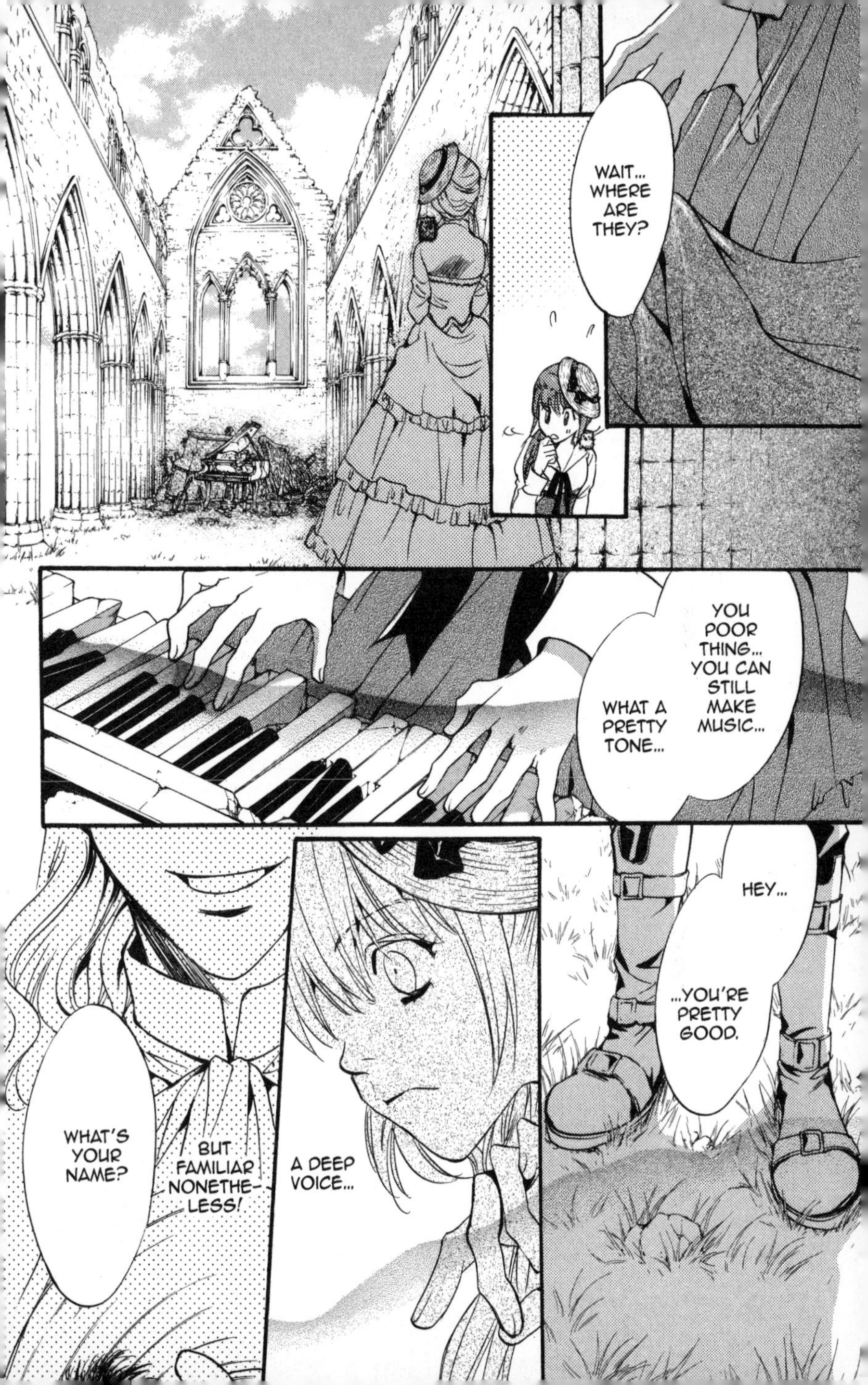
WAIT... WHERE ARE THEY?
YOU POOR THING... YOU CAN STILL MAKE MUSIC...
WHAT A PRETTY TONE...
HEY...
...YOU'RE PRETTY GOOD.
A DEEP VOICE...
BUT FAMILIAR NONETHE-LESS!
WHAT'S YOUR NAME?

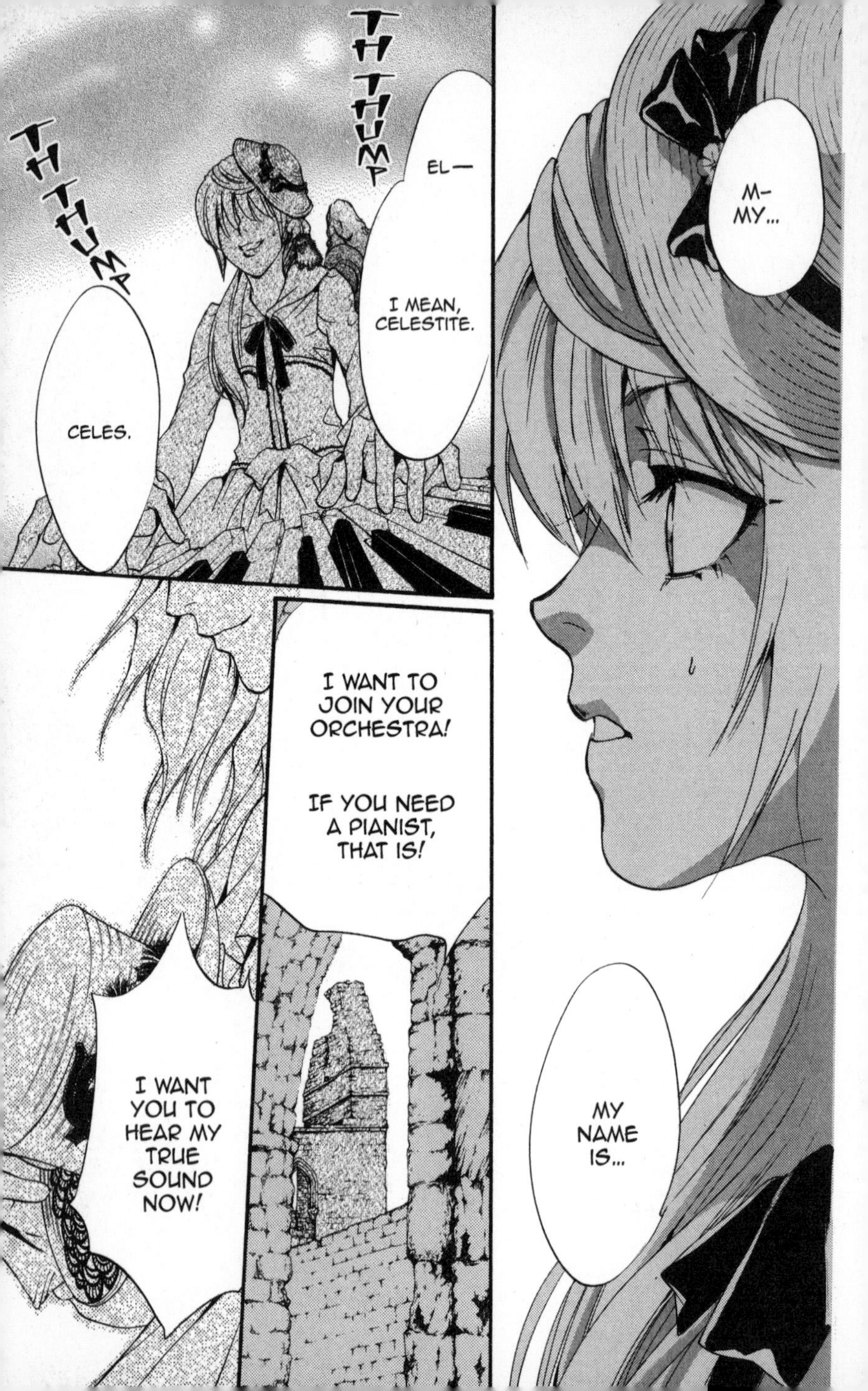
M-
MY...
MY NAME IS...
THTHUMP
EL—
I MEAN, CELESTITE.
THTHUMP
CELES.
I WANT TO JOIN YOUR ORCHESTRA!
IF YOU NEED A PIANIST, THAT IS!
I WANT YOU TO HEAR MY TRUE SOUND NOW!

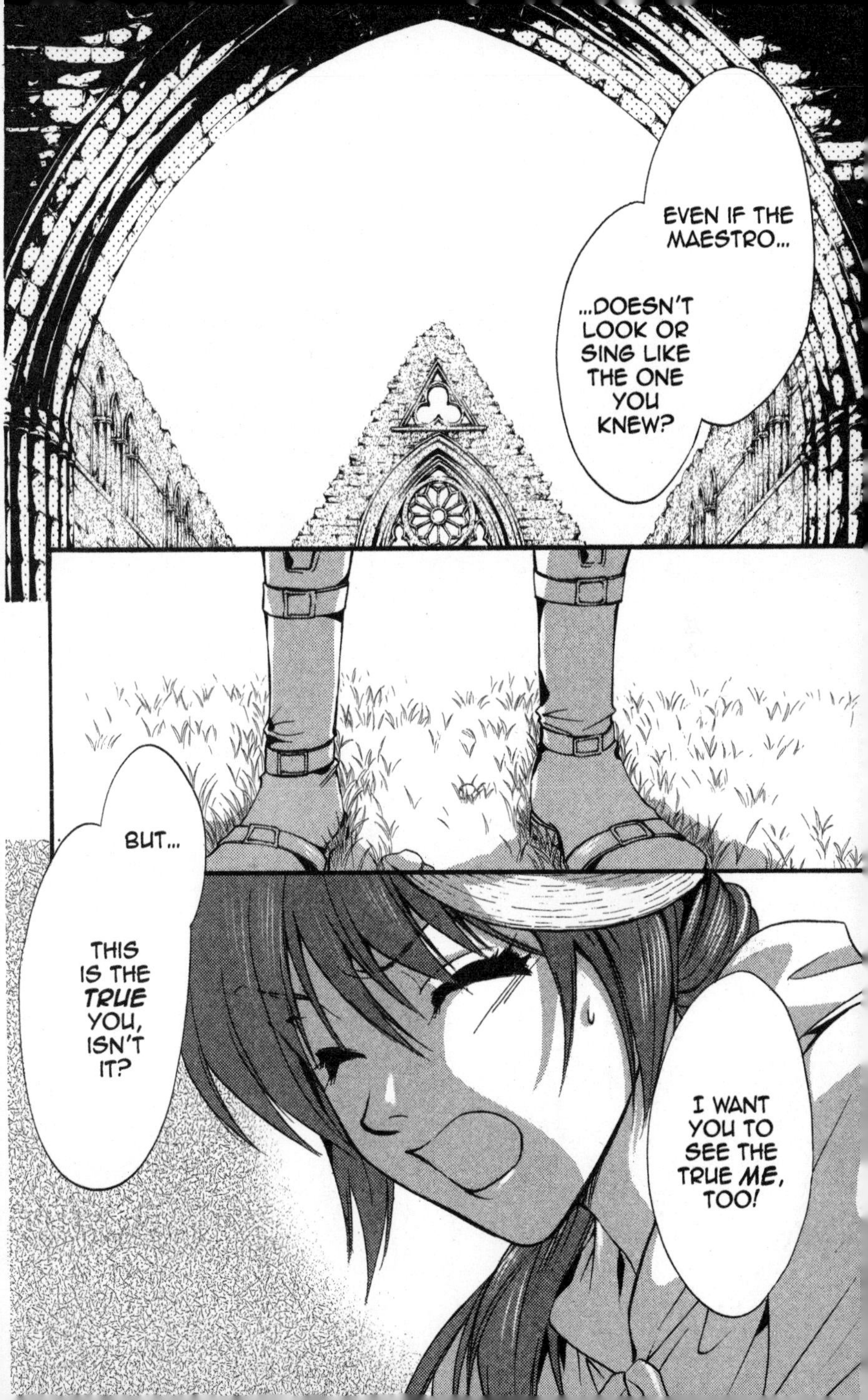
EVEN IF THE MAESTRO...
...DOESN'T LOOK OR SING LIKE THE ONE YOU KNEW?
BUT...
I WANT YOU TO SEE THE TRUE *ME*, TOO!
THIS IS THE *TRUE* YOU, ISN'T IT?

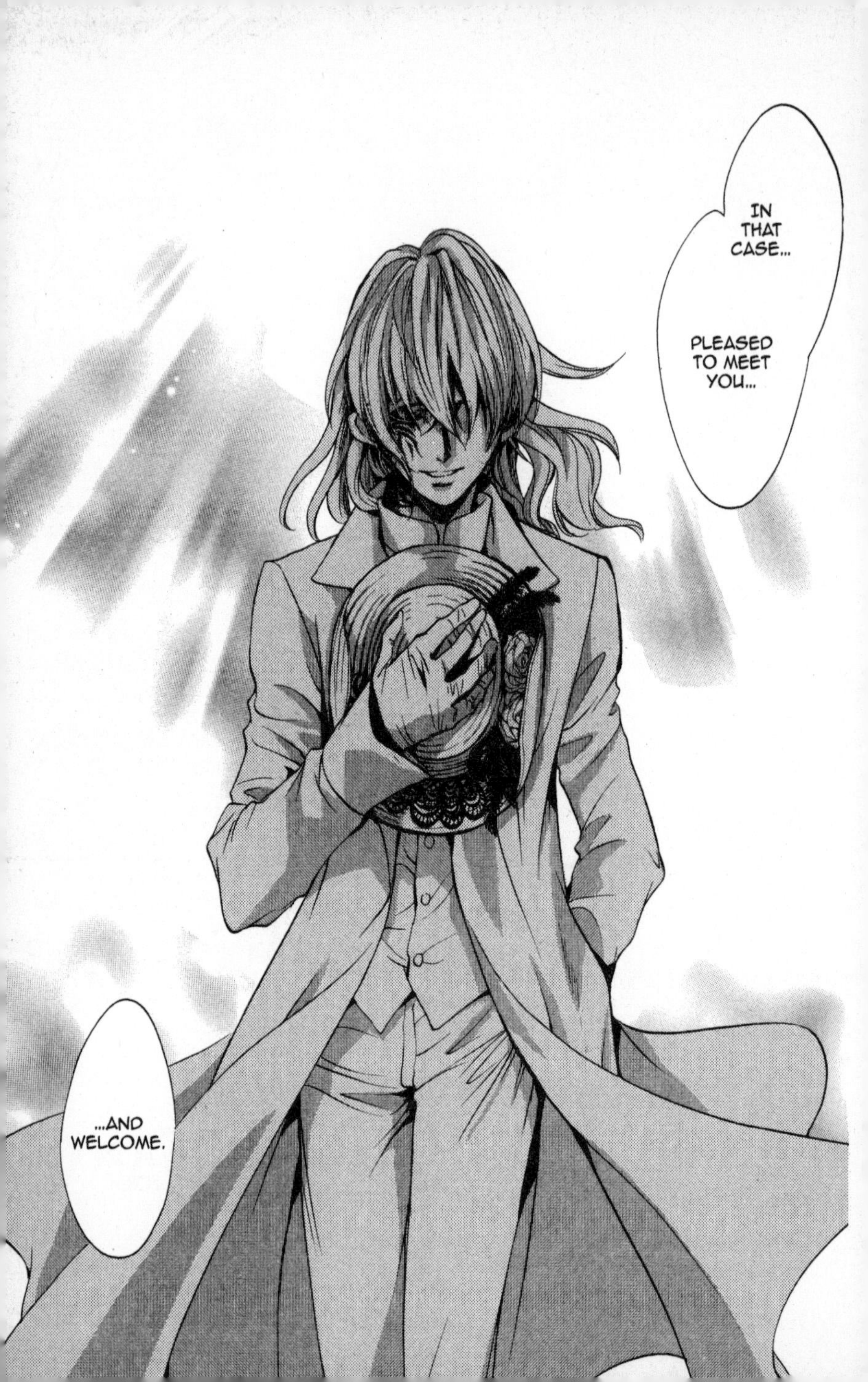
IN THAT CASE...
PLEASED TO MEET YOU...
...AND WELCOME.

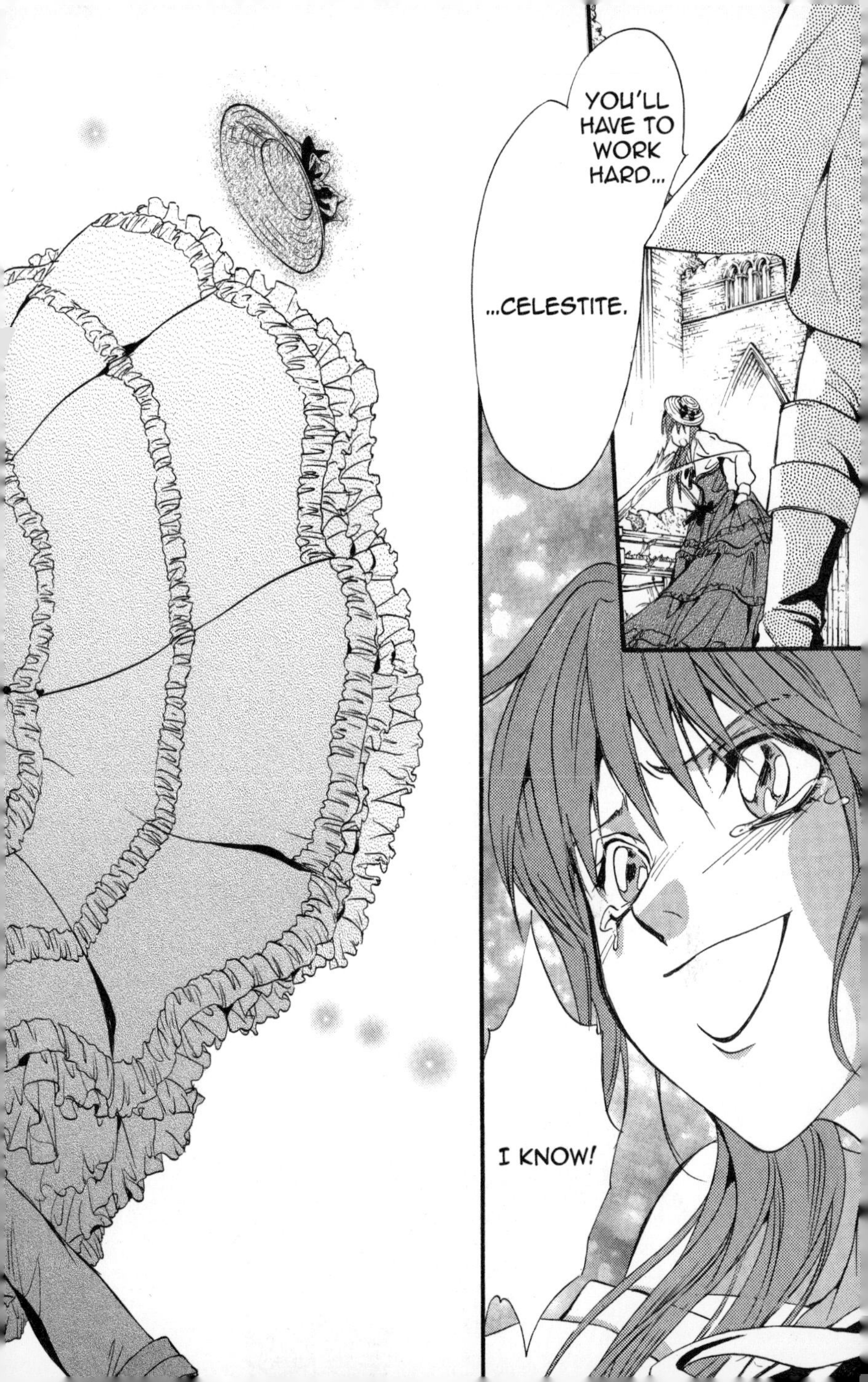
YOU'LL HAVE TO WORK HARD...
...CELESTITE.
I KNOW!

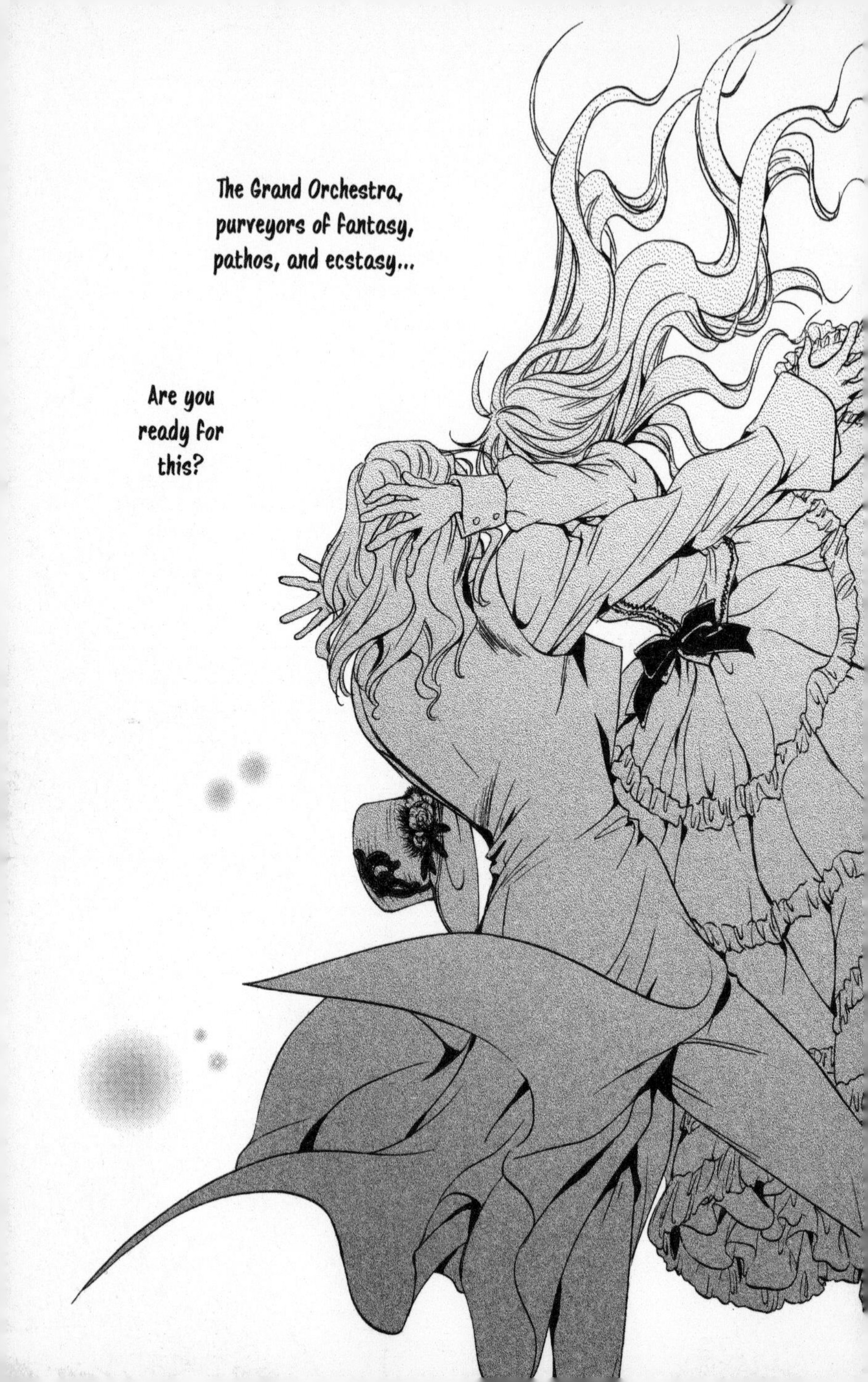
The Grand Orchestra, purveyors of fantasy, pathos, and ecstasy...
Are you ready for this?

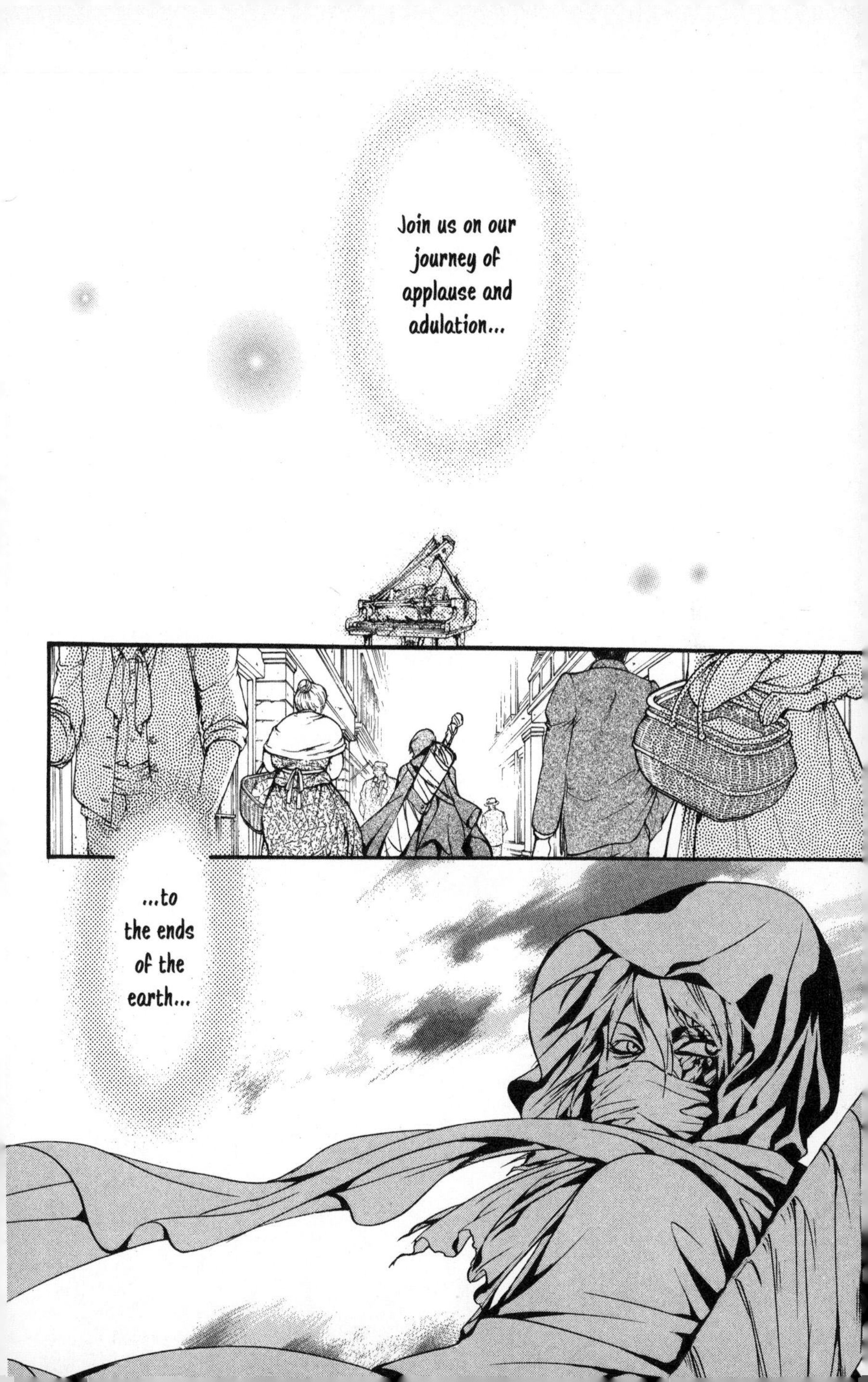
Join us on our journey of applause and adulation...
...to the ends of the earth...

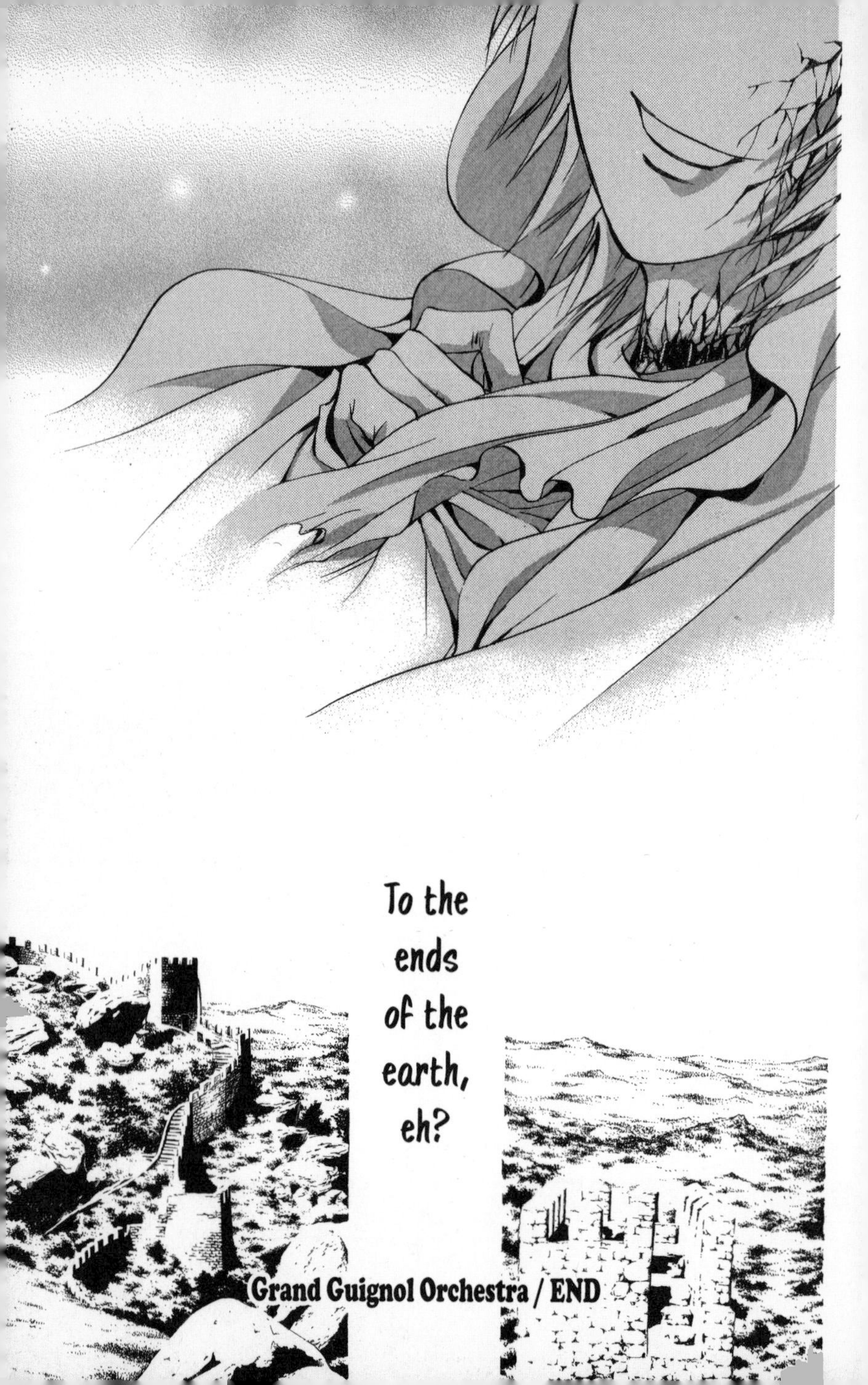
To the ends of the earth, eh?
Grand Guignol Orchestra / END

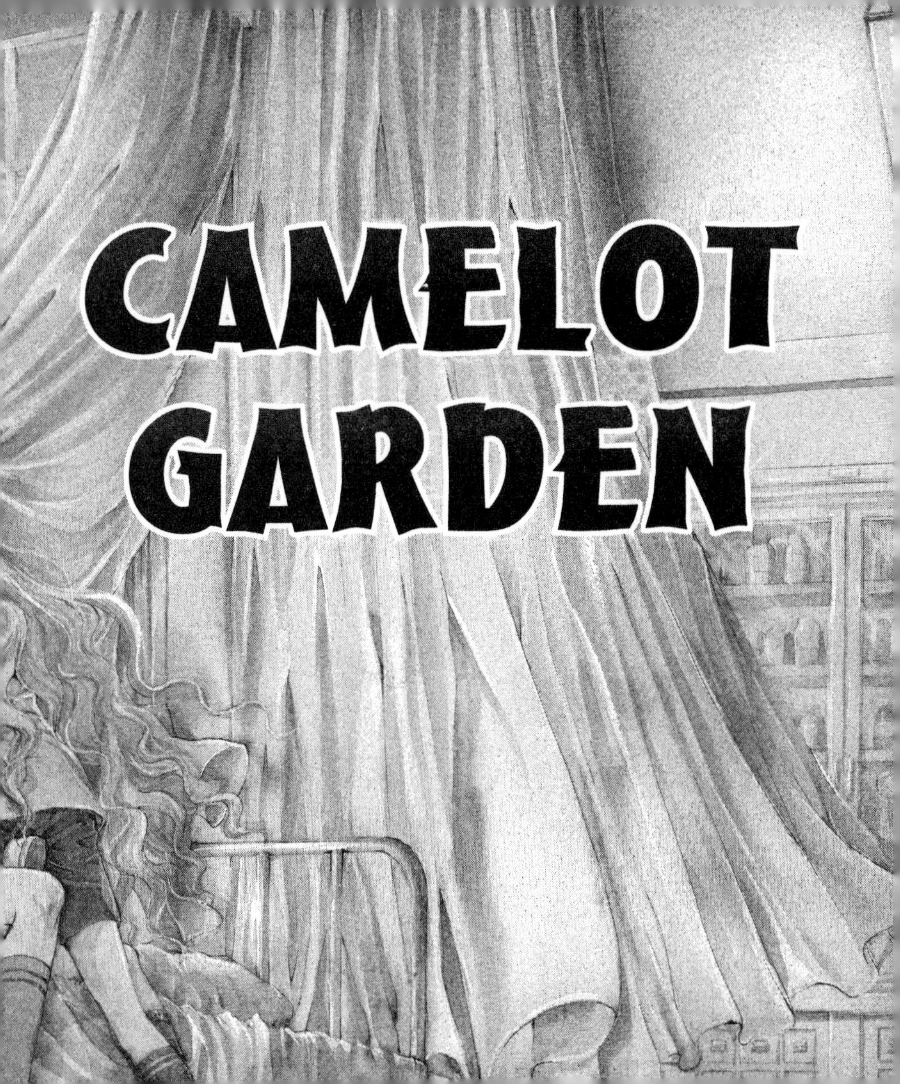
CAMELOT
GARDEN

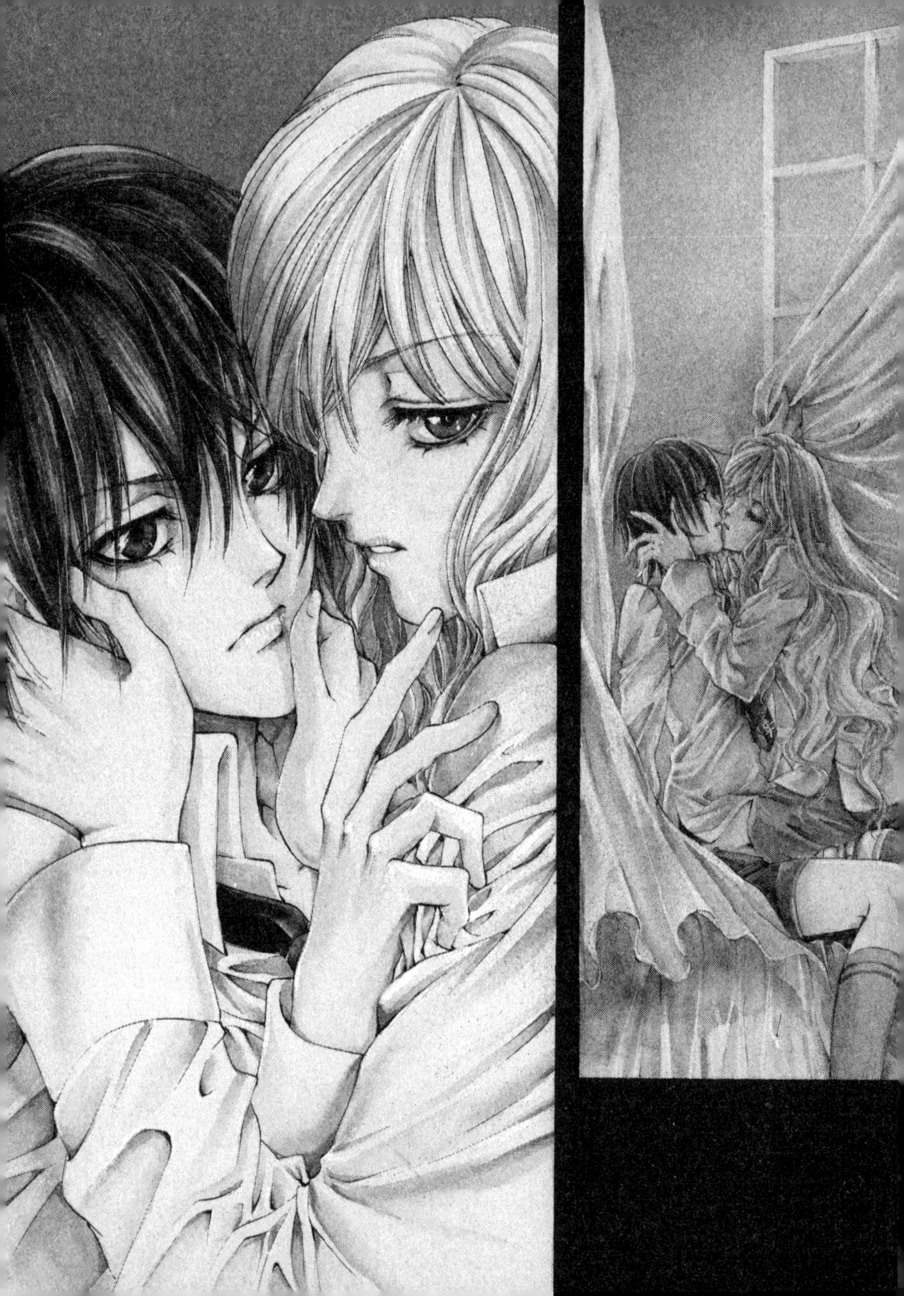

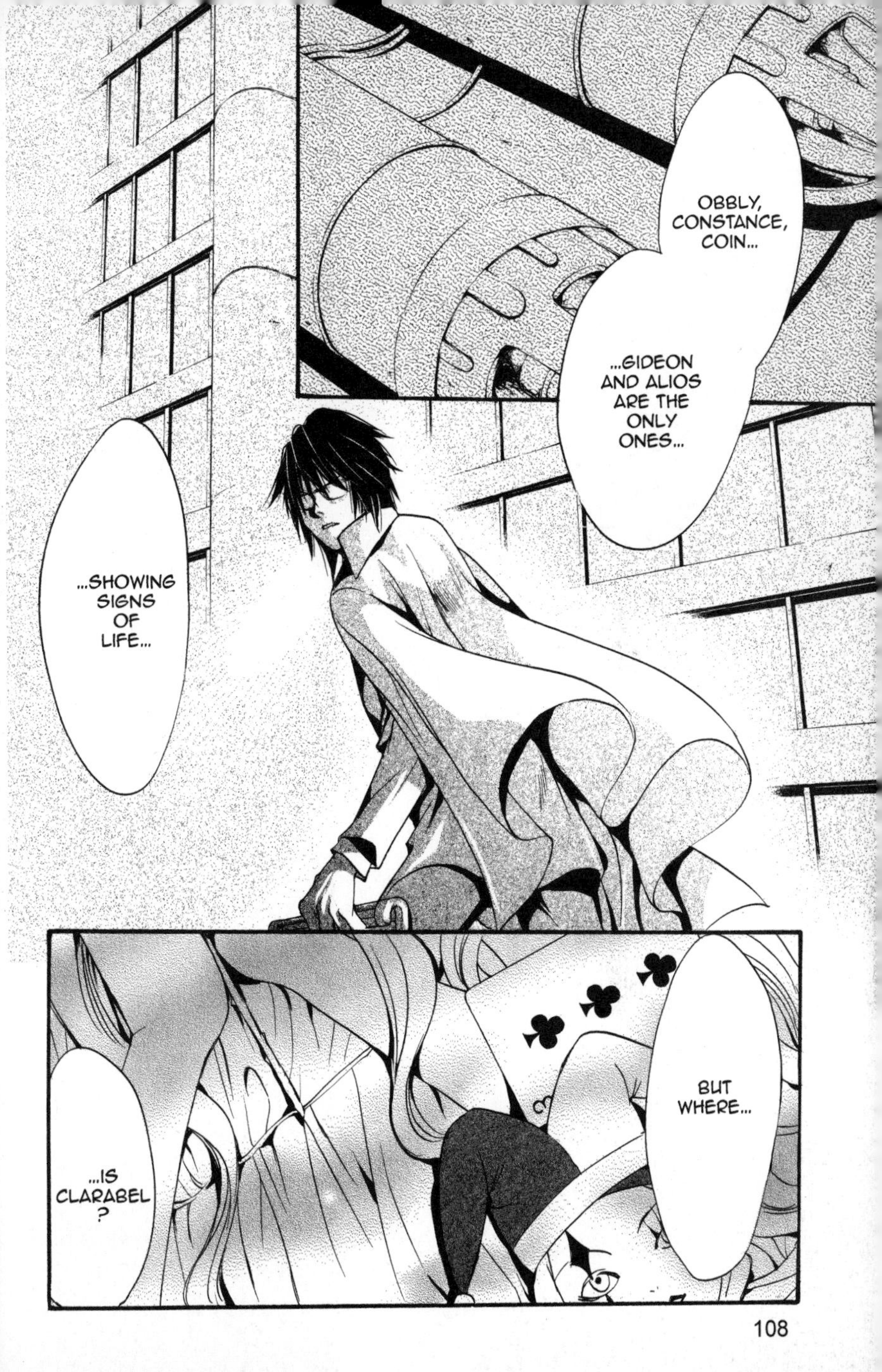
OBBLY, CONSTANCE, COIN...
...GIDEON AND ALIOS ARE THE ONLY ONES...
...SHOWING SIGNS OF LIFE...
BUT WHERE...
...IS CLARABEL?

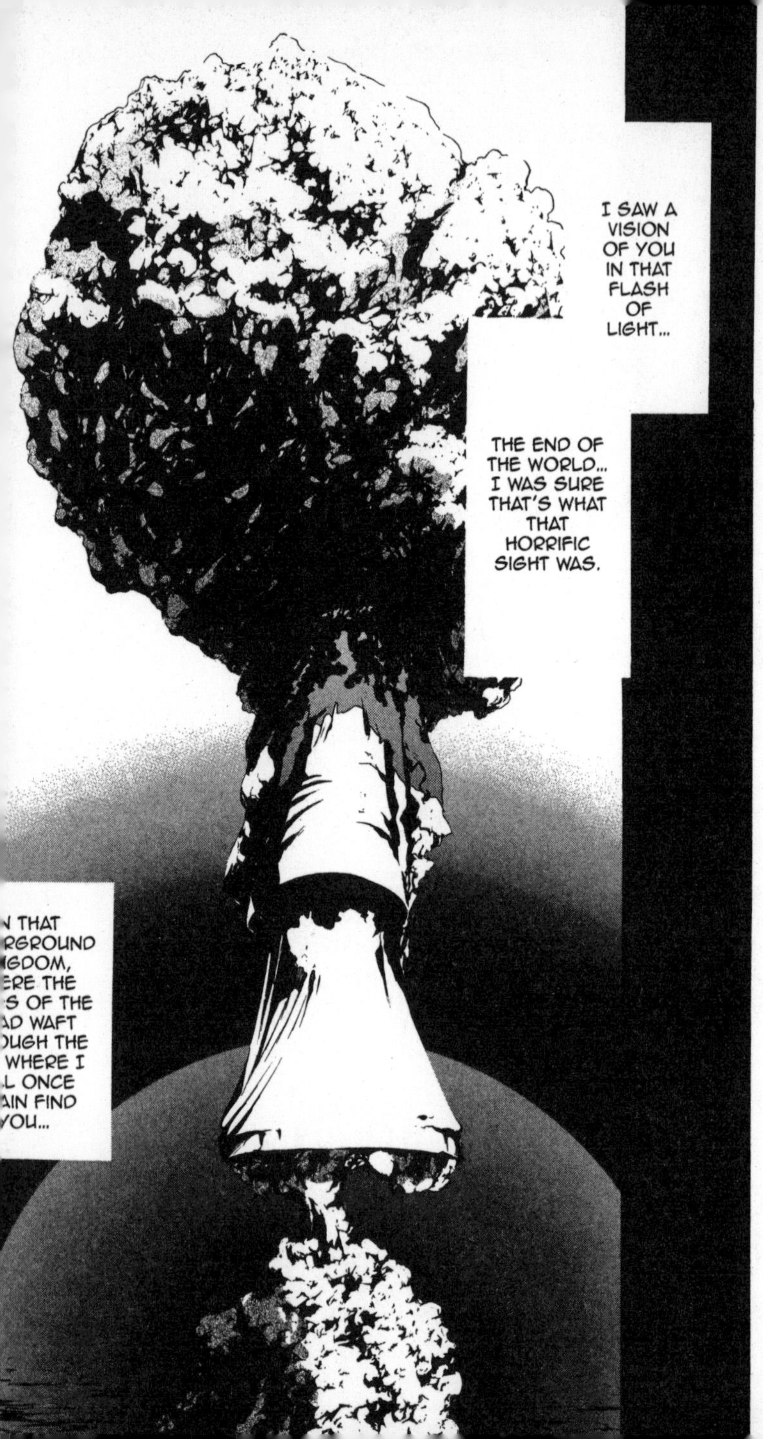
I SAW A VISION OF YOU IN THAT FLASH OF LIGHT...
THE END OF THE WORLD... I WAS SURE THAT'S WHAT THAT HORRIFIC SIGHT WAS.
N THAT RGROUND GDOM, ERE THE S OF THE AD WAFT OUGH THE WHERE I L ONCE AIN FIND YOU...

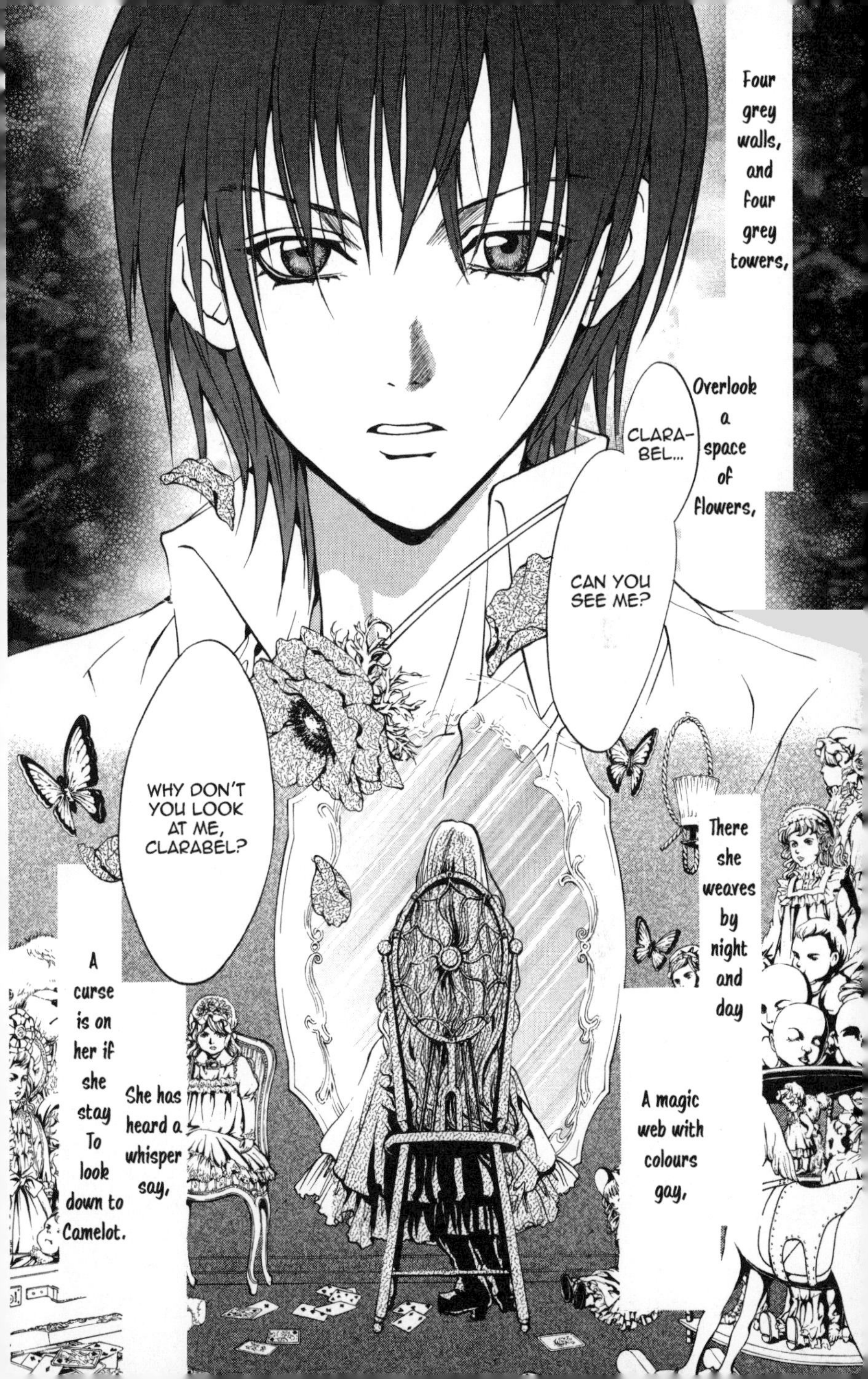
Four grey walls, and four grey towers,
Overlook a space of flowers,
CLARA-BEL...
CAN YOU SEE ME?
WHY DON'T YOU LOOK AT ME, CLARABEL?
There she weaves by night and day
A magic web with colours gay,
She has heard a whisper say,
A curse is on her if she stay To look down to Camelot.

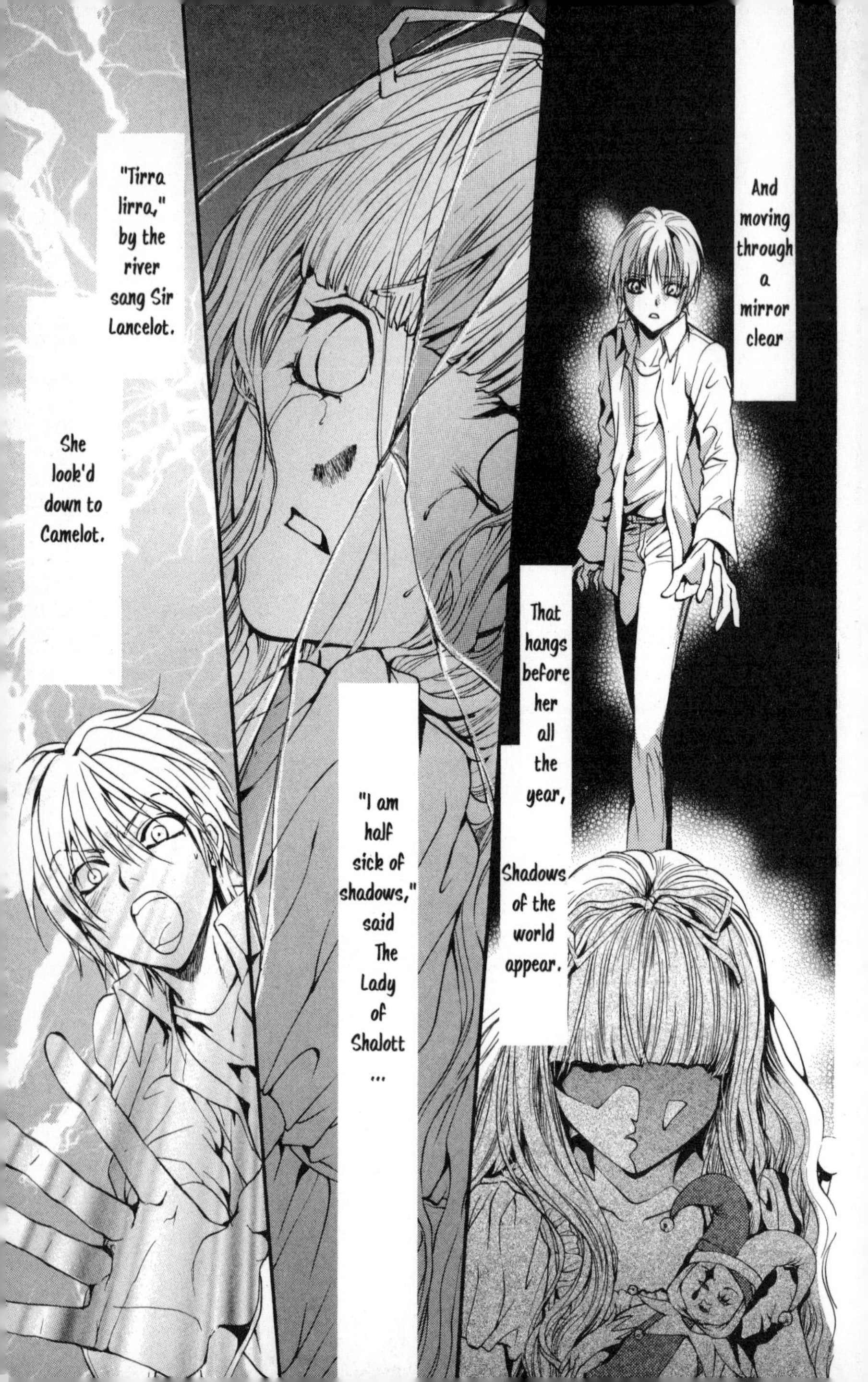
And moving through a mirror clear
That hangs before her all the year,
Shadows of the world appear.
"I am half sick of shadows," said The Lady of Shalott ...
"Tirra lirra," by the river sang Sir Lancelot.
She look'd down to Camelot.

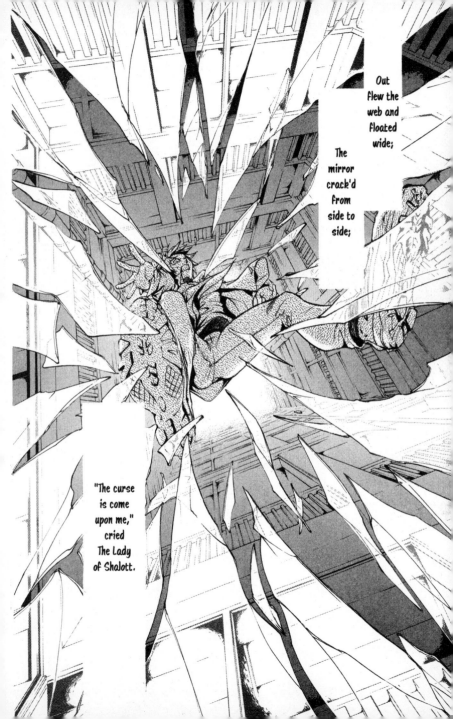

Out flew the web and floated wide;

The mirror crack'd from side to side;

"The curse is come upon me," cried The Lady of Shalott.

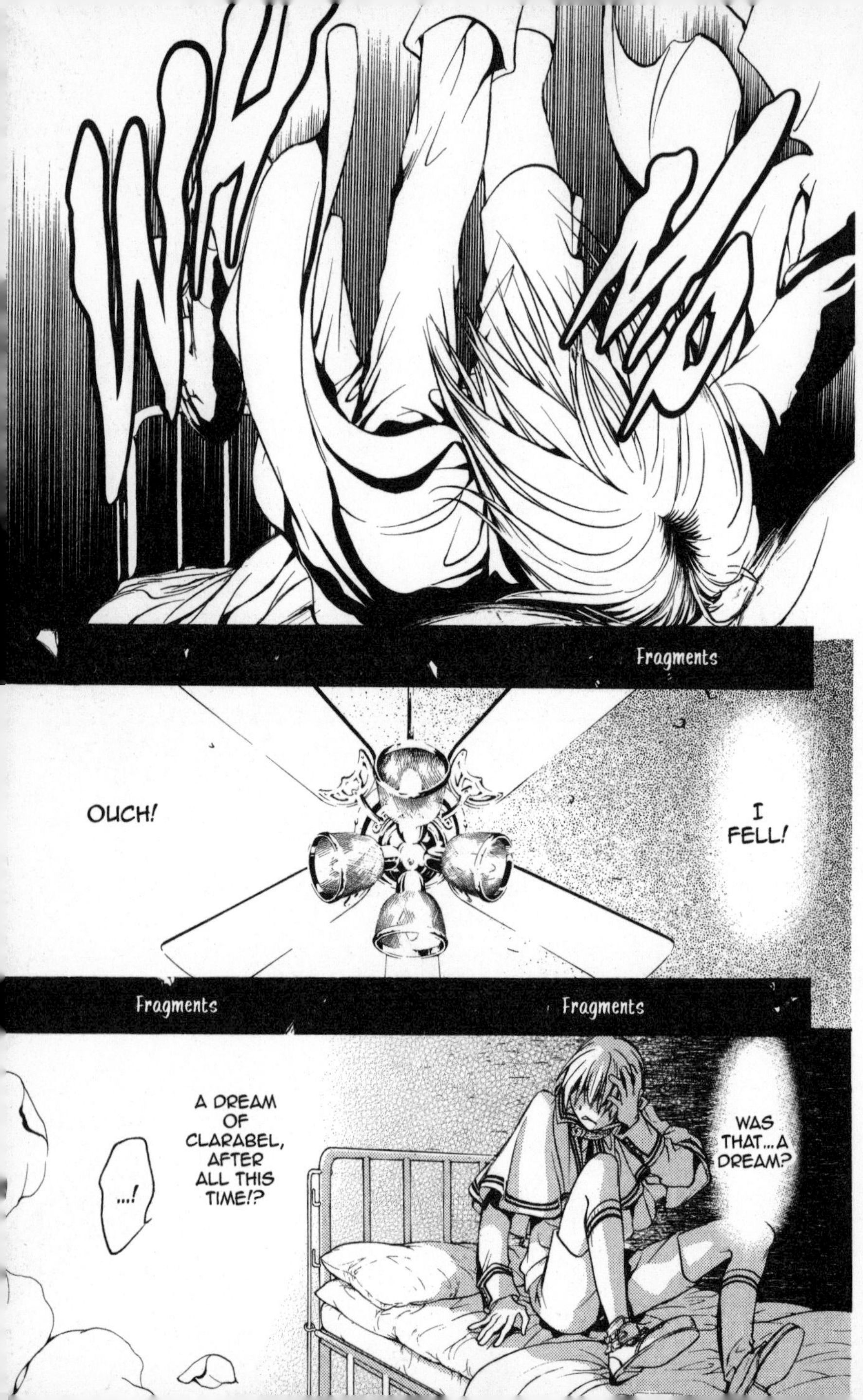
Fragments
I FELL!
OUCH!
Fragments
Fragments
WAS THAT...A DREAM?
A DREAM OF CLARABEL, AFTER ALL THIS TIME!?
...!

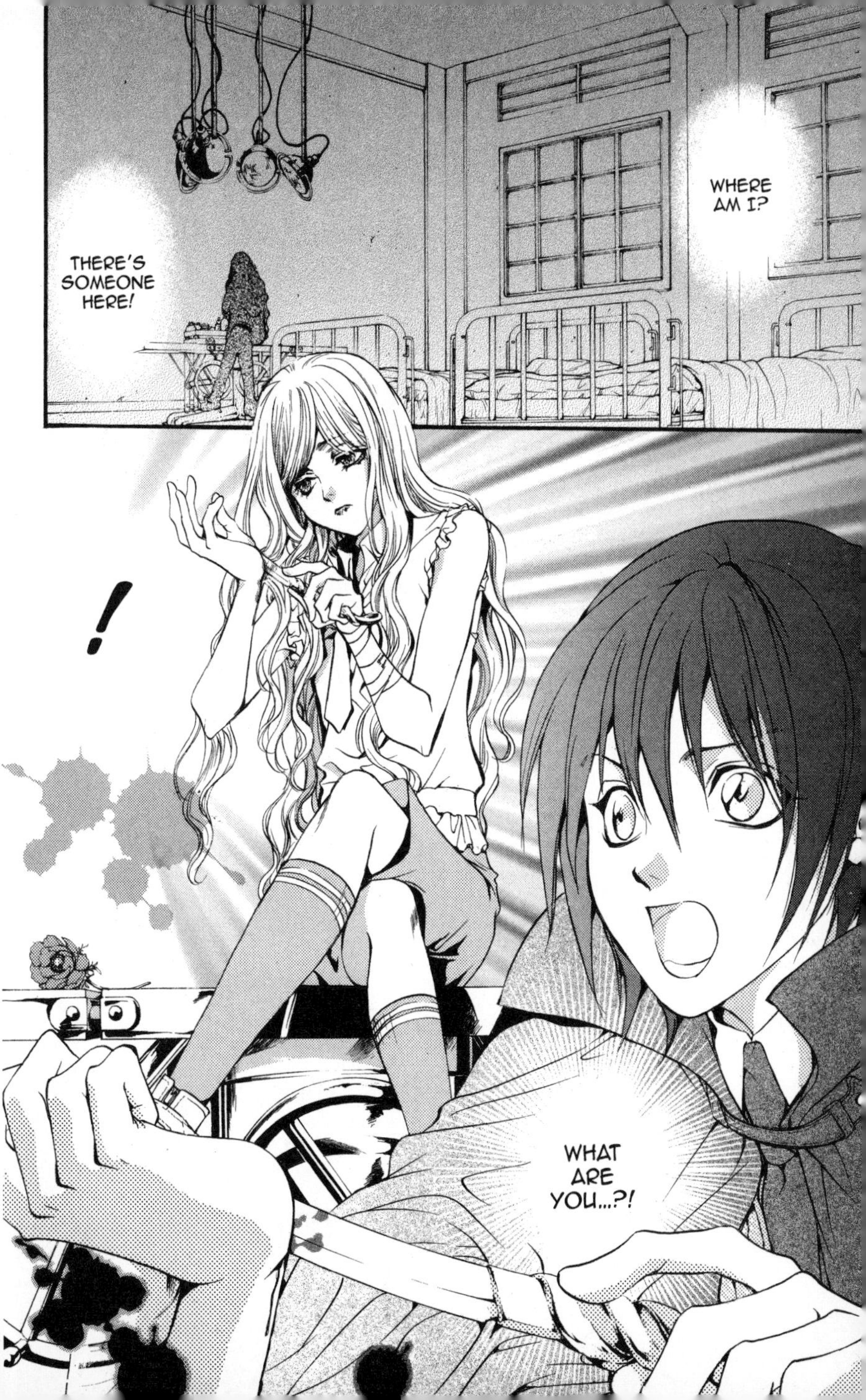
WHERE AM I?
THERE'S SOMEONE HERE!
!
WHAT ARE YOU...?!

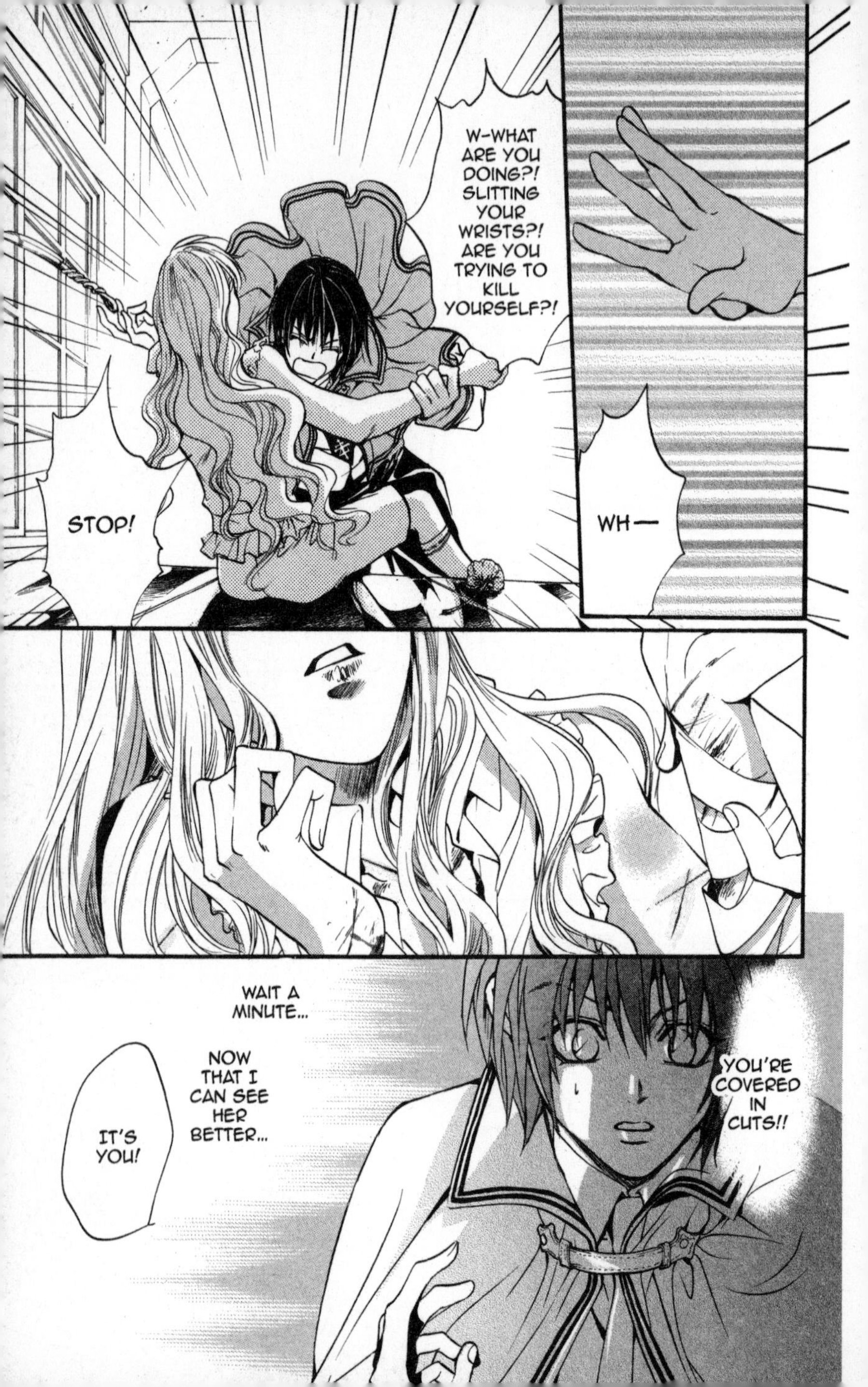
WH—
W-WHAT ARE YOU DOING?! SLITTING YOUR WRISTS?! ARE YOU TRYING TO KILL YOURSELF?!
STOP!
WAIT A MINUTE...
NOW THAT I CAN SEE HER BETTER...
YOU'RE COVERED IN CUTS!!
IT'S YOU!

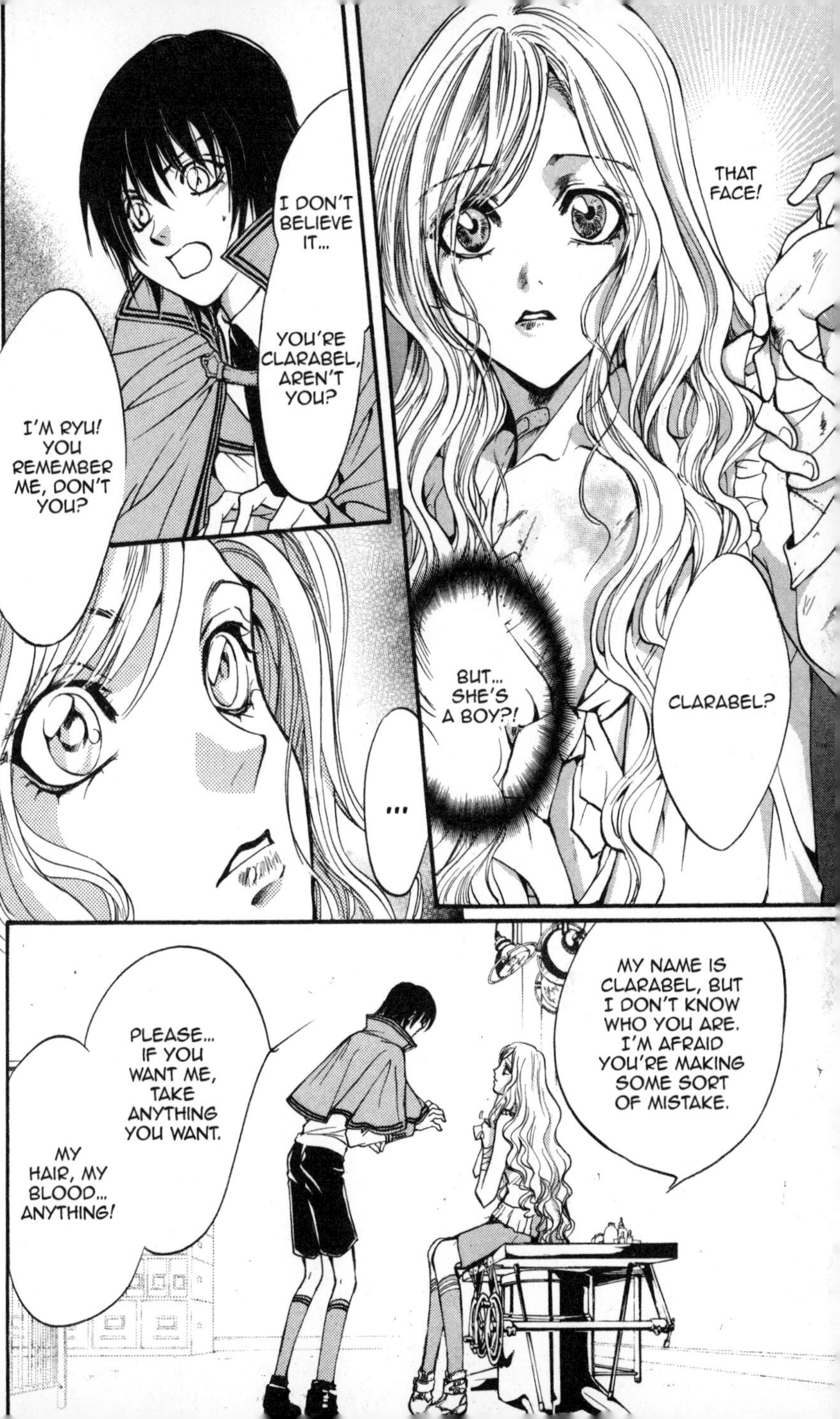

THAT FACE!
CLARABEL?
BUT... SHE'S A BOY?!
I DON'T BELIEVE IT...
YOU'RE CLARABEL, AREN'T YOU?
I'M RYU! YOU REMEMBER ME, DON'T YOU?
...
MY NAME IS CLARABEL, BUT I DON'T KNOW WHO YOU ARE. I'M AFRAID YOU'RE MAKING SOME SORT OF MISTAKE.
PLEASE... IF YOU WANT ME, TAKE ANYTHING YOU WANT.
MY HAIR, MY BLOOD... ANYTHING!

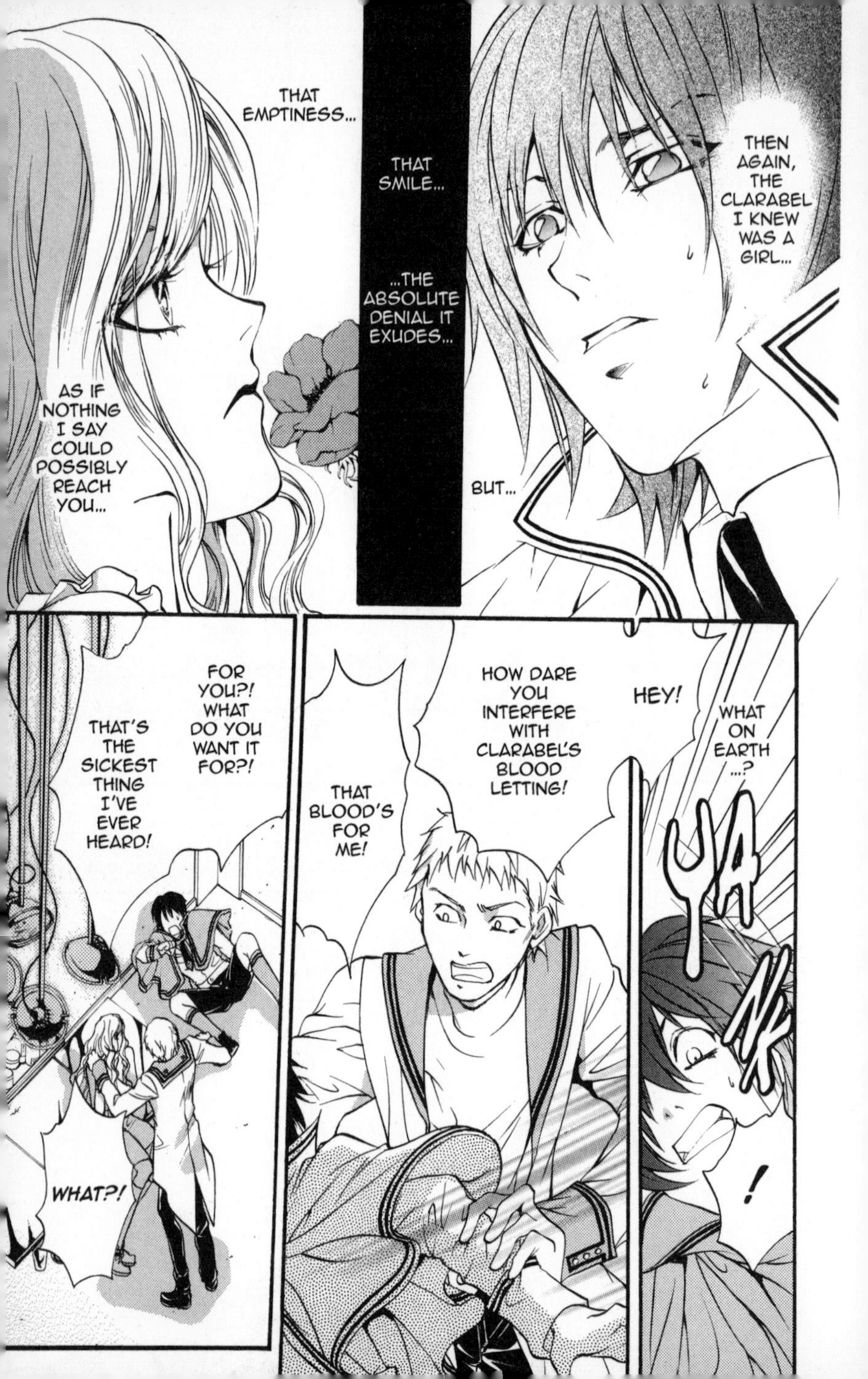
THEN AGAIN, THE CLARABEL I KNEW WAS A GIRL...
BUT...
THAT EMPTINESS...
THAT SMILE...
...THE ABSOLUTE DENIAL IT EXUDES...
AS IF NOTHING I SAY COULD POSSIBLY REACH YOU...
WHAT ON EARTH ...?
YANK
!
HEY!
HOW DARE YOU INTERFERE WITH CLARABEL'S BLOOD LETTING!
THAT BLOOD'S FOR ME!
FOR YOU?! WHAT DO YOU WANT IT FOR?!
THAT'S THE SICKEST THING I'VE EVER HEARD!
WHAT?!

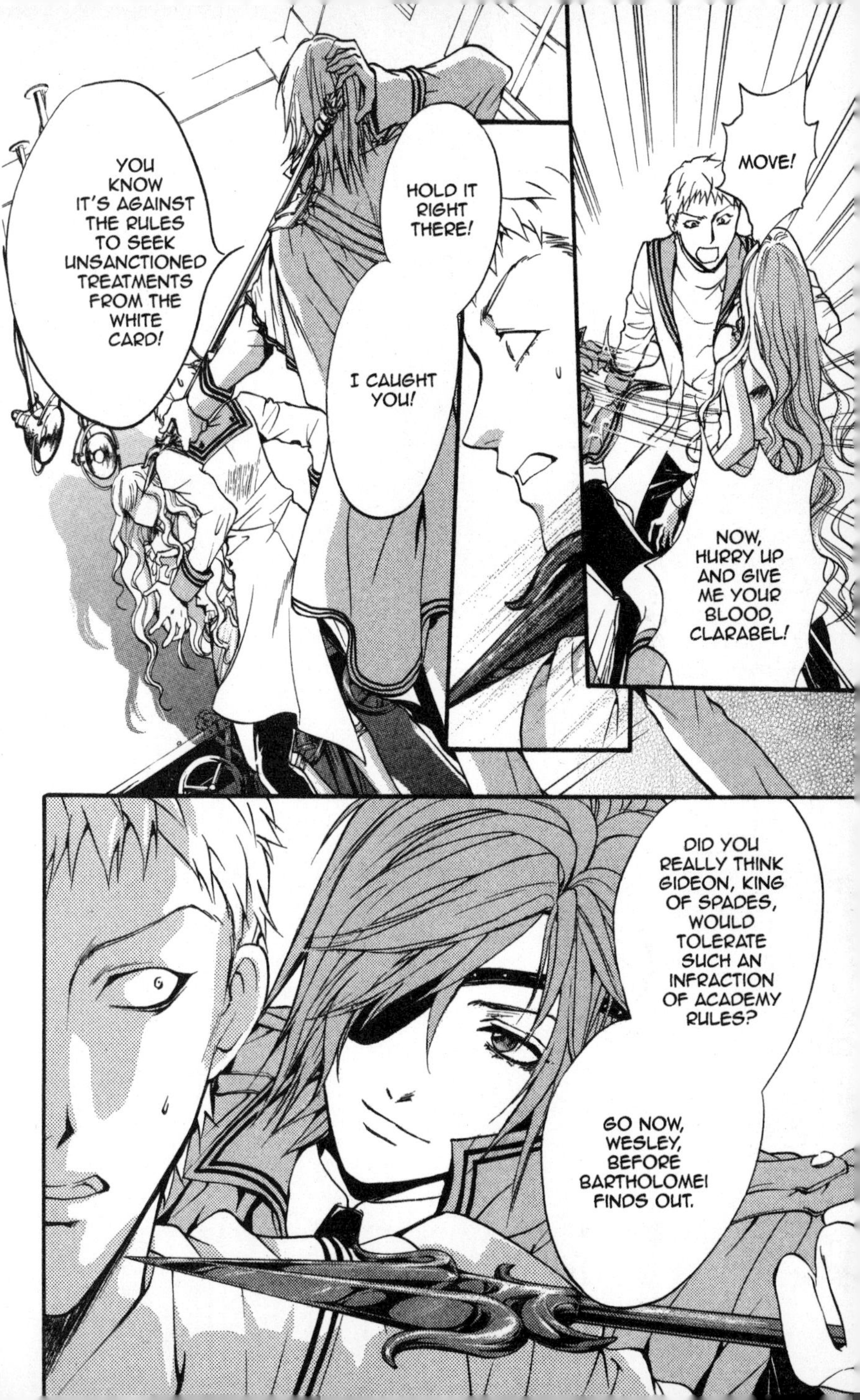
MOVE!
NOW, HURRY UP AND GIVE ME YOUR BLOOD, CLARABEL!
HOLD IT RIGHT THERE!
I CAUGHT YOU!
YOU KNOW IT'S AGAINST THE RULES TO SEEK UNSANCTIONED TREATMENTS FROM THE WHITE CARD!
DID YOU REALLY THINK GIDEON, KING OF SPADES, WOULD TOLERATE SUCH AN INFRACTION OF ACADEMY RULES?
GO NOW, WESLEY, BEFORE BARTHOLOMEI FINDS OUT.

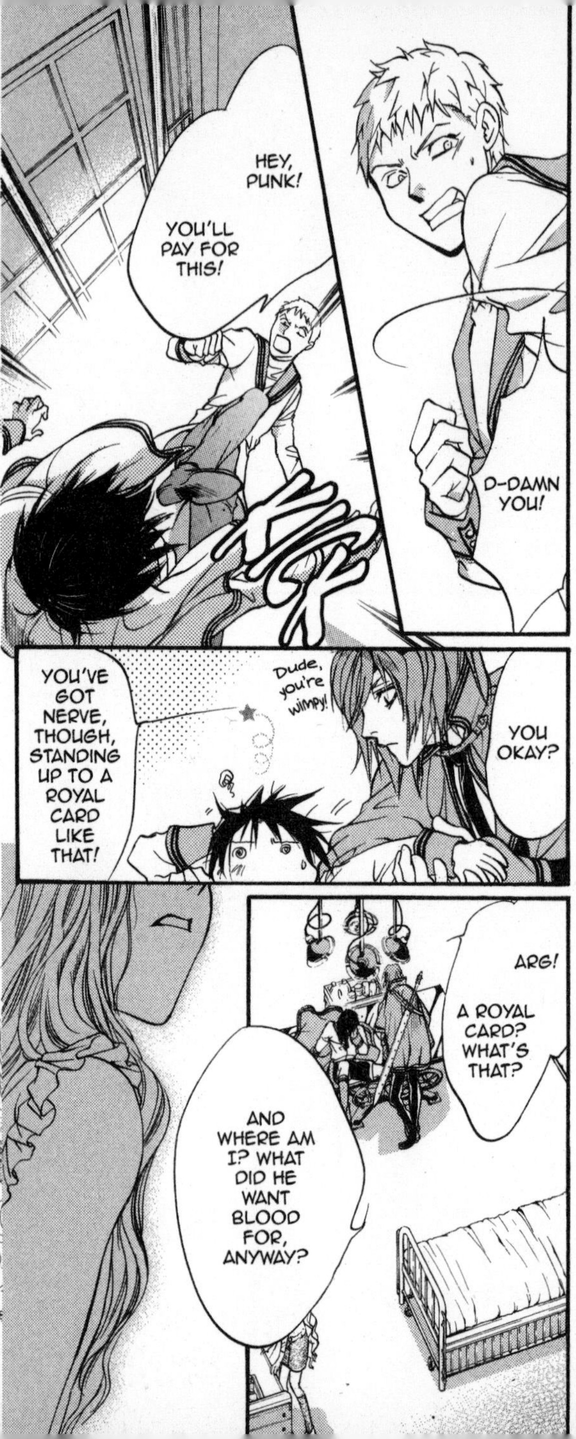
D-DAMN YOU!
HEY, PUNK!
YOU'LL PAY FOR THIS!
KICK
YOU OKAY?
Dude, you're wimpy!
YOU'VE GOT NERVE, THOUGH, STANDING UP TO A ROYAL CARD LIKE THAT!
ARG!
A ROYAL CARD? WHAT'S THAT?
AND WHERE AM I? WHAT DID HE WANT BLOOD FOR, ANYWAY?

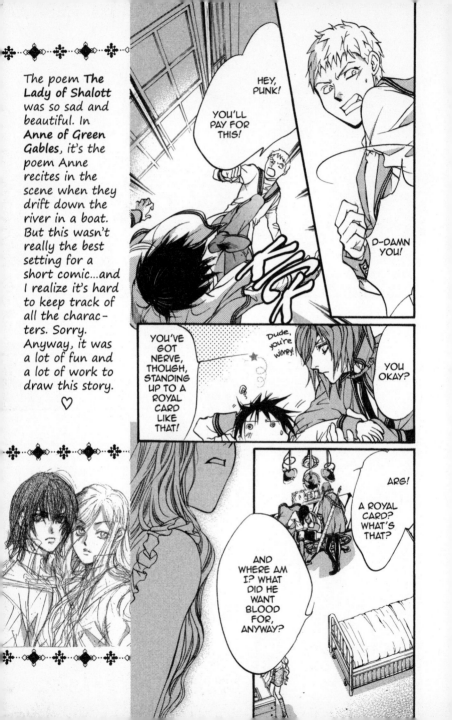

The poem **The Lady of Shalott** was so sad and beautiful. In **Anne of Green Gables**, it's the poem Anne recites in the scene when they drift down the river in a boat. But this wasn't really the best setting for a short comic...and I realize it's hard to keep track of all the charac-ters. Sorry. Anyway, it was a lot of fun and a lot of work to draw this story. ♡

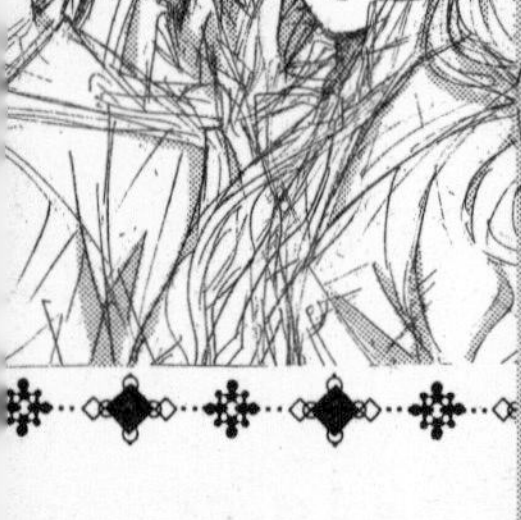

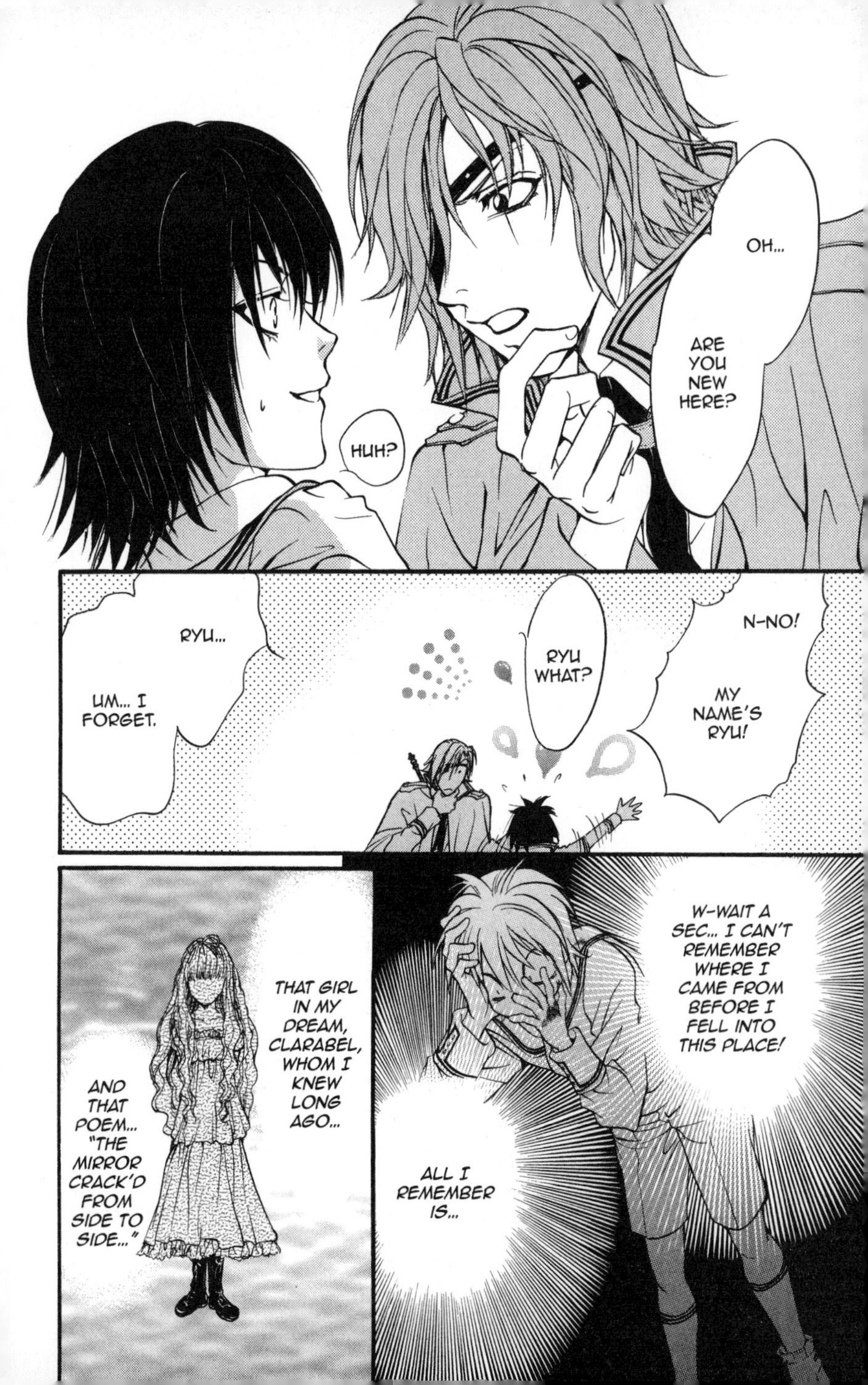
OH...
ARE YOU NEW HERE?
HUH?
N-NO!
MY NAME'S RYU!
RYU WHAT?
RYU...
UM... I FORGET.
W-WAIT A SEC... I CAN'T REMEMBER WHERE I CAME FROM BEFORE I FELL INTO THIS PLACE!
ALL I REMEMBER IS...
THAT GIRL IN MY DREAM, CLARABEL, WHOM I KNEW LONG AGO...
AND THAT POEM... "THE MIRROR CRACK'D FROM SIDE TO SIDE..."

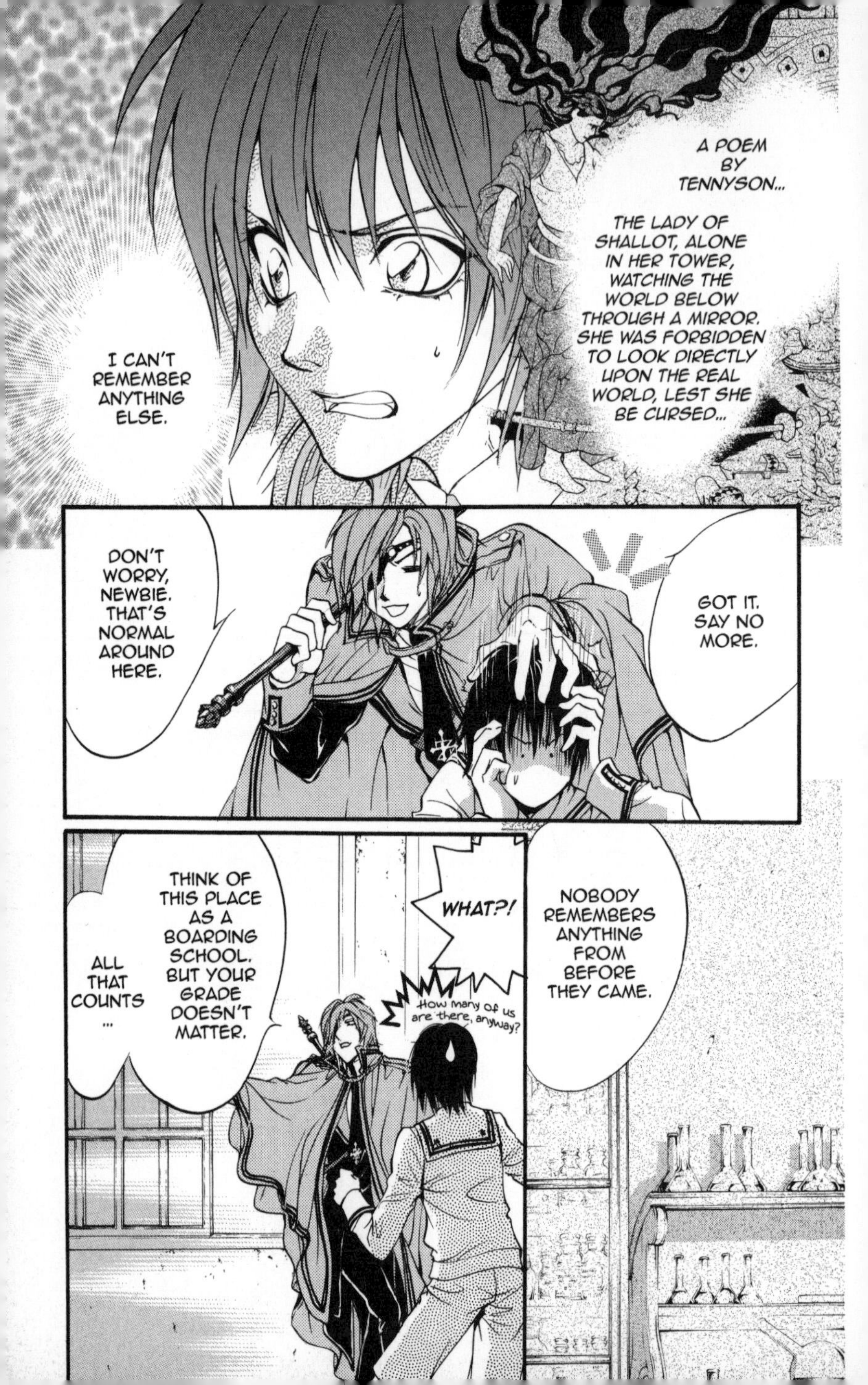
A POEM BY TENNYSON...
THE LADY OF SHALLOT, ALONE IN HER TOWER, WATCHING THE WORLD BELOW THROUGH A MIRROR. SHE WAS FORBIDDEN TO LOOK DIRECTLY UPON THE REAL WORLD, LEST SHE BE CURSED...
I CAN'T REMEMBER ANYTHING ELSE.
GOT IT. SAY NO MORE.
DON'T WORRY, NEWBIE. THAT'S NORMAL AROUND HERE.
NOBODY REMEMBERS ANYTHING FROM BEFORE THEY CAME.
WHAT?!
How many of us are there, anyway?
THINK OF THIS PLACE AS A BOARDING SCHOOL. BUT YOUR GRADE DOESN'T MATTER.
ALL THAT COUNTS ...

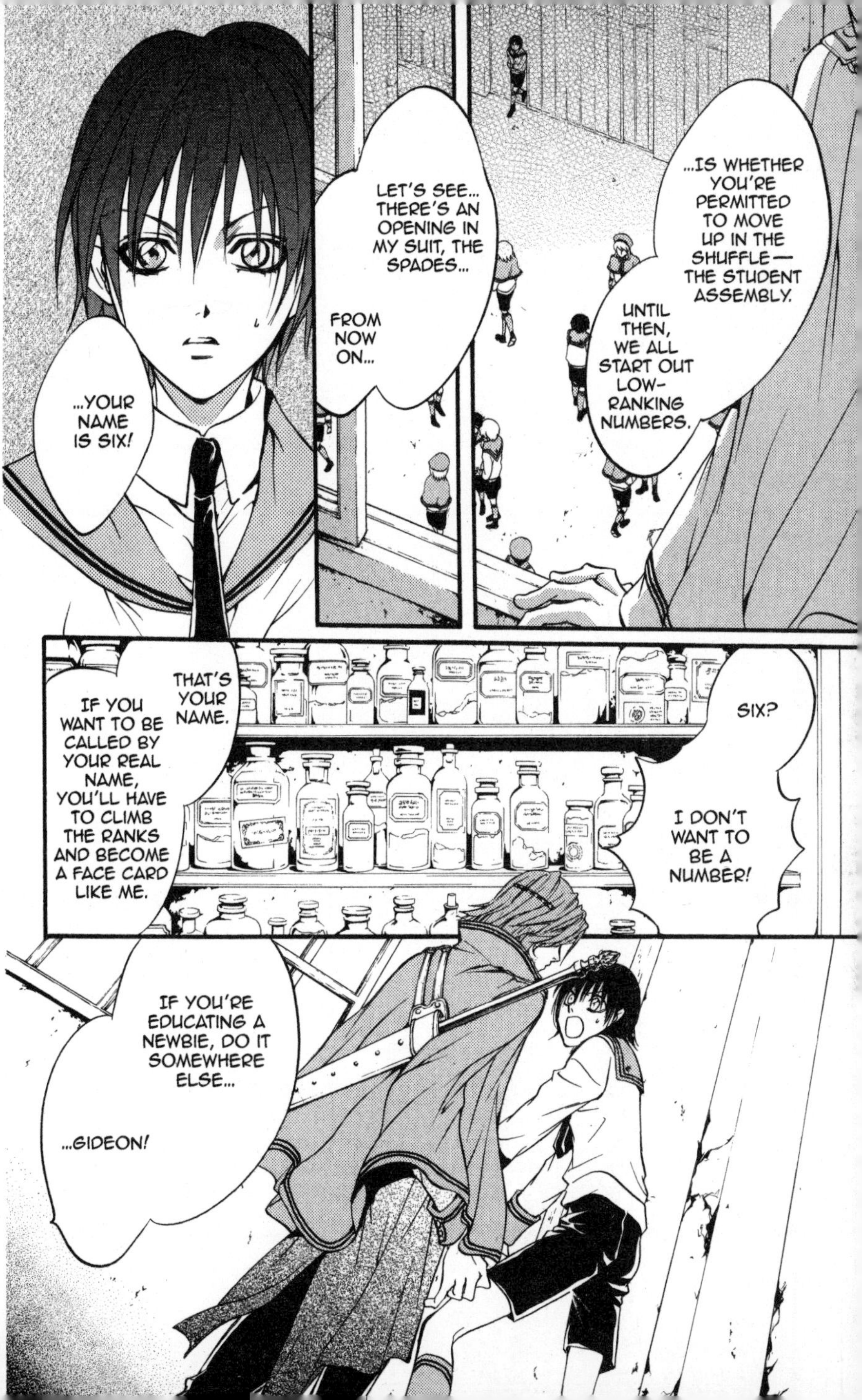
...IS WHETHER YOU'RE PERMITTED TO MOVE UP IN THE SHUFFLE— THE STUDENT ASSEMBLY.
UNTIL THEN, WE ALL START OUT LOW-RANKING NUMBERS.
LET'S SEE... THERE'S AN OPENING IN MY SUIT, THE SPADES...
FROM NOW ON...
...YOUR NAME IS SIX!
SIX?
I DON'T WANT TO BE A NUMBER!
THAT'S YOUR NAME.
IF YOU WANT TO BE CALLED BY YOUR REAL NAME, YOU'LL HAVE TO CLIMB THE RANKS AND BECOME A FACE CARD LIKE ME.
IF YOU'RE EDUCATING A NEWBIE, DO IT SOMEWHERE ELSE...
...GIDEON!

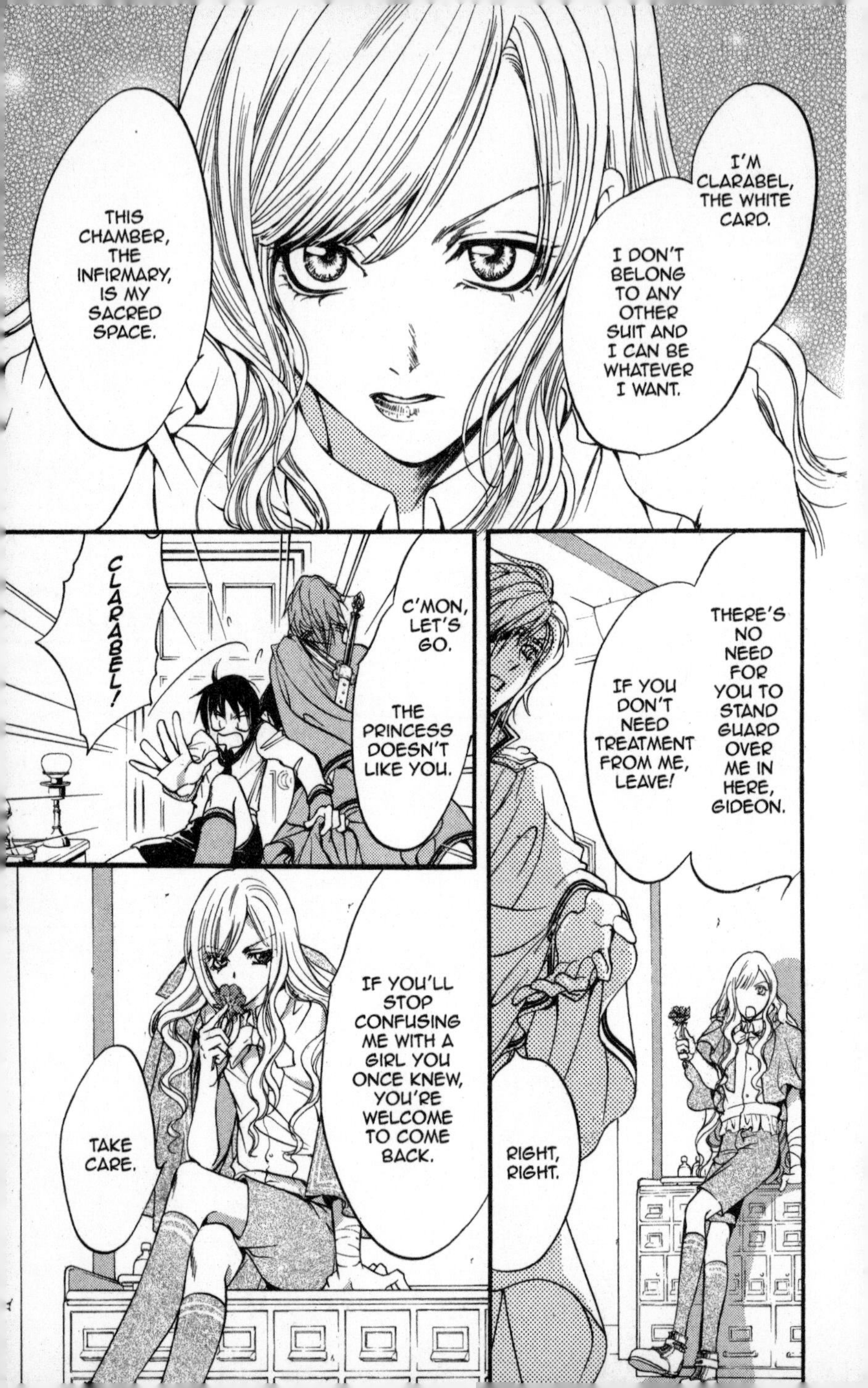
I'M CLARABEL, THE WHITE CARD.
I DON'T BELONG TO ANY OTHER SUIT AND I CAN BE WHATEVER I WANT.
THIS CHAMBER, THE INFIRMARY, IS MY SACRED SPACE.
THERE'S NO NEED FOR YOU TO STAND GUARD OVER ME IN HERE, GIDEON.
IF YOU DON'T NEED TREATMENT FROM ME, LEAVE!
RIGHT, RIGHT.
C'MON, LET'S GO.
THE PRINCESS DOESN'T LIKE YOU.
CLARABEL!
IF YOU'LL STOP CONFUSING ME WITH A GIRL YOU ONCE KNEW, YOU'RE WELCOME TO COME BACK.
TAKE CARE.

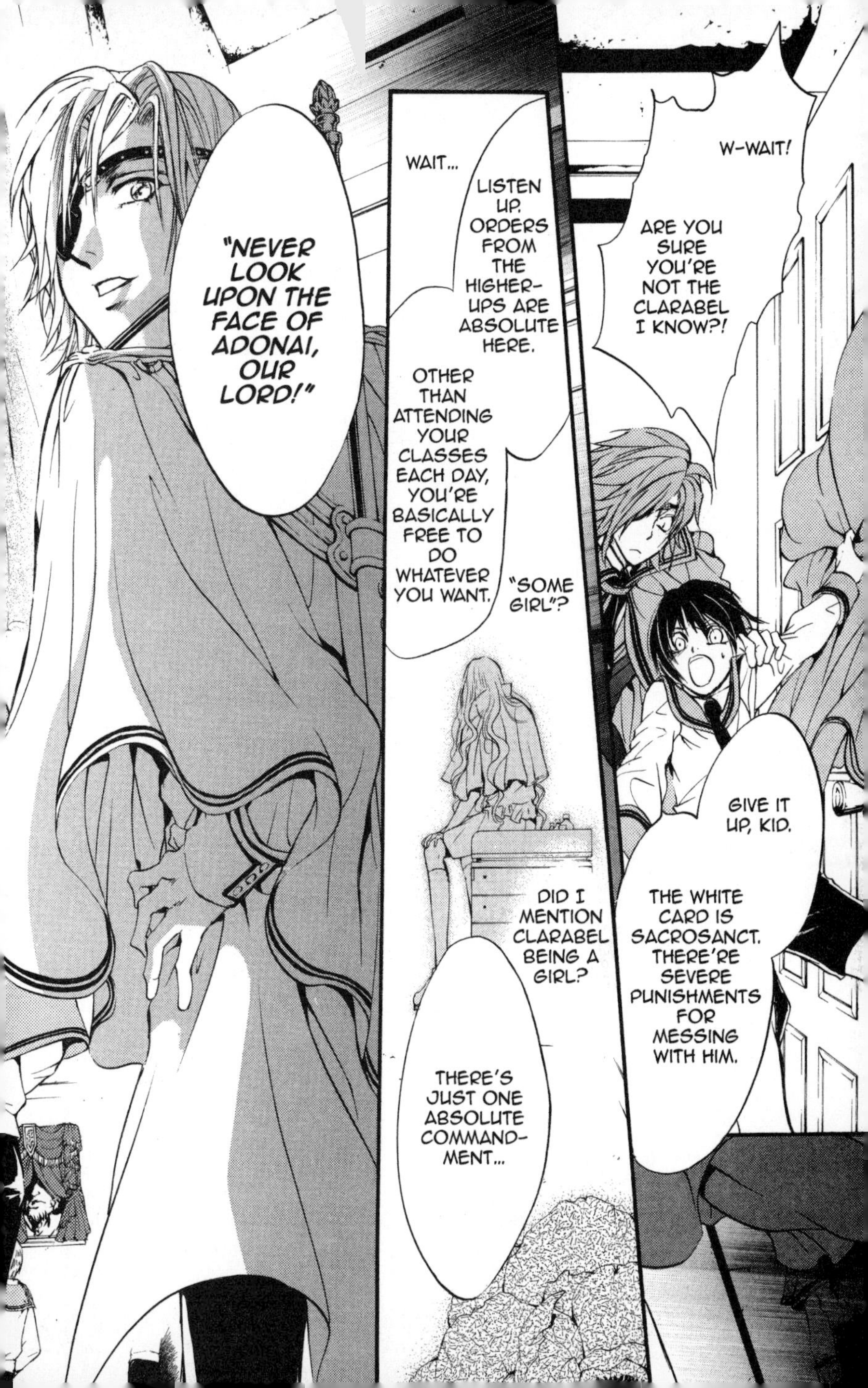
W-WAIT!
ARE YOU SURE YOU'RE NOT THE CLARABEL I KNOW?!
GIVE IT UP, KID.
THE WHITE CARD IS SACROSANCT. THERE'RE SEVERE PUNISHMENTS FOR MESSING WITH HIM.
"SOME GIRL"?
DID I MENTION CLARABEL BEING A GIRL?
WAIT...
LISTEN UP. ORDERS FROM THE HIGHER-UPS ARE ABSOLUTE HERE.
OTHER THAN ATTENDING YOUR CLASSES EACH DAY, YOU'RE BASICALLY FREE TO DO WHATEVER YOU WANT.
THERE'S JUST ONE ABSOLUTE COMMANDMENT...
"NEVER LOOK UPON THE FACE OF ADONAI, OUR LORD!"

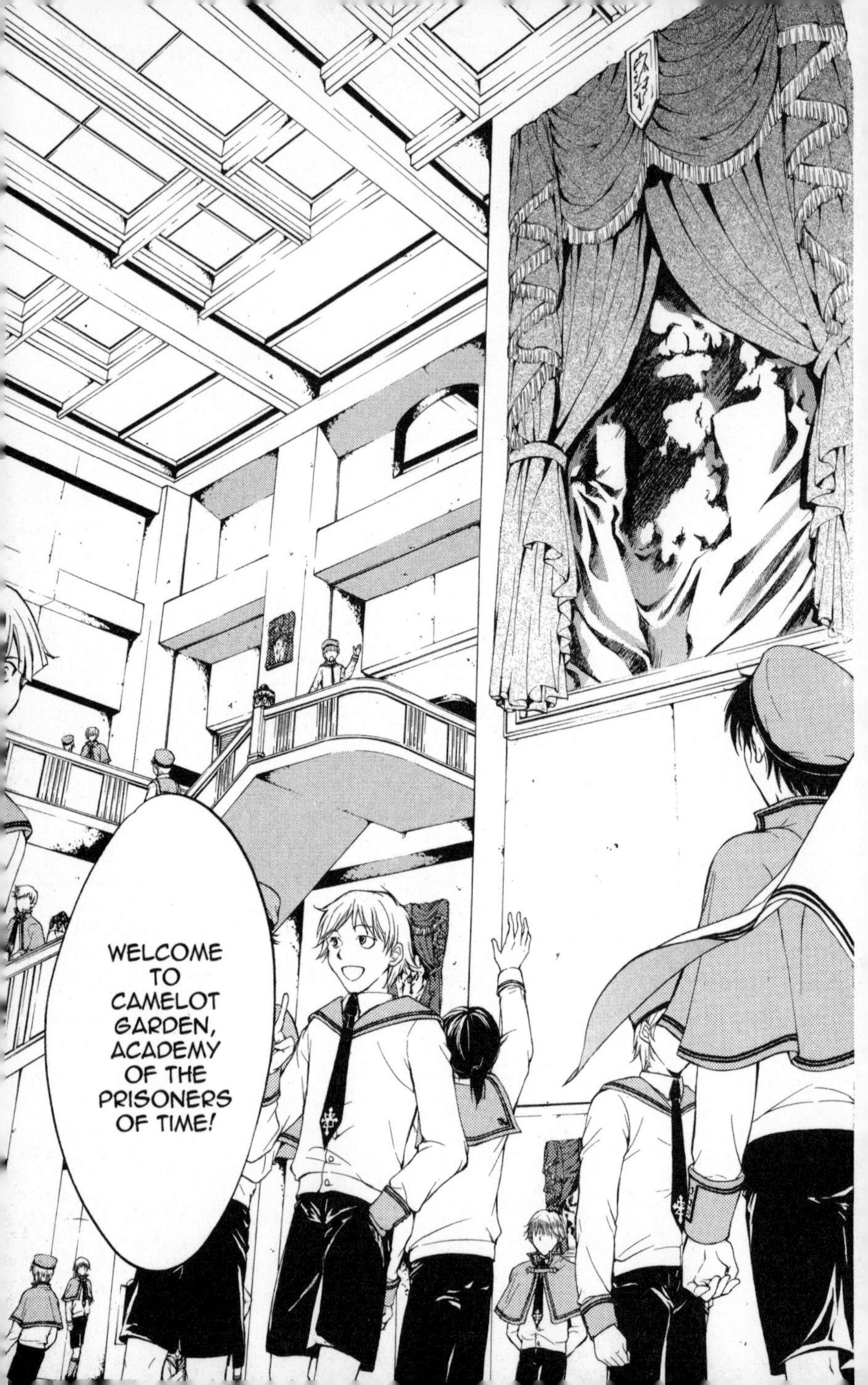
WELCOME TO CAMELOT GARDEN, ACADEMY OF THE PRISONERS OF TIME!

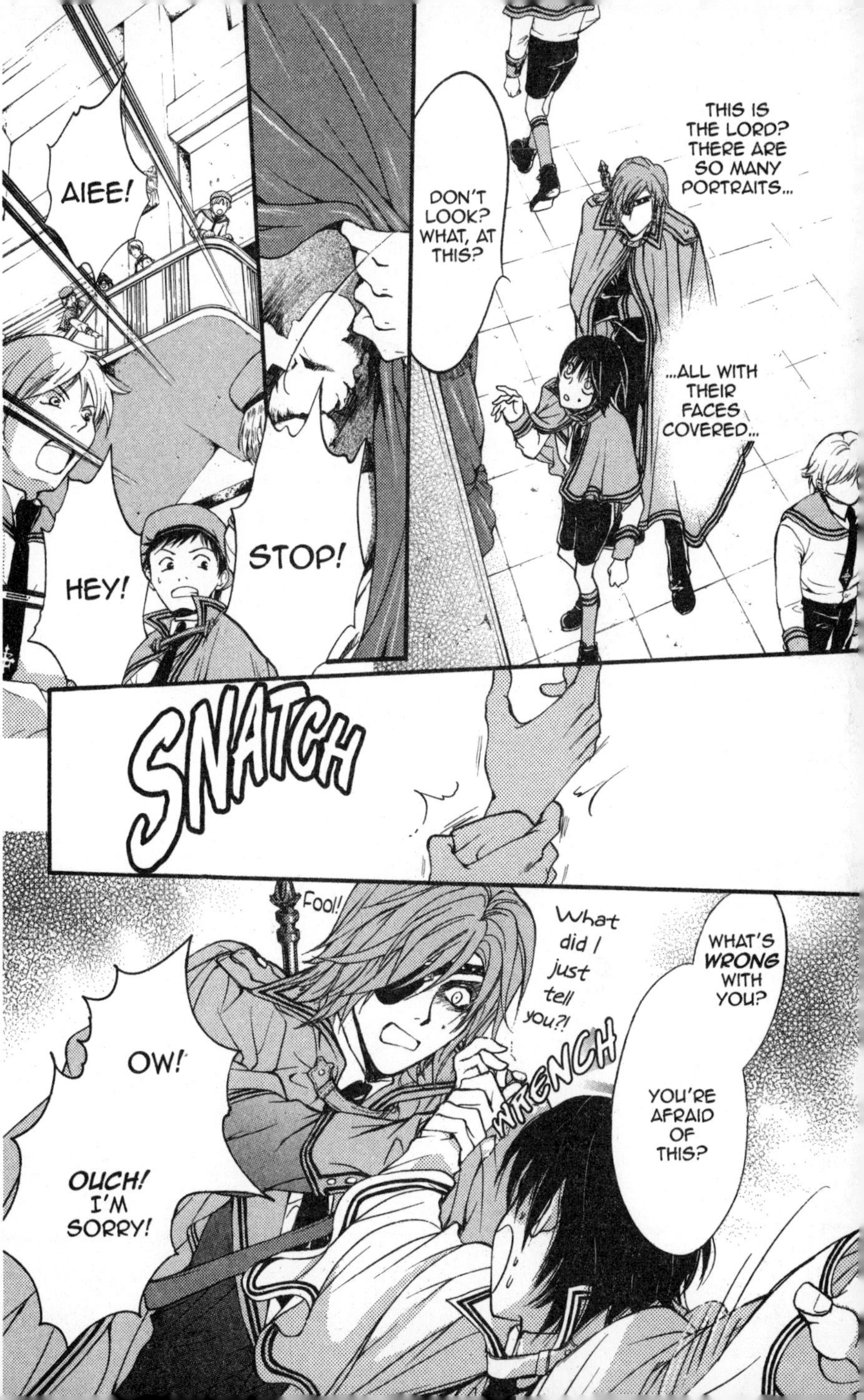
THIS IS THE LORD? THERE ARE SO MANY PORTRAITS...
...ALL WITH THEIR FACES COVERED...
DON'T LOOK? WHAT, AT THIS?
STOP!
AIEE!
HEY!
SNATCH
WHAT'S **WRONG** WITH YOU?
YOU'RE AFRAID OF THIS?
What did I just tell you?!
Fool!
WRENCH
OW!
OUCH! I'M SORRY!

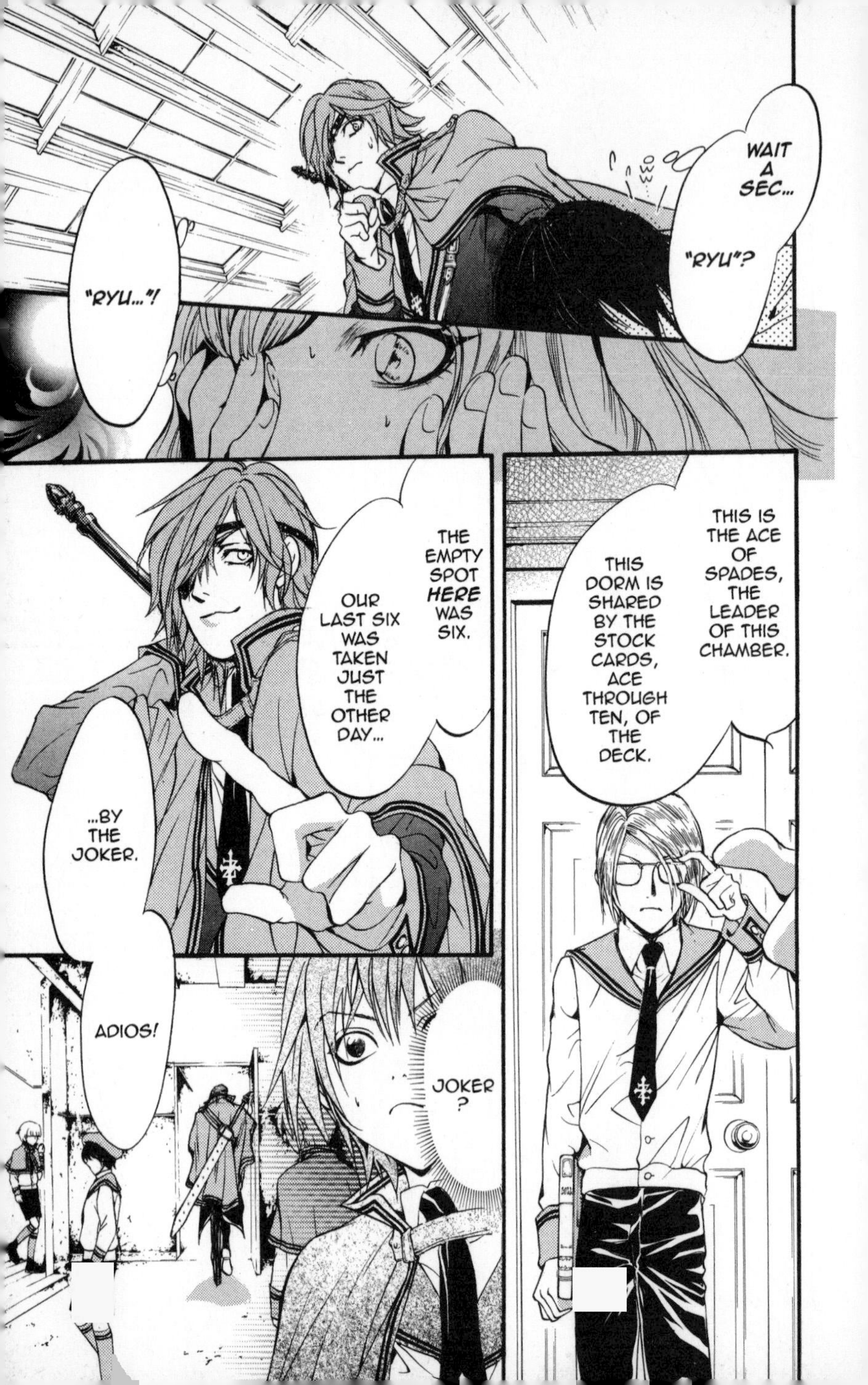
WAIT A SEC...
"RYU"?
"RYU..."!
THIS IS THE ACE OF SPADES, THE LEADER OF THIS CHAMBER.
THIS DORM IS SHARED BY THE STOCK CARDS, ACE THROUGH TEN, OF THE DECK.
THE EMPTY SPOT HERE WAS SIX.
OUR LAST SIX WAS TAKEN JUST THE OTHER DAY...
...BY THE JOKER.
JOKER?
ADIOS!

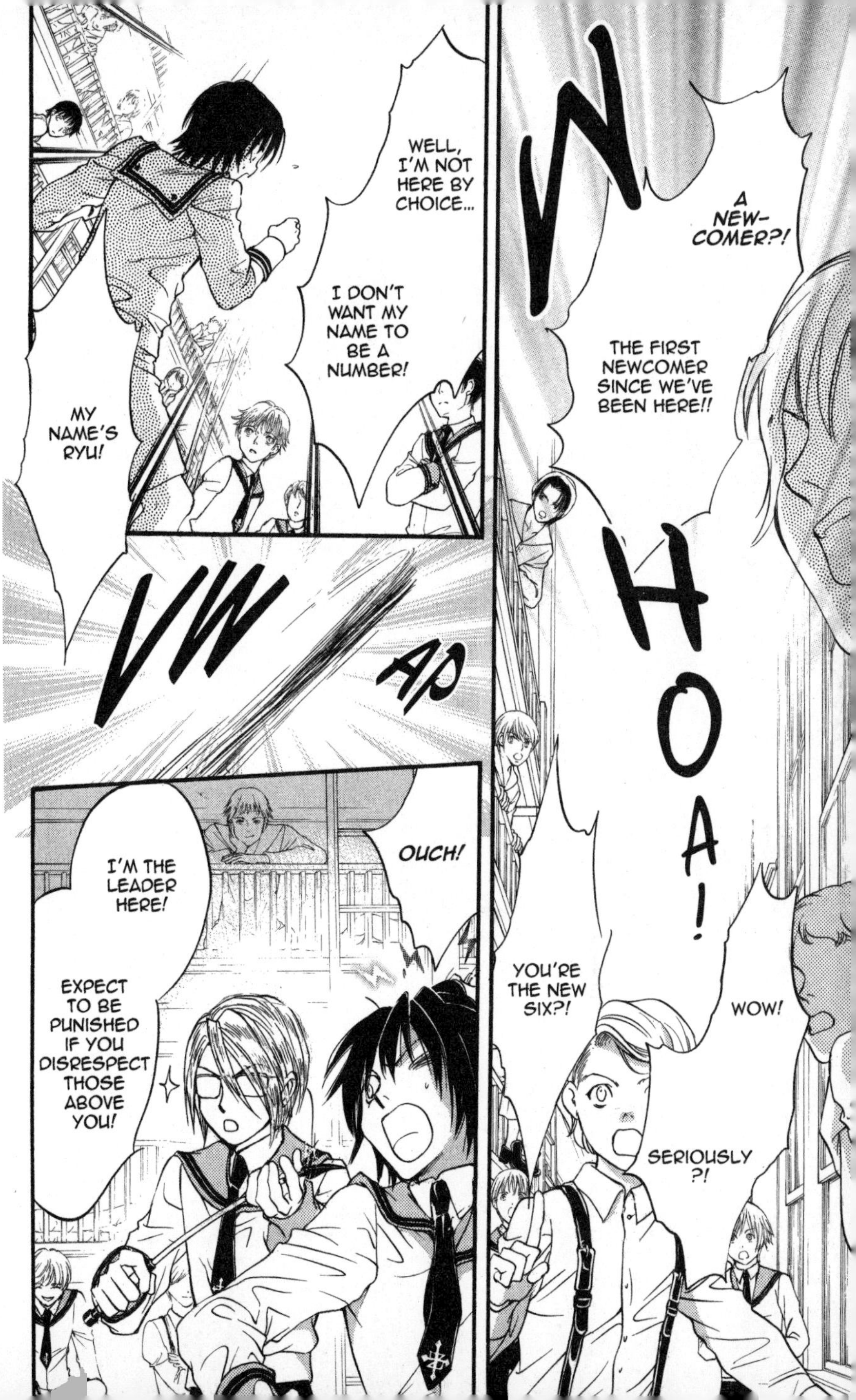
WHOA!
A NEW-COMER?!
THE FIRST NEWCOMER SINCE WE'VE BEEN HERE!!
WOW!
YOU'RE THE NEW SIX?!
SERIOUSLY ?!
WELL, I'M NOT HERE BY CHOICE...
I DON'T WANT MY NAME TO BE A NUMBER!
MY NAME'S RYU!
VWAP
OUCH!
I'M THE LEADER HERE!
EXPECT TO BE PUNISHED IF YOU DISRESPECT THOSE ABOVE YOU!

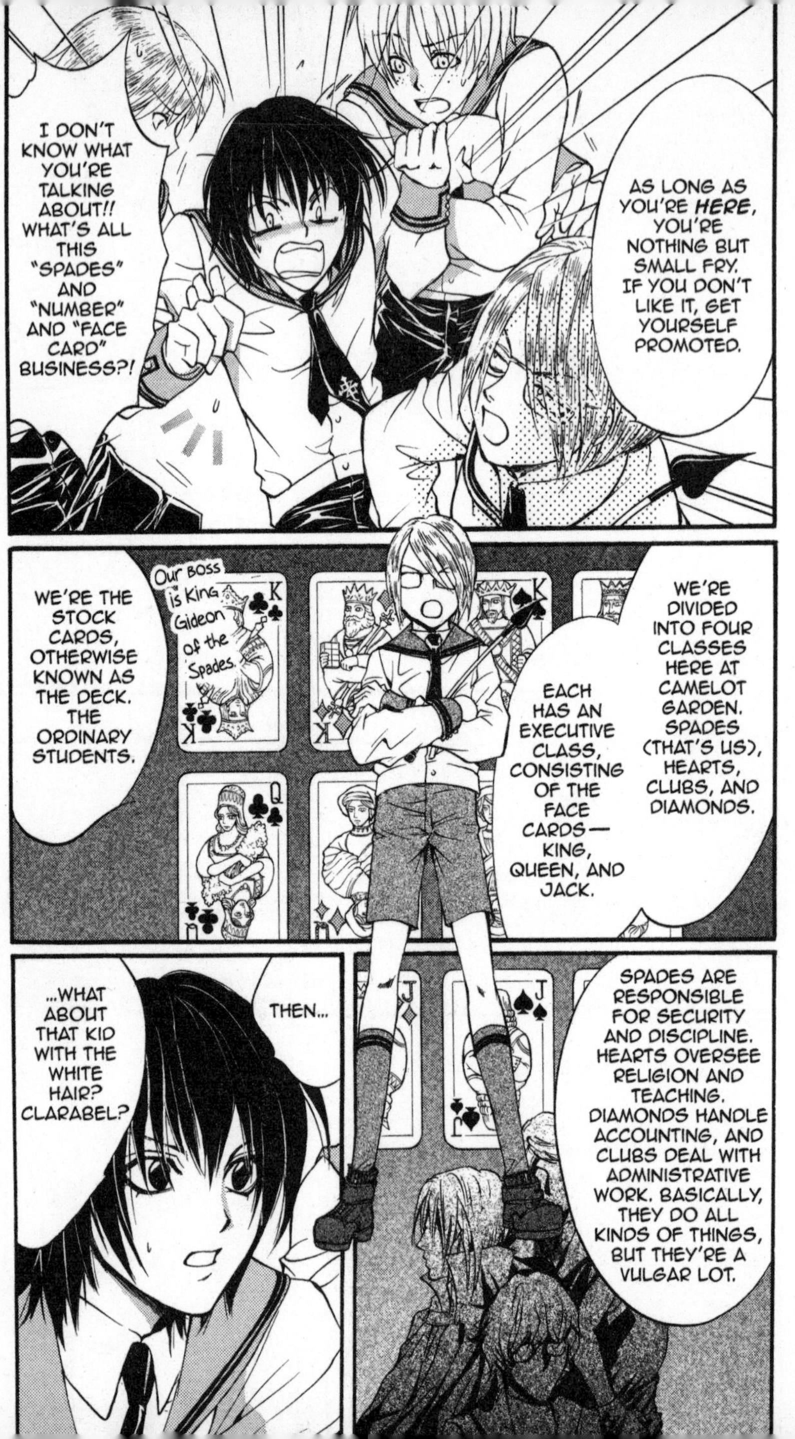
AS LONG AS YOU'RE *HERE*, YOU'RE NOTHING BUT SMALL FRY. IF YOU DON'T LIKE IT, GET YOURSELF PROMOTED.
I DON'T KNOW WHAT YOU'RE TALKING ABOUT!! WHAT'S ALL THIS "SPADES" AND "NUMBER" AND "FACE CARD" BUSINESS?!
WE'RE DIVIDED INTO FOUR CLASSES HERE AT CAMELOT GARDEN. SPADES (THAT'S US), HEARTS, CLUBS, AND DIAMONDS.
EACH HAS AN EXECUTIVE CLASS, CONSISTING OF THE FACE CARDS— KING, QUEEN, AND JACK.
Our boss is King Gideon of the Spades.
WE'RE THE STOCK CARDS, OTHERWISE KNOWN AS THE DECK. THE ORDINARY STUDENTS.
SPADES ARE RESPONSIBLE FOR SECURITY AND DISCIPLINE. HEARTS OVERSEE RELIGION AND TEACHING. DIAMONDS HANDLE ACCOUNTING, AND CLUBS DEAL WITH ADMINISTRATIVE WORK. BASICALLY, THEY DO ALL KINDS OF THINGS, BUT THEY'RE A VULGAR LOT.
THEN...
...WHAT ABOUT THAT KID WITH THE WHITE HAIR? CLARABEL?

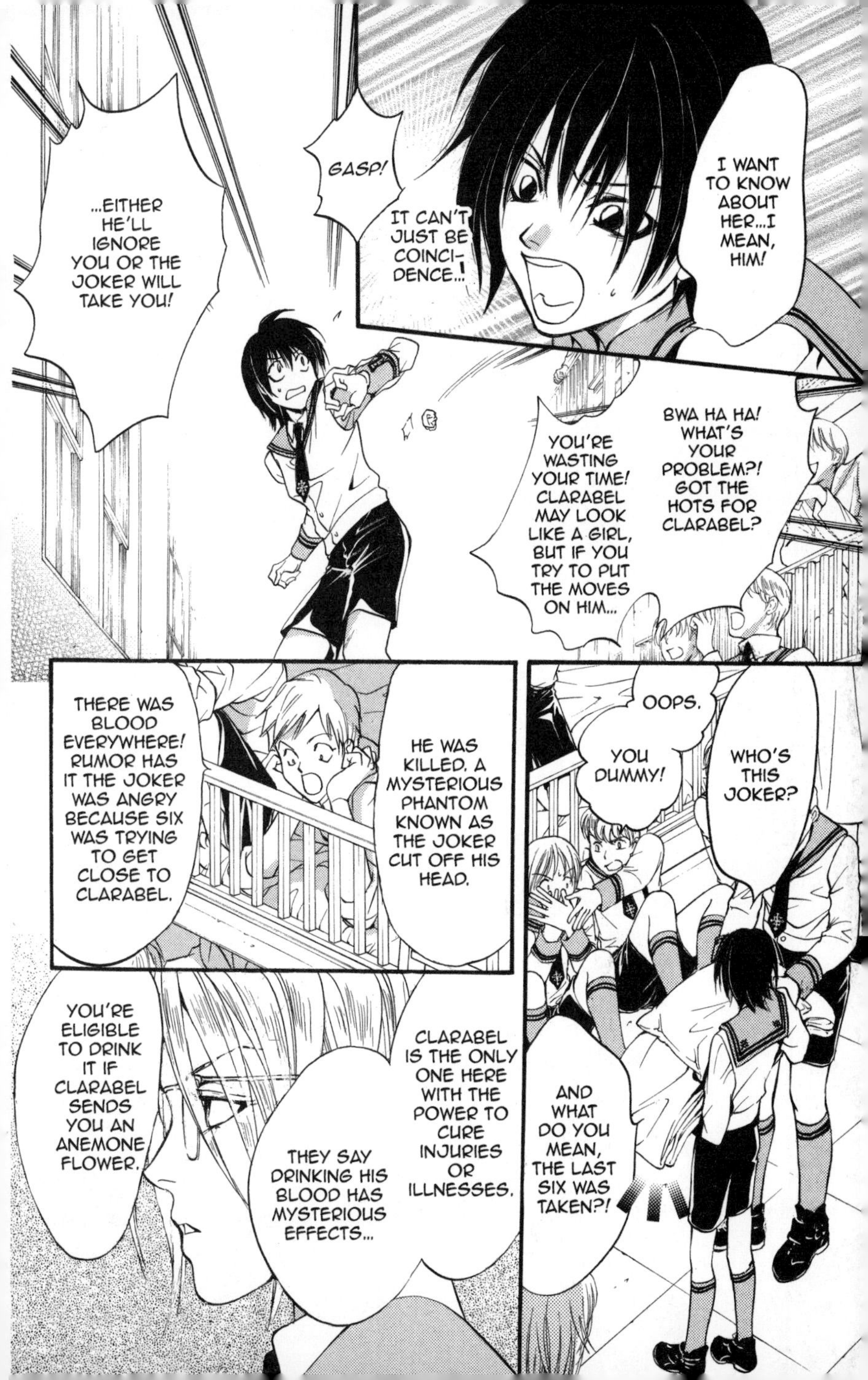
I WANT TO KNOW ABOUT HER...I MEAN, HIM!
IT CAN'T JUST BE COINCIDENCE...!
BWA HA HA! WHAT'S YOUR PROBLEM?! GOT THE HOTS FOR CLARABEL?
YOU'RE WASTING YOUR TIME! CLARABEL MAY LOOK LIKE A GIRL, BUT IF YOU TRY TO PUT THE MOVES ON HIM...
...EITHER HE'LL IGNORE YOU OR THE JOKER WILL TAKE YOU!
GASP!
WHO'S THIS JOKER?
OOPS.
YOU DUMMY!
AND WHAT DO YOU MEAN, THE LAST SIX WAS TAKEN?!
HE WAS KILLED. A MYSTERIOUS PHANTOM KNOWN AS THE JOKER CUT OFF HIS HEAD.
THERE WAS BLOOD EVERYWHERE! RUMOR HAS IT THE JOKER WAS ANGRY BECAUSE SIX WAS TRYING TO GET CLOSE TO CLARABEL.
CLARABEL IS THE ONLY ONE HERE WITH THE POWER TO CURE INJURIES OR ILLNESSES.
THEY SAY DRINKING HIS BLOOD HAS MYSTERIOUS EFFECTS...
YOU'RE ELIGIBLE TO DRINK IT IF CLARABEL SENDS YOU AN ANEMONE FLOWER.

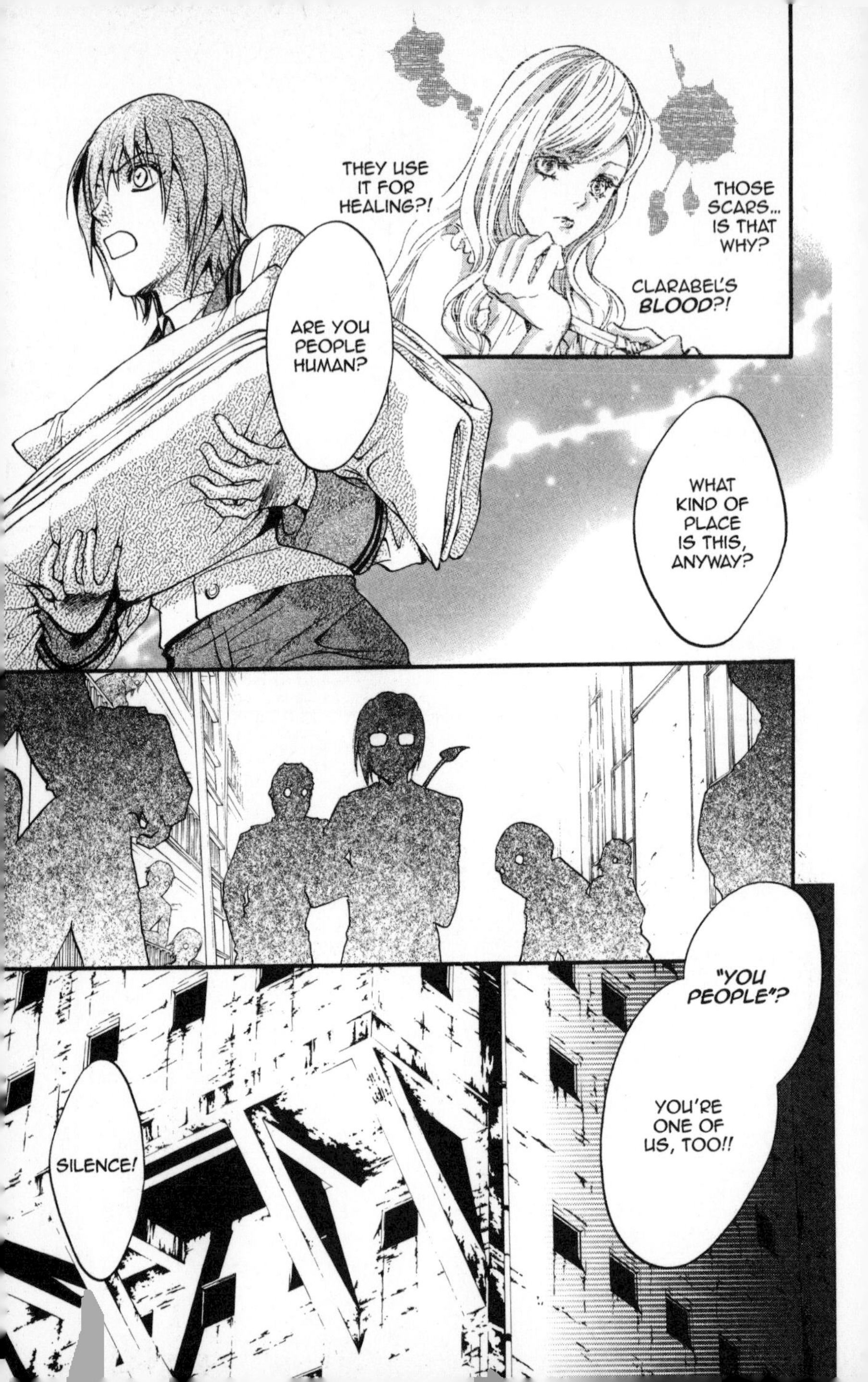
THOSE SCARS... IS THAT WHY?
CLARABEL'S *BLOOD*?!
THEY USE IT FOR HEALING?!
ARE YOU PEOPLE HUMAN?
WHAT KIND OF PLACE IS THIS, ANYWAY?
"YOU PEOPLE"?
YOU'RE ONE OF US, TOO!!
SILENCE!

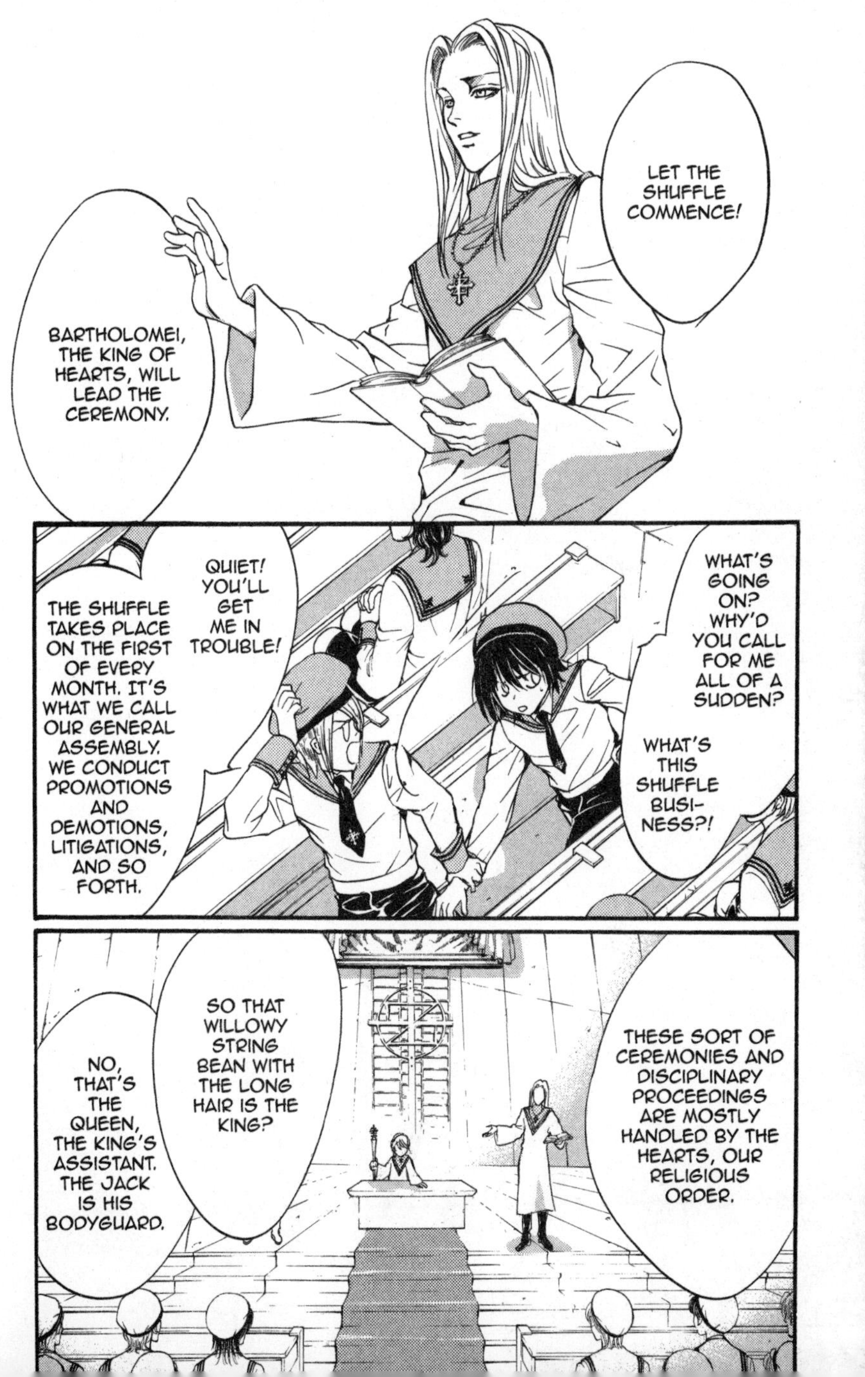
LET THE SHUFFLE COMMENCE!
BARTHOLOMEI, THE KING OF HEARTS, WILL LEAD THE CEREMONY.
WHAT'S GOING ON? WHY'D YOU CALL FOR ME ALL OF A SUDDEN?
WHAT'S THIS SHUFFLE BUSI-NESS?!
QUIET! YOU'LL GET ME IN TROUBLE!
THE SHUFFLE TAKES PLACE ON THE FIRST OF EVERY MONTH. IT'S WHAT WE CALL OUR GENERAL ASSEMBLY. WE CONDUCT PROMOTIONS AND DEMOTIONS, LITIGATIONS, AND SO FORTH.
THESE SORT OF CEREMONIES AND DISCIPLINARY PROCEEDINGS ARE MOSTLY HANDLED BY THE HEARTS, OUR RELIGIOUS ORDER.
SO THAT WILLOWY STRING BEAN WITH THE LONG HAIR IS THE KING?
NO, THAT'S THE QUEEN, THE KING'S ASSISTANT. THE JACK IS HIS BODYGUARD.

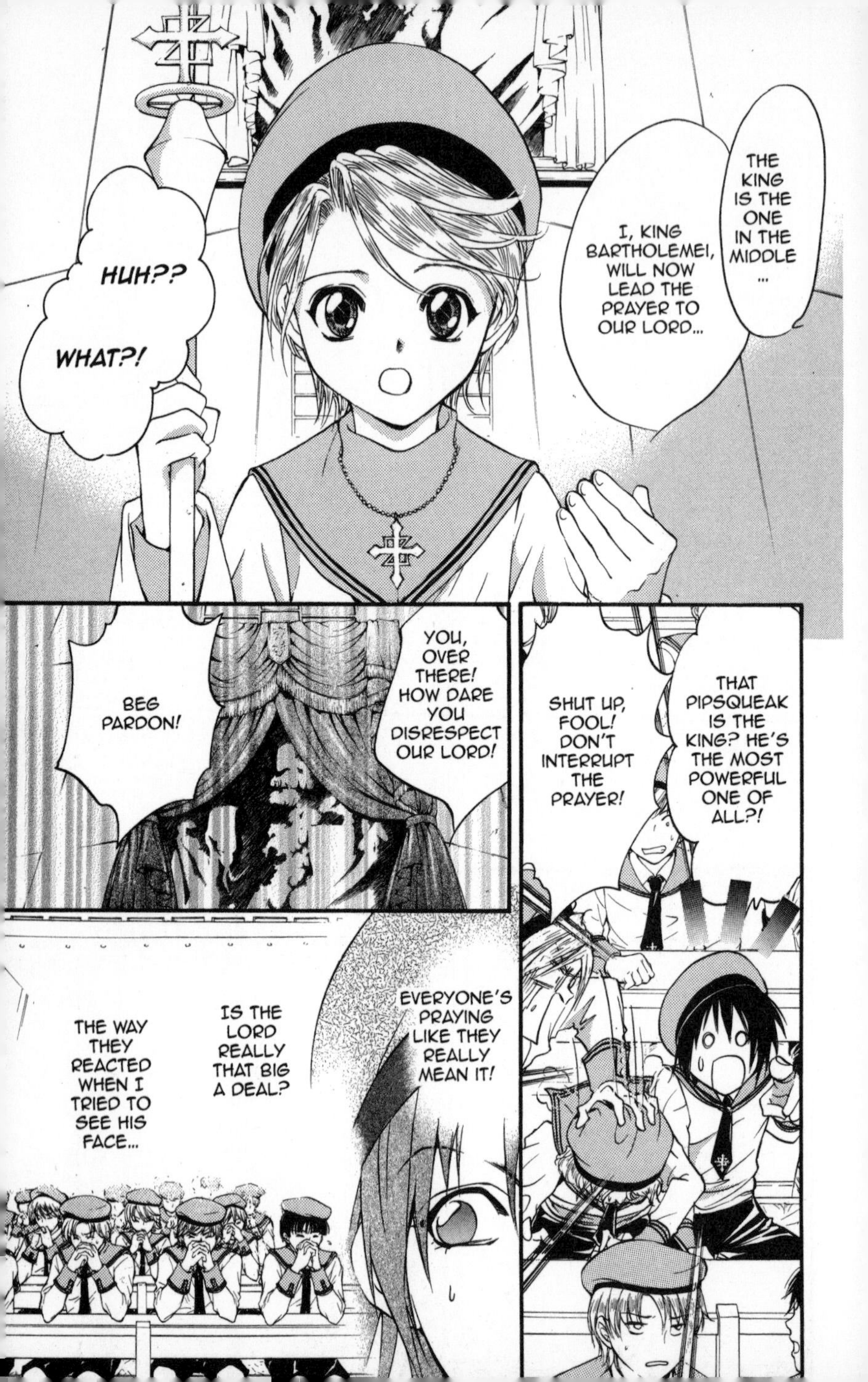
THE KING IS THE ONE IN THE MIDDLE ...
I, KING BARTHOLEMEI, WILL NOW LEAD THE PRAYER TO OUR LORD...
HUH?? WHAT?!
THAT PIPSQUEAK IS THE KING? HE'S THE MOST POWERFUL ONE OF ALL?!
SHUT UP, FOOL! DON'T INTERRUPT THE PRAYER!
YOU, OVER THERE! HOW DARE YOU DISRESPECT OUR LORD!
BEG PARDON!
EVERYONE'S PRAYING LIKE THEY REALLY MEAN IT!
IS THE LORD REALLY THAT BIG A DEAL?
THE WAY THEY REACTED WHEN I TRIED TO SEE HIS FACE...

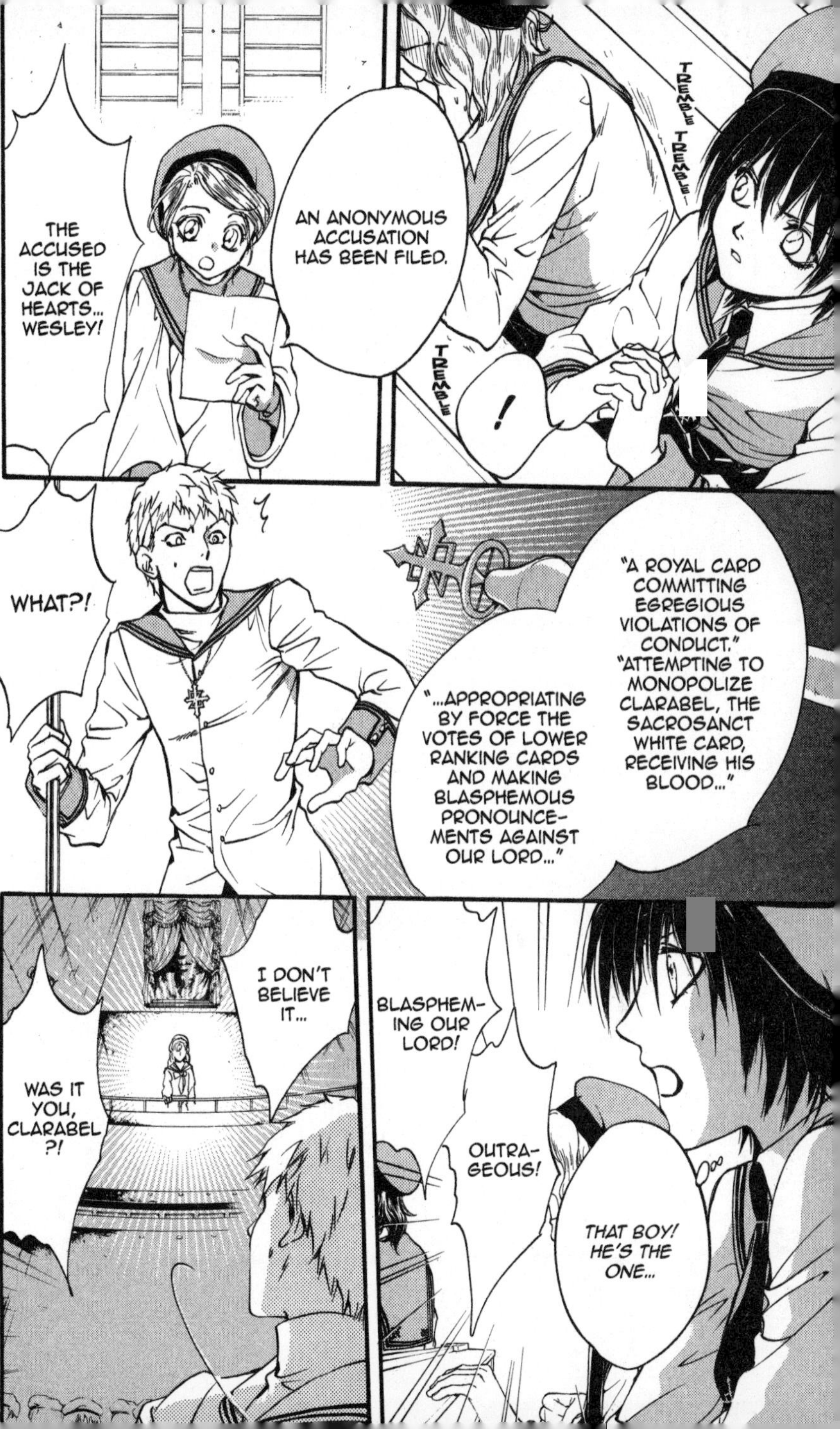
AN ANONYMOUS ACCUSATION HAS BEEN FILED.
TREMBLE TREMBLE
TREMBLE
!
THE ACCUSED IS THE JACK OF HEARTS... WESLEY!
"A ROYAL CARD COMMITTING EGREGIOUS VIOLATIONS OF CONDUCT." "ATTEMPTING TO MONOPOLIZE CLARABEL, THE SACROSANCT WHITE CARD, RECEIVING HIS BLOOD..."
"...APPROPRIATING BY FORCE THE VOTES OF LOWER RANKING CARDS AND MAKING BLASPHEMOUS PRONOUNCE-MENTS AGAINST OUR LORD..."
WHAT?!
BLASPHEM-ING OUR LORD!
OUTRA-GEOUS!
THAT BOY! HE'S THE ONE...
I DON'T BELIEVE IT...
WAS IT YOU, CLARABEL?!

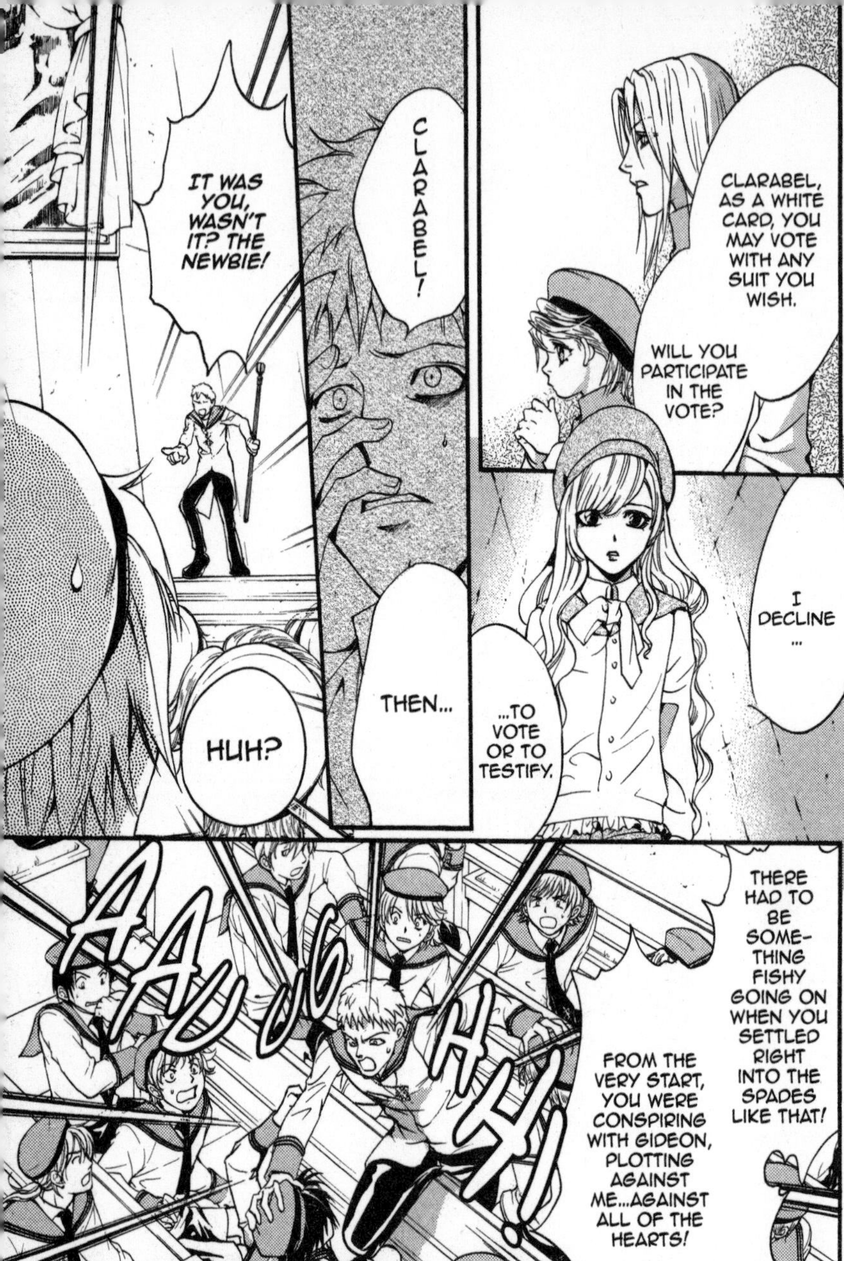
CLARABEL, AS A WHITE CARD, YOU MAY VOTE WITH ANY SUIT YOU WISH.
WILL YOU PARTICIPATE IN THE VOTE?
I DECLINE...
...TO VOTE OR TO TESTIFY.
CLARABEL!
THEN...
IT WAS YOU, WASN'T IT? THE NEWBIE!
HUH?
THERE HAD TO BE SOMETHING FISHY GOING ON WHEN YOU SETTLED RIGHT INTO THE SPADES LIKE THAT!
FROM THE VERY START, YOU WERE CONSPIRING WITH GIDEON, PLOTTING AGAINST ME...AGAINST ALL OF THE HEARTS!
AAUGHH!

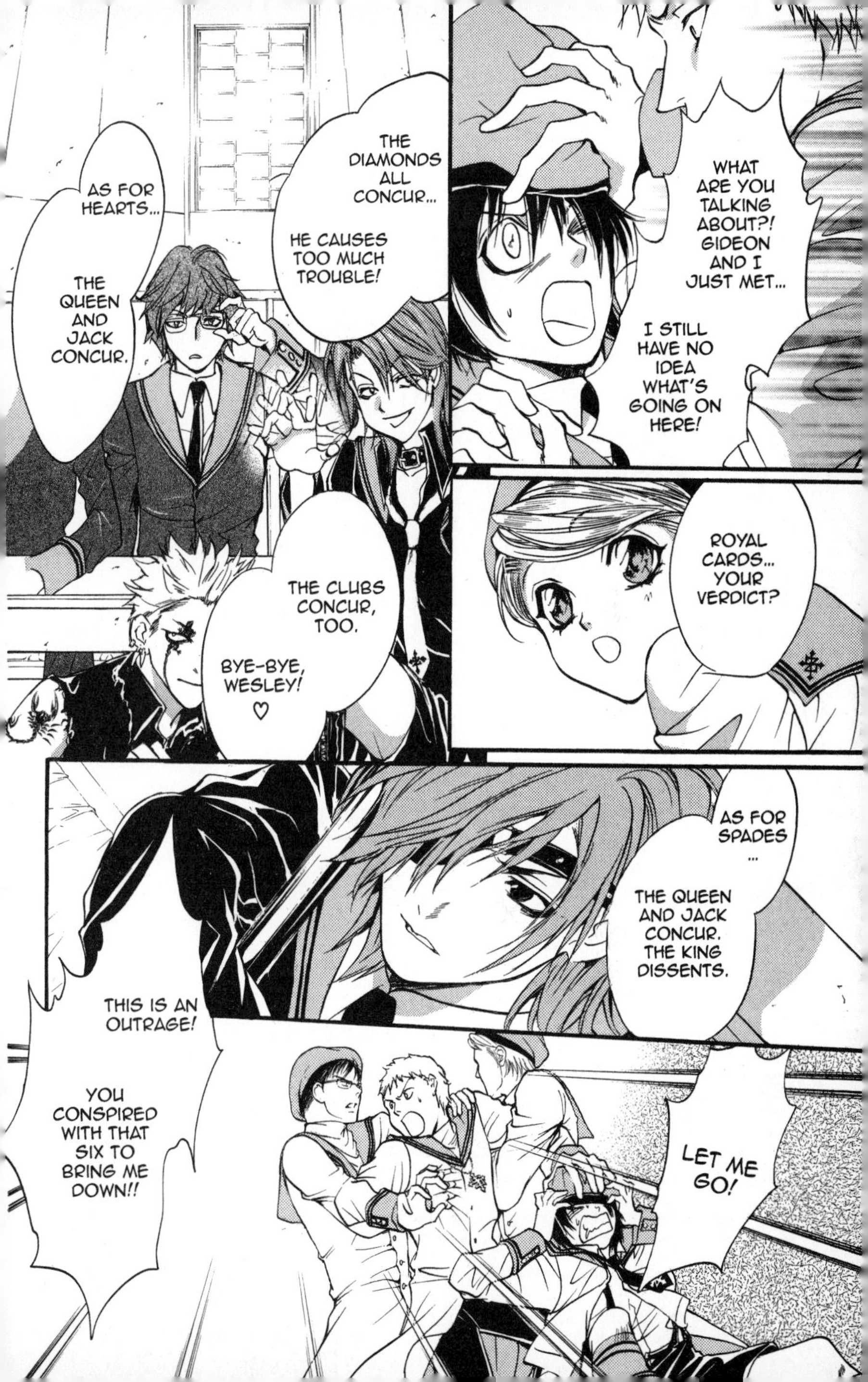

WHAT ARE YOU TALKING ABOUT?! GIDEON AND I JUST MET...
I STILL HAVE NO IDEA WHAT'S GOING ON HERE!
ROYAL CARDS... YOUR VERDICT?
THE DIAMONDS ALL CONCUR...
HE CAUSES TOO MUCH TROUBLE!
AS FOR HEARTS...
THE QUEEN AND JACK CONCUR.
THE CLUBS CONCUR, TOO.
BYE-BYE, WESLEY! ♡
AS FOR SPADES ...
THE QUEEN AND JACK CONCUR. THE KING DISSENTS.
LET ME GO!
THIS IS AN OUTRAGE!
YOU CONSPIRED WITH THAT SIX TO BRING ME DOWN!!

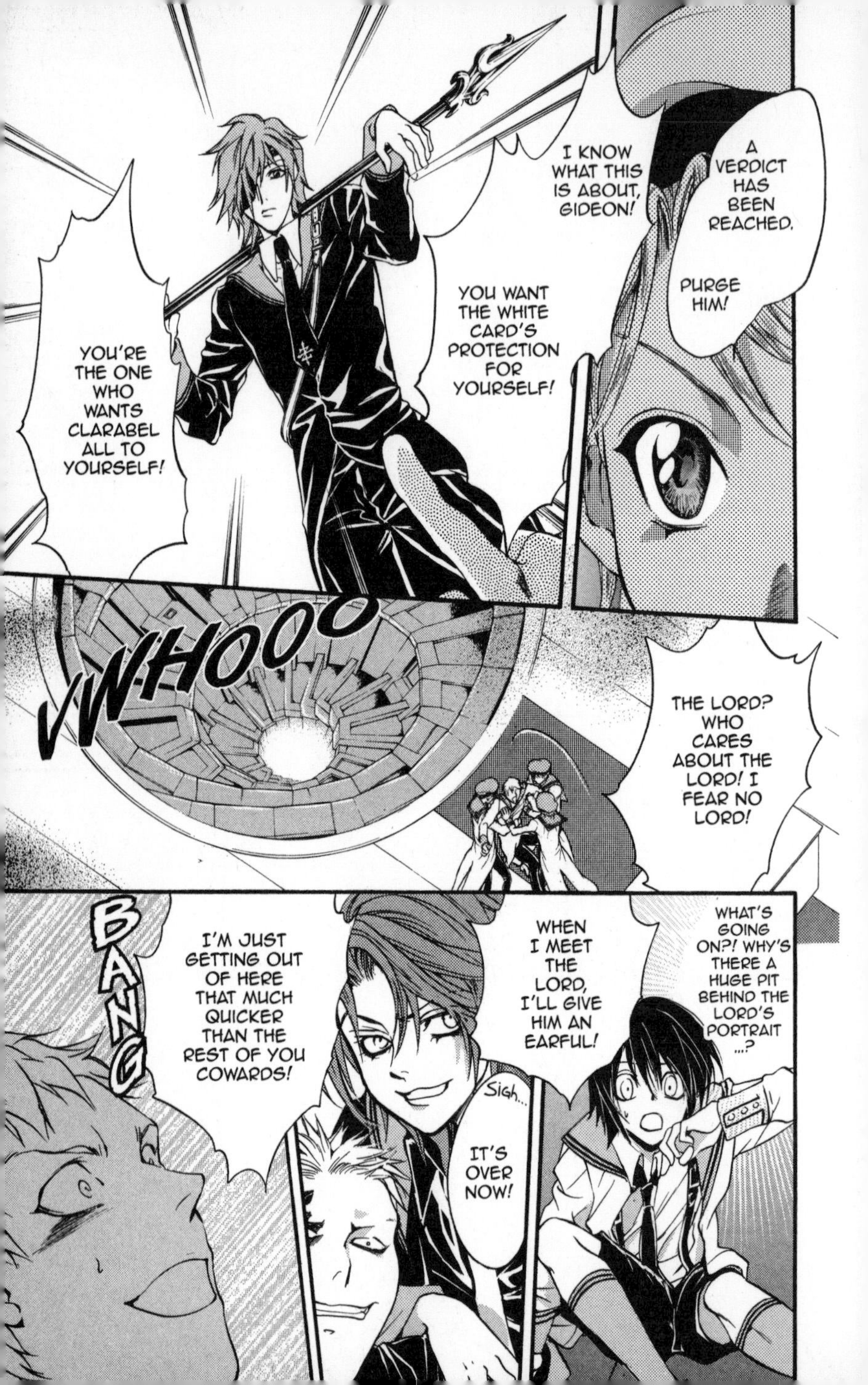
A VERDICT HAS BEEN REACHED.
PURGE HIM!
I KNOW WHAT THIS IS ABOUT, GIDEON!
YOU WANT THE WHITE CARD'S PROTECTION FOR YOURSELF!
YOU'RE THE ONE WHO WANTS CLARABEL ALL TO YOURSELF!
THE LORD? WHO CARES ABOUT THE LORD! I FEAR NO LORD!
VWHOOOO
WHAT'S GOING ON?! WHY'S THERE A HUGE PIT BEHIND THE LORD'S PORTRAIT ...?
WHEN I MEET THE LORD, I'LL GIVE HIM AN EARFUL!
I'M JUST GETTING OUT OF HERE THAT MUCH QUICKER THAN THE REST OF YOU COWARDS!
BANG
Sigh...
IT'S OVER NOW!

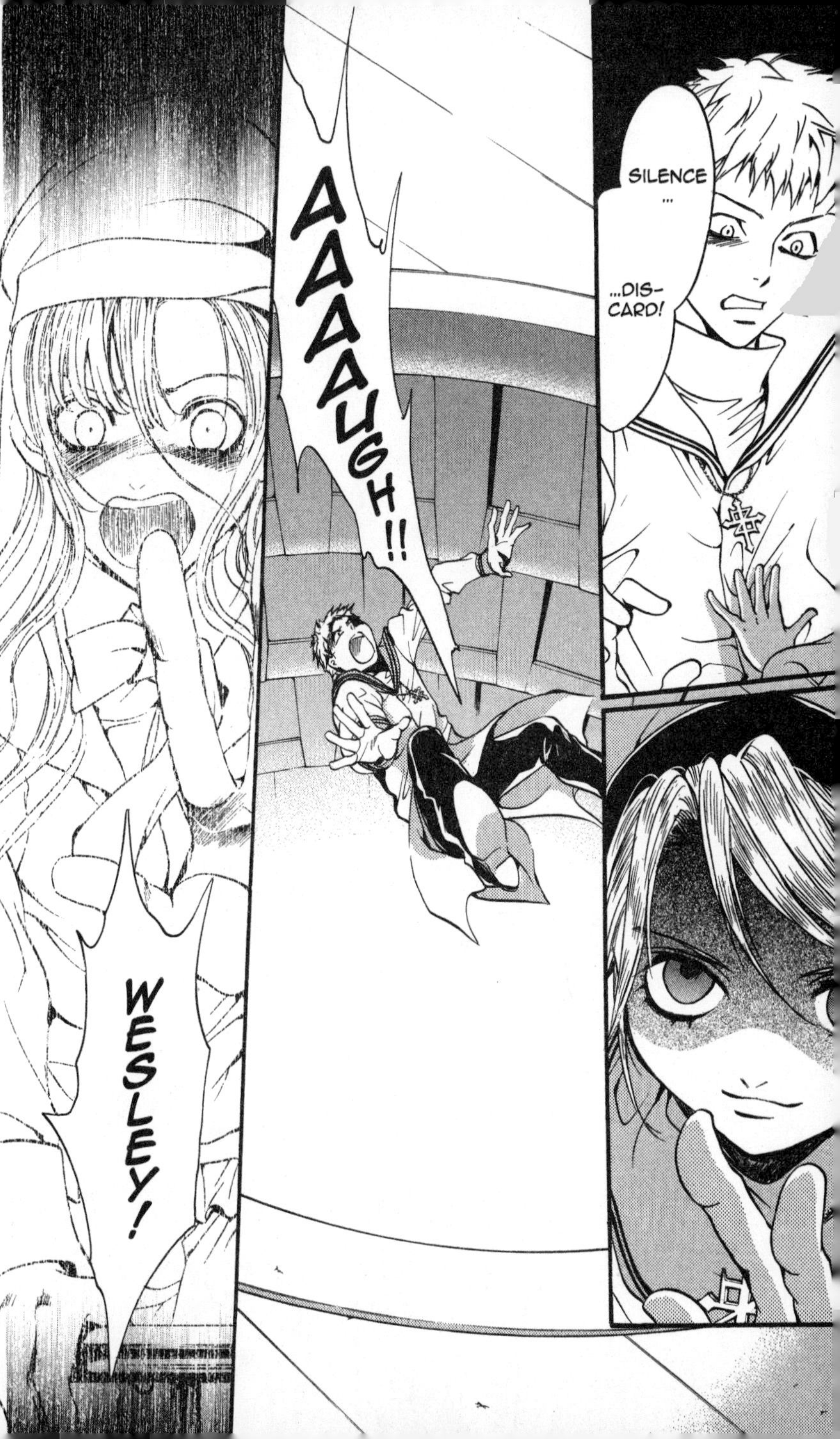
SILENCE ...
...DIS-CARD!
AAAAAUGH!!
WESLEY!

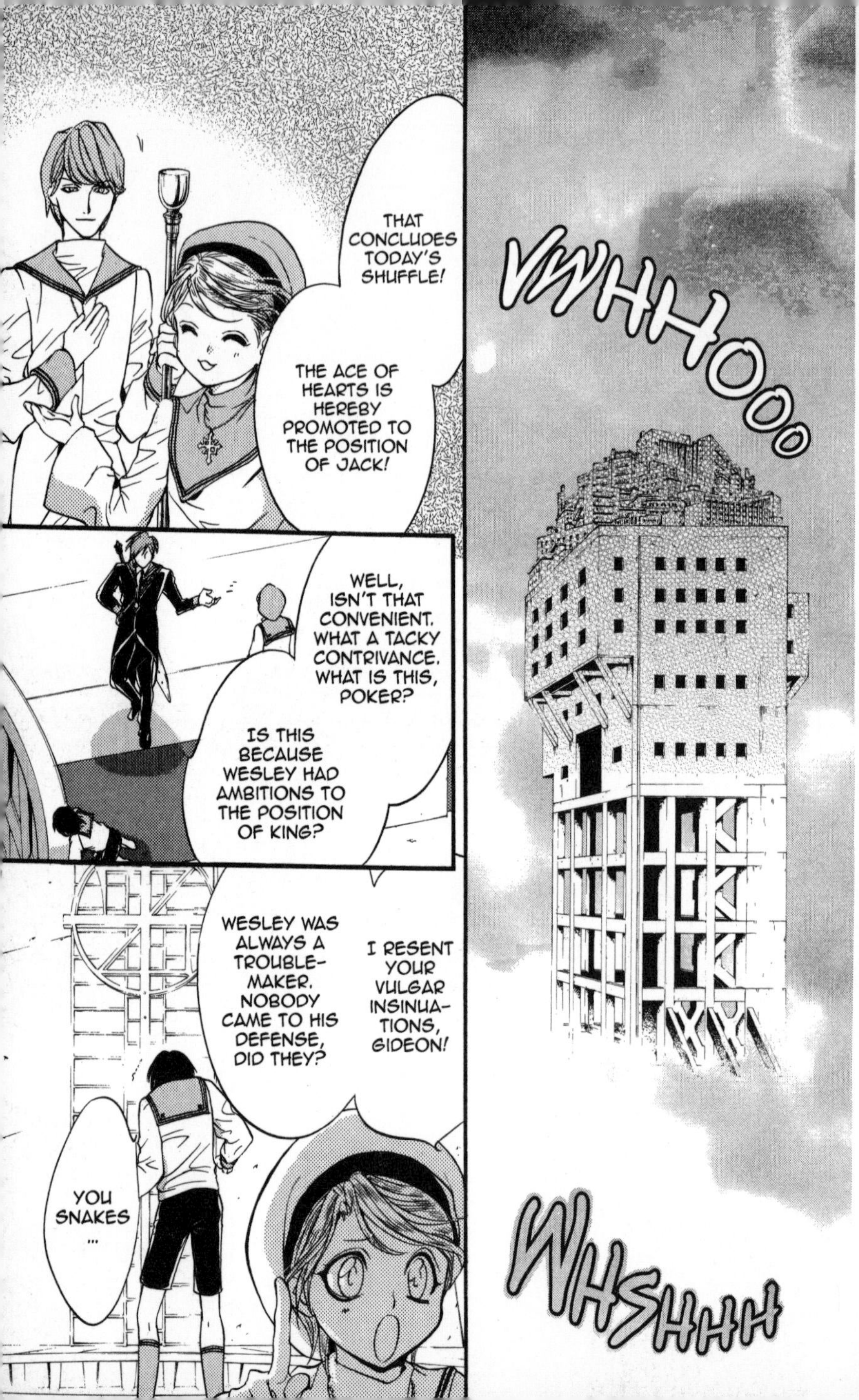
VWHHOOO
WHSHHH
THAT CONCLUDES TODAY'S SHUFFLE!
THE ACE OF HEARTS IS HEREBY PROMOTED TO THE POSITION OF JACK!
WELL, ISN'T THAT CONVENIENT. WHAT A TACKY CONTRIVANCE. WHAT IS THIS, POKER?
IS THIS BECAUSE WESLEY HAD AMBITIONS TO THE POSITION OF KING?
I RESENT YOUR VULGAR INSINUATIONS, GIDEON!
WESLEY WAS ALWAYS A TROUBLE-MAKER. NOBODY CAME TO HIS DEFENSE, DID THEY?
YOU SNAKES ...

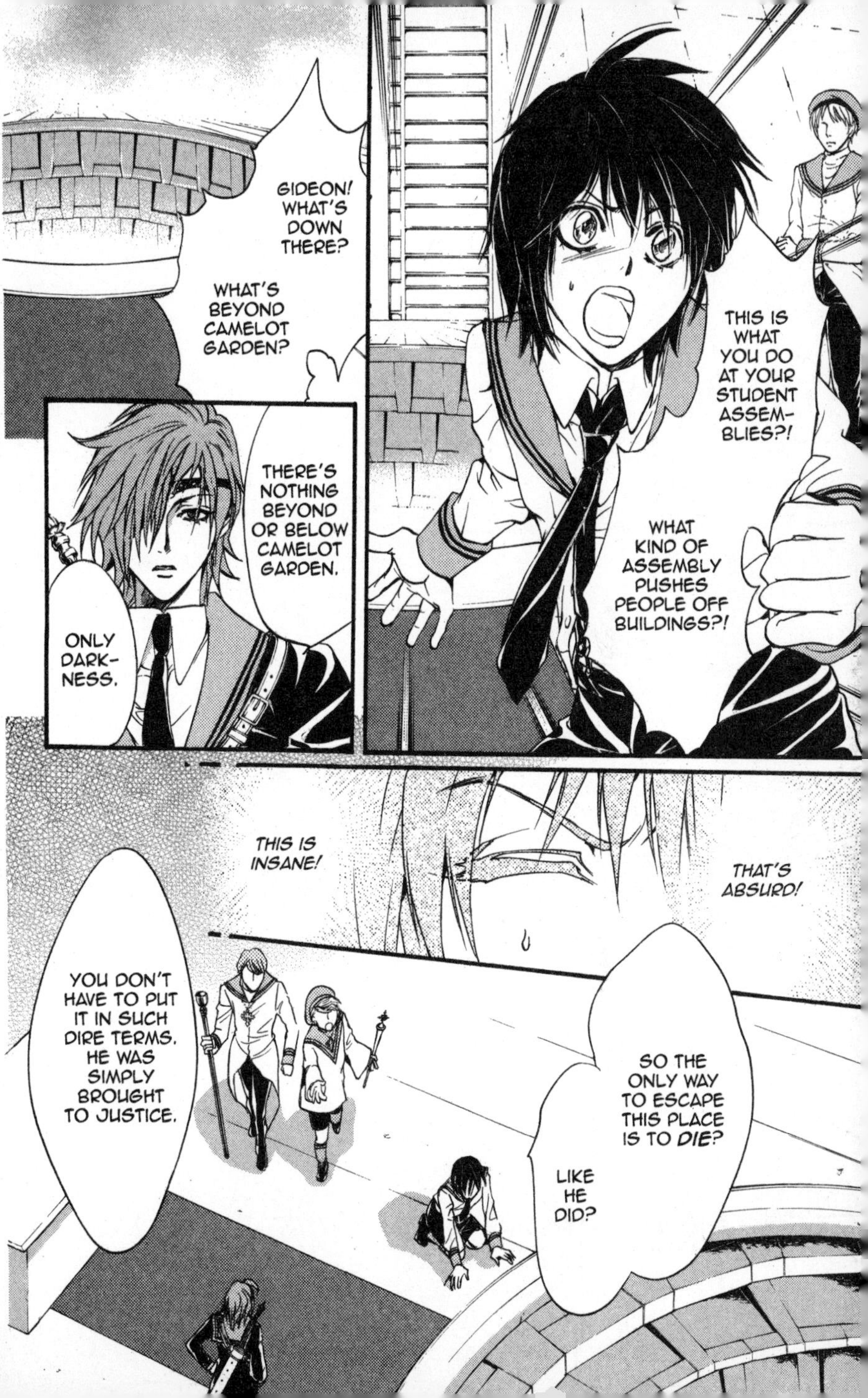
THIS IS WHAT YOU DO AT YOUR STUDENT ASSEMBLIES?!
WHAT KIND OF ASSEMBLY PUSHES PEOPLE OFF BUILDINGS?!
GIDEON! WHAT'S DOWN THERE?
WHAT'S BEYOND CAMELOT GARDEN?
THERE'S NOTHING BEYOND OR BELOW CAMELOT GARDEN.
ONLY DARKNESS.
THAT'S ABSURD!
THIS IS INSANE!
SO THE ONLY WAY TO ESCAPE THIS PLACE IS TO *DIE*?
LIKE HE DID?
YOU DON'T HAVE TO PUT IT IN SUCH DIRE TERMS. HE WAS SIMPLY BROUGHT TO JUSTICE.

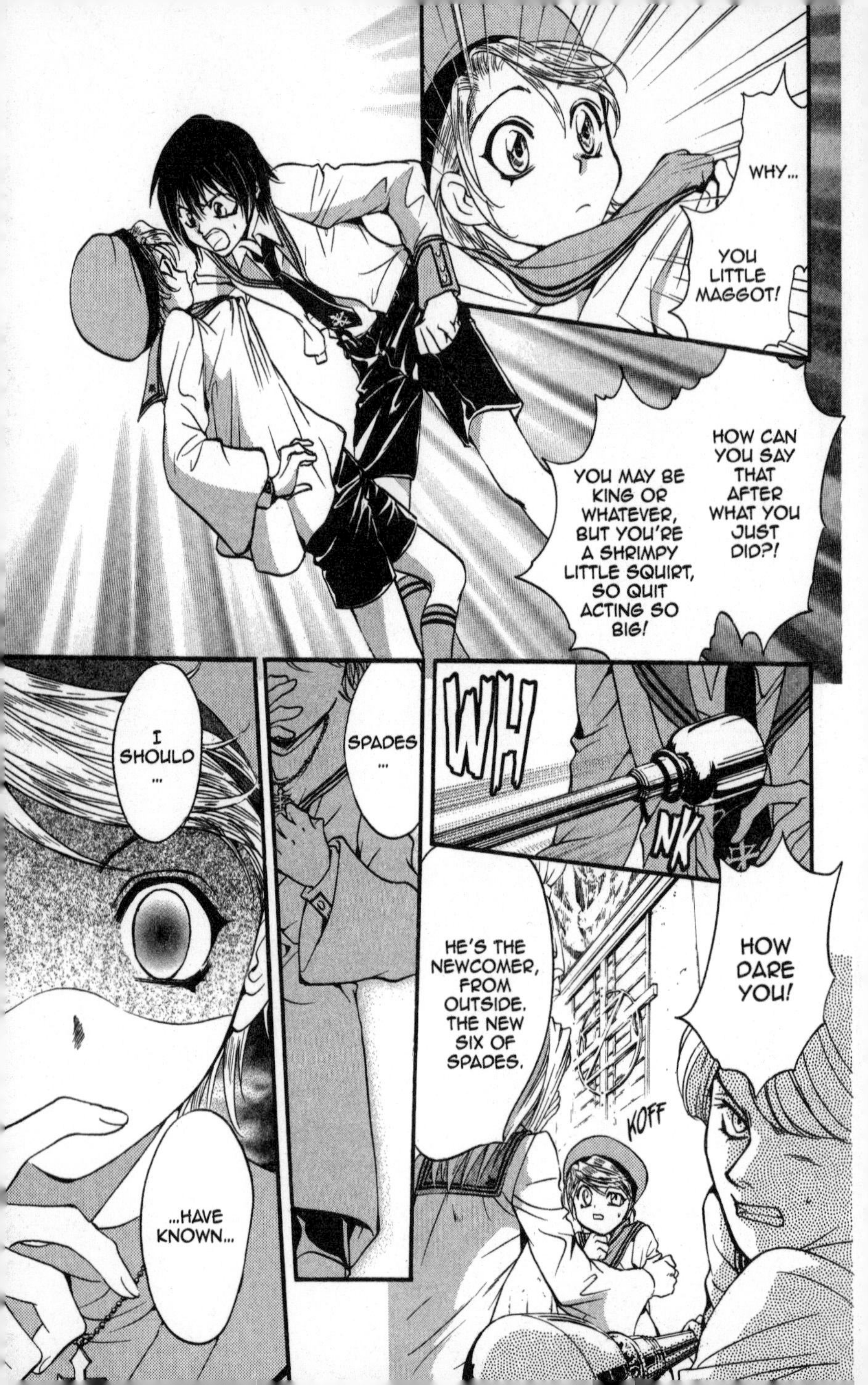
WHY...
YOU LITTLE MAGGOT!
HOW CAN YOU SAY THAT AFTER WHAT YOU JUST DID?!
YOU MAY BE KING OR WHATEVER, BUT YOU'RE A SHRIMPY LITTLE SQUIRT, SO QUIT ACTING SO BIG!
WH
NK
HOW DARE YOU!
HE'S THE NEWCOMER, FROM OUTSIDE. THE NEW SIX OF SPADES.
KOFF
SPADES...
I SHOULD...
...HAVE KNOWN...

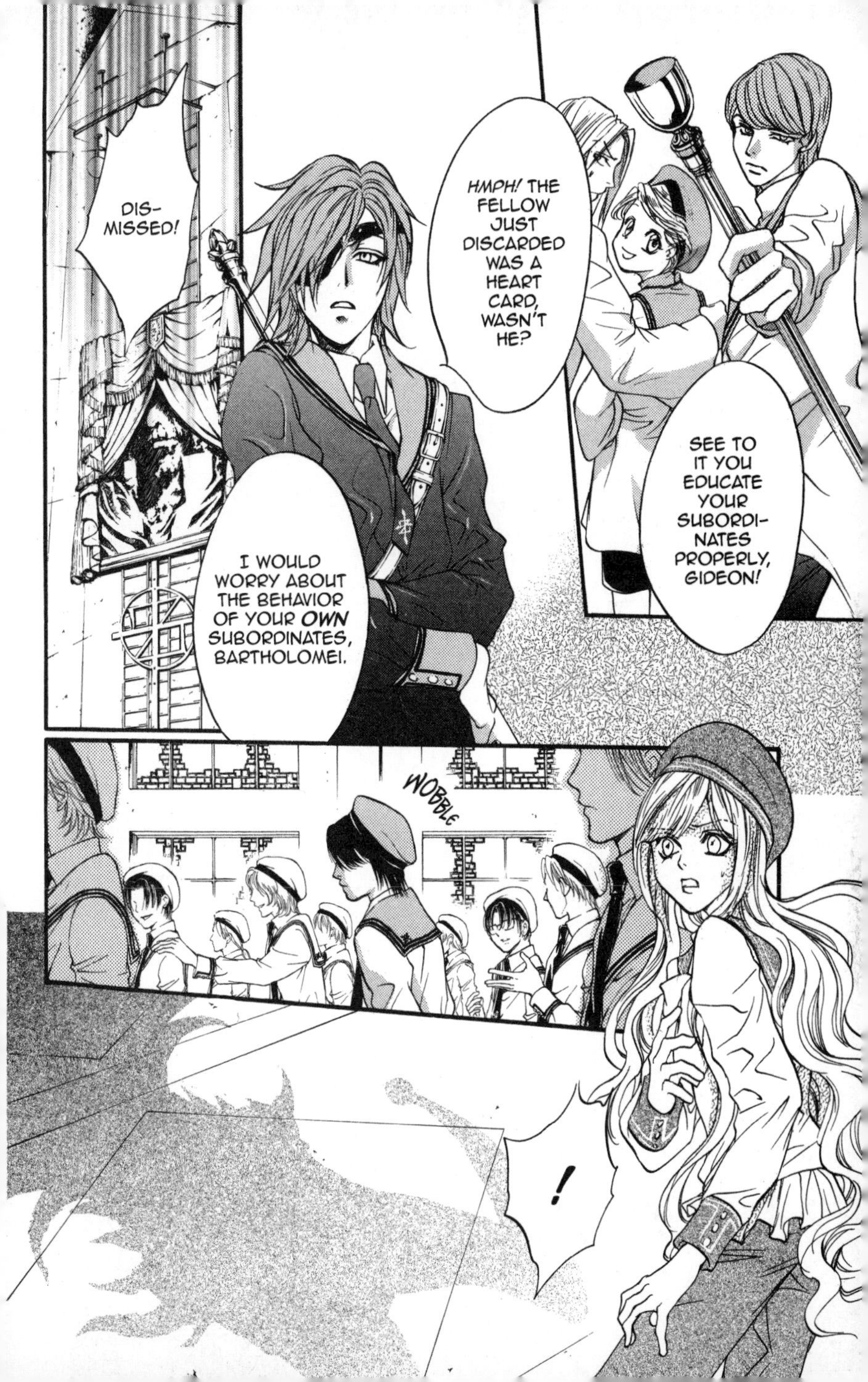
HMPH! THE FELLOW JUST DISCARDED WAS A HEART CARD, WASN'T HE?
SEE TO IT YOU EDUCATE YOUR SUBORDI-NATES PROPERLY, GIDEON!
DIS-MISSED!
I WOULD WORRY ABOUT THE BEHAVIOR OF YOUR OWN SUBORDINATES, BARTHOLOMEI.
WOBBLE
!

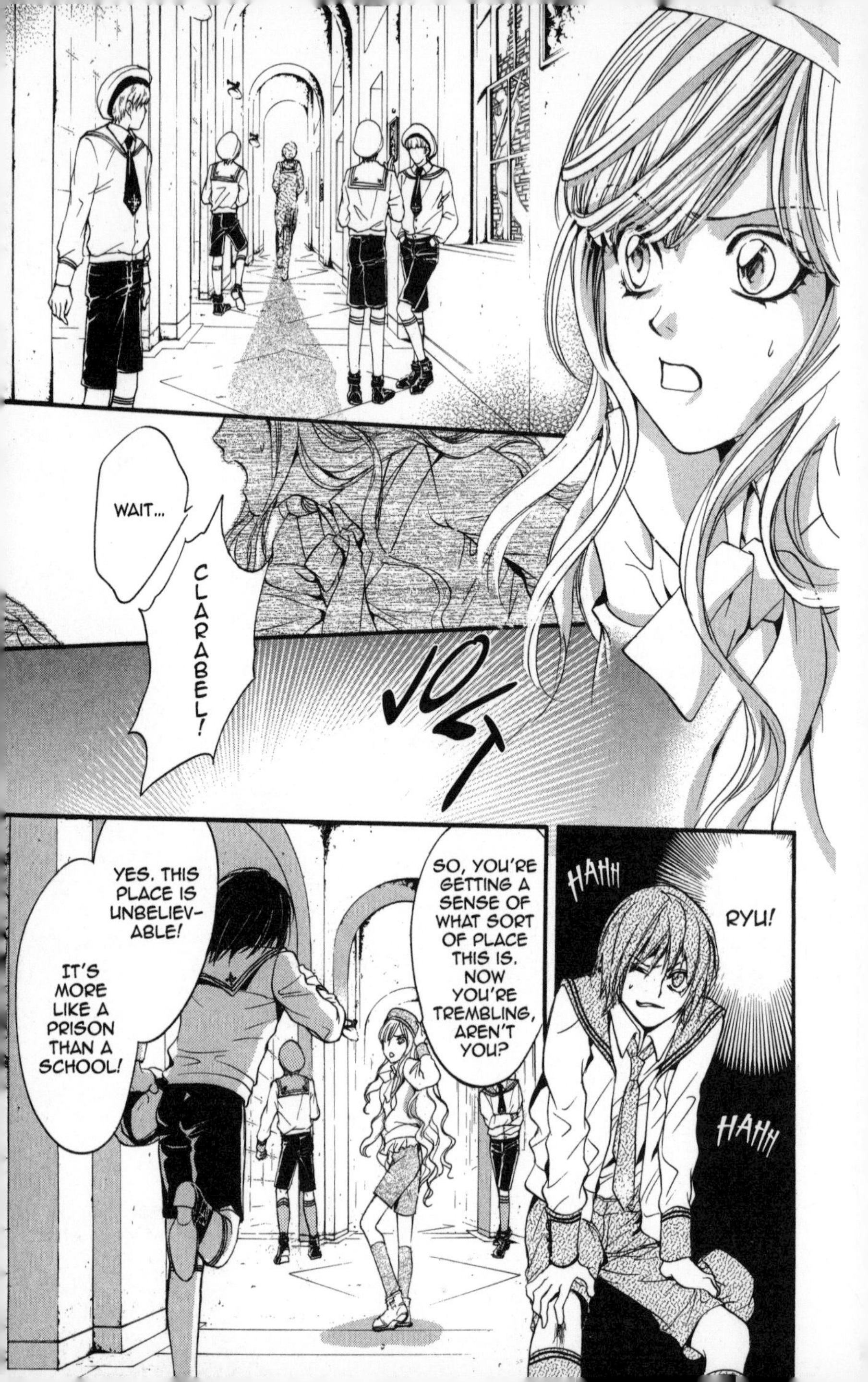
WAIT...
CLARABEL!
JOLT
HAHH
RYU!
HAHH
SO, YOU'RE GETTING A SENSE OF WHAT SORT OF PLACE THIS IS. NOW YOU'RE TREMBLING, AREN'T YOU?
YES. THIS PLACE IS UNBELIEV-ABLE!
IT'S MORE LIKE A PRISON THAN A SCHOOL!

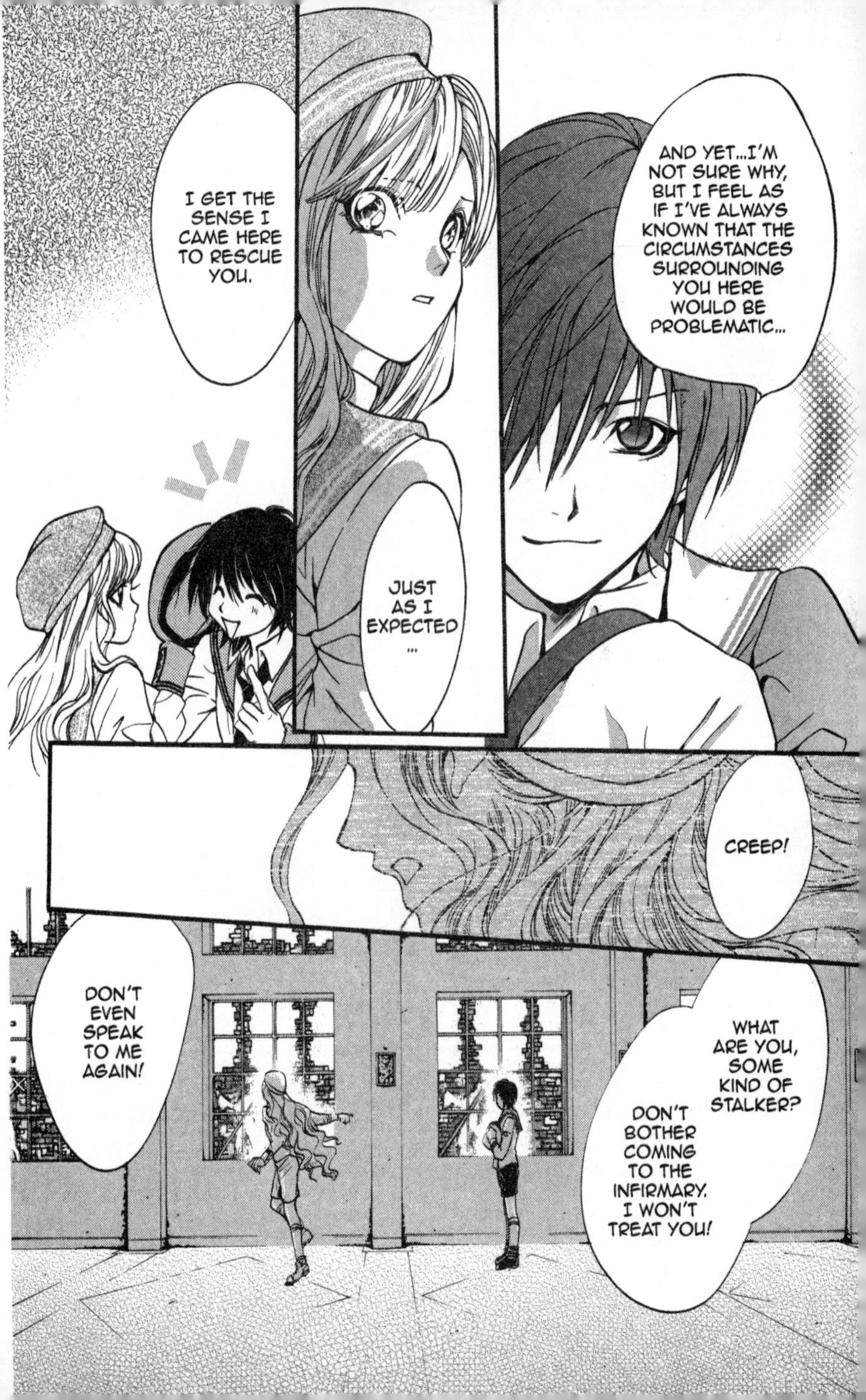
AND YET...I'M NOT SURE WHY, BUT I FEEL AS IF I'VE ALWAYS KNOWN THAT THE CIRCUMSTANCES SURROUNDING YOU HERE WOULD BE PROBLEMATIC...
JUST AS I EXPECTED ...
I GET THE SENSE I CAME HERE TO RESCUE YOU.
CREEP!
WHAT ARE YOU, SOME KIND OF STALKER?
DON'T BOTHER COMING TO THE INFIRMARY. I WON'T TREAT YOU!
DON'T EVEN SPEAK TO ME AGAIN!

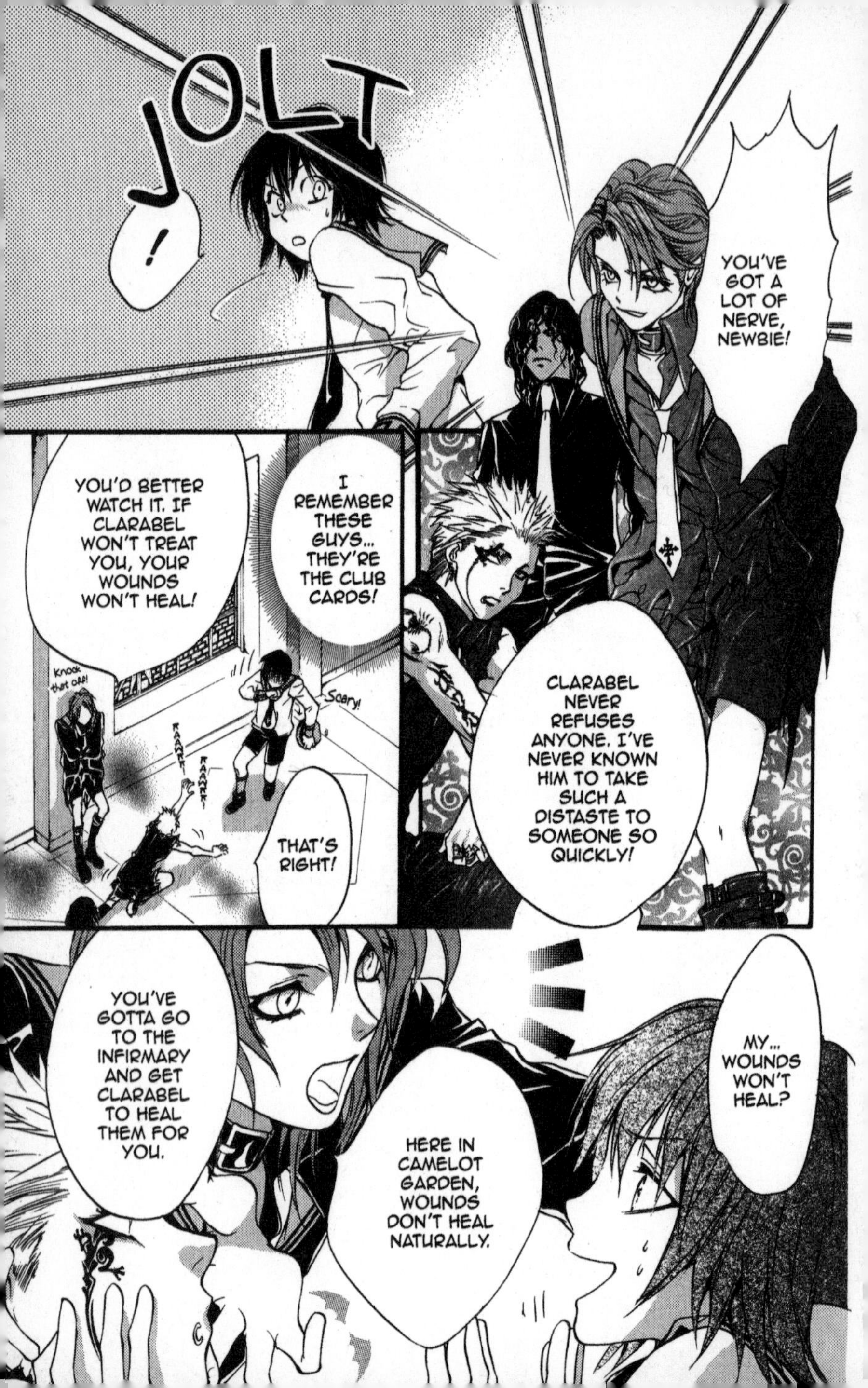
JOLT
!
YOU'VE GOT A LOT OF NERVE, NEWBIE!
CLARABEL NEVER REFUSES ANYONE. I'VE NEVER KNOWN HIM TO TAKE SUCH A DISTASTE TO SOMEONE SO QUICKLY!
I REMEMBER THESE GUYS... THEY'RE THE CLUB CARDS!
YOU'D BETTER WATCH IT. IF CLARABEL WON'T TREAT YOU, YOUR WOUNDS WON'T HEAL!
Scary!
RAAWR! RAAWR!
Knock that off!
THAT'S RIGHT!
MY... WOUNDS WON'T HEAL?
HERE IN CAMELOT GARDEN, WOUNDS DON'T HEAL NATURALLY.
YOU'VE GOTTA GO TO THE INFIRMARY AND GET CLARABEL TO HEAL THEM FOR YOU.

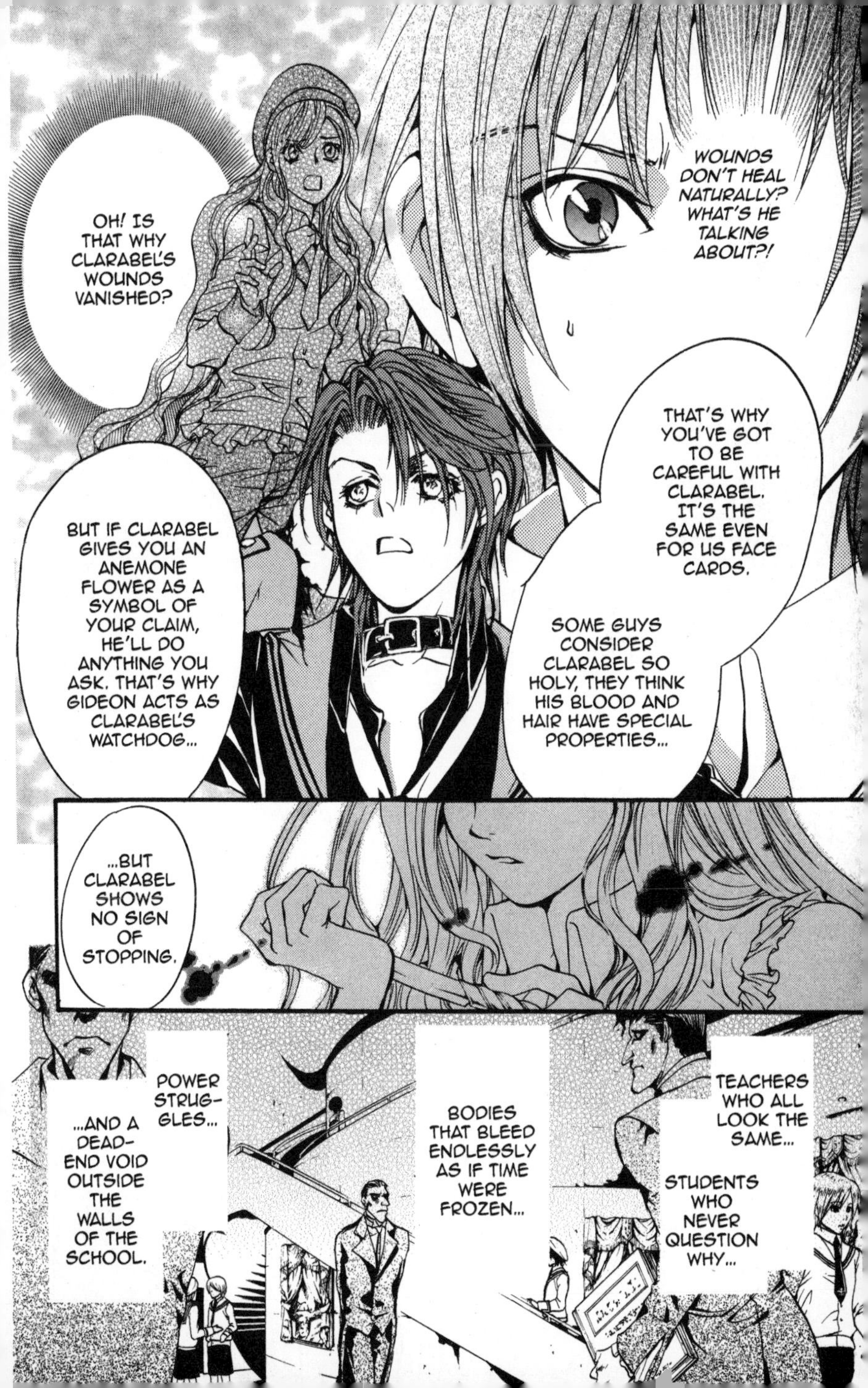
WOUNDS DON'T HEAL NATURALLY? WHAT'S HE TALKING ABOUT?!
OH! IS THAT WHY CLARABEL'S WOUNDS VANISHED?
THAT'S WHY YOU'VE GOT TO BE CAREFUL WITH CLARABEL. IT'S THE SAME EVEN FOR US FACE CARDS.
SOME GUYS CONSIDER CLARABEL SO HOLY, THEY THINK HIS BLOOD AND HAIR HAVE SPECIAL PROPERTIES...
BUT IF CLARABEL GIVES YOU AN ANEMONE FLOWER AS A SYMBOL OF YOUR CLAIM, HE'LL DO ANYTHING YOU ASK. THAT'S WHY GIDEON ACTS AS CLARABEL'S WATCHDOG...
...BUT CLARABEL SHOWS NO SIGN OF STOPPING.
TEACHERS WHO ALL LOOK THE SAME...
STUDENTS WHO NEVER QUESTION WHY...
BODIES THAT BLEED ENDLESSLY AS IF TIME WERE FROZEN...
POWER STRUG-GLES...
...AND A DEAD-END VOID OUTSIDE THE WALLS OF THE SCHOOL.

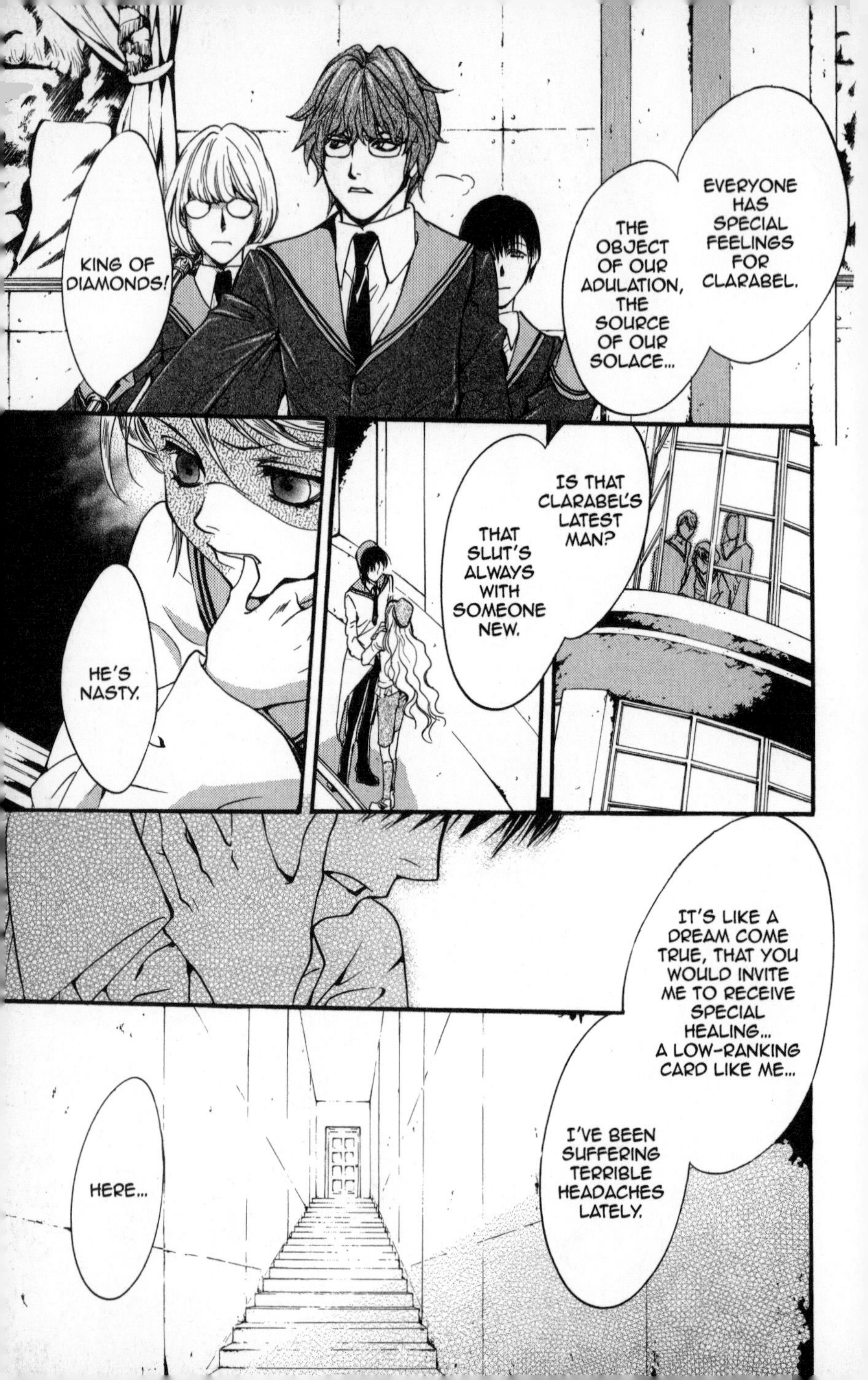
EVERYONE HAS SPECIAL FEELINGS FOR CLARABEL.
THE OBJECT OF OUR ADULATION, THE SOURCE OF OUR SOLACE...
KING OF DIAMONDS!
IS THAT CLARABEL'S LATEST MAN?
THAT SLUT'S ALWAYS WITH SOMEONE NEW.
HE'S NASTY.
IT'S LIKE A DREAM COME TRUE, THAT YOU WOULD INVITE ME TO RECEIVE SPECIAL HEALING... A LOW-RANKING CARD LIKE ME...
I'VE BEEN SUFFERING TERRIBLE HEADACHES LATELY.
HERE...

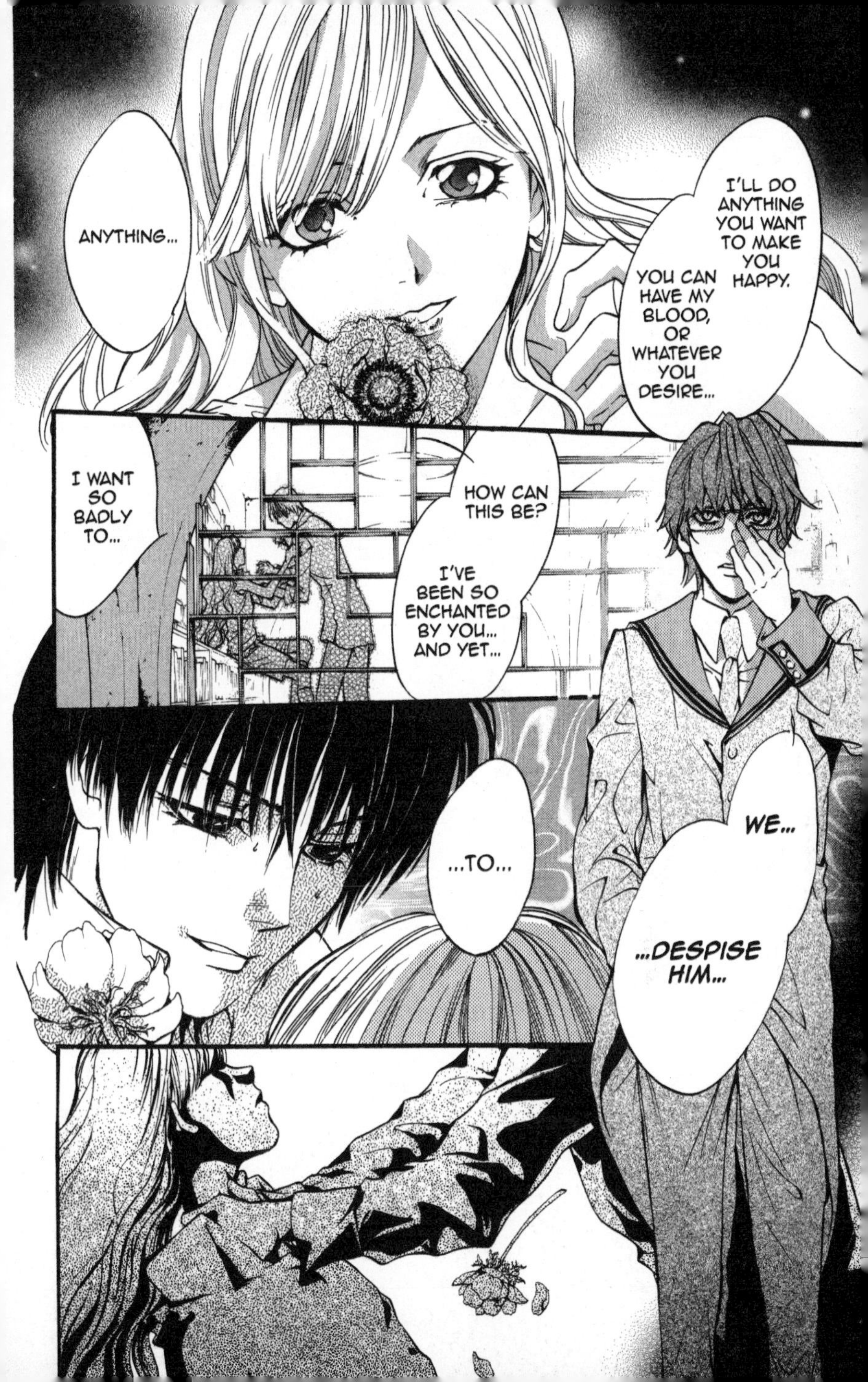
I'LL DO ANYTHING YOU WANT TO MAKE YOU HAPPY.
YOU CAN HAVE MY BLOOD, OR WHATEVER YOU DESIRE...
ANYTHING...
HOW CAN THIS BE?
I'VE BEEN SO ENCHANTED BY YOU... AND YET...
I WANT SO BADLY TO...
...TO...
WE...
...DESPISE HIM...

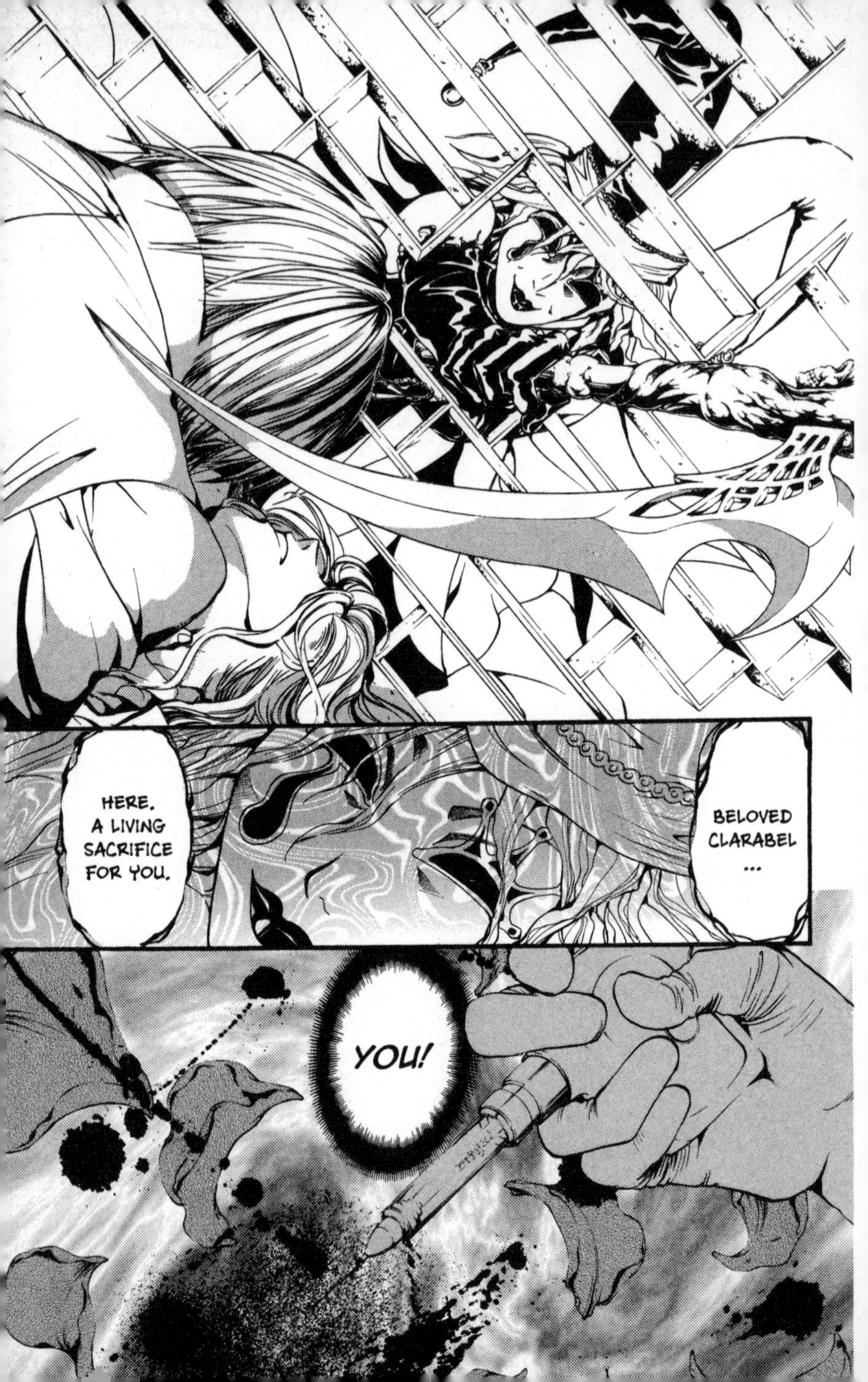
BELOVED CLARABEL ...
HERE. A LIVING SACRIFICE FOR YOU.
YOU!

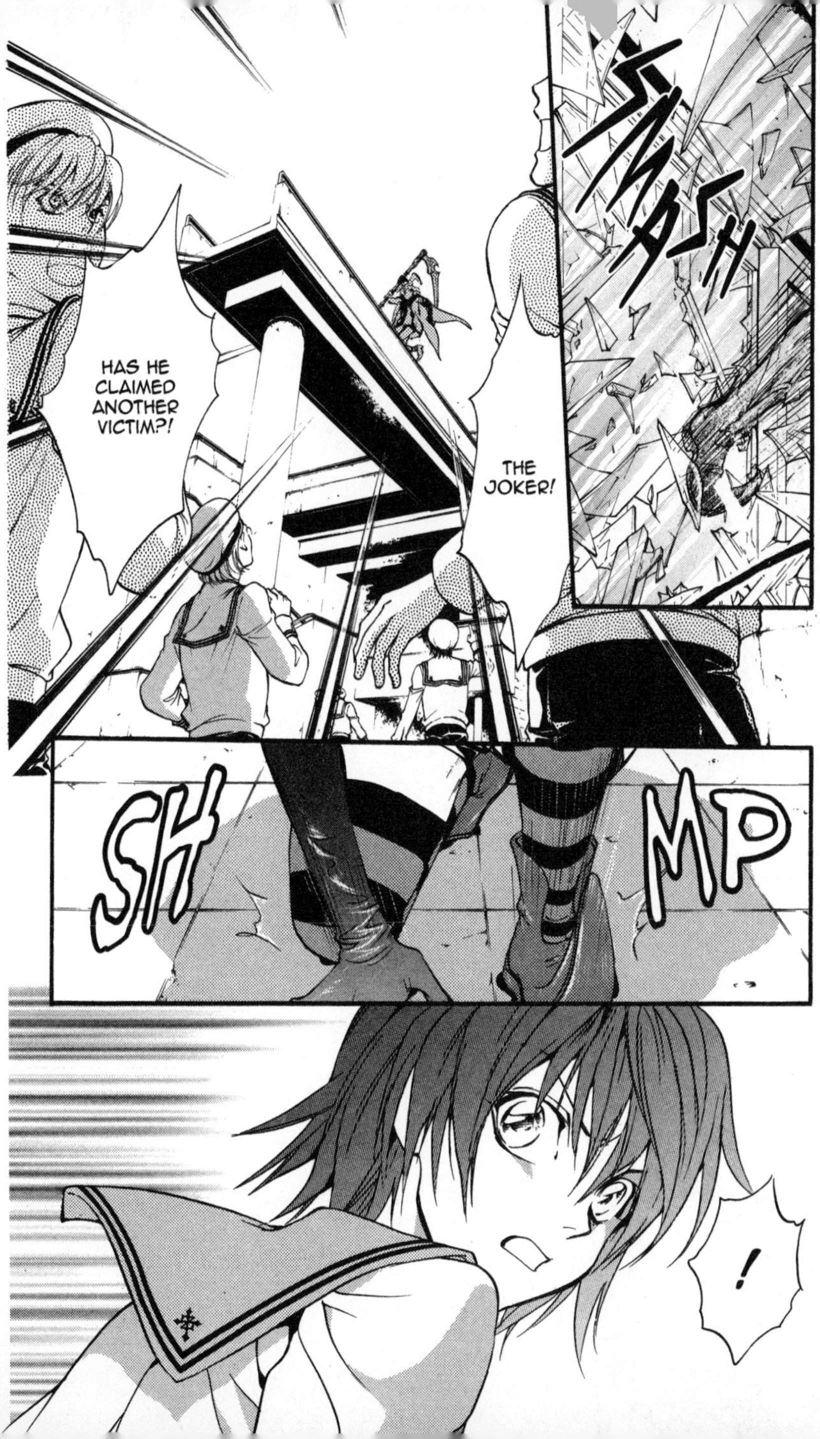
SMASH
THE JOKER!
HAS HE CLAIMED ANOTHER VICTIM?!
SH
MP
!

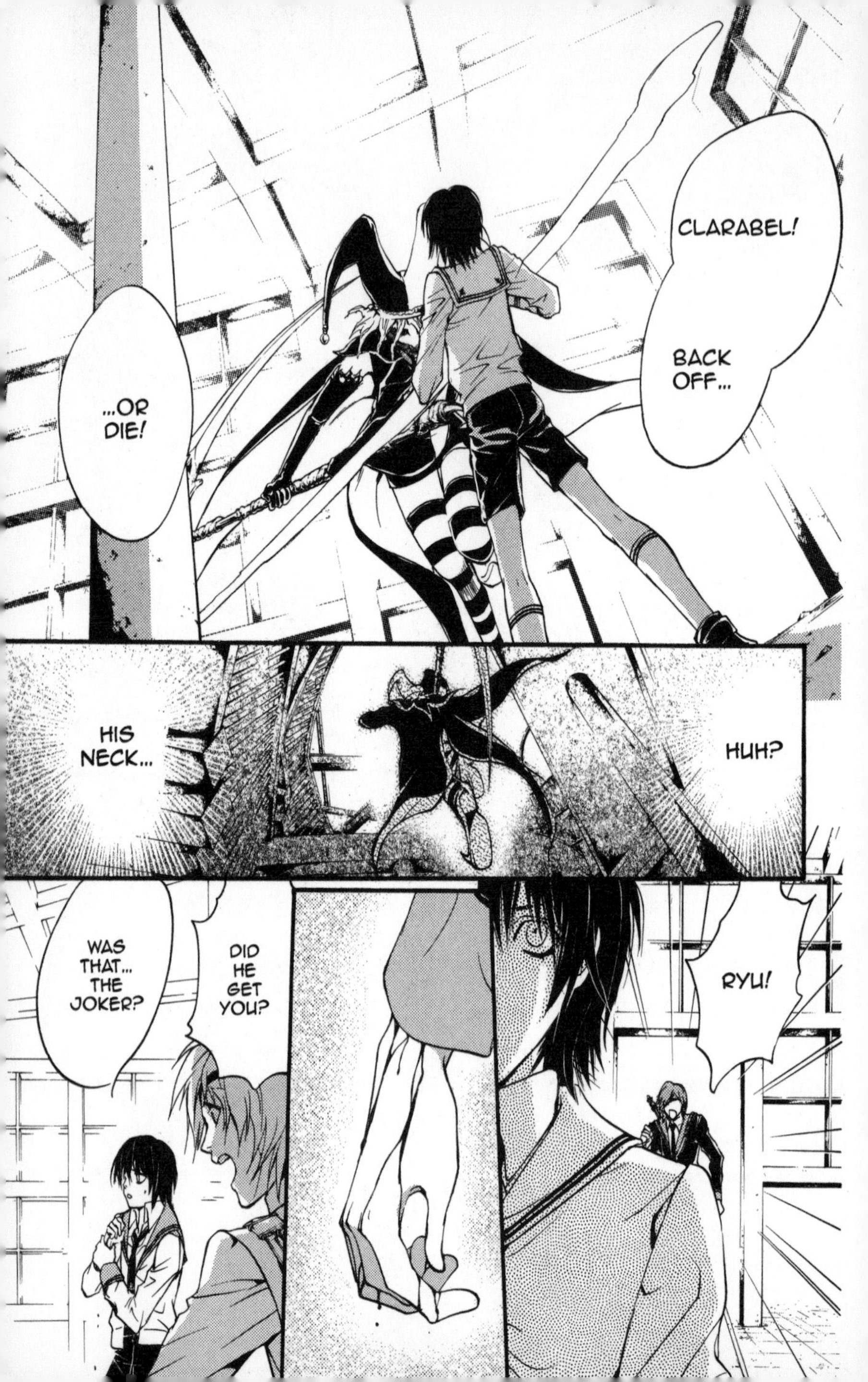
CLARABEL!
BACK OFF...
...OR DIE!
HUH?
HIS NECK...
RYU!
DID HE GET YOU?
WAS THAT... THE JOKER?

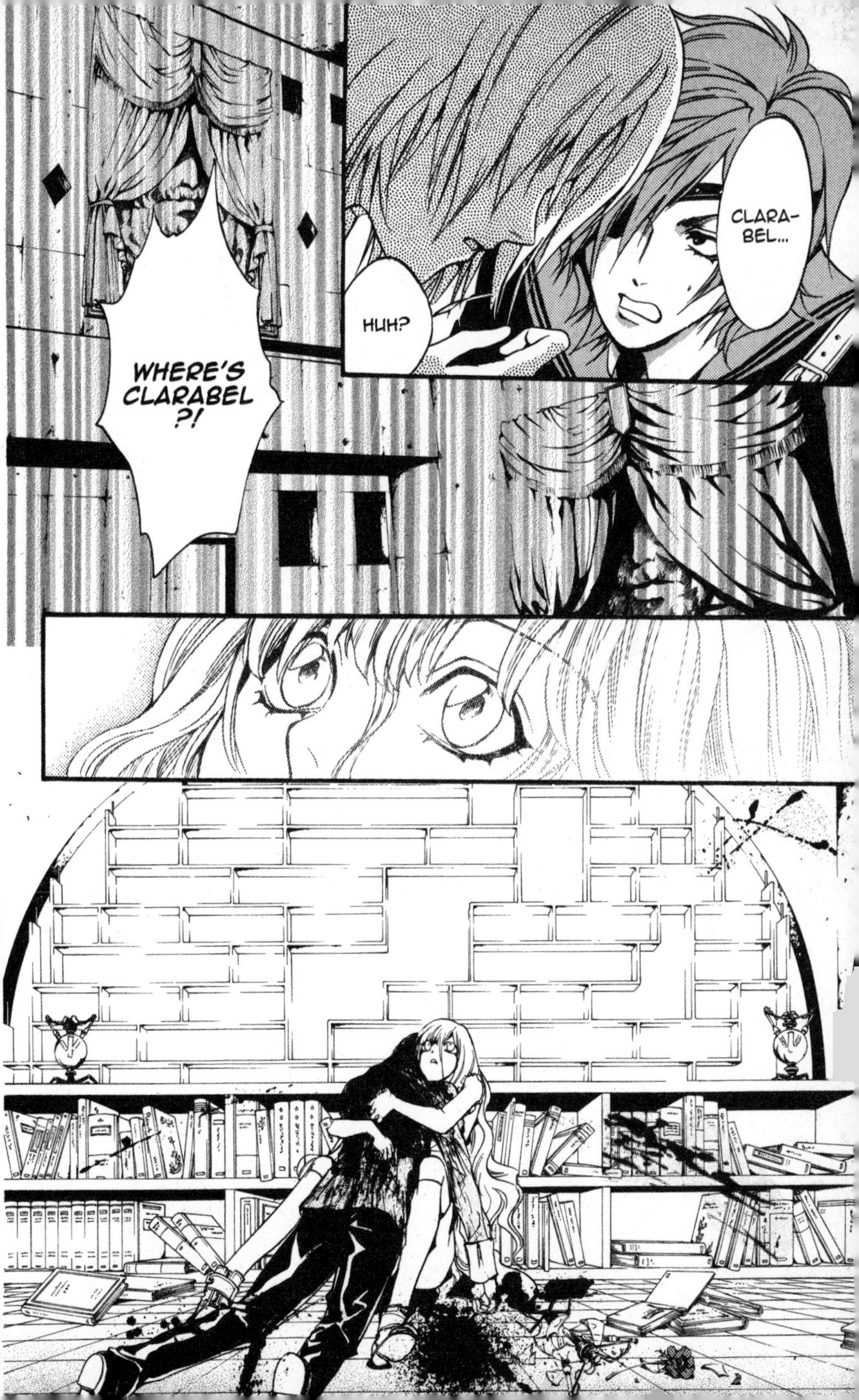
CLARA-BEL...
HUH?
WHERE'S CLARABEL ?!

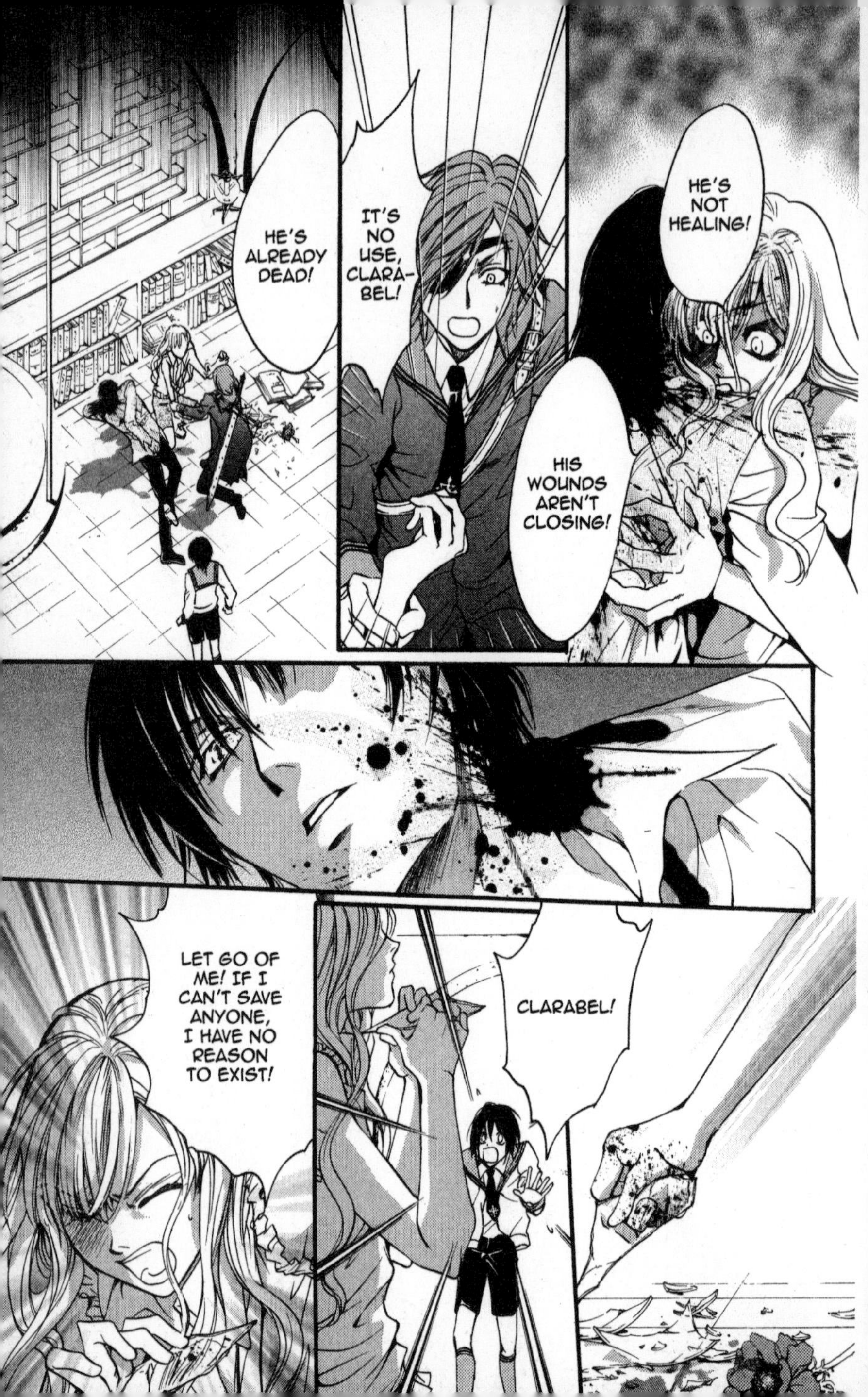
HE'S NOT HEALING!
HIS WOUNDS AREN'T CLOSING!
IT'S NO USE, CLARA-BEL!
HE'S ALREADY DEAD!
CLARABEL!
LET GO OF ME! IF I CAN'T SAVE ANYONE, I HAVE NO REASON TO EXIST!

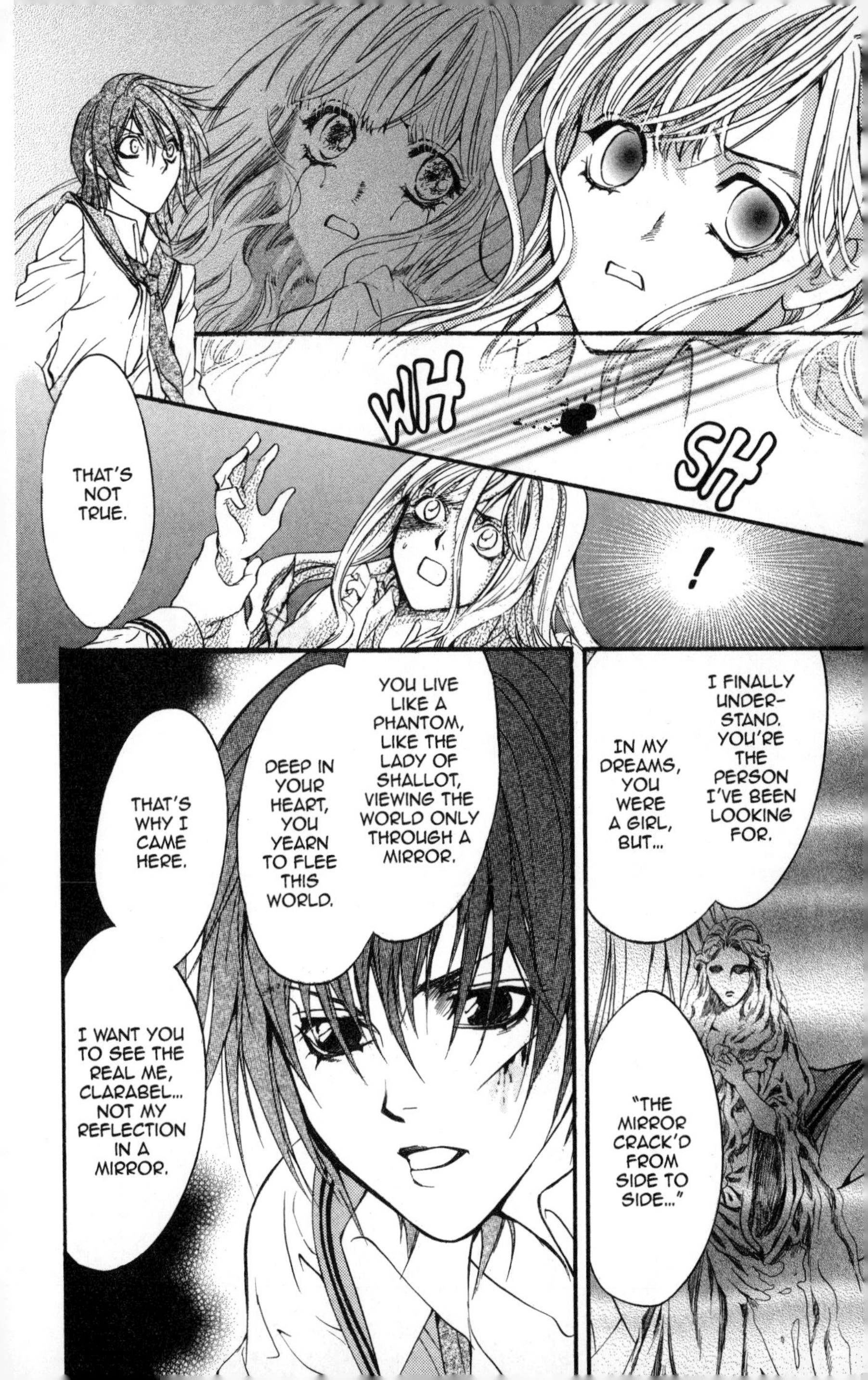
WH
SH
!
THAT'S NOT TRUE.
I FINALLY UNDER-STAND. YOU'RE THE PERSON I'VE BEEN LOOKING FOR.
IN MY DREAMS, YOU WERE A GIRL, BUT...
"THE MIRROR CRACK'D FROM SIDE TO SIDE..."
YOU LIVE LIKE A PHANTOM, LIKE THE LADY OF SHALLOT, VIEWING THE WORLD ONLY THROUGH A MIRROR.
DEEP IN YOUR HEART, YOU YEARN TO FLEE THIS WORLD.
THAT'S WHY I CAME HERE.
I WANT YOU TO SEE THE REAL ME, CLARABEL... NOT MY REFLECTION IN A MIRROR.

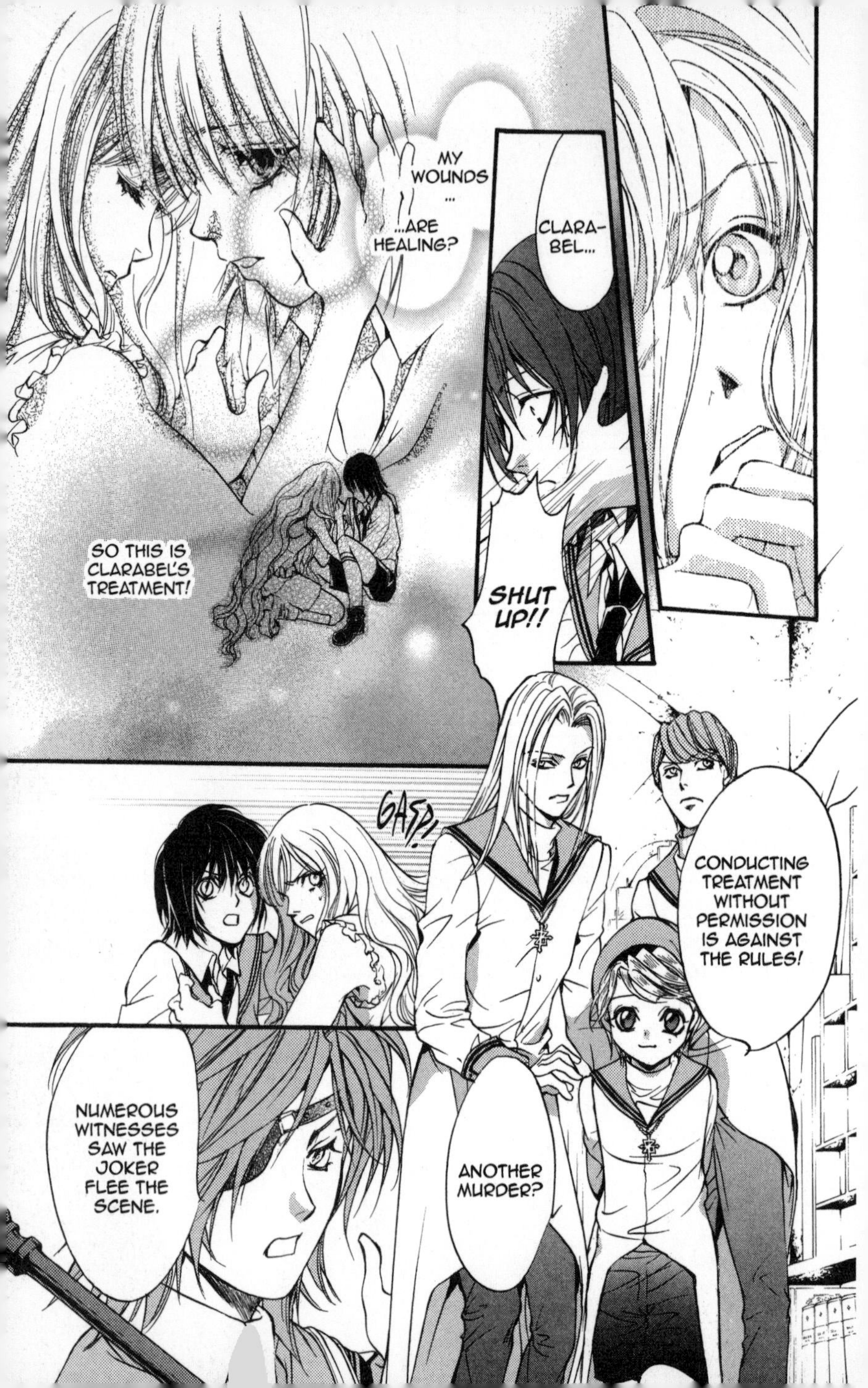
CLARA-BEL...
SHUT UP!!
MY WOUNDS ...
...ARE HEALING?
SO THIS IS CLARABEL'S TREATMENT!
CONDUCTING TREATMENT WITHOUT PERMISSION IS AGAINST THE RULES!
GASP!
ANOTHER MURDER?
NUMEROUS WITNESSES SAW THE JOKER FLEE THE SCENE.

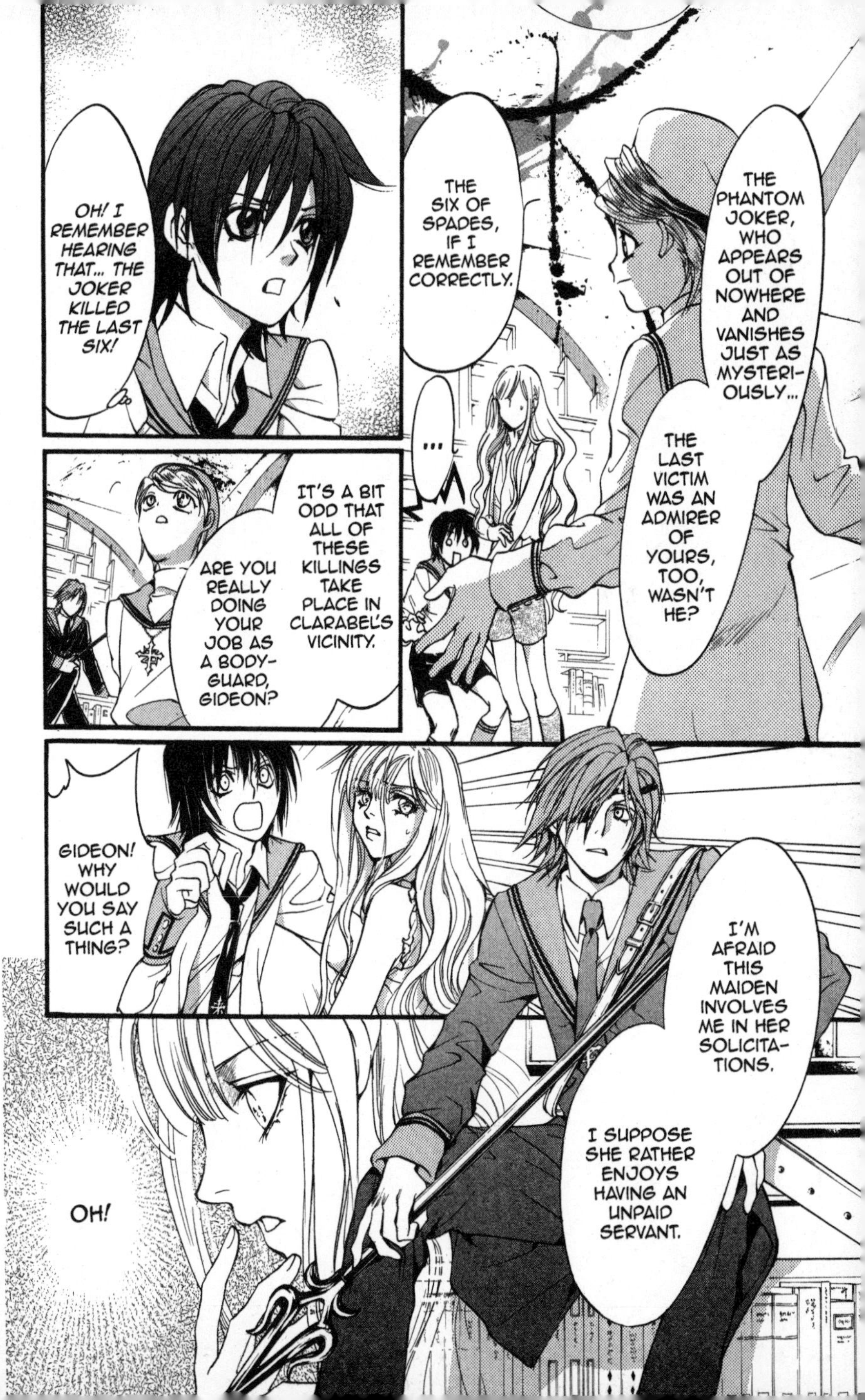
THE PHANTOM JOKER, WHO APPEARS OUT OF NOWHERE AND VANISHES JUST AS MYSTERIOUSLY...
THE SIX OF SPADES, IF I REMEMBER CORRECTLY.
THE LAST VICTIM WAS AN ADMIRER OF YOURS, TOO, WASN'T HE?
...
OH! I REMEMBER HEARING THAT... THE JOKER KILLED THE LAST SIX!
IT'S A BIT ODD THAT ALL OF THESE KILLINGS TAKE PLACE IN CLARABEL'S VICINITY.
ARE YOU REALLY DOING YOUR JOB AS A BODY-GUARD, GIDEON?
GIDEON! WHY WOULD YOU SAY SUCH A THING?
I'M AFRAID THIS MAIDEN INVOLVES ME IN HER SOLICITA-TIONS.
I SUPPOSE SHE RATHER ENJOYS HAVING AN UNPAID SERVANT.
OH!

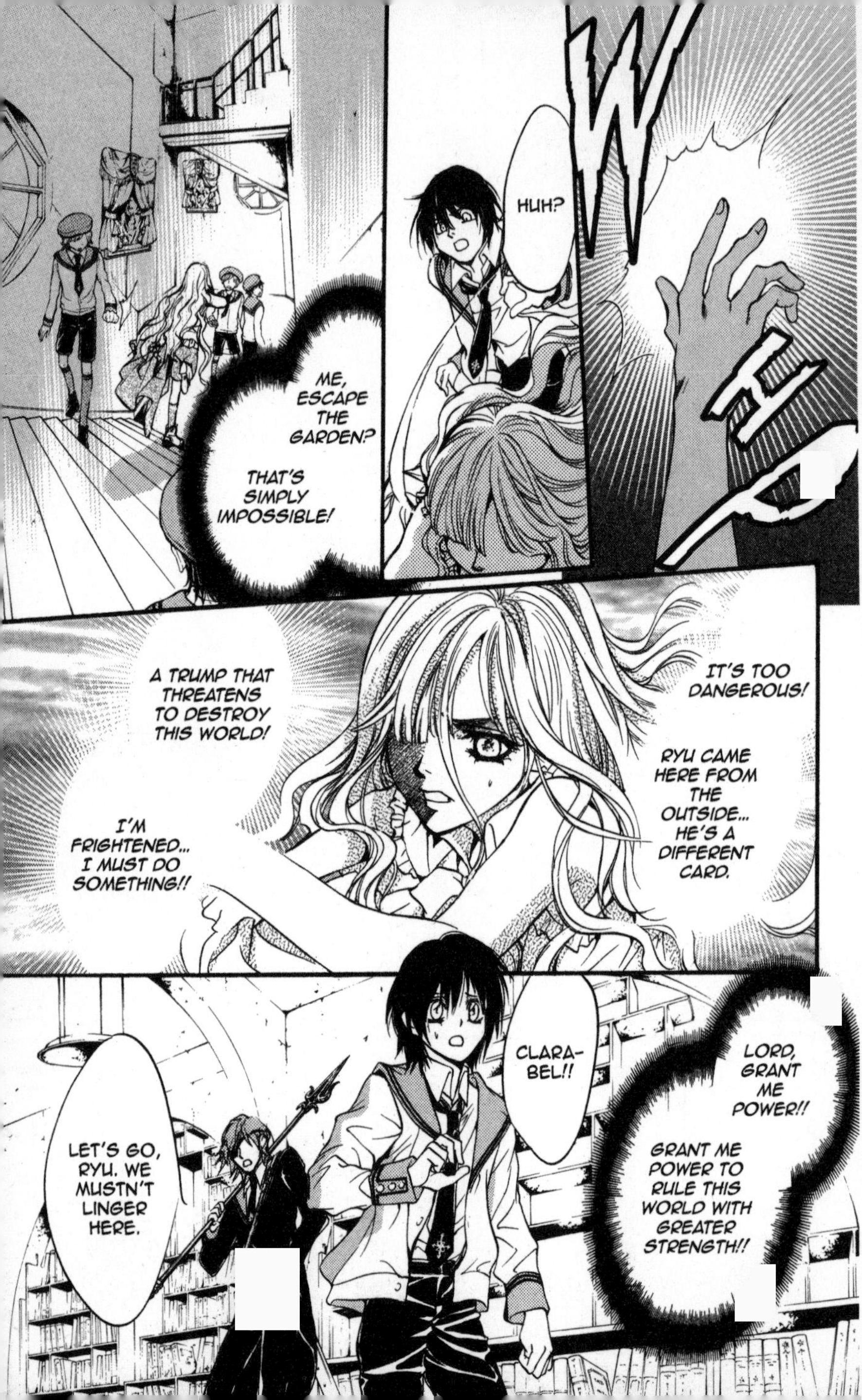
HUH?
ME, ESCAPE THE GARDEN?
THAT'S SIMPLY IMPOSSIBLE!
IT'S TOO DANGEROUS!
RYU CAME HERE FROM THE OUTSIDE... HE'S A DIFFERENT CARD.
A TRUMP THAT THREATENS TO DESTROY THIS WORLD!
I'M FRIGHTENED... I MUST DO SOMETHING!!
LORD, GRANT ME POWER!!
GRANT ME POWER TO RULE THIS WORLD WITH GREATER STRENGTH!!
CLARA-BEL!!
LET'S GO, RYU. WE MUSTN'T LINGER HERE.

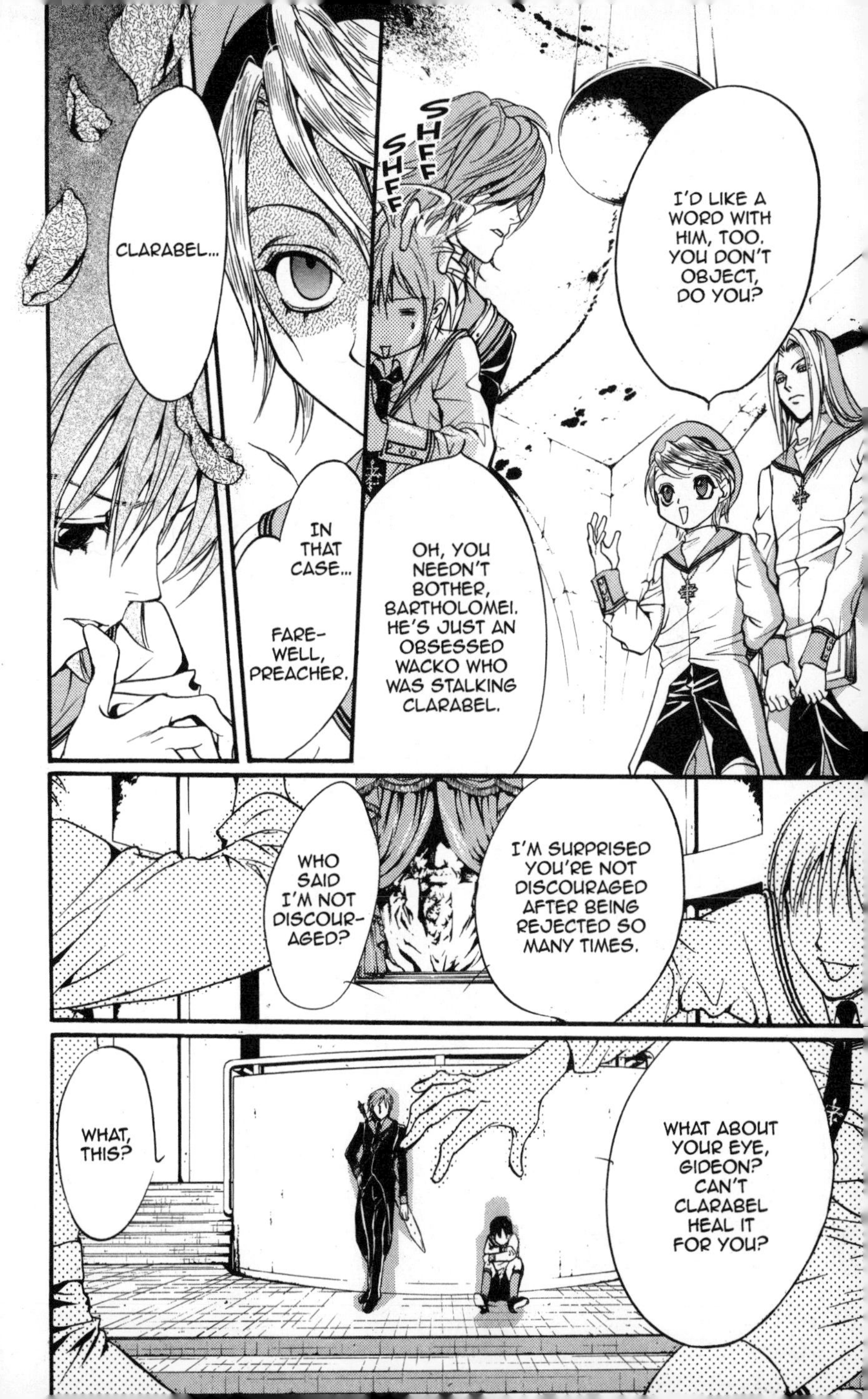
I'D LIKE A WORD WITH HIM, TOO. YOU DON'T OBJECT, DO YOU?
SHFF
SHFF
OH, YOU NEEDN'T BOTHER, BARTHOLOMEI. HE'S JUST AN OBSESSED WACKO WHO WAS STALKING CLARABEL.
IN THAT CASE...
FARE-WELL, PREACHER.
CLARABEL...
I'M SURPRISED YOU'RE NOT DISCOURAGED AFTER BEING REJECTED SO MANY TIMES.
WHO SAID I'M NOT DISCOUR-AGED?
WHAT ABOUT YOUR EYE, GIDEON? CAN'T CLARABEL HEAL IT FOR YOU?
WHAT, THIS?

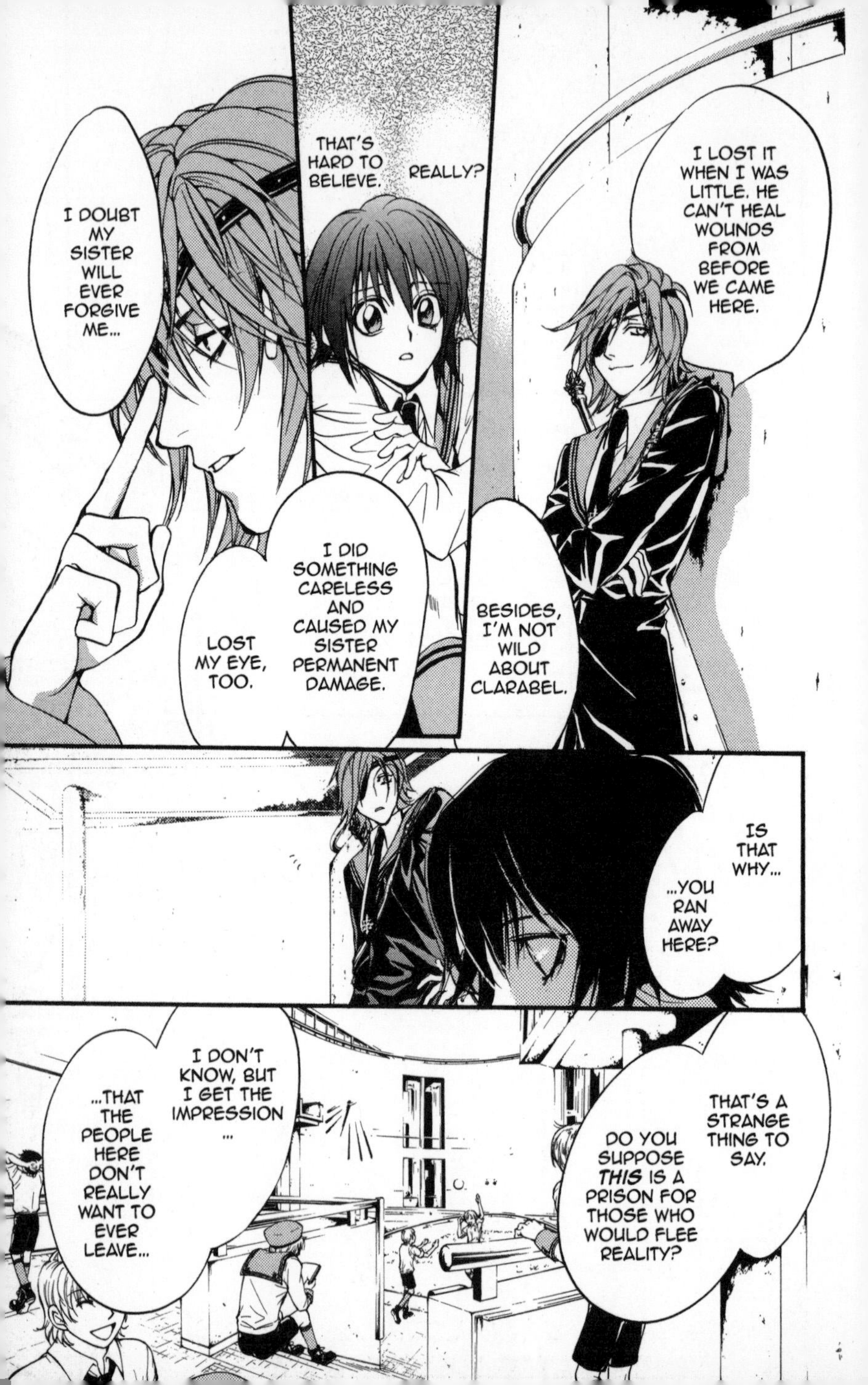
I LOST IT WHEN I WAS LITTLE. HE CAN'T HEAL WOUNDS FROM BEFORE WE CAME HERE.
BESIDES, I'M NOT WILD ABOUT CLARABEL.
REALLY?
THAT'S HARD TO BELIEVE.
I DID SOMETHING CARELESS AND CAUSED MY SISTER PERMANENT DAMAGE.
LOST MY EYE, TOO.
I DOUBT MY SISTER WILL EVER FORGIVE ME...
IS THAT WHY...
...YOU RAN AWAY HERE?
THAT'S A STRANGE THING TO SAY.
DO YOU SUPPOSE *THIS* IS A PRISON FOR THOSE WHO WOULD FLEE REALITY?
I DON'T KNOW, BUT I GET THE IMPRESSION...
...THAT THE PEOPLE HERE DON'T REALLY WANT TO EVER LEAVE...

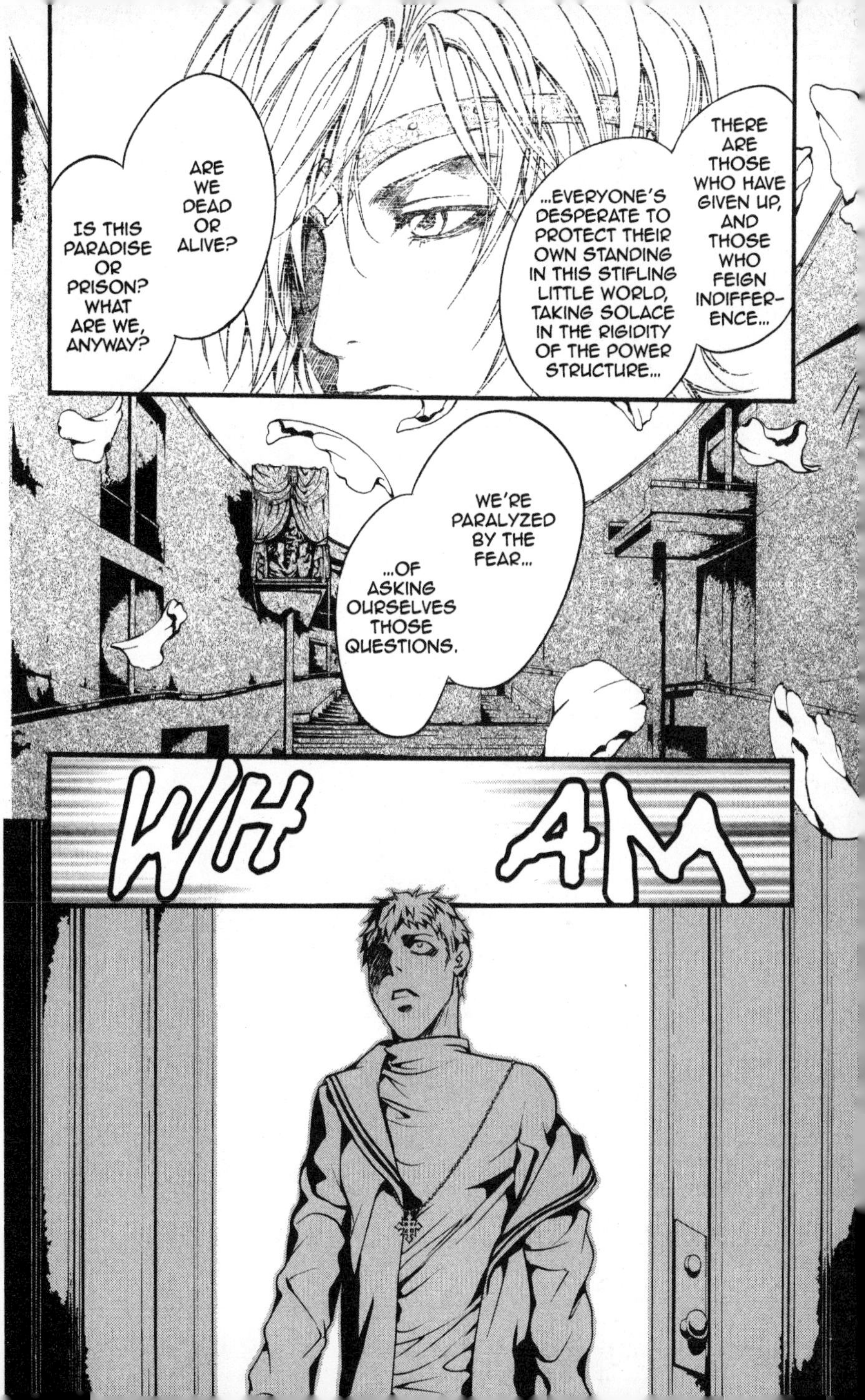
THERE ARE THOSE WHO HAVE GIVEN UP, AND THOSE WHO FEIGN INDIFFER-ENCE...
...EVERYONE'S DESPERATE TO PROTECT THEIR OWN STANDING IN THIS STIFLING LITTLE WORLD, TAKING SOLACE IN THE RIGIDITY OF THE POWER STRUCTURE...
ARE WE DEAD OR ALIVE?
IS THIS PARADISE OR PRISON? WHAT ARE WE, ANYWAY?
WE'RE PARALYZED BY THE FEAR...
...OF ASKING OURSELVES THOSE QUESTIONS.
WH AM

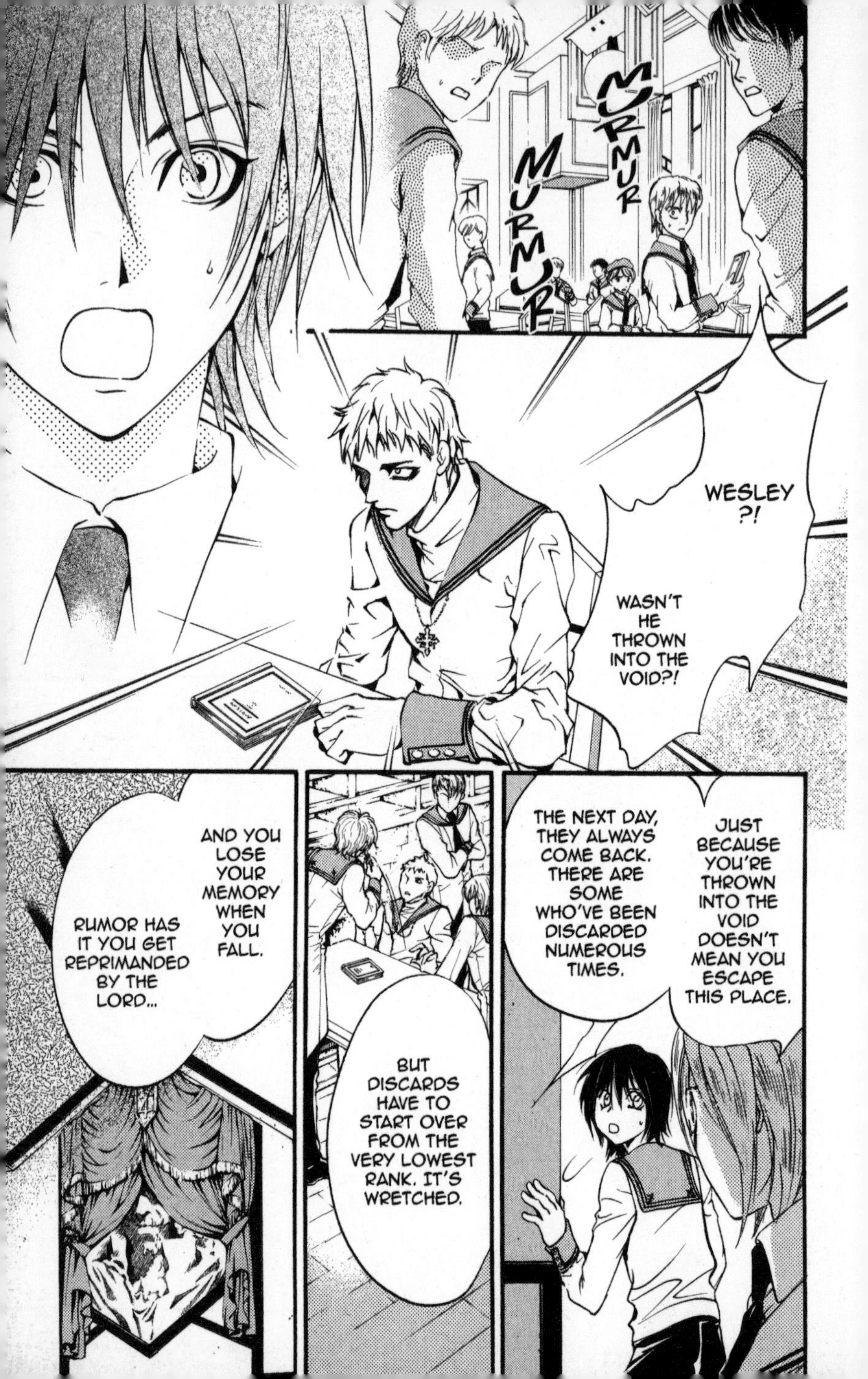
MURMUR
MURMUR
WESLEY?!
WASN'T HE THROWN INTO THE VOID?!
JUST BECAUSE YOU'RE THROWN INTO THE VOID DOESN'T MEAN YOU ESCAPE THIS PLACE.
THE NEXT DAY, THEY ALWAYS COME BACK. THERE ARE SOME WHO'VE BEEN DISCARDED NUMEROUS TIMES.
BUT DISCARDS HAVE TO START OVER FROM THE VERY LOWEST RANK. IT'S WRETCHED.
RUMOR HAS IT YOU GET REPRIMANDED BY THE LORD...
AND YOU LOSE YOUR MEMORY WHEN YOU FALL.

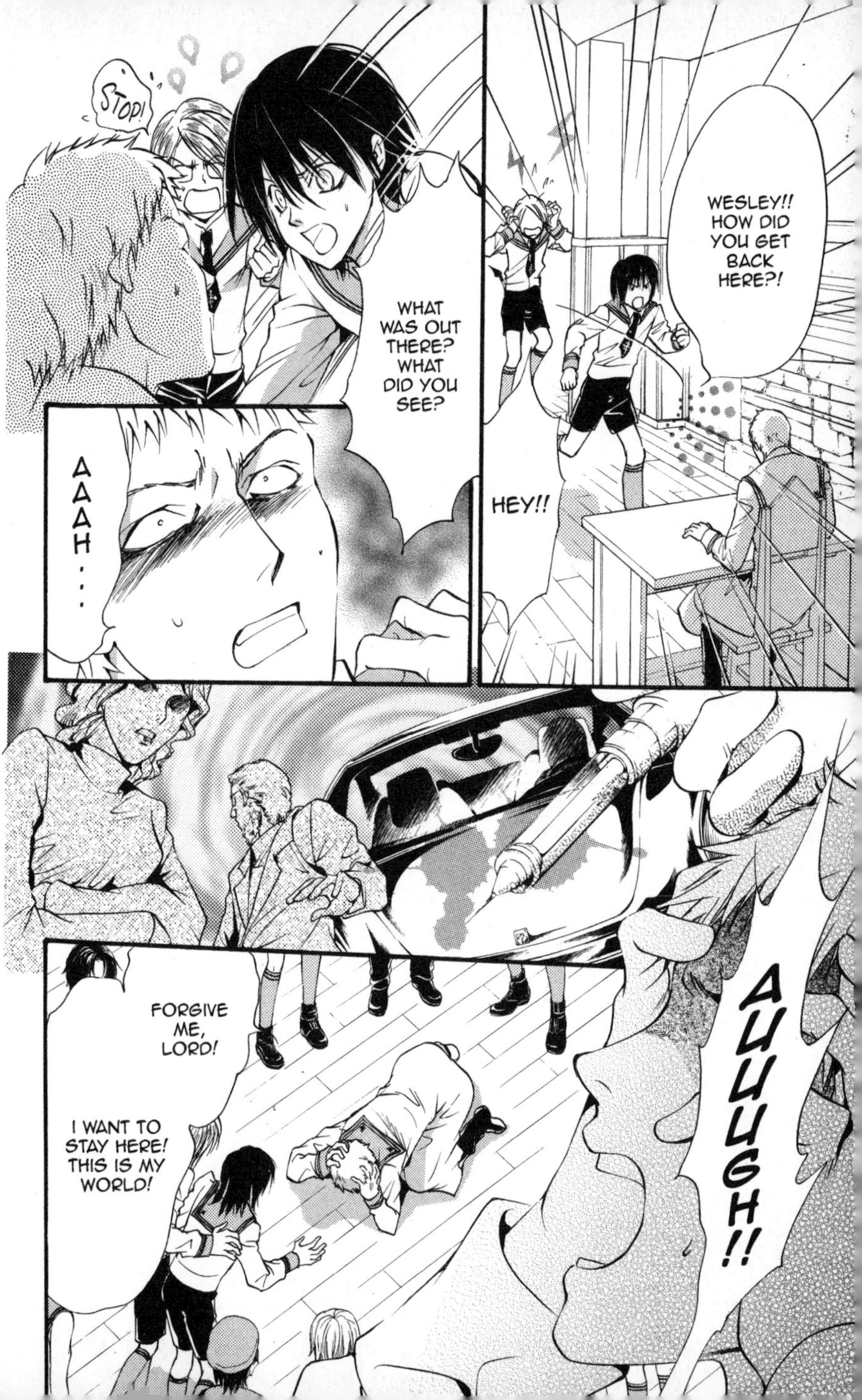
WESLEY!! HOW DID YOU GET BACK HERE?!
HEY!!
STOP!
WHAT WAS OUT THERE? WHAT DID YOU SEE?
AAAH...
AUUUGH!!
FORGIVE ME, LORD!
I WANT TO STAY HERE! THIS IS MY WORLD!

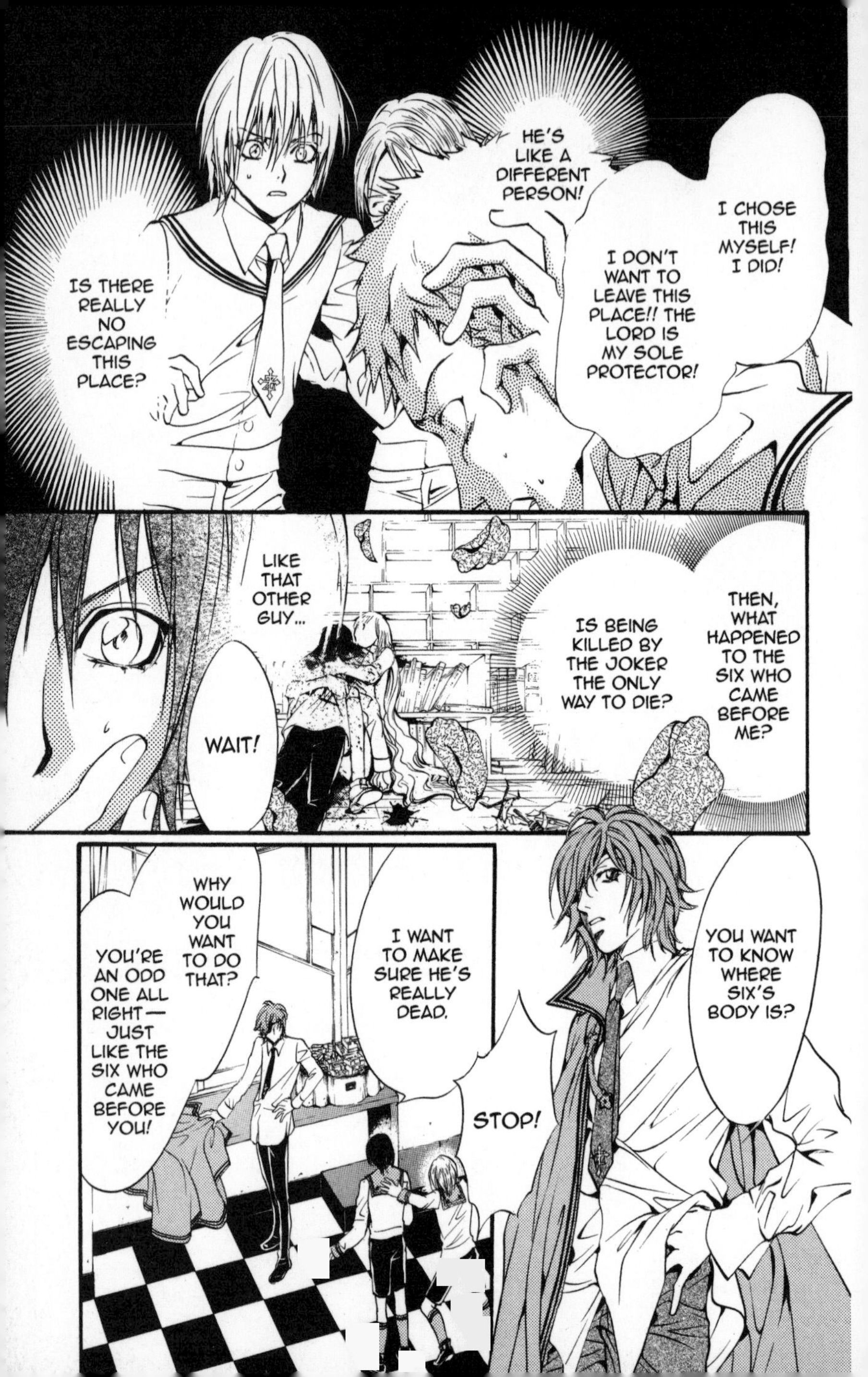
I CHOSE THIS MYSELF! I DID!
I DON'T WANT TO LEAVE THIS PLACE!! THE LORD IS MY SOLE PROTECTOR!
HE'S LIKE A DIFFERENT PERSON!
IS THERE REALLY NO ESCAPING THIS PLACE?
THEN, WHAT HAPPENED TO THE SIX WHO CAME BEFORE ME?
IS BEING KILLED BY THE JOKER THE ONLY WAY TO DIE?
LIKE THAT OTHER GUY...
WAIT!
YOU WANT TO KNOW WHERE SIX'S BODY IS?
STOP!
I WANT TO MAKE SURE HE'S REALLY DEAD.
WHY WOULD YOU WANT TO DO THAT?
YOU'RE AN ODD ONE ALL RIGHT—JUST LIKE THE SIX WHO CAME BEFORE YOU!

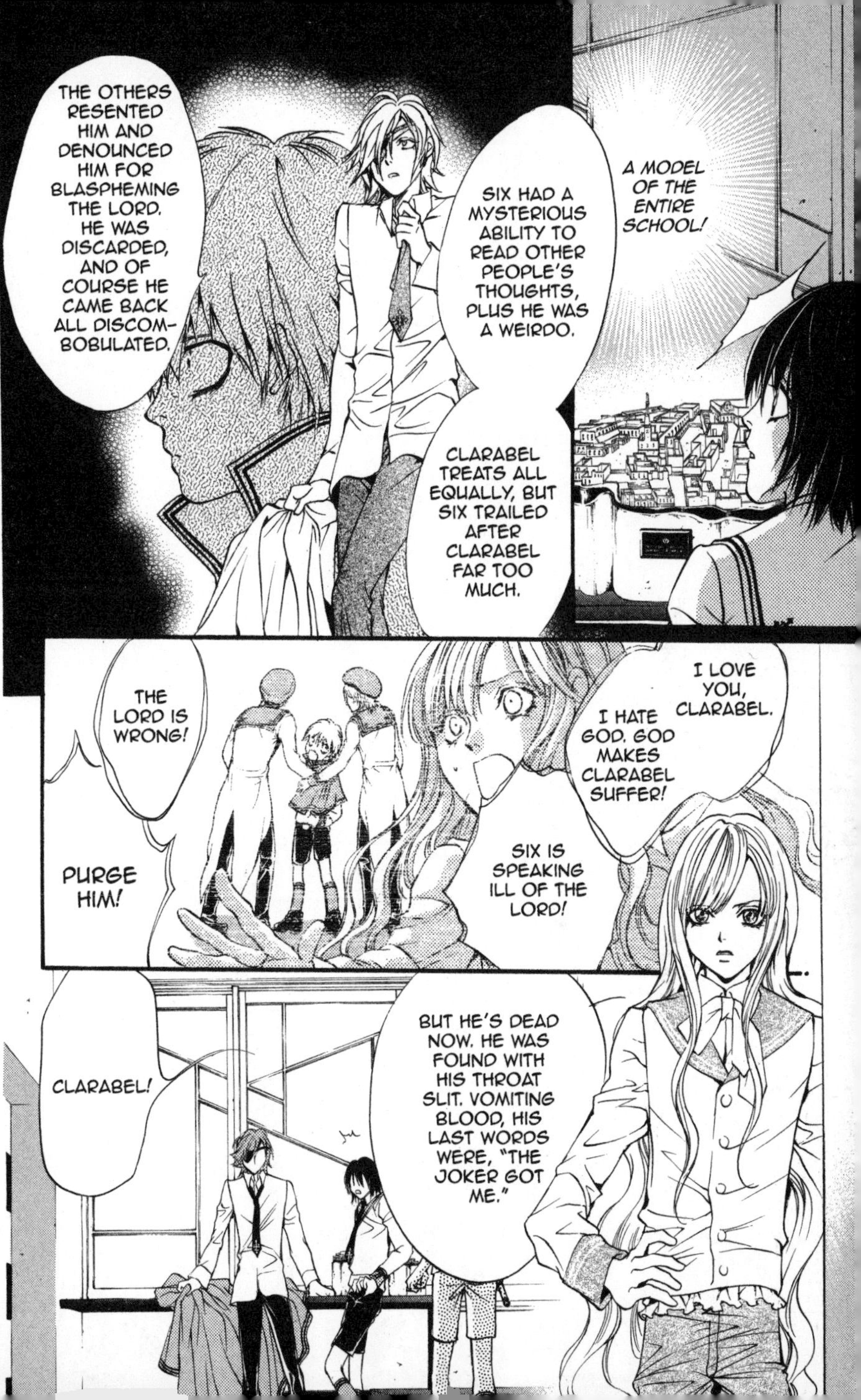
A MODEL OF THE ENTIRE SCHOOL!
SIX HAD A MYSTERIOUS ABILITY TO READ OTHER PEOPLE'S THOUGHTS, PLUS HE WAS A WEIRDO.
CLARABEL TREATS ALL EQUALLY, BUT SIX TRAILED AFTER CLARABEL FAR TOO MUCH.
THE OTHERS RESENTED HIM AND DENOUNCED HIM FOR BLASPHEMING THE LORD. HE WAS DISCARDED, AND OF COURSE HE CAME BACK ALL DISCOMBOBULATED.
I LOVE YOU, CLARABEL.
I HATE GOD. GOD MAKES CLARABEL SUFFER!
SIX IS SPEAKING ILL OF THE LORD!
THE LORD IS WRONG!
PURGE HIM!
BUT HE'S DEAD NOW. HE WAS FOUND WITH HIS THROAT SLIT. VOMITING BLOOD, HIS LAST WORDS WERE, "THE JOKER GOT ME."
CLARABEL!

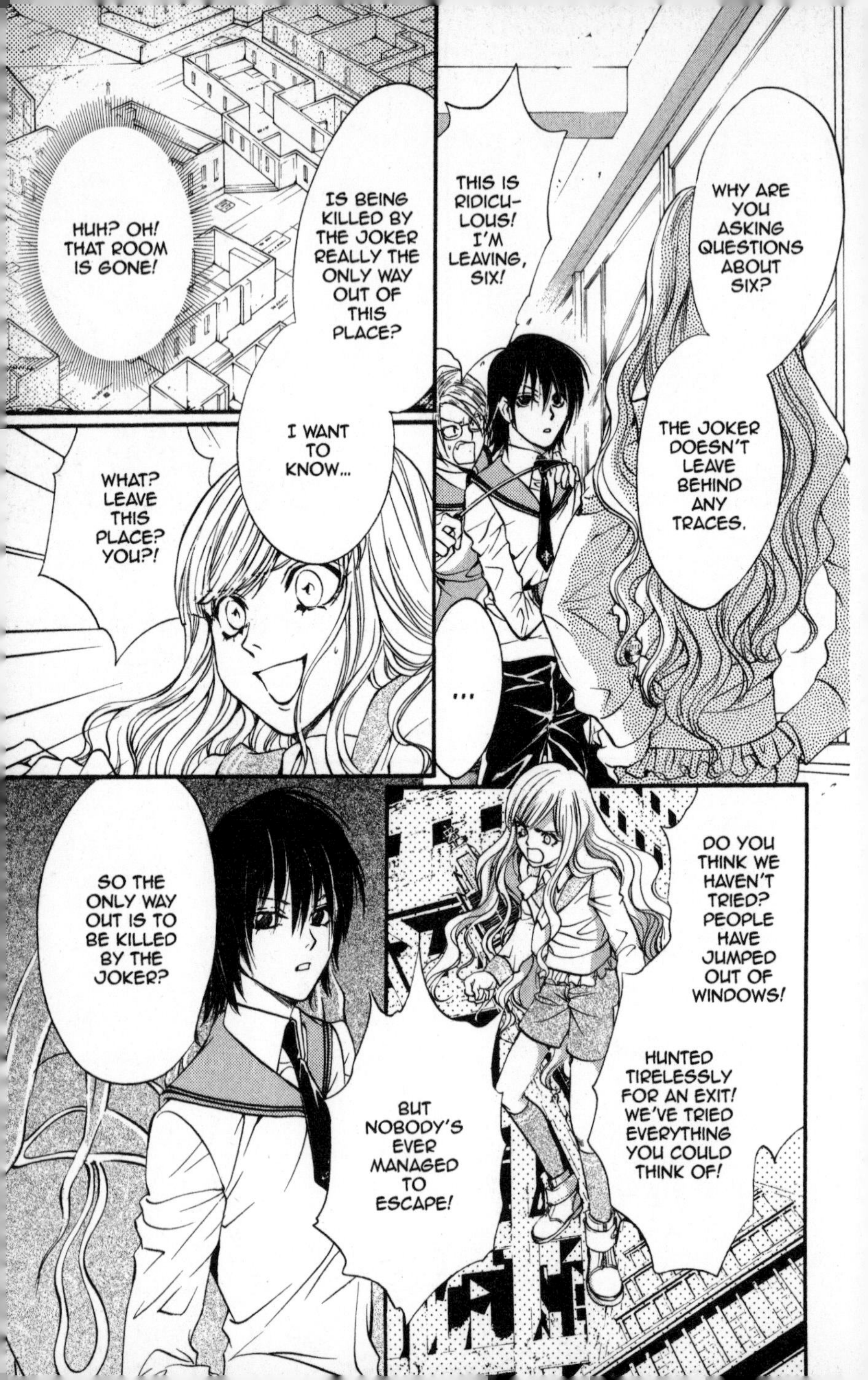
WHY ARE YOU ASKING QUESTIONS ABOUT SIX?
THE JOKER DOESN'T LEAVE BEHIND ANY TRACES.
THIS IS RIDICU-LOUS! I'M LEAVING, SIX!
...
HUH? OH! THAT ROOM IS GONE!
I WANT TO KNOW...
IS BEING KILLED BY THE JOKER REALLY THE ONLY WAY OUT OF THIS PLACE?
WHAT? LEAVE THIS PLACE? YOU?!
DO YOU THINK WE HAVEN'T TRIED? PEOPLE HAVE JUMPED OUT OF WINDOWS!
HUNTED TIRELESSLY FOR AN EXIT! WE'VE TRIED EVERYTHING YOU COULD THINK OF!
BUT NOBODY'S EVER MANAGED TO ESCAPE!
SO THE ONLY WAY OUT IS TO BE KILLED BY THE JOKER?

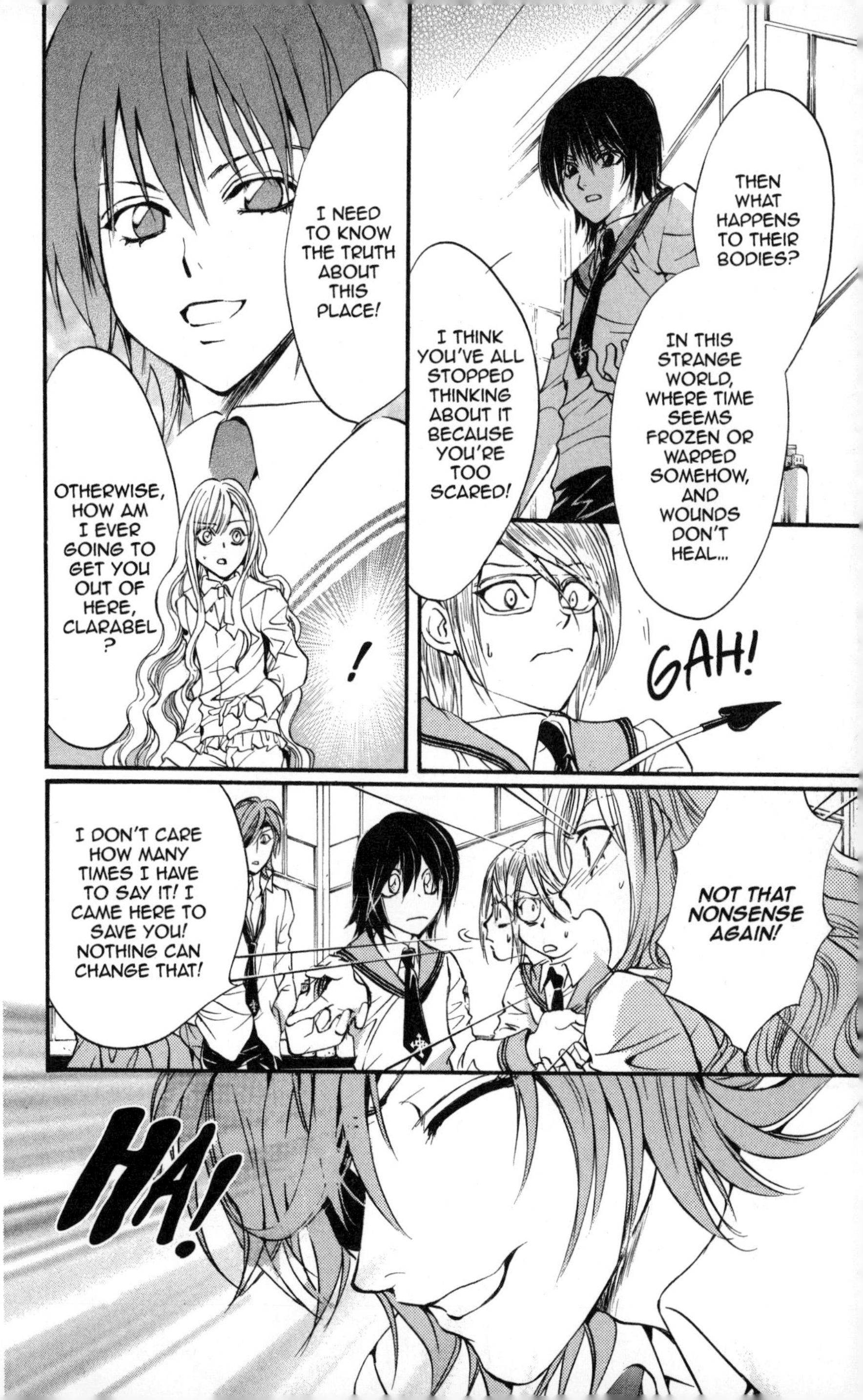
THEN WHAT HAPPENS TO THEIR BODIES?
IN THIS STRANGE WORLD, WHERE TIME SEEMS FROZEN OR WARPED SOMEHOW, AND WOUNDS DON'T HEAL...
I THINK YOU'VE ALL STOPPED THINKING ABOUT IT BECAUSE YOU'RE TOO SCARED!
GAH!
I NEED TO KNOW THE TRUTH ABOUT THIS PLACE!
OTHERWISE, HOW AM I EVER GOING TO GET YOU OUT OF HERE, CLARABEL?
!
NOT THAT NONSENSE AGAIN!
I DON'T CARE HOW MANY TIMES I HAVE TO SAY IT! I CAME HERE TO SAVE YOU! NOTHING CAN CHANGE THAT!
HA!

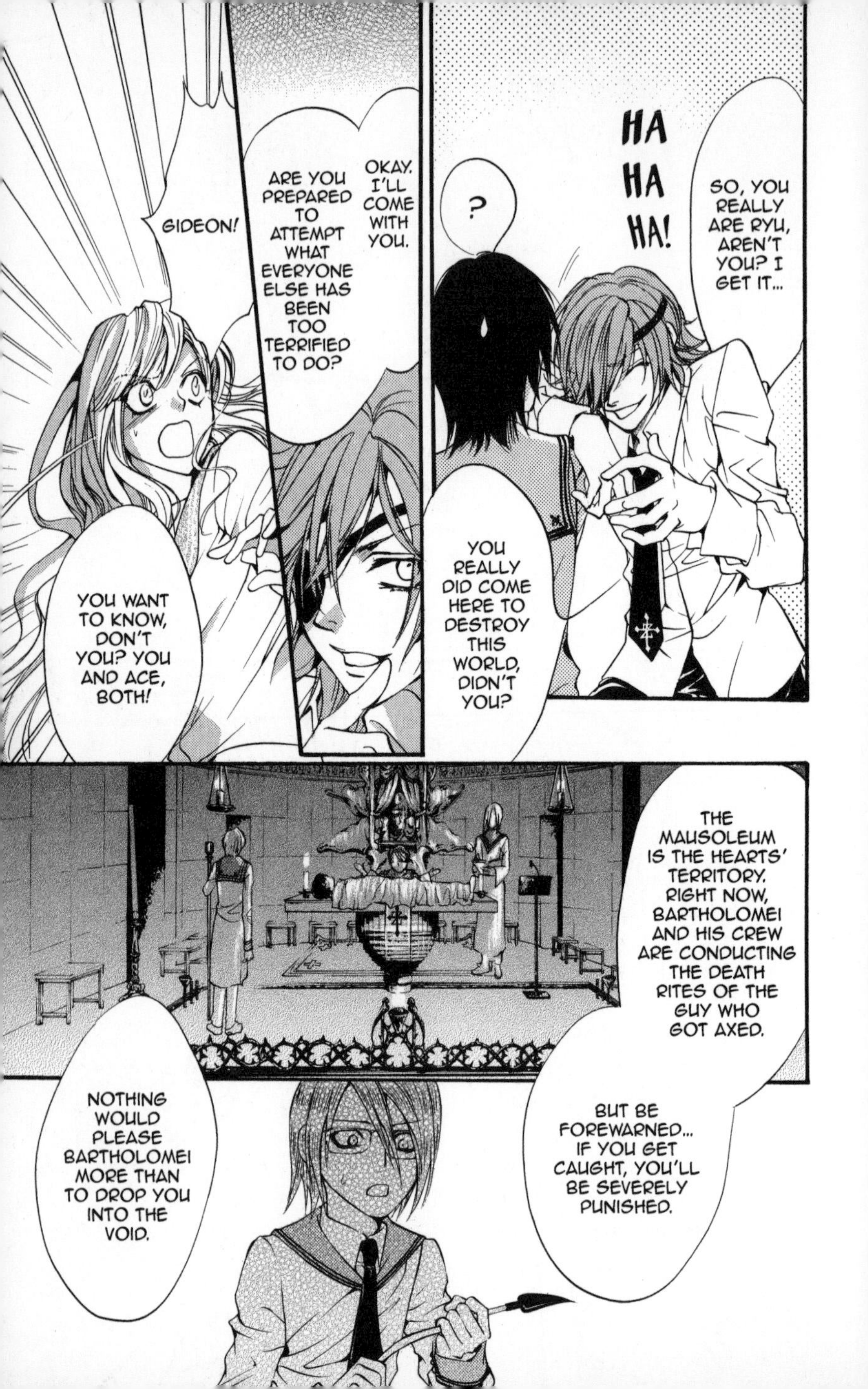
SO, YOU REALLY ARE RYU, AREN'T YOU? I GET IT...
HA HA HA!
?
YOU REALLY DID COME HERE TO DESTROY THIS WORLD, DIDN'T YOU?
OKAY. I'LL COME WITH YOU.
ARE YOU PREPARED TO ATTEMPT WHAT EVERYONE ELSE HAS BEEN TOO TERRIFIED TO DO?
GIDEON!
YOU WANT TO KNOW, DON'T YOU? YOU AND ACE, BOTH!
THE MAUSOLEUM IS THE HEARTS' TERRITORY. RIGHT NOW, BARTHOLOMEI AND HIS CREW ARE CONDUCTING THE DEATH RITES OF THE GUY WHO GOT AXED.
BUT BE FOREWARNED... IF YOU GET CAUGHT, YOU'LL BE SEVERELY PUNISHED.
NOTHING WOULD PLEASE BARTHOLOMEI MORE THAN TO DROP YOU INTO THE VOID.

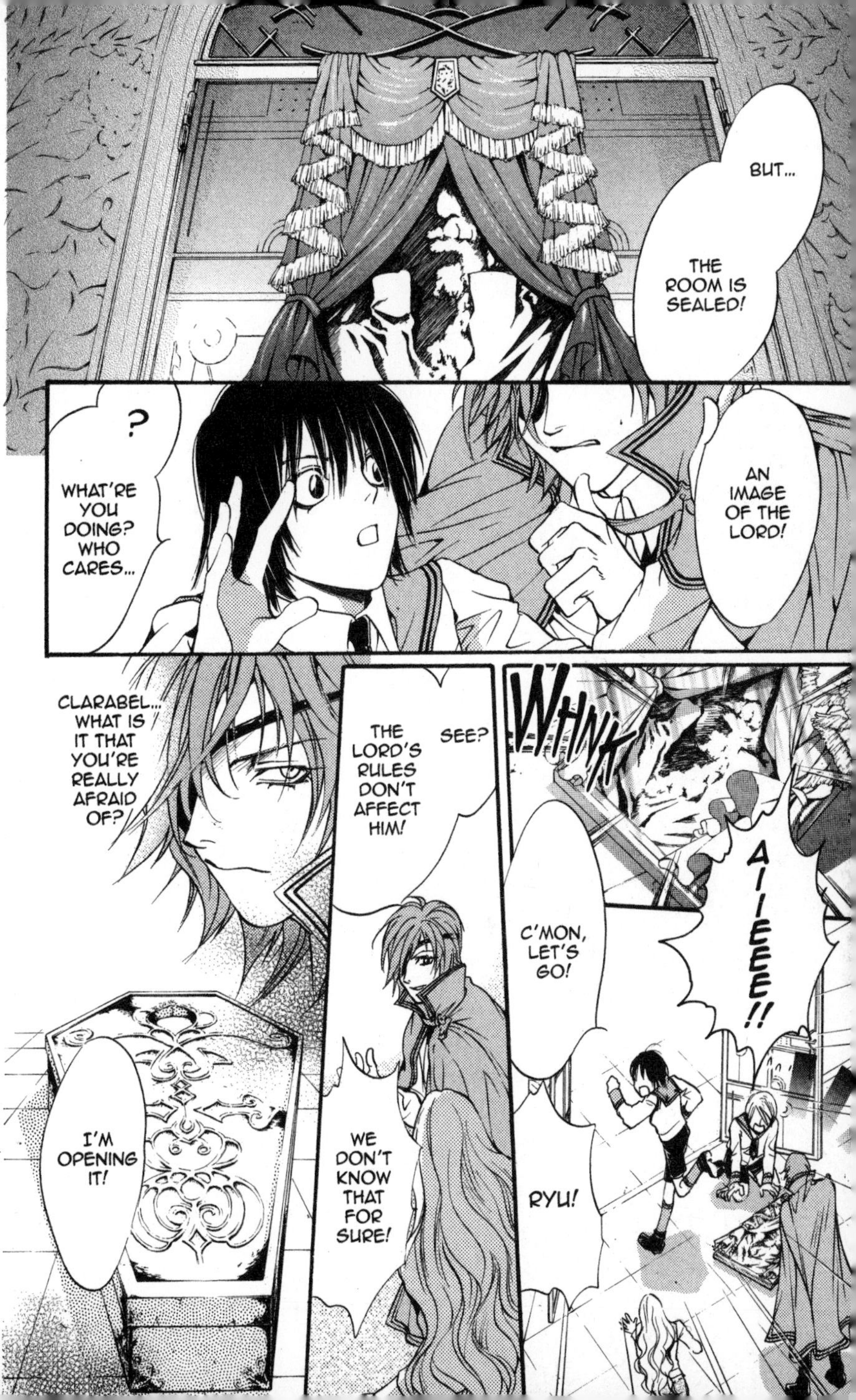
BUT...
THE ROOM IS SEALED!
AN IMAGE OF THE LORD!
?
WHAT'RE YOU DOING? WHO CARES...
WHNK
AIIEEEE!!
C'MON, LET'S GO!
RYU!
SEE?
THE LORD'S RULES DON'T AFFECT HIM!
WE DON'T KNOW THAT FOR SURE!
CLARABEL... WHAT IS IT THAT YOU'RE REALLY AFRAID OF?
I'M OPENING IT!

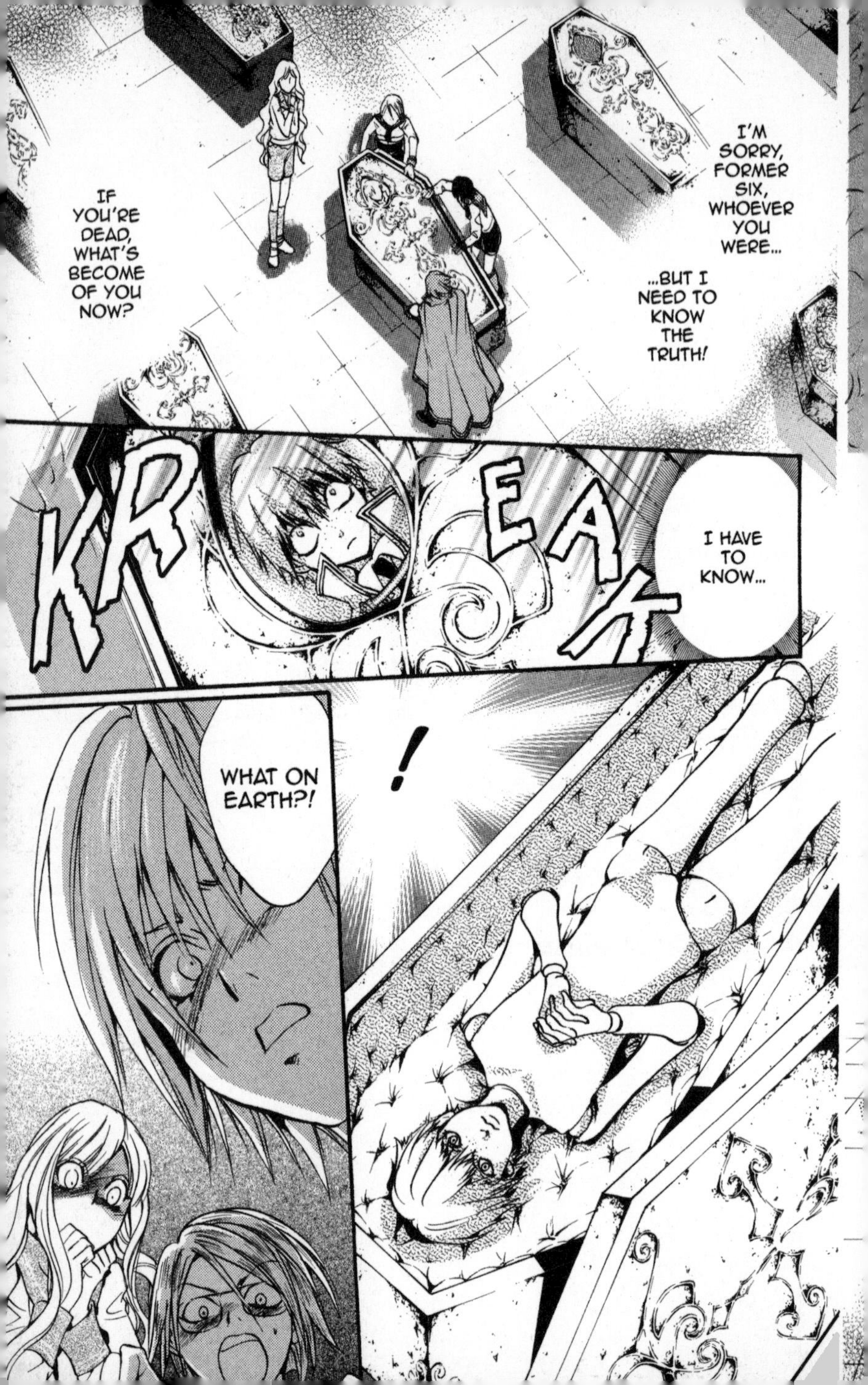
I'M SORRY, FORMER SIX, WHOEVER YOU WERE...
...BUT I NEED TO KNOW THE TRUTH!
IF YOU'RE DEAD, WHAT'S BECOME OF YOU NOW?
I HAVE TO KNOW...
KREAK
!
WHAT ON EARTH?!

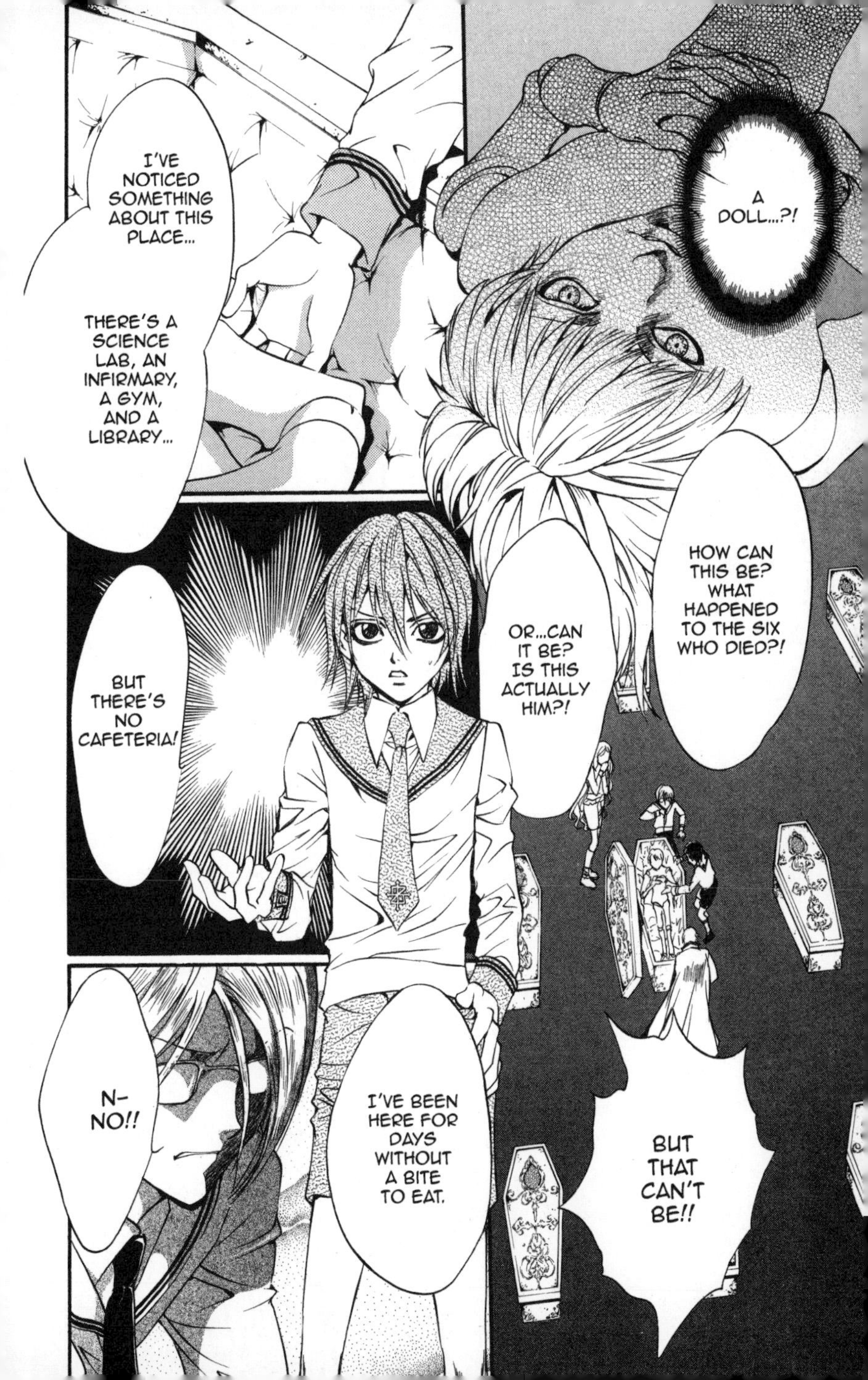
A DOLL...?!
HOW CAN THIS BE? WHAT HAPPENED TO THE SIX WHO DIED?!
OR...CAN IT BE? IS THIS ACTUALLY HIM?!
BUT THAT CAN'T BE!!
I'VE NOTICED SOMETHING ABOUT THIS PLACE...
THERE'S A SCIENCE LAB, AN INFIRMARY, A GYM, AND A LIBRARY...
BUT THERE'S NO CAFETERIA!
I'VE BEEN HERE FOR DAYS WITHOUT A BITE TO EAT.
N-NO!!

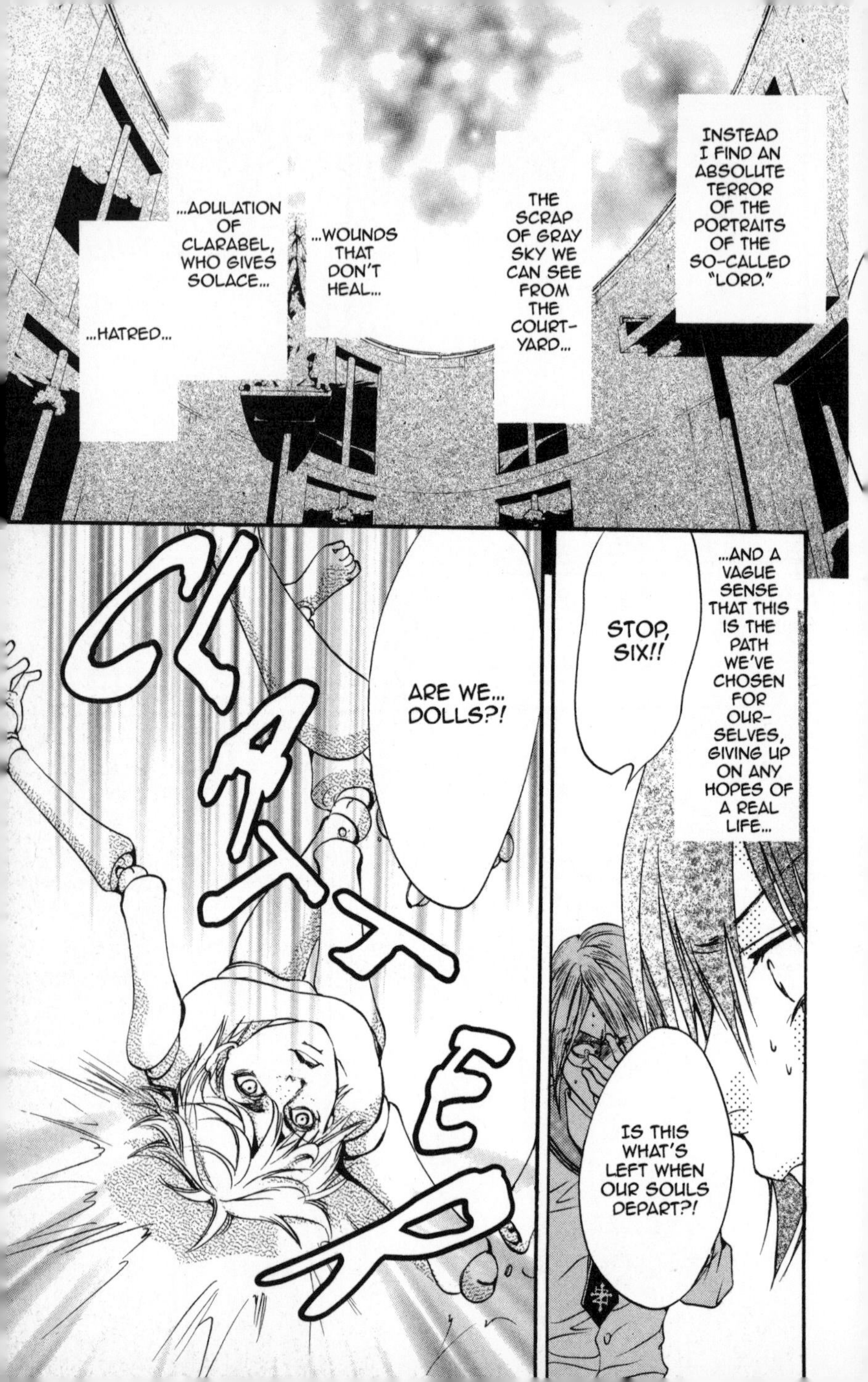
INSTEAD I FIND AN ABSOLUTE TERROR OF THE PORTRAITS OF THE SO-CALLED "LORD."
THE SCRAP OF GRAY SKY WE CAN SEE FROM THE COURT-YARD...
...WOUNDS THAT DON'T HEAL...
...ADULATION OF CLARABEL, WHO GIVES SOLACE...
...HATRED...
...AND A VAGUE SENSE THAT THIS IS THE PATH WE'VE CHOSEN FOR OUR-SELVES, GIVING UP ON ANY HOPES OF A REAL LIFE...
STOP, SIX!!
IS THIS WHAT'S LEFT WHEN OUR SOULS DEPART?!
ARE WE... DOLLS?!
CLATTER

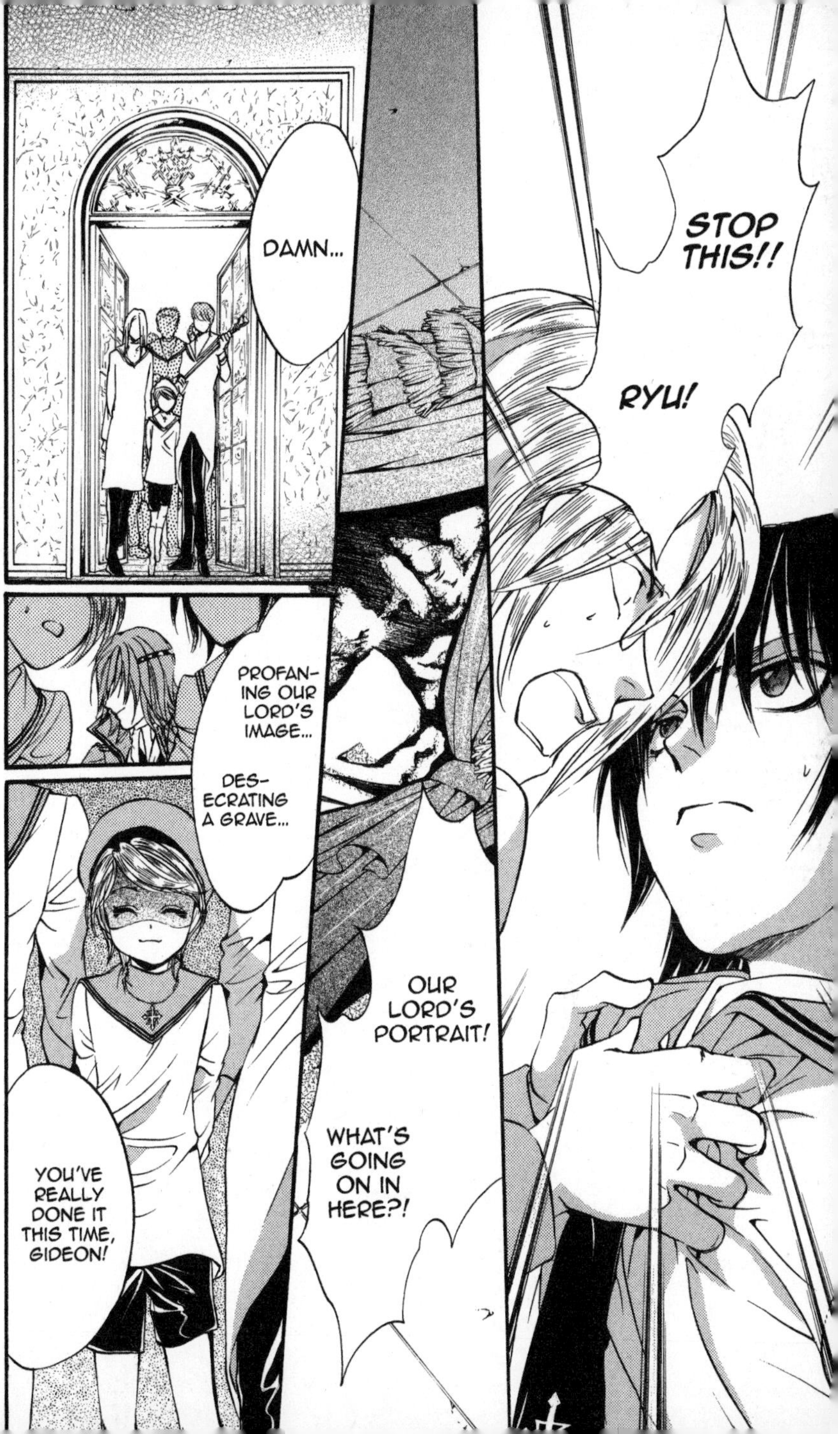
STOP THIS!!
RYU!
DAMN...
OUR LORD'S PORTRAIT!
WHAT'S GOING ON IN HERE?!
PROFANING OUR LORD'S IMAGE...
DESECRATING A GRAVE...
YOU'VE REALLY DONE IT THIS TIME, GIDEON!

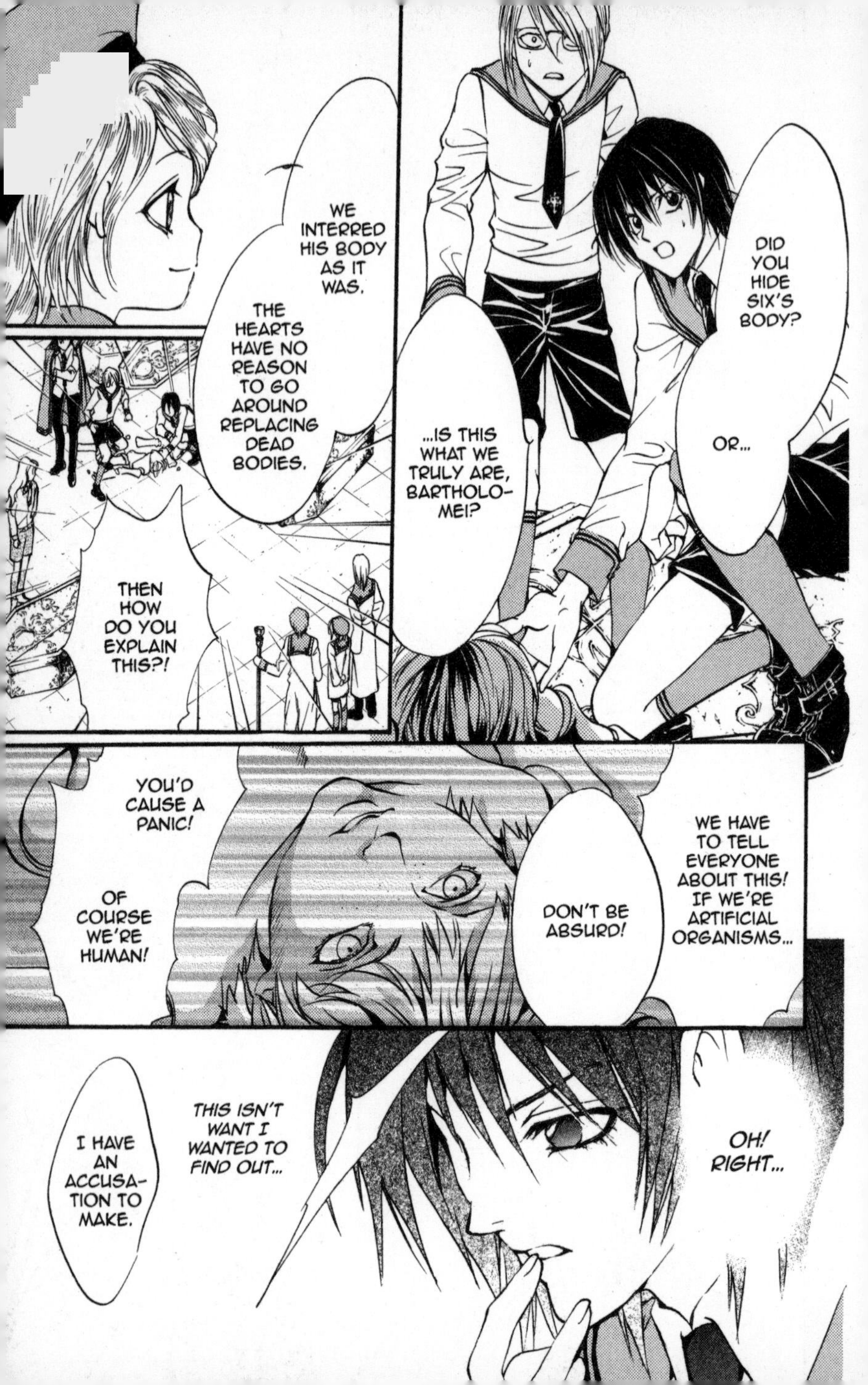
DID YOU HIDE SIX'S BODY?
OR...
...IS THIS WHAT WE TRULY ARE, BARTHOLOMEI?
WE INTERRED HIS BODY AS IT WAS.
THE HEARTS HAVE NO REASON TO GO AROUND REPLACING DEAD BODIES.
THEN HOW DO YOU EXPLAIN THIS?!
WE HAVE TO TELL EVERYONE ABOUT THIS! IF WE'RE ARTIFICIAL ORGANISMS...
DON'T BE ABSURD!
YOU'D CAUSE A PANIC!
OF COURSE WE'RE HUMAN!
OH! RIGHT...
THIS ISN'T WANT I WANTED TO FIND OUT...
I HAVE AN ACCUSATION TO MAKE.

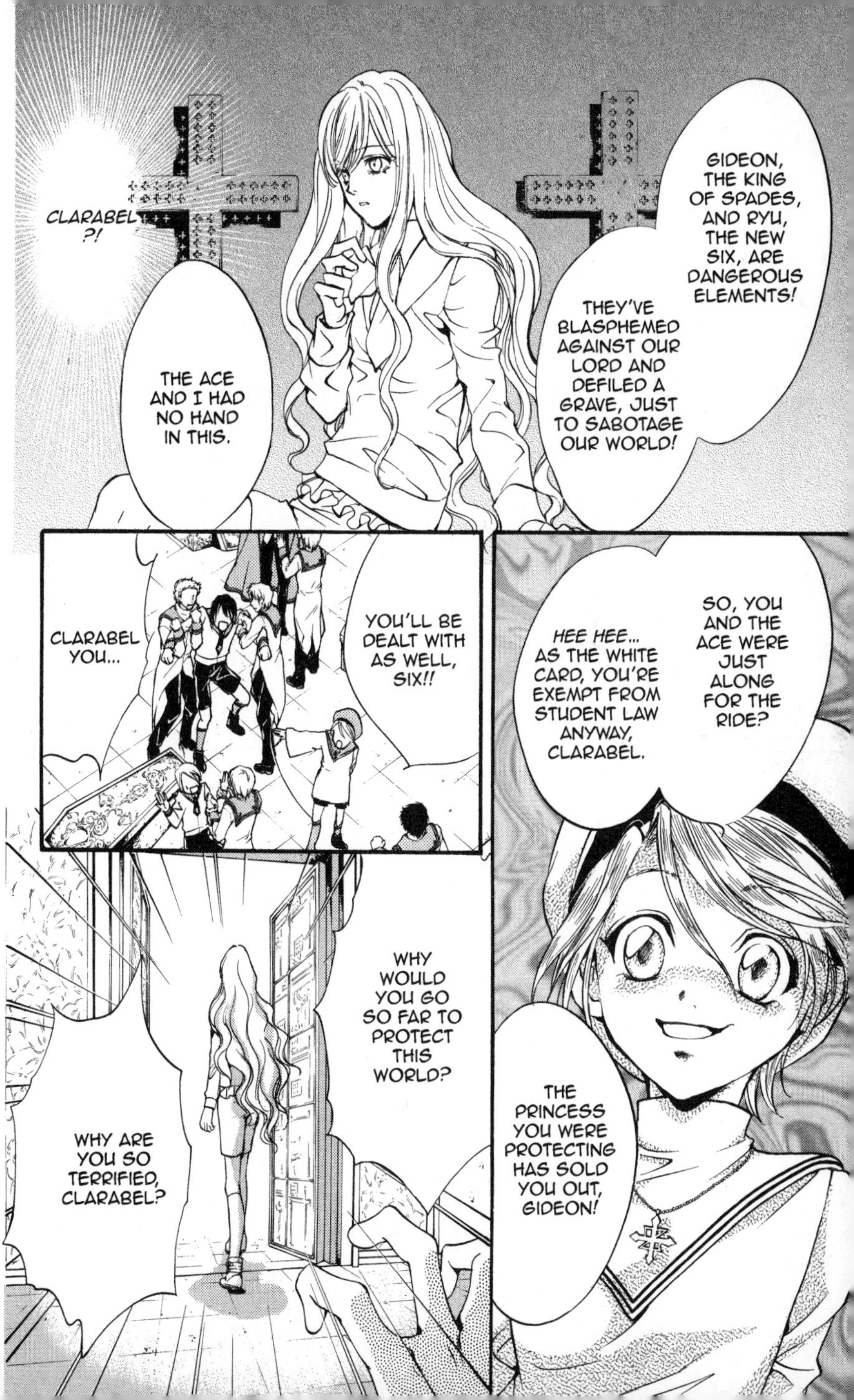
GIDEON, THE KING OF SPADES, AND RYU, THE NEW SIX, ARE DANGEROUS ELEMENTS!
THEY'VE BLASPHEMED AGAINST OUR LORD AND DEFILED A GRAVE, JUST TO SABOTAGE OUR WORLD!
CLARABEL ?!
THE ACE AND I HAD NO HAND IN THIS.
SO, YOU AND THE ACE WERE JUST ALONG FOR THE RIDE?
HEE HEE... AS THE WHITE CARD, YOU'RE EXEMPT FROM STUDENT LAW ANYWAY, CLARABEL.
THE PRINCESS YOU WERE PROTECTING HAS SOLD YOU OUT, GIDEON!
YOU'LL BE DEALT WITH AS WELL, SIX!!
CLARABEL YOU...
WHY WOULD YOU GO SO FAR TO PROTECT THIS WORLD?
WHY ARE YOU SO TERRIFIED, CLARABEL?

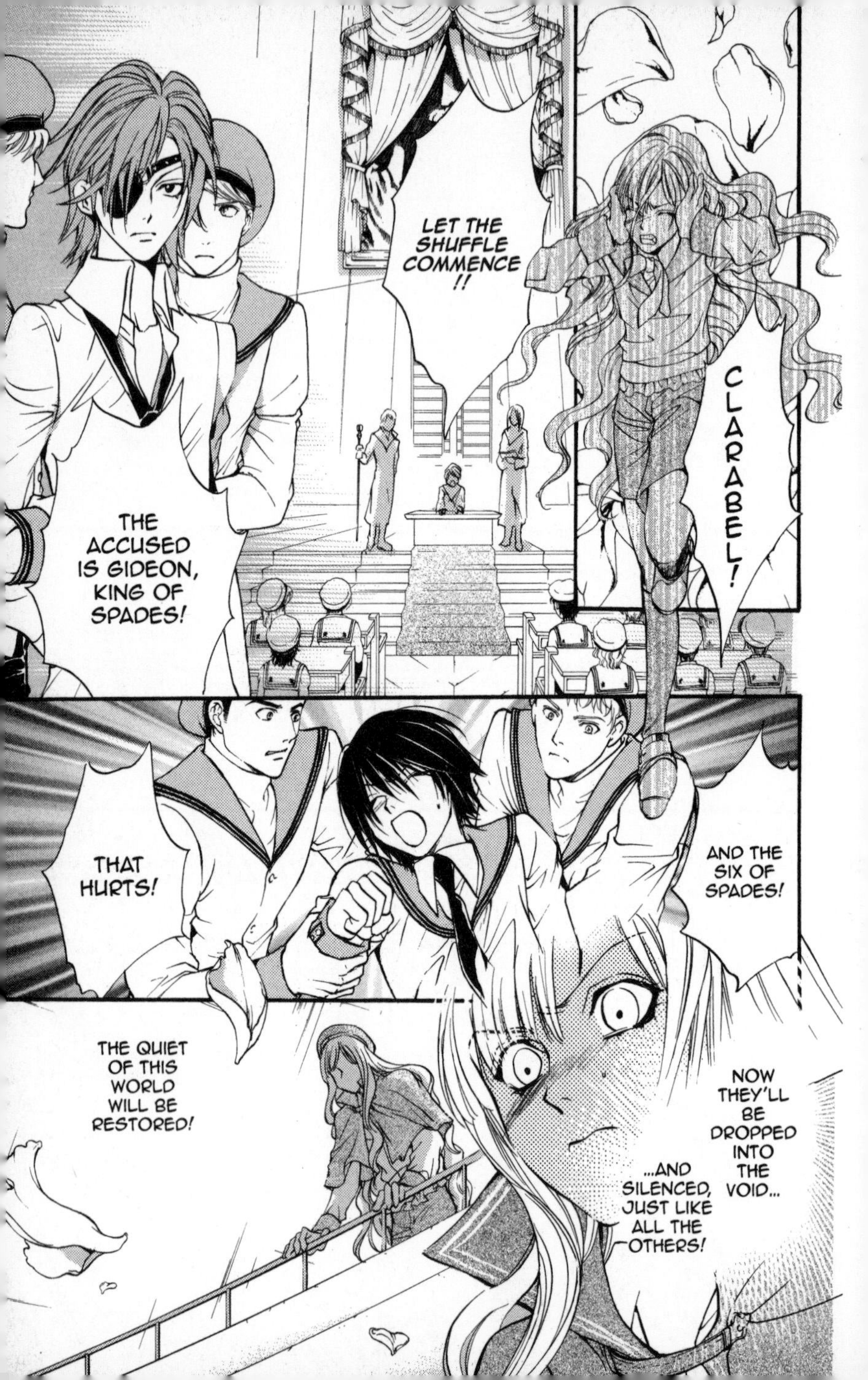
CLARABEL!
LET THE SHUFFLE COMMENCE!!
THE ACCUSED IS GIDEON, KING OF SPADES!
AND THE SIX OF SPADES!
THAT HURTS!
NOW THEY'LL BE DROPPED INTO THE VOID...
...AND SILENCED, JUST LIKE ALL THE OTHERS!
THE QUIET OF THIS WORLD WILL BE RESTORED!

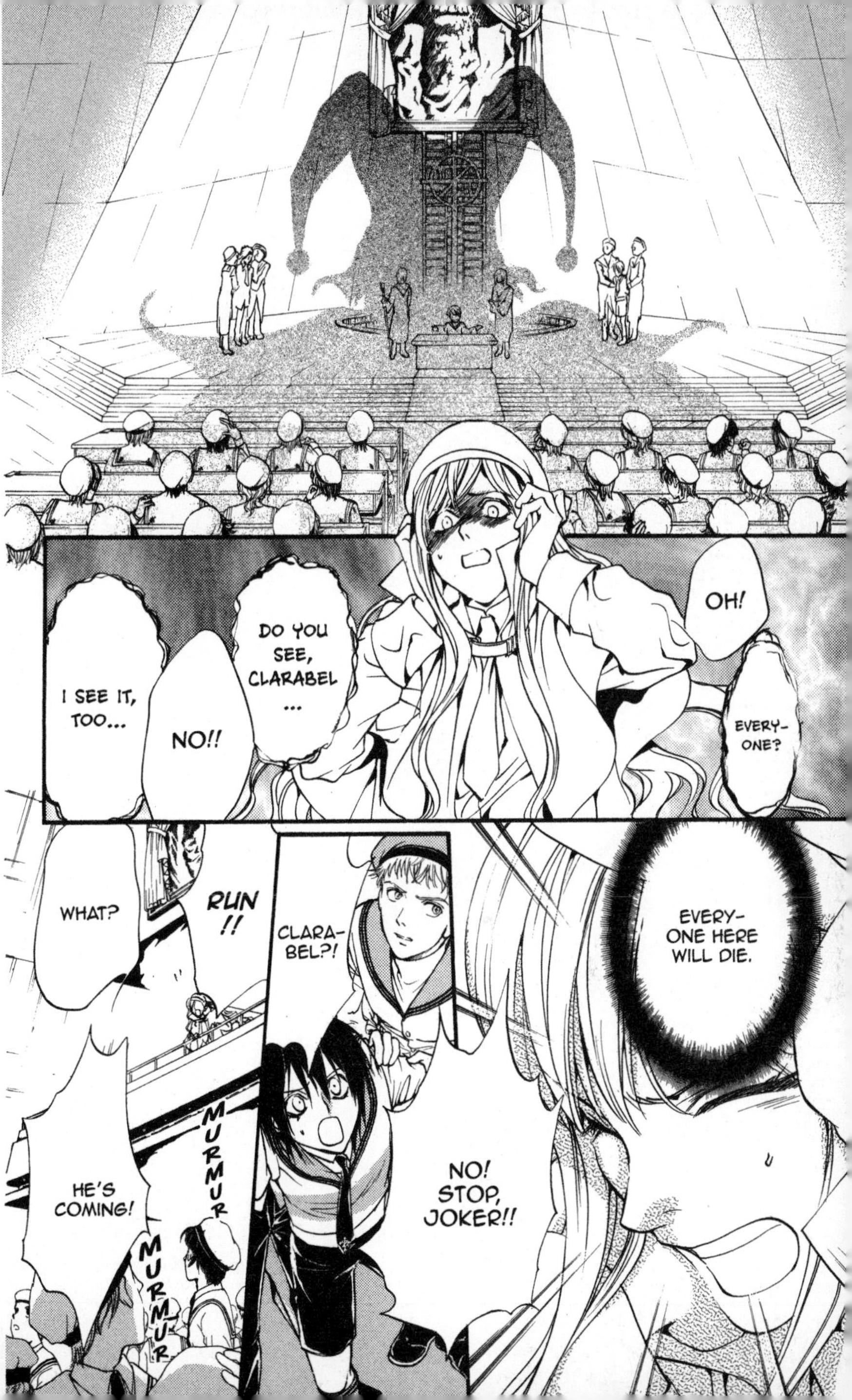
OH!
EVERY-ONE?
DO YOU SEE, CLARABEL...
NO!!
I SEE IT, TOO...
EVERY-ONE HERE WILL DIE.
CLARA-BEL?!
NO! STOP, JOKER!!
RUN!!
WHAT?
MURMUR
HE'S COMING!
MURMUR

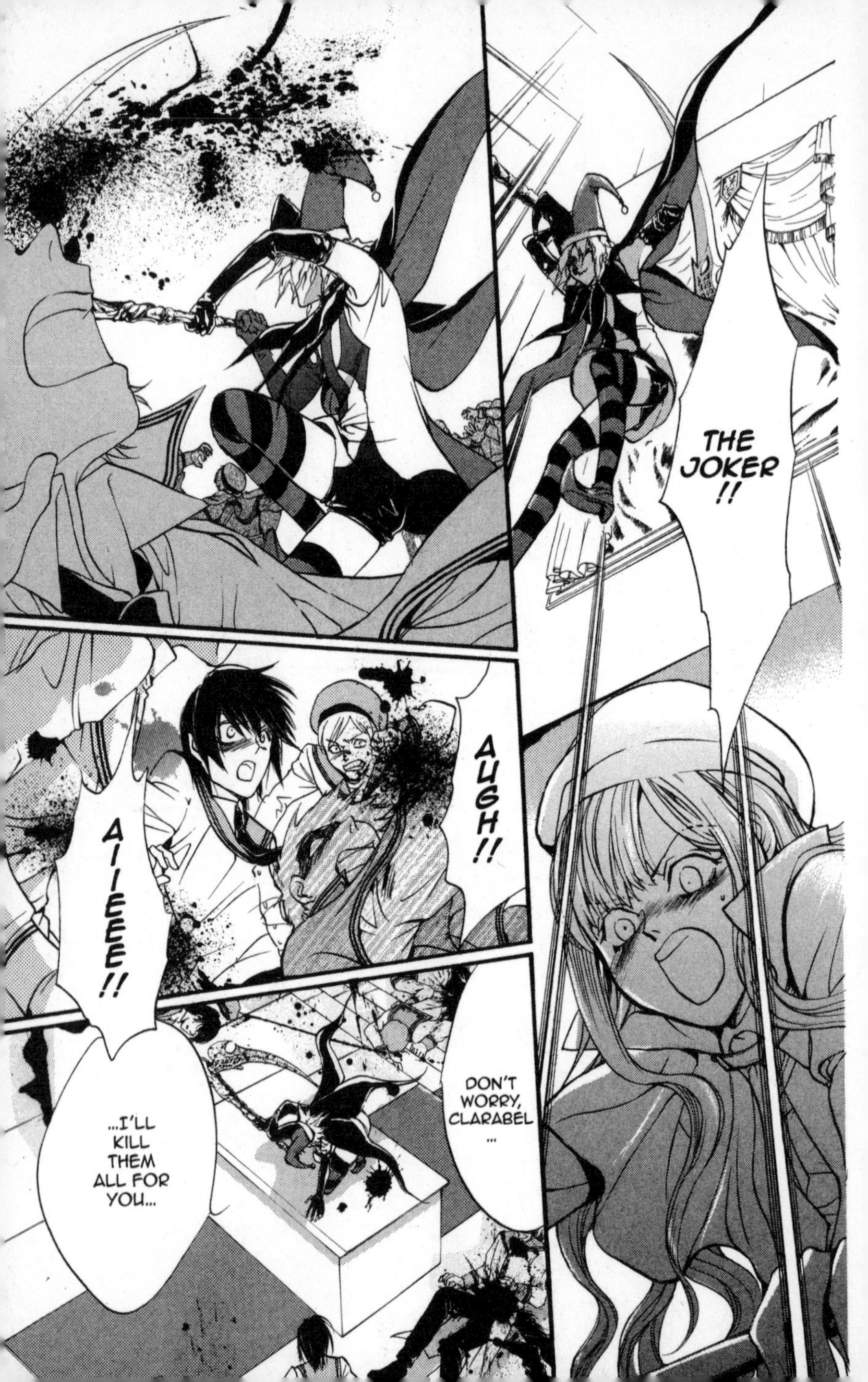
THE JOKER !!
AUGH!!
AIIEEEE!!
DON'T WORRY, CLARABEL ...
...I'LL KILL THEM ALL FOR YOU...

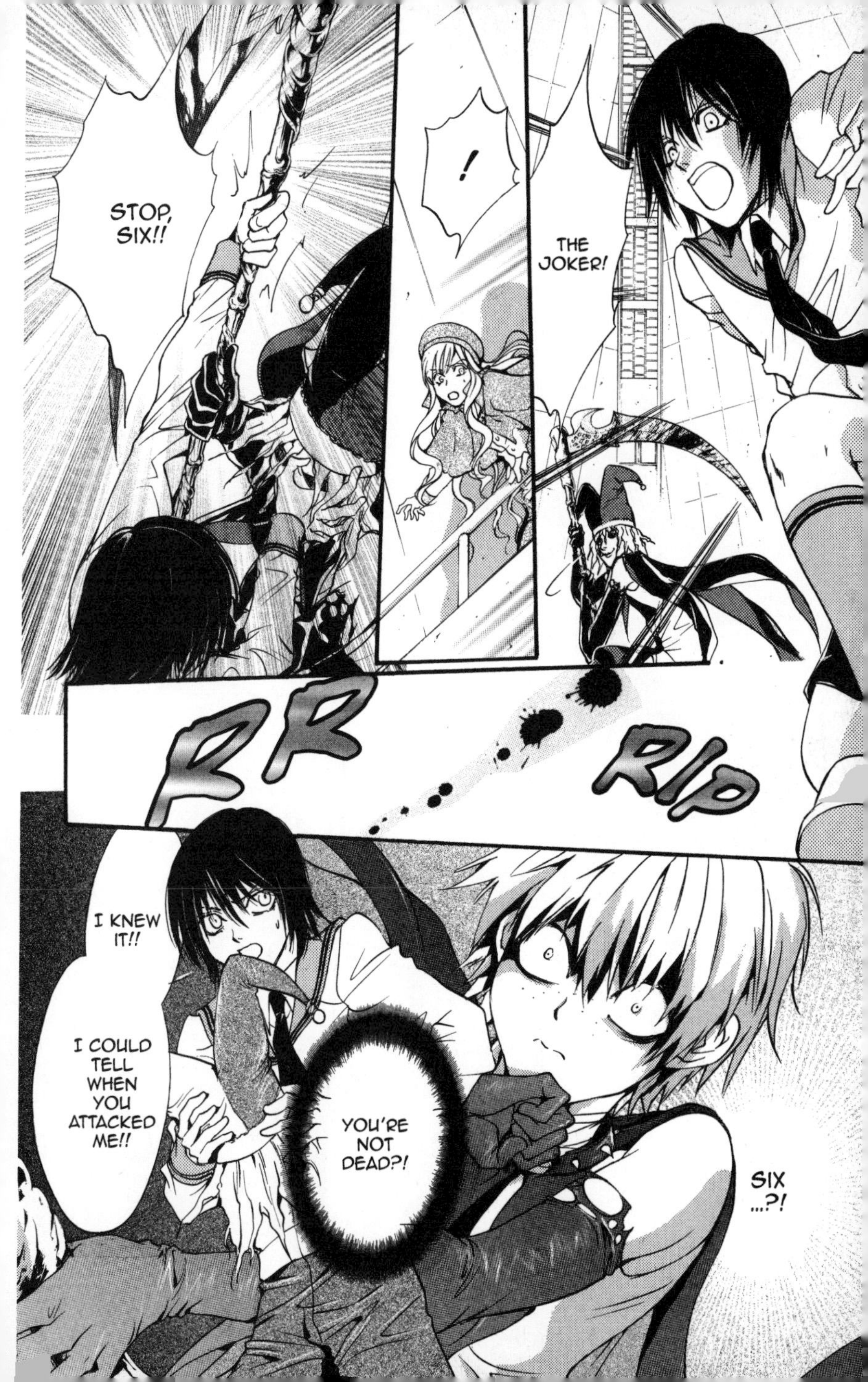
THE JOKER!
!
STOP, SIX!!
RR RIP
SIX ...?!
YOU'RE NOT DEAD?!
I KNEW IT!!
I COULD TELL WHEN YOU ATTACKED ME!!

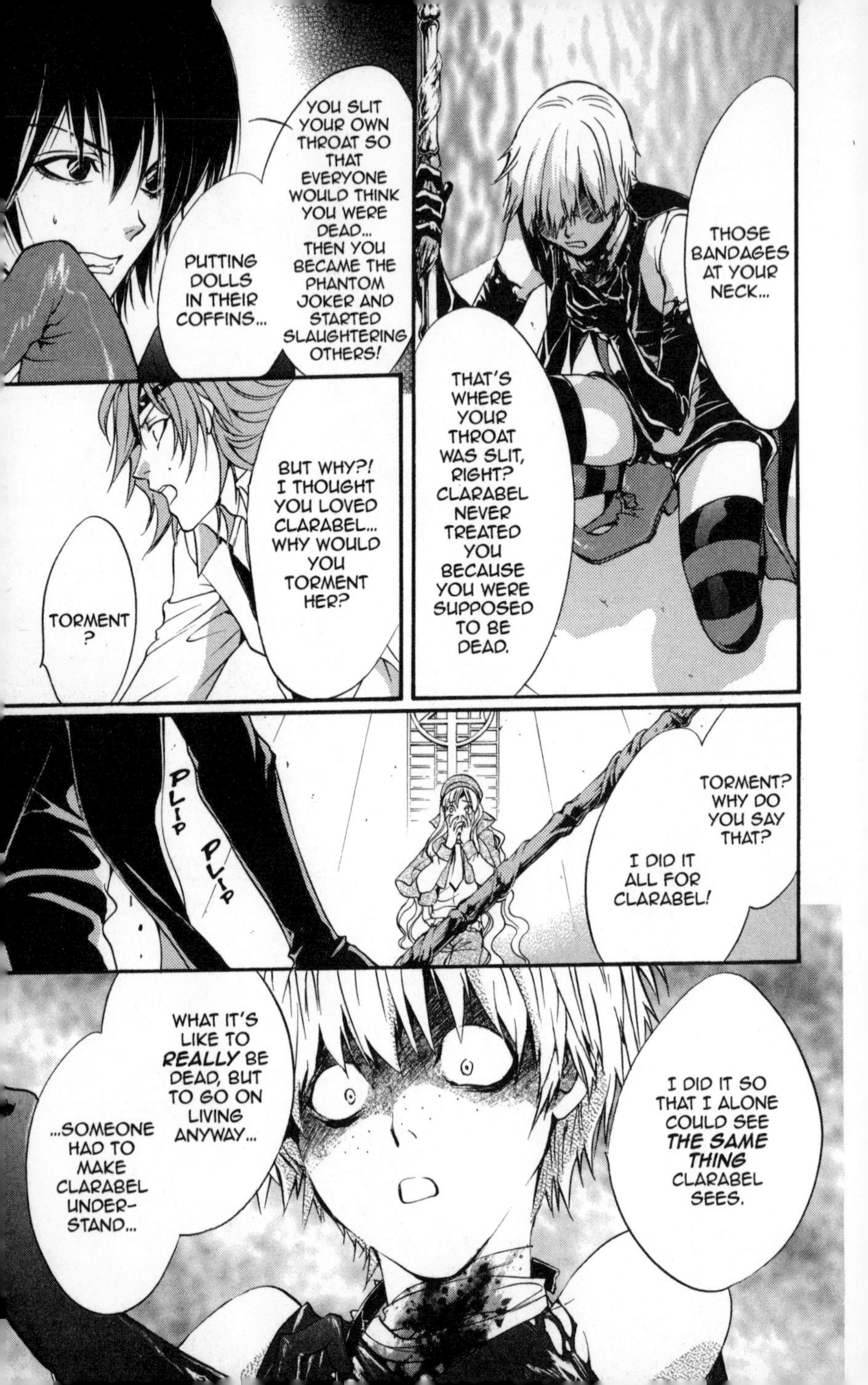
THOSE BANDAGES AT YOUR NECK...
THAT'S WHERE YOUR THROAT WAS SLIT, RIGHT? CLARABEL NEVER TREATED YOU BECAUSE YOU WERE SUPPOSED TO BE DEAD.
YOU SLIT YOUR OWN THROAT SO THAT EVERYONE WOULD THINK YOU WERE DEAD... THEN YOU BECAME THE PHANTOM JOKER AND STARTED SLAUGHTERING OTHERS!
PUTTING DOLLS IN THEIR COFFINS...
BUT WHY?! I THOUGHT YOU LOVED CLARABEL... WHY WOULD YOU TORMENT HER?
TORMENT?
TORMENT? WHY DO YOU SAY THAT?
I DID IT ALL FOR CLARABEL!
PLIP
PLIP
I DID IT SO THAT I ALONE COULD SEE **THE SAME THING** CLARABEL SEES.
WHAT IT'S LIKE TO ***REALLY*** BE DEAD, BUT TO GO ON LIVING ANYWAY...
...SOMEONE HAD TO MAKE CLARABEL UNDER-STAND...

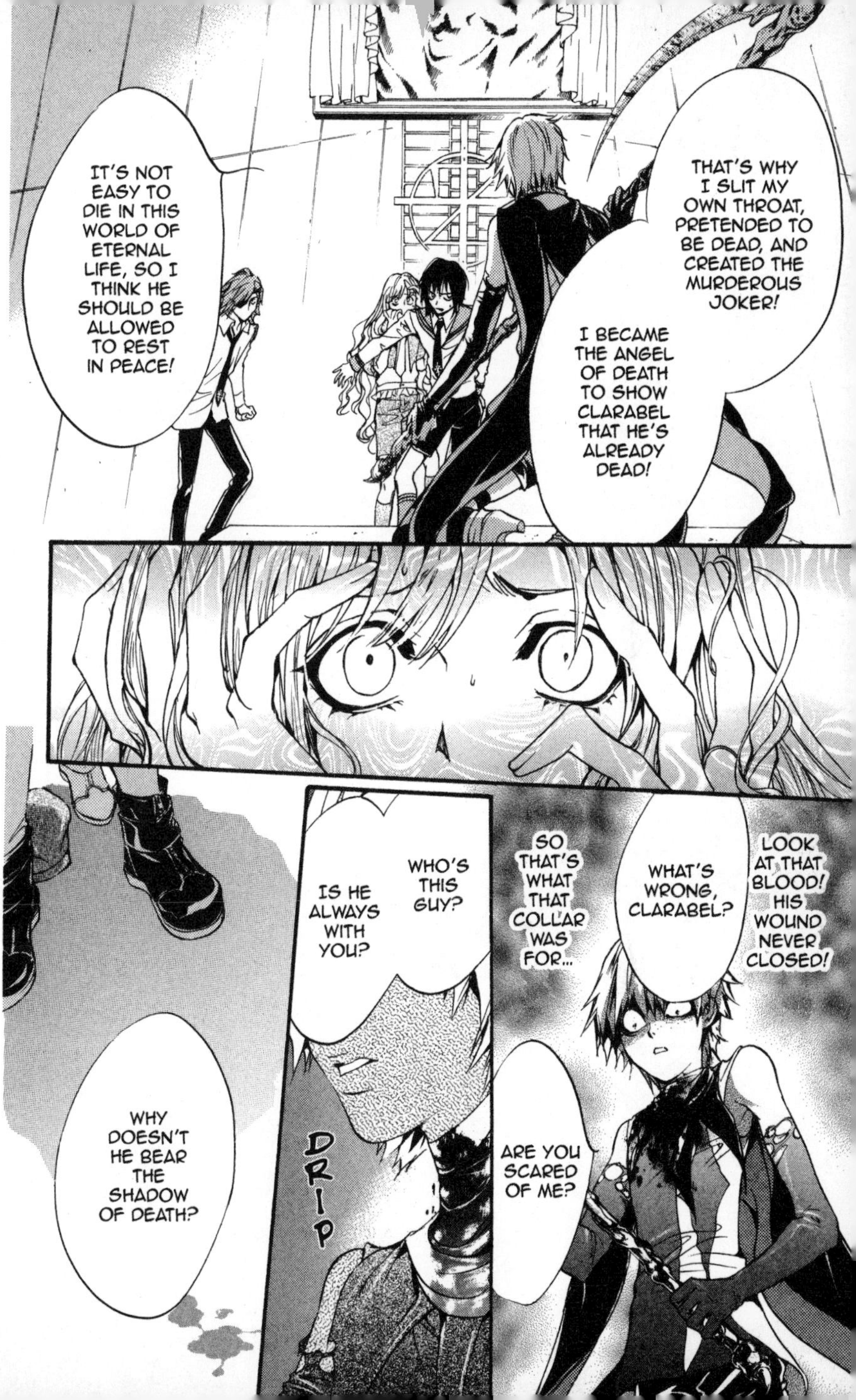
THAT'S WHY I SLIT MY OWN THROAT, PRETENDED TO BE DEAD, AND CREATED THE MURDEROUS JOKER!
I BECAME THE ANGEL OF DEATH TO SHOW CLARABEL THAT HE'S ALREADY DEAD!
IT'S NOT EASY TO DIE IN THIS WORLD OF ETERNAL LIFE, SO I THINK HE SHOULD BE ALLOWED TO REST IN PEACE!
LOOK AT THAT BLOOD! HIS WOUND NEVER CLOSED!
WHAT'S WRONG, CLARABEL?
SO THAT'S WHAT THAT COLLAR WAS FOR...
ARE YOU SCARED OF ME?
WHO'S THIS GUY?
IS HE ALWAYS WITH YOU?
DRIP
WHY DOESN'T HE BEAR THE SHADOW OF DEATH?

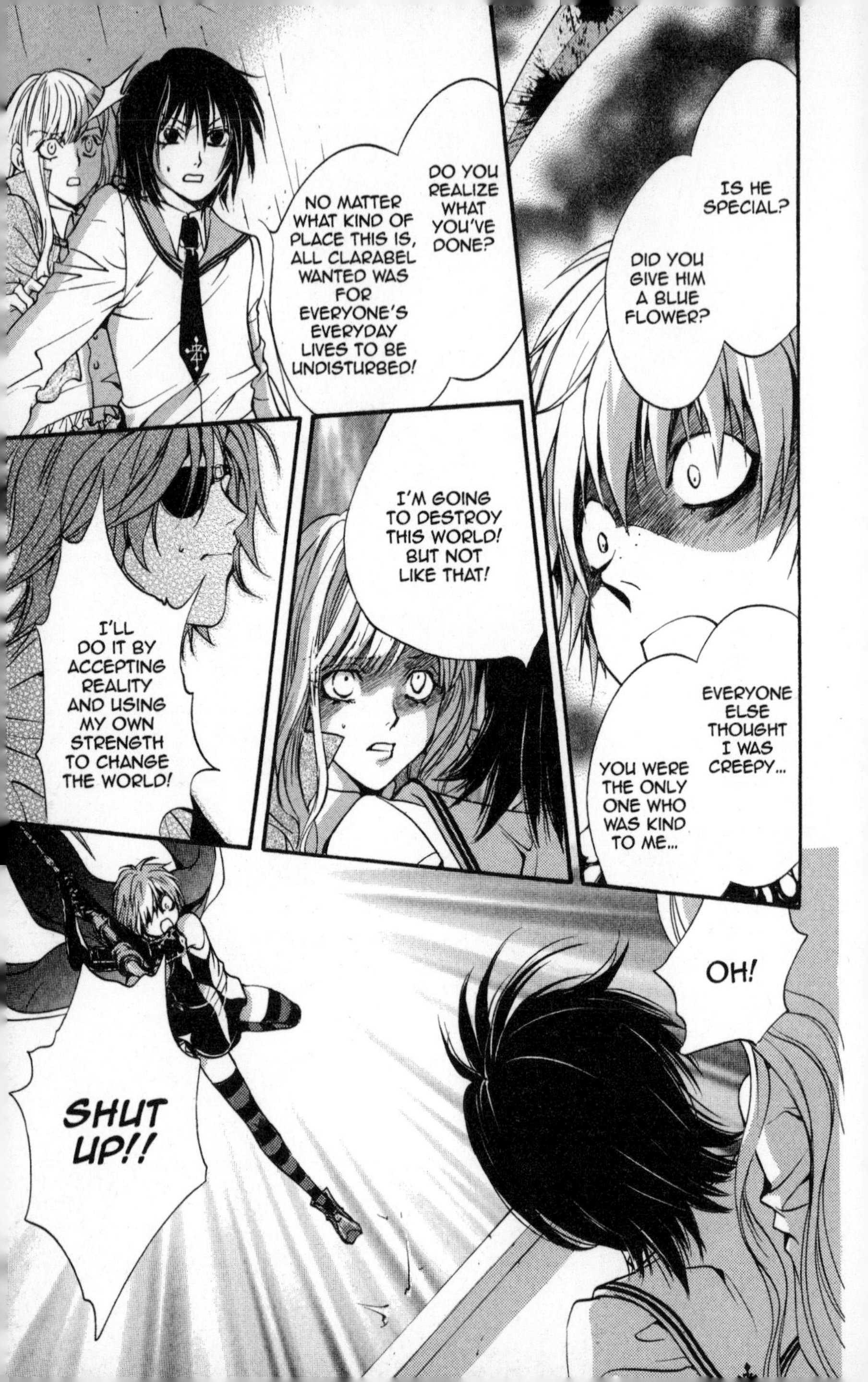
IS HE SPECIAL?
DID YOU GIVE HIM A BLUE FLOWER?
EVERYONE ELSE THOUGHT I WAS CREEPY...
YOU WERE THE ONLY ONE WHO WAS KIND TO ME...
DO YOU REALIZE WHAT YOU'VE DONE?
NO MATTER WHAT KIND OF PLACE THIS IS, ALL CLARABEL WANTED WAS FOR EVERYONE'S EVERYDAY LIVES TO BE UNDISTURBED!
I'M GOING TO DESTROY THIS WORLD! BUT NOT LIKE THAT!
I'LL DO IT BY ACCEPTING REALITY AND USING MY OWN STRENGTH TO CHANGE THE WORLD!
OH!
SHUT UP!!

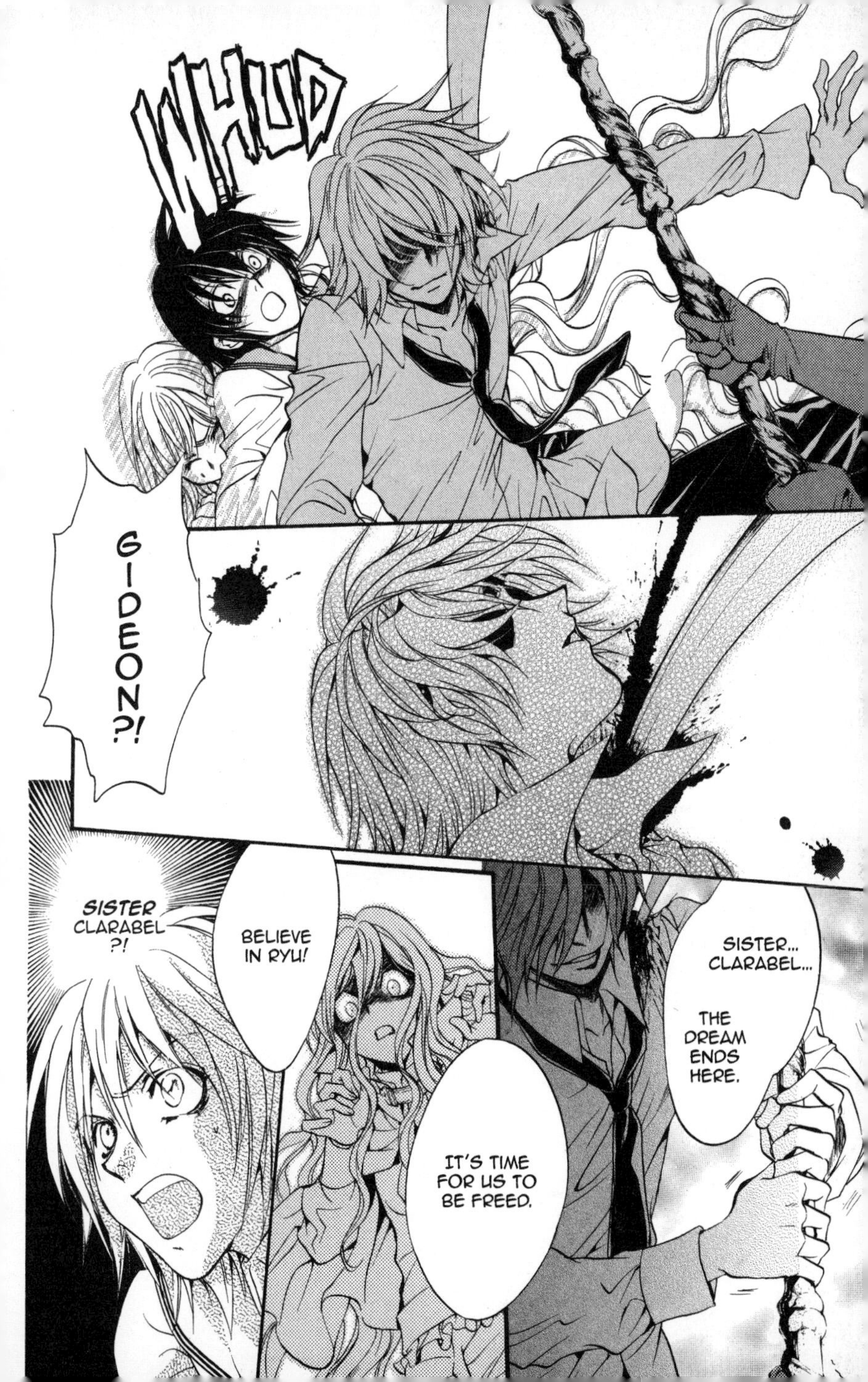
WHUD
GIDEON?!
SISTER... CLARABEL...
THE DREAM ENDS HERE.
IT'S TIME FOR US TO BE FREED.
BELIEVE IN RYU!
SISTER CLARABEL?!

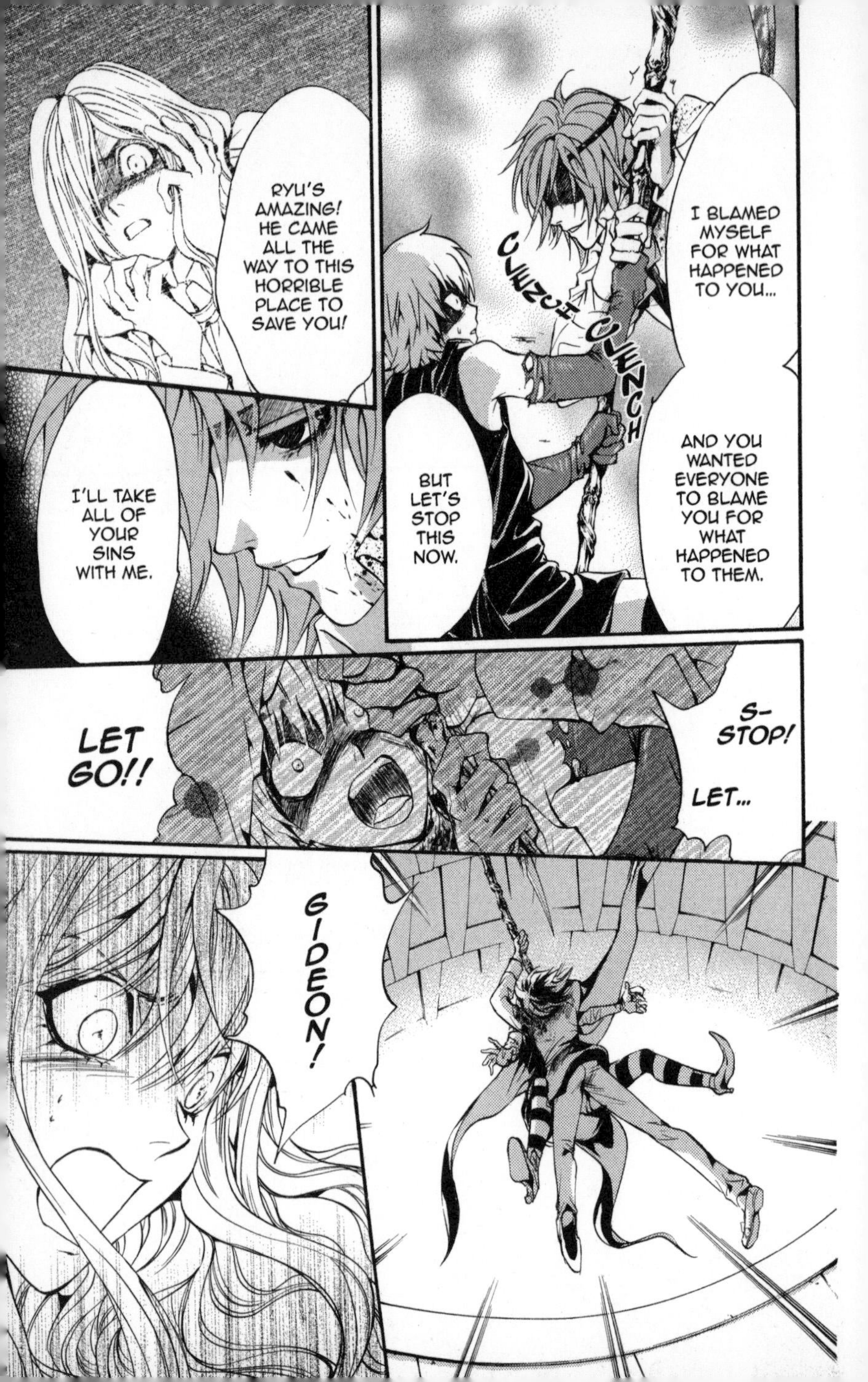
I BLAMED MYSELF FOR WHAT HAPPENED TO YOU...
CLENCH CLENCH
AND YOU WANTED EVERYONE TO BLAME YOU FOR WHAT HAPPENED TO THEM.
BUT LET'S STOP THIS NOW.
RYU'S AMAZING! HE CAME ALL THE WAY TO THIS HORRIBLE PLACE TO SAVE YOU!
I'LL TAKE ALL OF YOUR SINS WITH ME.
S-STOP!
LET...
LET GO!!
GIDEON!

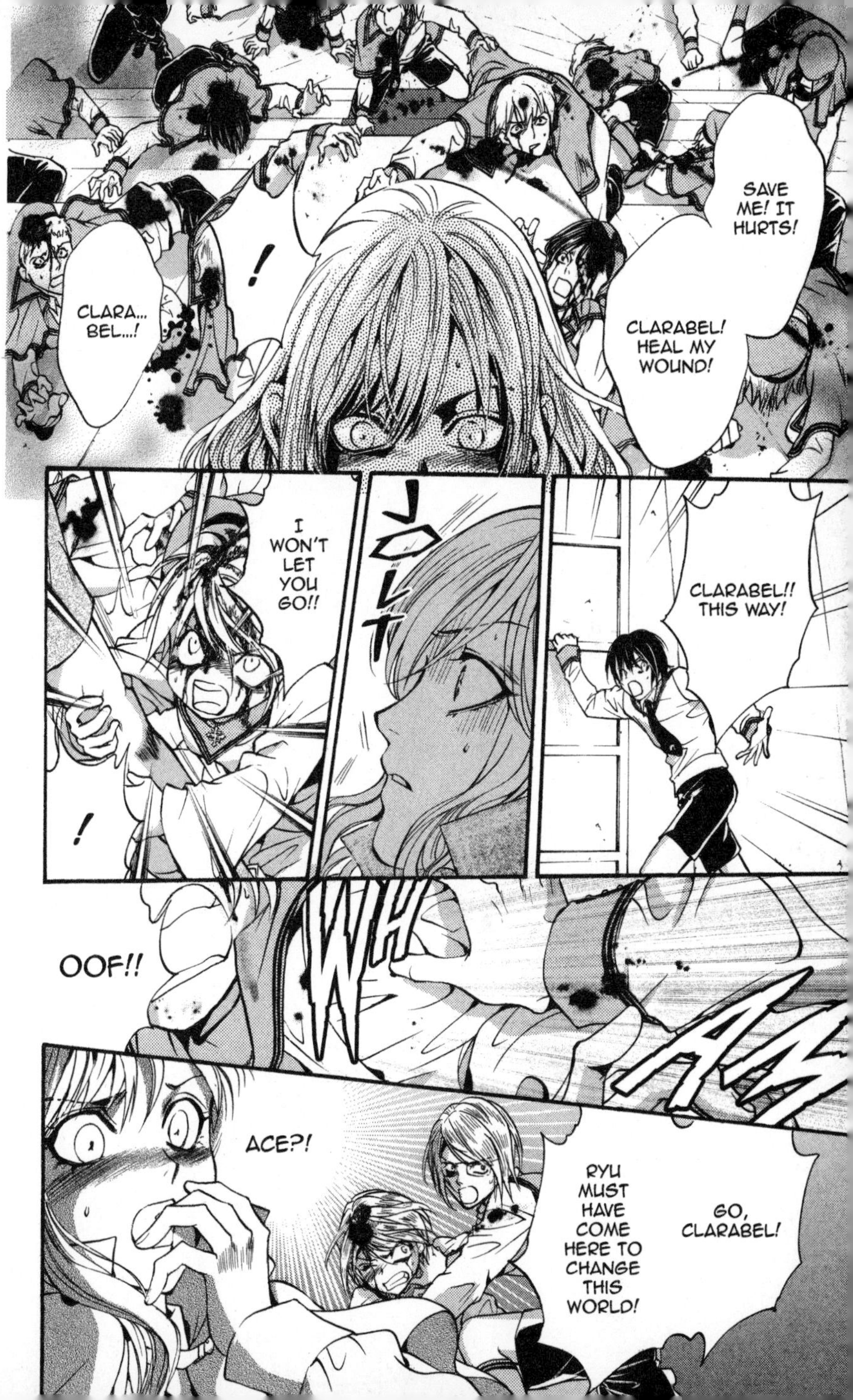
SAVE ME! IT HURTS!
CLARABEL! HEAL MY WOUND!
!
CLARA... BEL...!
CLARABEL!! THIS WAY!
JOLT
I WON'T LET YOU GO!!
!
WHAM
OOF!!
GO, CLARABEL!
RYU MUST HAVE COME HERE TO CHANGE THIS WORLD!
ACE?!

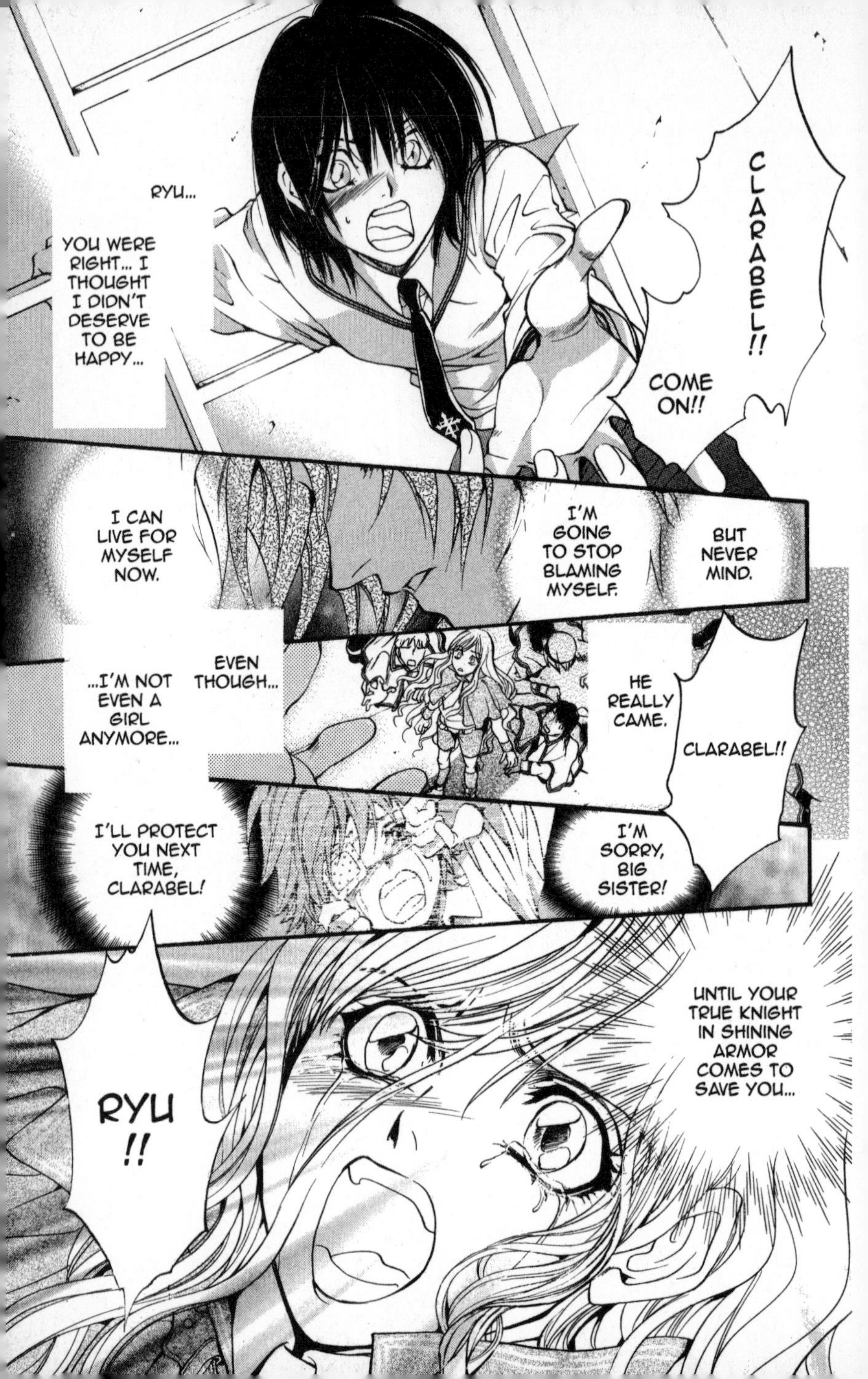
CLARABEL!!
COME ON!!
RYU...
YOU WERE RIGHT... I THOUGHT I DIDN'T DESERVE TO BE HAPPY...
BUT NEVER MIND.
I'M GOING TO STOP BLAMING MYSELF.
I CAN LIVE FOR MYSELF NOW.
HE REALLY CAME.
CLARABEL!!
EVEN THOUGH...
...I'M NOT EVEN A GIRL ANYMORE...
I'M SORRY, BIG SISTER!
I'LL PROTECT YOU NEXT TIME, CLARABEL!
UNTIL YOUR TRUE KNIGHT IN SHINING ARMOR COMES TO SAVE YOU...
RYU!!

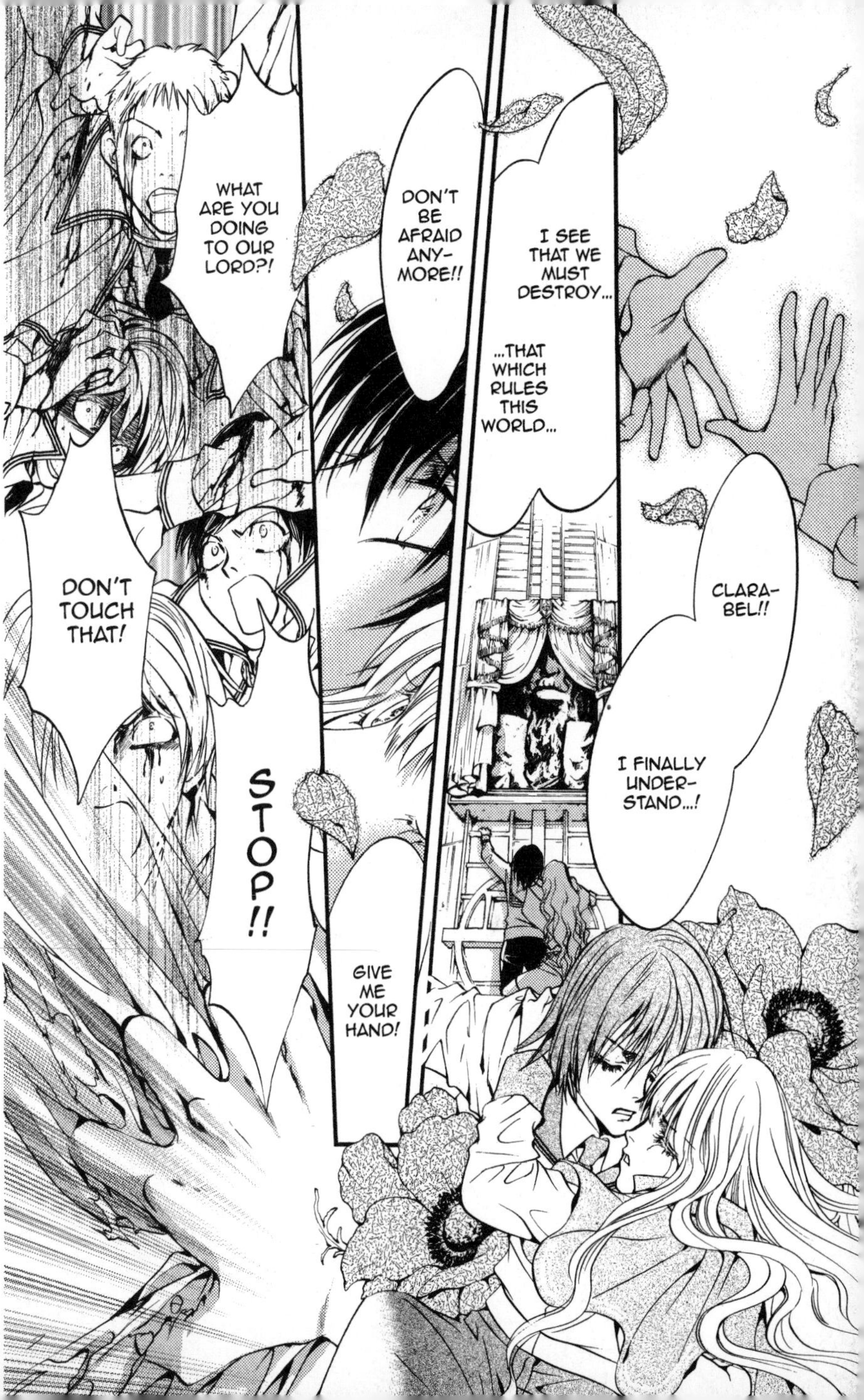
CLARA-BEL!!
I FINALLY UNDER-STAND...!
I SEE THAT WE MUST DESTROY...
...THAT WHICH RULES THIS WORLD...
DON'T BE AFRAID ANY-MORE!!
GIVE ME YOUR HAND!
WHAT ARE YOU DOING TO OUR LORD?!
DON'T TOUCH THAT!
STOP!!

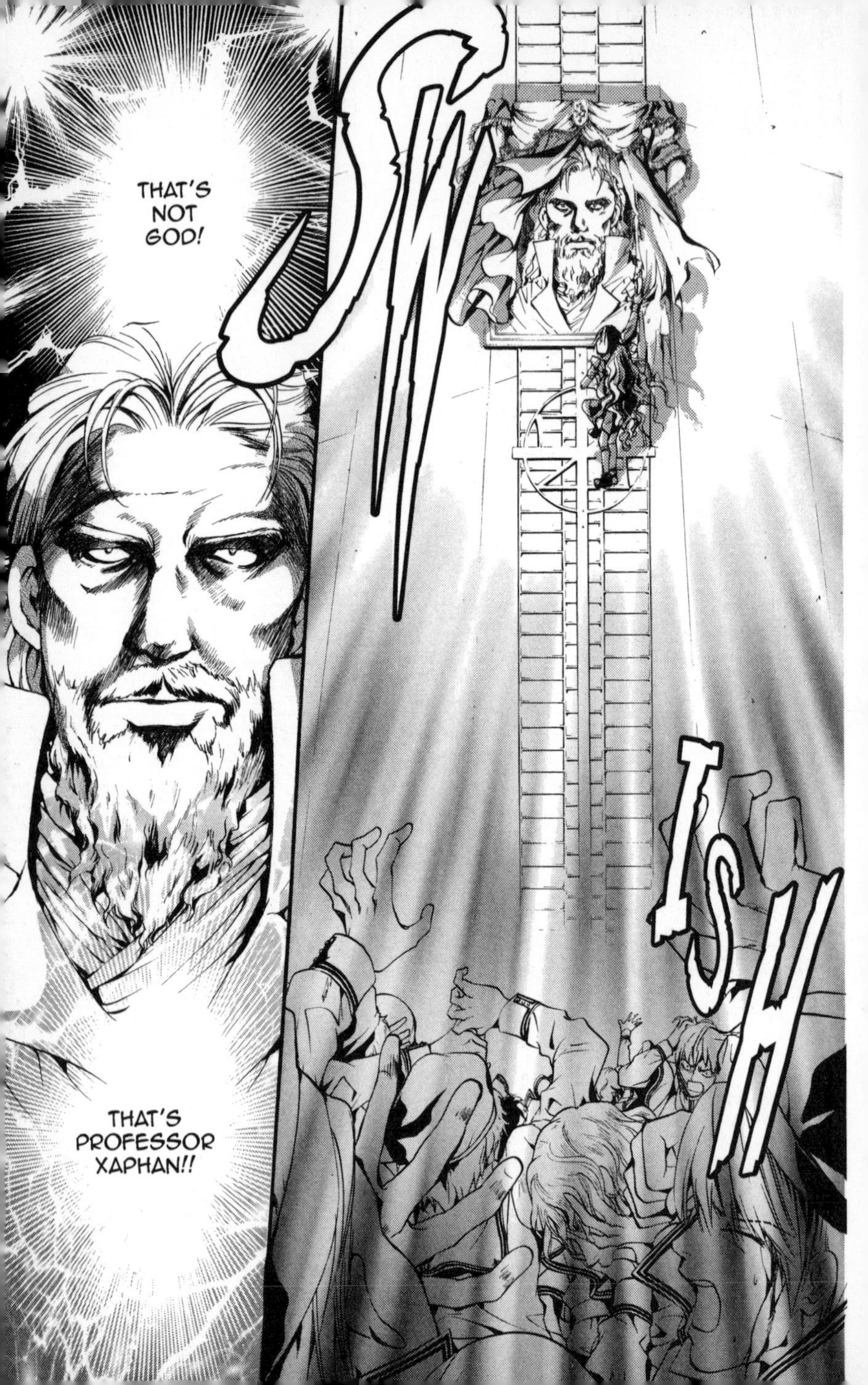
SW
ISH
THAT'S NOT GOD!
THAT'S PROFESSOR XAPHAN!!

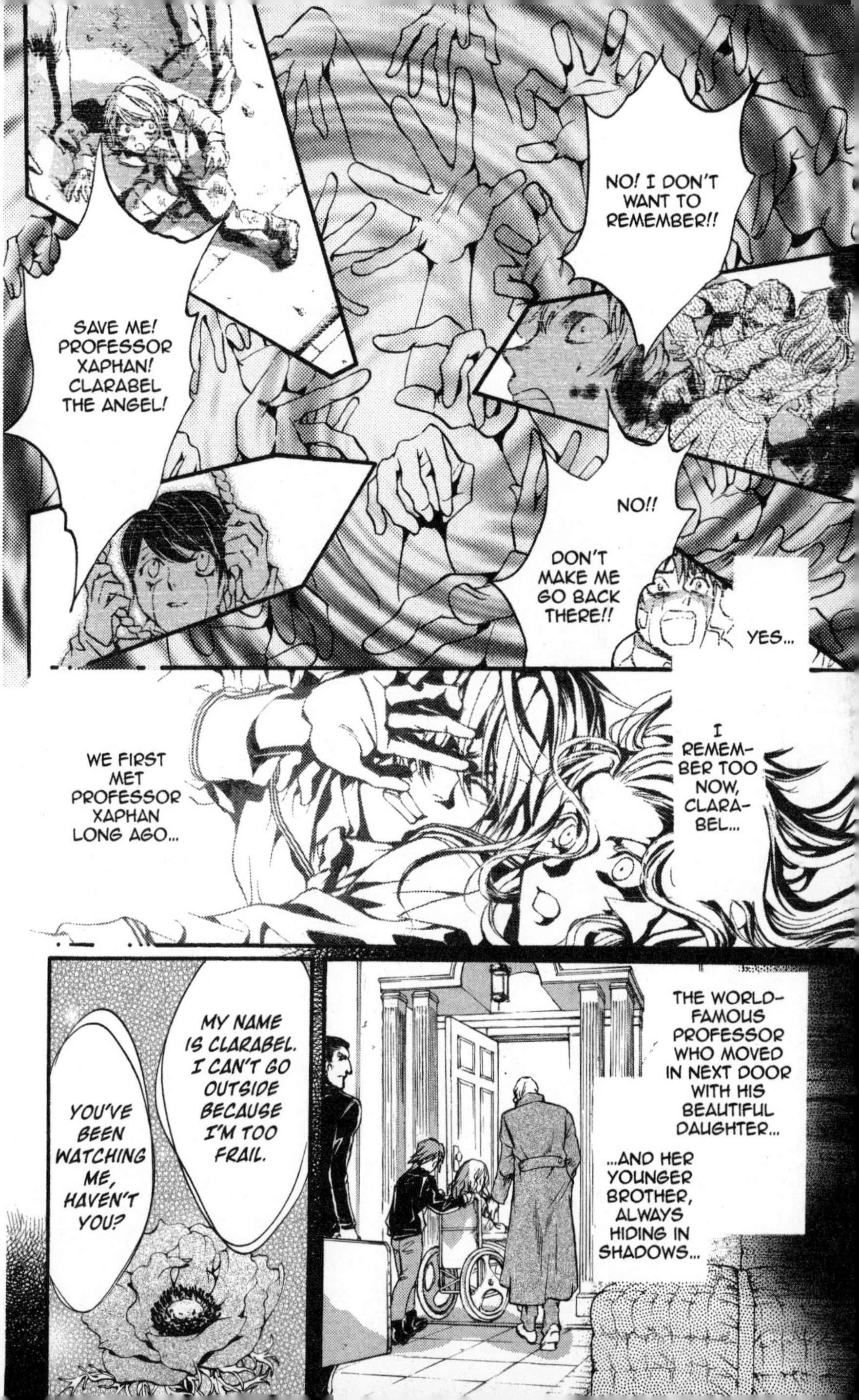
NO! I DON'T WANT TO REMEMBER!!
NO!!
DON'T MAKE ME GO BACK THERE!!
SAVE ME! PROFESSOR XAPHAN! CLARABEL THE ANGEL!
YES...
I REMEMBER TOO NOW, CLARABEL...
WE FIRST MET PROFESSOR XAPHAN LONG AGO...
THE WORLD-FAMOUS PROFESSOR WHO MOVED IN NEXT DOOR WITH HIS BEAUTIFUL DAUGHTER...
...AND HER YOUNGER BROTHER, ALWAYS HIDING IN SHADOWS...
MY NAME IS CLARABEL. I CAN'T GO OUTSIDE BECAUSE I'M TOO FRAIL.
YOU'VE BEEN WATCHING ME, HAVEN'T YOU?

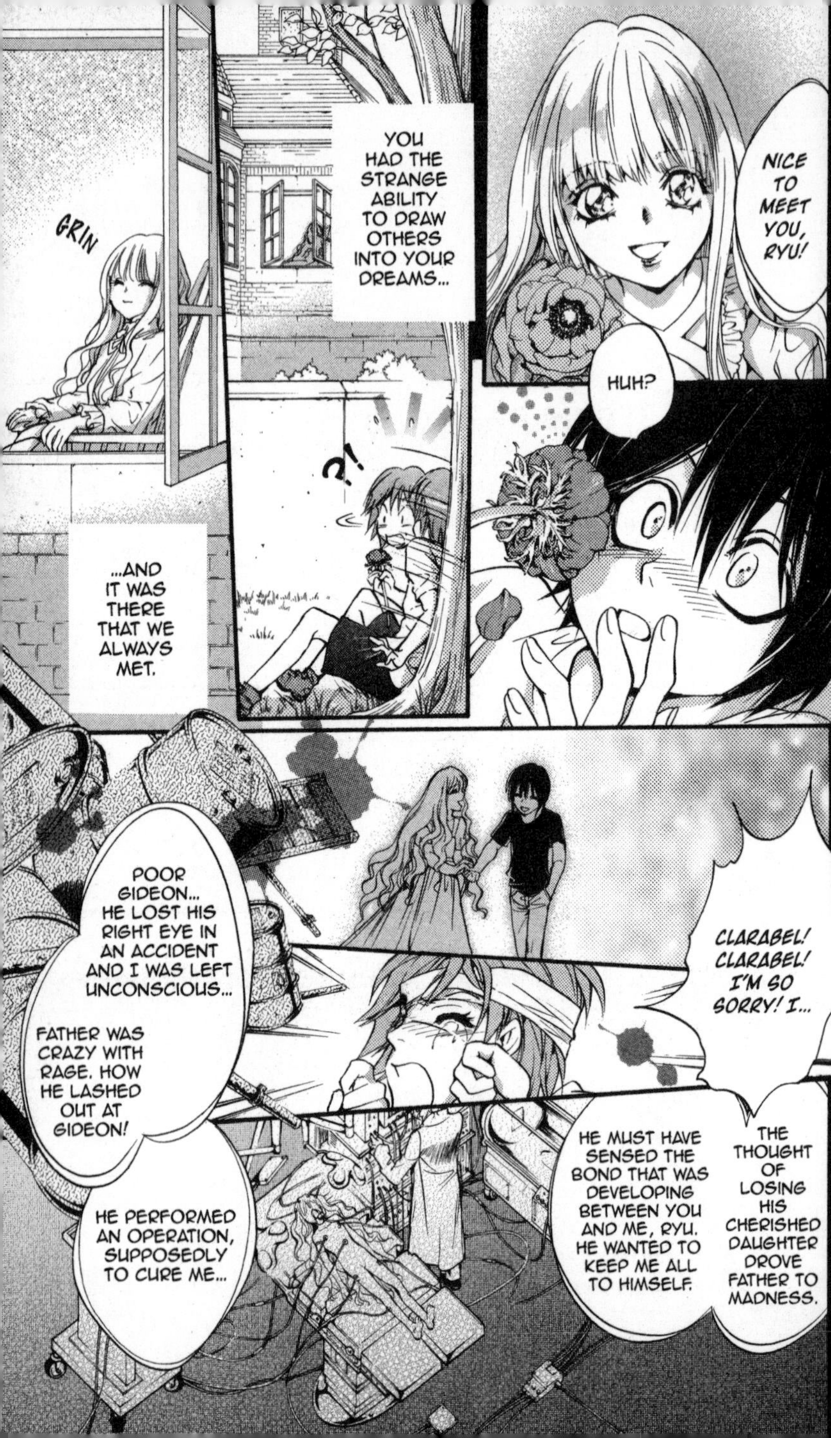
NICE TO MEET YOU, RYU!
YOU HAD THE STRANGE ABILITY TO DRAW OTHERS INTO YOUR DREAMS...
HUH?
?!
GRIN
...AND IT WAS THERE THAT WE ALWAYS MET.
CLARABEL! CLARABEL! I'M SO SORRY! I...
THE THOUGHT OF LOSING HIS CHERISHED DAUGHTER DROVE FATHER TO MADNESS.
HE MUST HAVE SENSED THE BOND THAT WAS DEVELOPING BETWEEN YOU AND ME, RYU. HE WANTED TO KEEP ME ALL TO HIMSELF.
POOR GIDEON... HE LOST HIS RIGHT EYE IN AN ACCIDENT AND I WAS LEFT UNCONSCIOUS...
FATHER WAS CRAZY WITH RAGE. HOW HE LASHED OUT AT GIDEON!
HE PERFORMED AN OPERATION, SUPPOSEDLY TO CURE ME...

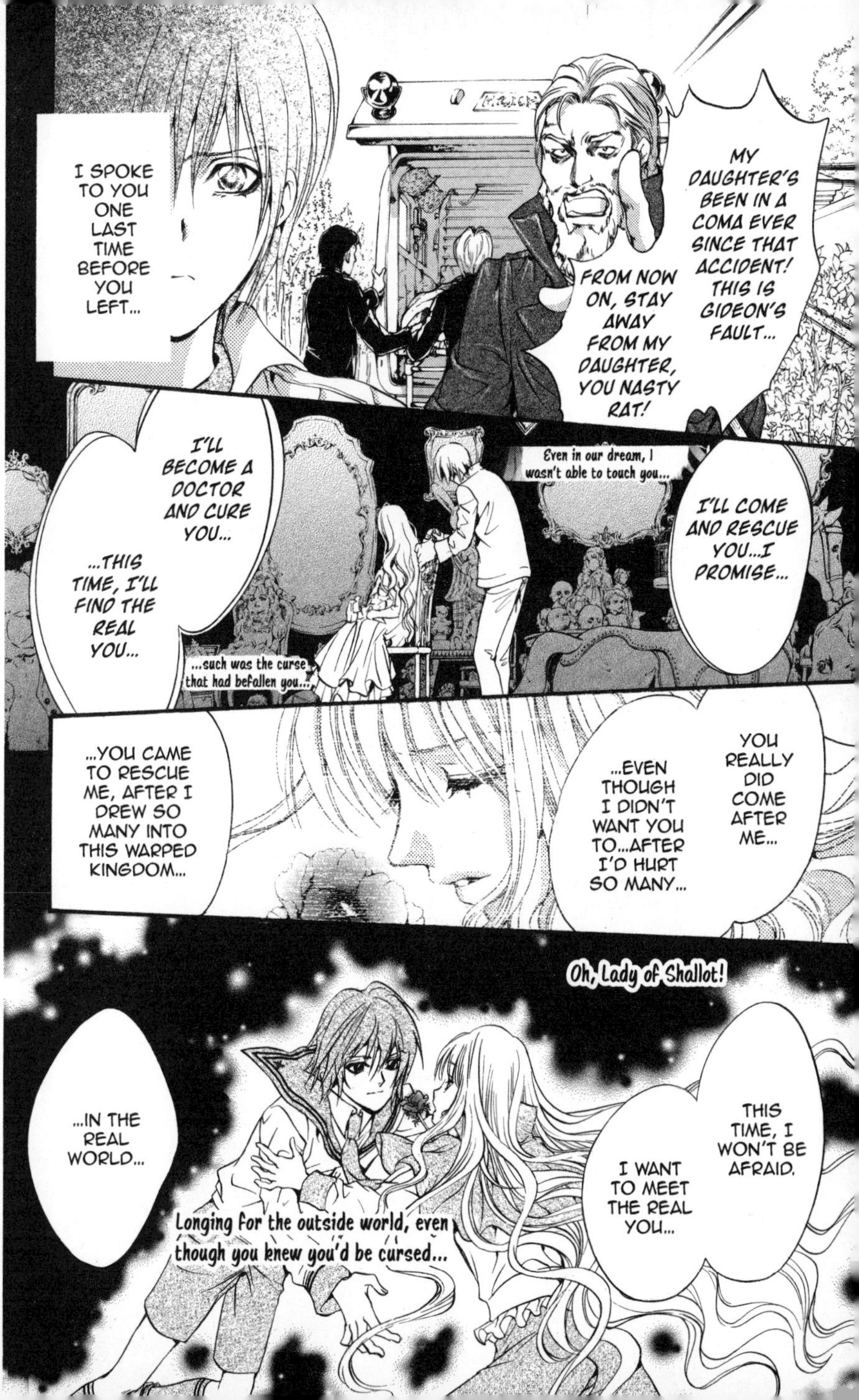
MY DAUGHTER'S BEEN IN A COMA EVER SINCE THAT ACCIDENT! THIS IS GIDEON'S FAULT...
FROM NOW ON, STAY AWAY FROM MY DAUGHTER, YOU NASTY RAT!
I SPOKE TO YOU ONE LAST TIME BEFORE YOU LEFT...
I'LL COME AND RESCUE YOU...I PROMISE...
Even in our dream, I wasn't able to touch you...
I'LL BECOME A DOCTOR AND CURE YOU...
...THIS TIME, I'LL FIND THE REAL YOU...
...such was the curse that had befallen you...
YOU REALLY DID COME AFTER ME...
...EVEN THOUGH I DIDN'T WANT YOU TO...AFTER I'D HURT SO MANY...
...YOU CAME TO RESCUE ME, AFTER I DREW SO MANY INTO THIS WARPED KINGDOM...
Oh, Lady of Shallot!
THIS TIME, I WON'T BE AFRAID.
I WANT TO MEET THE REAL YOU...
...IN THE REAL WORLD...
Longing for the outside world, even though you knew you'd be cursed...

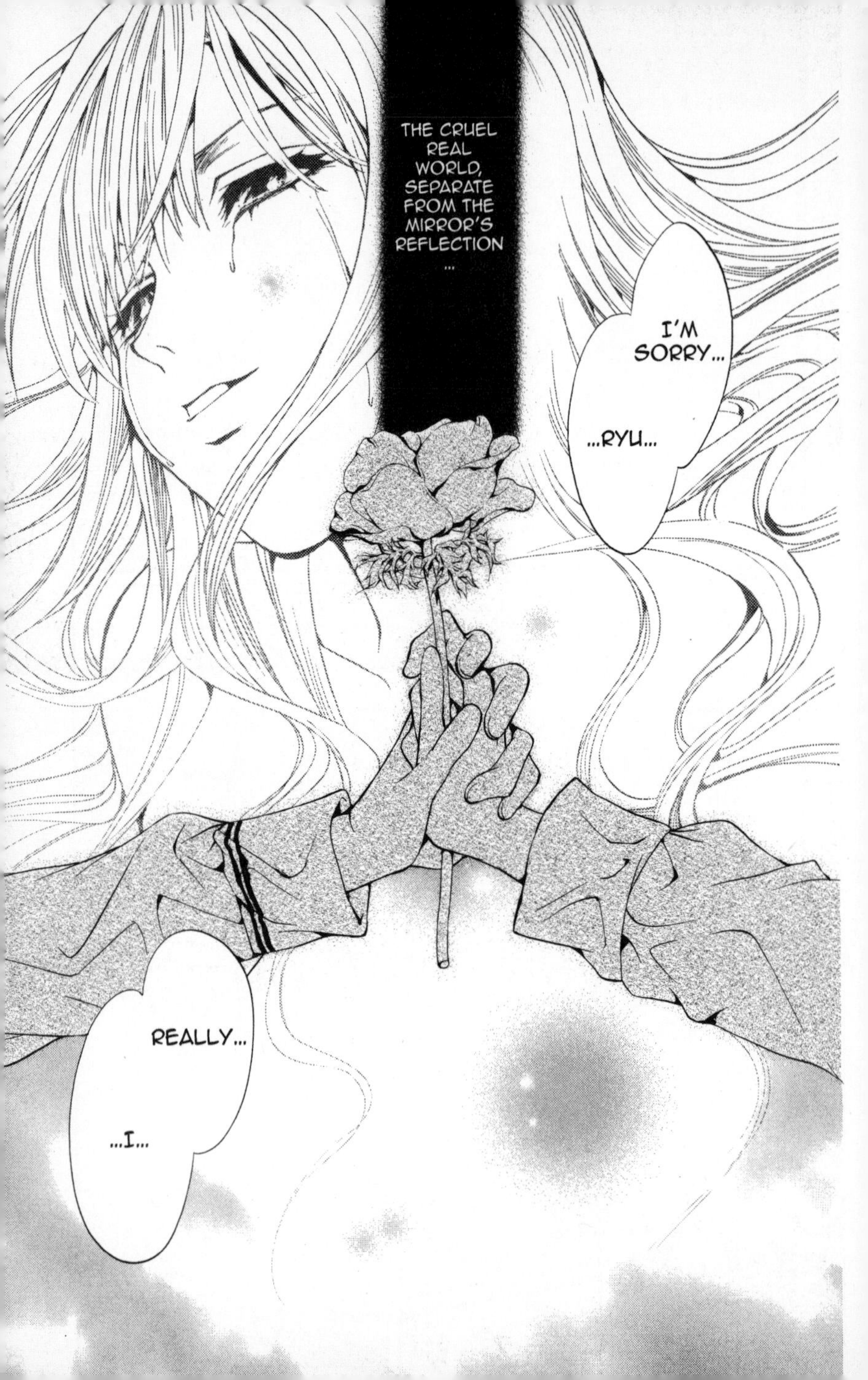
THE CRUEL REAL WORLD, SEPARATE FROM THE MIRROR'S REFLECTION ...
I'M SORRY... ...RYU...
REALLY... ...I...

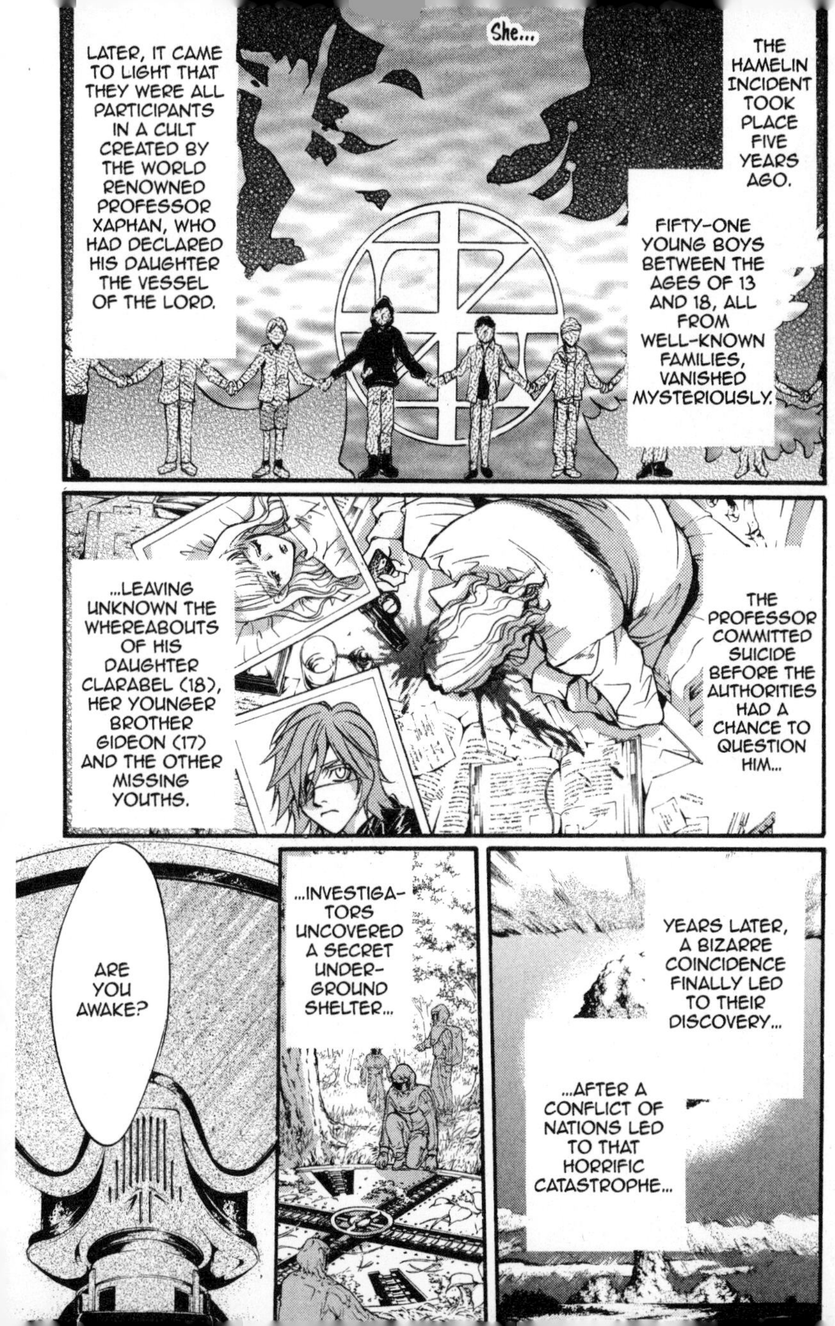
THE HAMELIN INCIDENT TOOK PLACE FIVE YEARS AGO.
She...
FIFTY-ONE YOUNG BOYS BETWEEN THE AGES OF 13 AND 18, ALL FROM WELL-KNOWN FAMILIES, VANISHED MYSTERIOUSLY.
LATER, IT CAME TO LIGHT THAT THEY WERE ALL PARTICIPANTS IN A CULT CREATED BY THE WORLD RENOWNED PROFESSOR XAPHAN, WHO HAD DECLARED HIS DAUGHTER THE VESSEL OF THE LORD.
THE PROFESSOR COMMITTED SUICIDE BEFORE THE AUTHORITIES HAD A CHANCE TO QUESTION HIM...
...LEAVING UNKNOWN THE WHEREABOUTS OF HIS DAUGHTER CLARABEL (18), HER YOUNGER BROTHER GIDEON (17) AND THE OTHER MISSING YOUTHS.
YEARS LATER, A BIZARRE COINCIDENCE FINALLY LED TO THEIR DISCOVERY...
...AFTER A CONFLICT OF NATIONS LED TO THAT HORRIFIC CATASTROPHE...
...INVESTIGATORS UNCOVERED A SECRET UNDERGROUND SHELTER...
ARE YOU AWAKE?

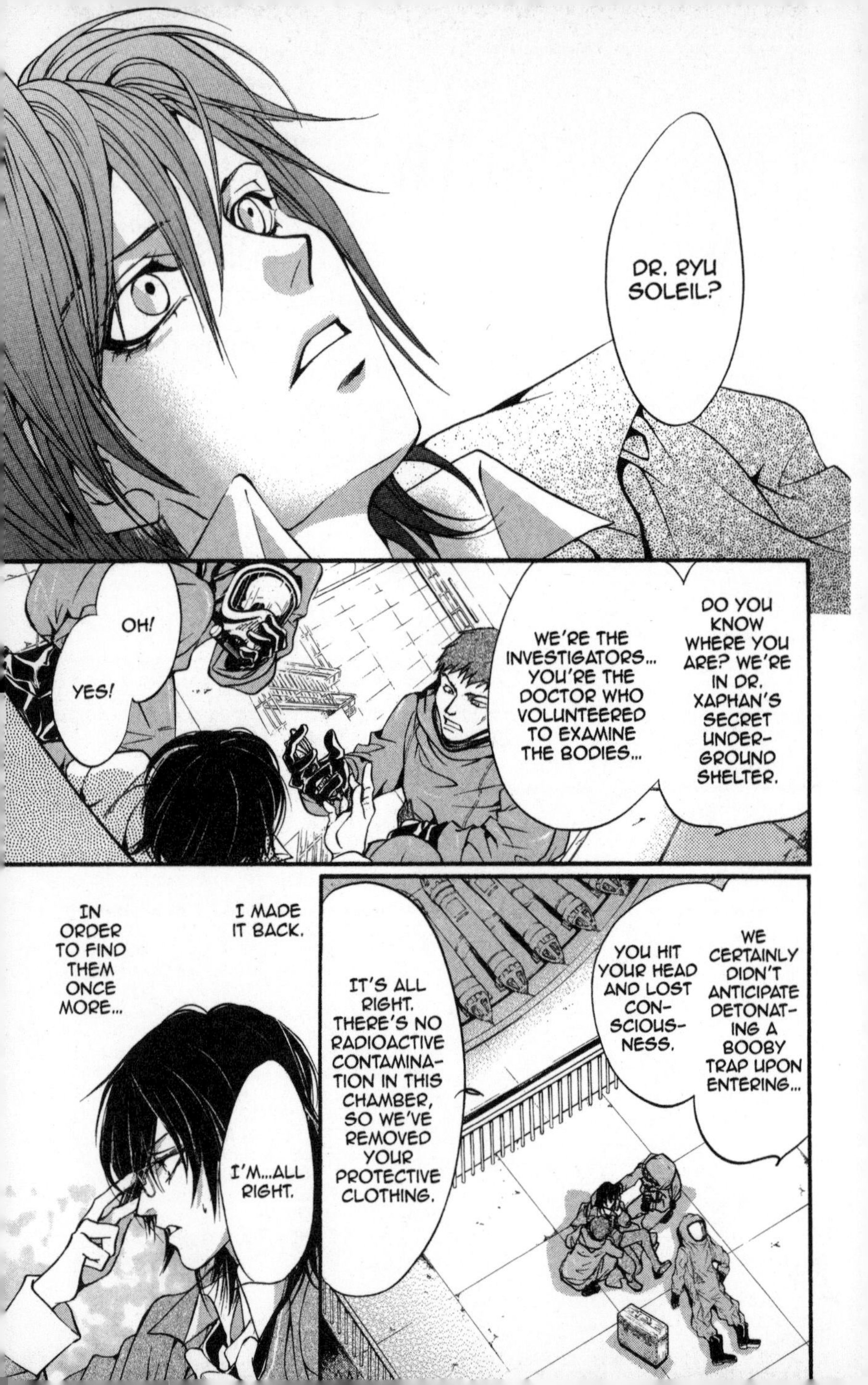
DR. RYU SOLEIL?
DO YOU KNOW WHERE YOU ARE? WE'RE IN DR. XAPHAN'S SECRET UNDER-GROUND SHELTER.
WE'RE THE INVESTIGATORS... YOU'RE THE DOCTOR WHO VOLUNTEERED TO EXAMINE THE BODIES...
OH!
YES!
WE CERTAINLY DIDN'T ANTICIPATE DETONAT-ING A BOOBY TRAP UPON ENTERING...
YOU HIT YOUR HEAD AND LOST CON-SCIOUS-NESS.
IT'S ALL RIGHT. THERE'S NO RADIOACTIVE CONTAMINA-TION IN THIS CHAMBER, SO WE'VE REMOVED YOUR PROTECTIVE CLOTHING.
I'M...ALL RIGHT.
I MADE IT BACK.
IN ORDER TO FIND THEM ONCE MORE...

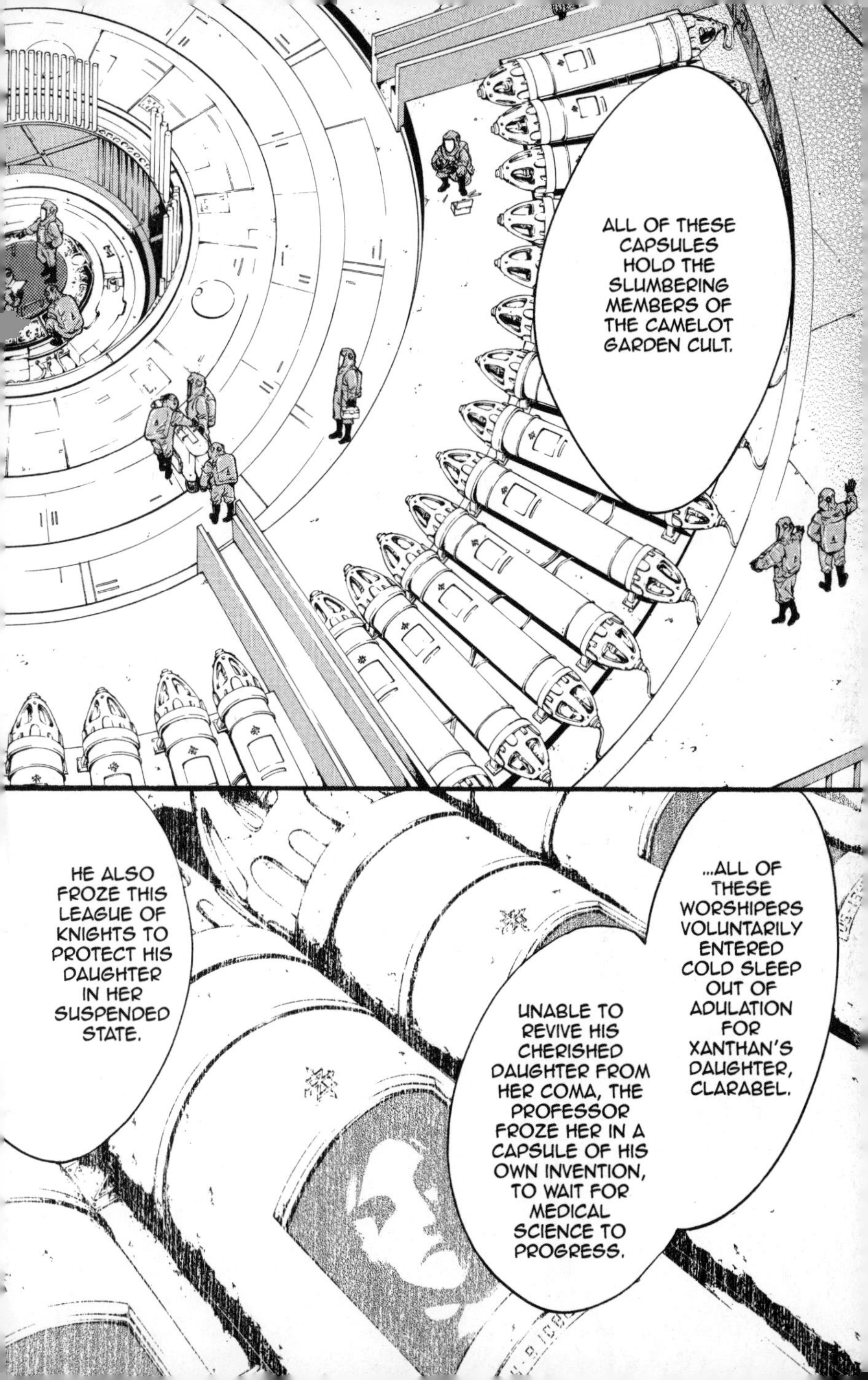
ALL OF THESE CAPSULES HOLD THE SLUMBERING MEMBERS OF THE CAMELOT GARDEN CULT.
...ALL OF THESE WORSHIPERS VOLUNTARILY ENTERED COLD SLEEP OUT OF ADULATION FOR XANTHAN'S DAUGHTER, CLARABEL.
UNABLE TO REVIVE HIS CHERISHED DAUGHTER FROM HER COMA, THE PROFESSOR FROZE HER IN A CAPSULE OF HIS OWN INVENTION, TO WAIT FOR MEDICAL SCIENCE TO PROGRESS.
HE ALSO FROZE THIS LEAGUE OF KNIGHTS TO PROTECT HIS DAUGHTER IN HER SUSPENDED STATE.

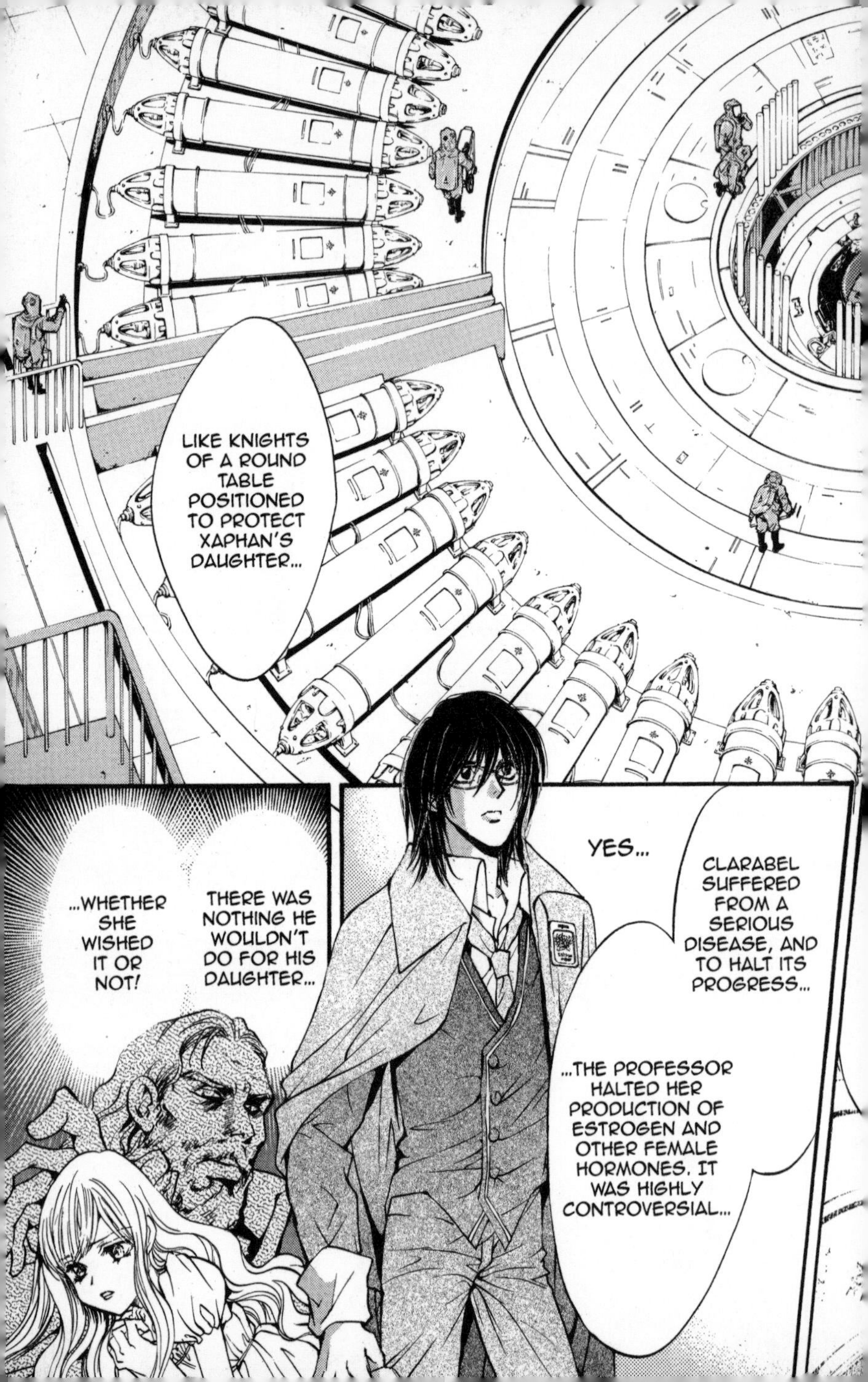
LIKE KNIGHTS OF A ROUND TABLE POSITIONED TO PROTECT XAPHAN'S DAUGHTER...
YES...
CLARABEL SUFFERED FROM A SERIOUS DISEASE, AND TO HALT ITS PROGRESS...
...THE PROFESSOR HALTED HER PRODUCTION OF ESTROGEN AND OTHER FEMALE HORMONES. IT WAS HIGHLY CONTROVERSIAL...
THERE WAS NOTHING HE WOULDN'T DO FOR HIS DAUGHTER...
...WHETHER SHE WISHED IT OR NOT!

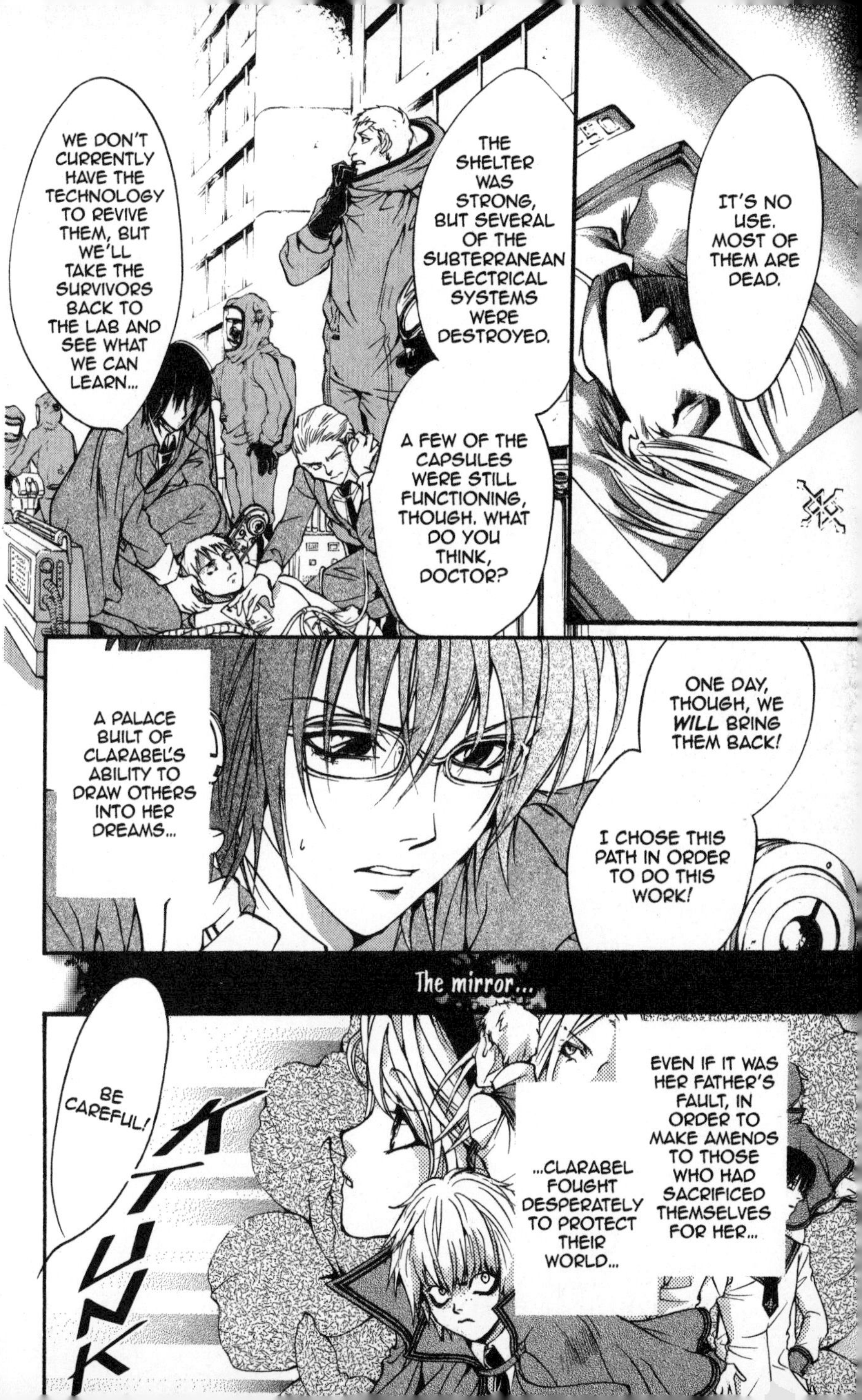
IT'S NO USE. MOST OF THEM ARE DEAD.
THE SHELTER WAS STRONG, BUT SEVERAL OF THE SUBTERRANEAN ELECTRICAL SYSTEMS WERE DESTROYED.
A FEW OF THE CAPSULES WERE STILL FUNCTIONING, THOUGH. WHAT DO YOU THINK, DOCTOR?
WE DON'T CURRENTLY HAVE THE TECHNOLOGY TO REVIVE THEM, BUT WE'LL TAKE THE SURVIVORS BACK TO THE LAB AND SEE WHAT WE CAN LEARN...
ONE DAY, THOUGH, WE *WILL* BRING THEM BACK!
I CHOSE THIS PATH IN ORDER TO DO THIS WORK!
A PALACE BUILT OF CLARABEL'S ABILITY TO DRAW OTHERS INTO HER DREAMS...
The mirror...
EVEN IF IT WAS HER FATHER'S FAULT, IN ORDER TO MAKE AMENDS TO THOSE WHO HAD SACRIFICED THEMSELVES FOR HER...
...CLARABEL FOUGHT DESPERATELY TO PROTECT THEIR WORLD...
BE CAREFUL!
KTUNK

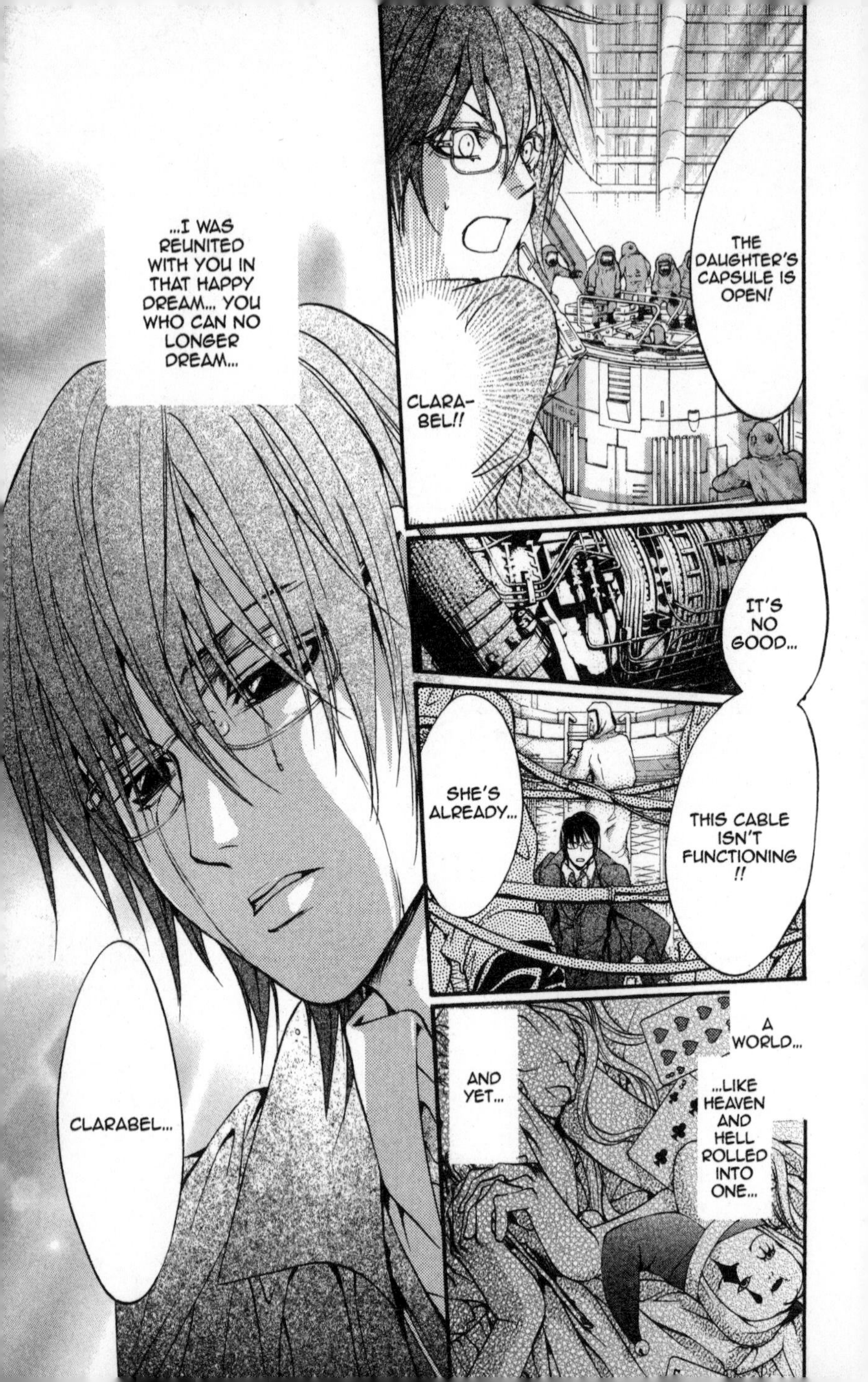
THE DAUGHTER'S CAPSULE IS OPEN!
CLARA-BEL!!
IT'S NO GOOD...
THIS CABLE ISN'T FUNCTIONING !!
SHE'S ALREADY...
A WORLD...
...LIKE HEAVEN AND HELL ROLLED INTO ONE...
AND YET...
...I WAS REUNITED WITH YOU IN THAT HAPPY DREAM... YOU WHO CAN NO LONGER DREAM...
CLARABEL...

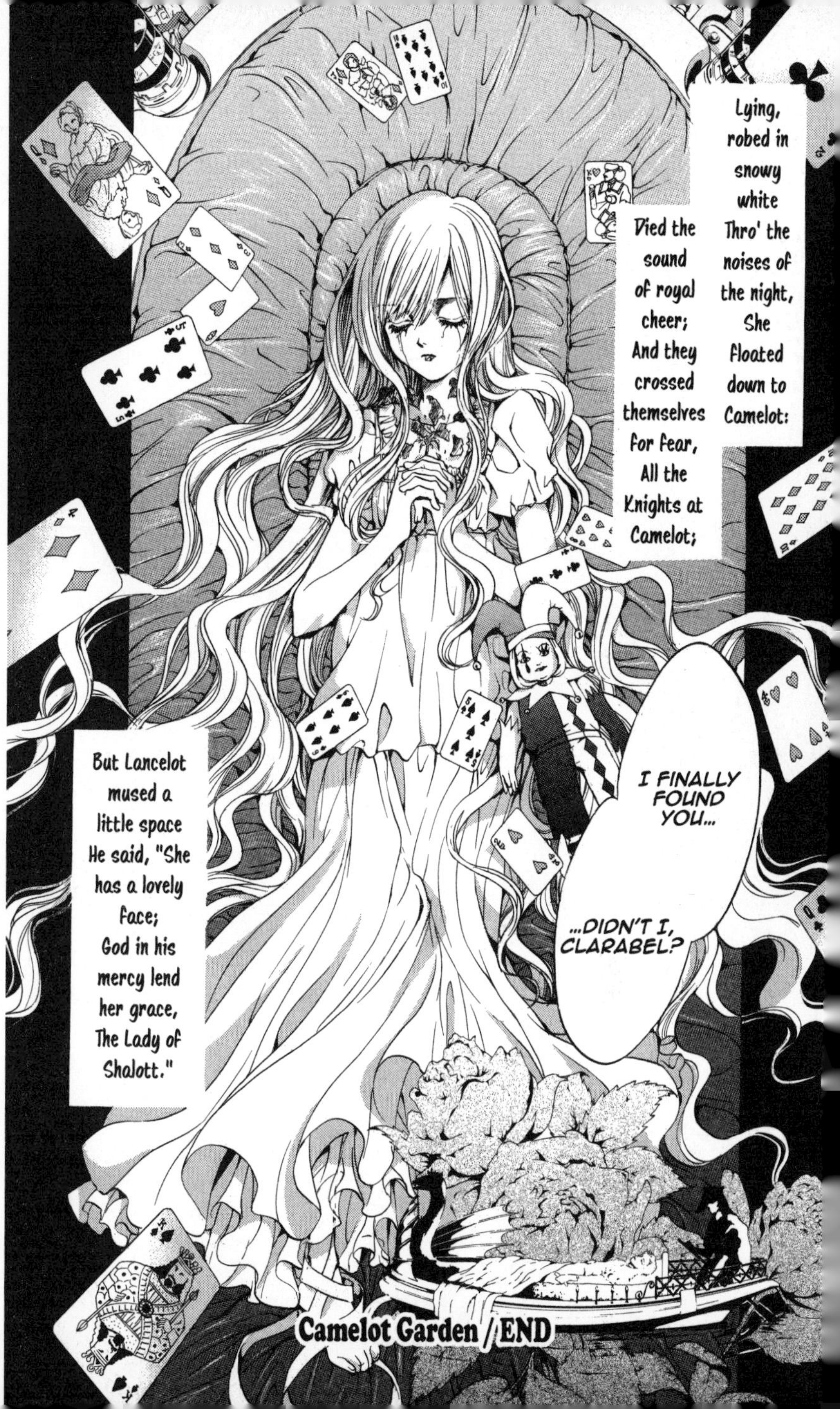
Lying, robed in snowy white Thro' the noises of the night, She floated down to Camelot:
Died the sound of royal cheer; And they crossed themselves for fear, All the Knights at Camelot;
I FINALLY FOUND YOU...
...DIDN'T I, CLARABEL?
But Lancelot mused a little space He said, "She has a lovely face; God in his mercy lend her grace, The Lady of Shalott."
Camelot Garden / END

Hello!
This was the final
chapter of *Grand
Guignol Orchestra*. You may
be wondering why Berthier is still
alive. Well, because he was revived by
Le Sénat, their bizarre experiment was
what gave him life. Carnelian survives because he
didn't benefit from the virus. Lucille reverts to his
unaltered state and his original, unenhanced voice. The
oratorio has left its mark on their bodies, but the
members of the Grand Orchestra won't let
that stop them! Maybe I'm getting
old—I seem to have developed
a fondness for happy
endings—or maybe
not? 'Till next
time!
♡

E PAGE
ER GARDEN
INGS ABOUT WORK,
NIKO NIKO ADDICTION,
WITH KIDS, ETC...
//WWW.YUKIKAORI.JP/TOP.PHP

TWITTER ACCOUNT:
ANGELAID
USERNAME:
由貴香織里

Creator:
Kaori Yuki

Date of Birth:
December 18

Blood Type:
B

Major Works:
Angel Sanctuary and *The Cain Saga*

 aori Yuki was born in Tokyo and started drawing at a very early age. Following her debut work, *Natsufuku no Erie* (Ellie in Summer Clothes), in the Japanese magazine *Bessatsu Hana to Yume*, she wrote a compelling series of short stories: *Zankoku na Douwatachi* (Cruel Fairy Tales), *Neji* (Screw) and *Sareki Ôkoku* (Gravel Kingdom).

As proven by her best-selling series *Angel Sanctuary*, *Godchild* and *Fairy Cube*, her celebrated body of work has etched an indelible mark on the Gothic comics genre. She likes mysteries and British films and is a fan of the movie *Dead Poets Society* and the show *Twin Peaks*.